The New Digital Storytelling

The New Digital Storytelling

Creating Narratives with New Media

Revised and Updated Edition

Bryan Alexander

 PRAEGER™

An Imprint of ABC-CLIO, LLC

Santa Barbara, California • Denver, Colorado

Library of Congress Cataloging-in-Publication Data

Names: Alexander, Bryan, 1967– author.
Title: The new digital storytelling : creating narratives with new media /
    Bryan Alexander.
Description: Revised and updated edition. | Santa Barbara, California : Praeger,
    an Imprint of ABC-CLIO, LLC, [2017] | Includes bibliographical references
    and index.
Identifiers: LCCN 2017009509 (print) | LCCN 2017010597 (ebook) |
    ISBN 9781440849602 (hard copy : alk. paper) | ISBN 9781440849619 (EISBN)
Subjects: LCSH: Interactive multimedia. | Digital storytelling. |
    Storytelling—Data processing.
Classification: LCC QA76.76.I59 A42 2017 (print) | LCC QA76.76.I59 (ebook) |
    DDC 006.7—dc23
LC record available at https://lccn.loc.gov/2017009509

ISBN: 978-1-4408-4960-2
EISBN: 978-1-4408-4961-9

21 20 19 18 17   1 2 3 4 5

This book is also available as an eBook.

Praeger
An Imprint of ABC-CLIO, LLC

ABC-CLIO, LLC
130 Cremona Drive, P.O. Box 1911
Santa Barbara, California 93116-1911
www.abc-clio.com

This book is printed on acid-free paper ∞

Manufactured in the United States of America

To my children, Gwynneth and Owain, for their love of stories, the stories they have created, and the ones they'll go on to tell.

And to my wife, Ceredwyn, for the story of our love. That's the best tale I know.

Our tendency to see and explain the world in common narratives is so deeply ingrained that we often don't notice it—even when we've written the words ourselves. In the Conceptual Age, however, we must awaken to the power of narrative.

—Daniel Pink

Make 'em cry, make 'em laugh, make 'em wait.

—attributed to Willkie Collins

Contents

Acknowledgments   xi

Introduction   xiii

Introduction to the Second Edition   xix

Part One   **Storytelling: A Tale of Two Generations**

Chapter 1   Storytelling for the 21st Century   3

Chapter 2   The First Wave of Digital Storytelling   17

Chapter 3   The Next Wave of Digital Storytelling Platforms   29

Part Two   **New Platforms for Tales and Telling**

Chapter 4   Storytelling with the Technology Formerly
                 Known as Web 2.0   47

Chapter 5   Social Media Storytelling   81

Chapter 6   Gaming: Storytelling on a Small Scale   97

Chapter 7   Gaming: Storytelling on a Large Scale   115

Part Three   **Combinatorial Storytelling; or, The Dawn
                 of New Narrative Forms**

Chapter 8   No Story Is a Single Thing; or, The Networked
                 Book   131

Chapter 9   Mobile Devices: The Birth of New Designs for
                 Small Screens   143

Chapter 10   Chaotic Fictions; or, Alternate Reality Games   155

Chapter 11   Augmented Reality: Telling Stories on
the Worldboard   167

Chapter 12   Storytelling through Virtual Reality   179

Part Four   Building Your Story

Chapter 13   Story Flow: Practical Lessons on Brainstorming,
Planning, and Development   187

Chapter 14   Communities, Resources, and Challenges   211

Chapter 15   Digital Storytelling in Education   223

Chapter 16   Coda: Toward the Next Wave of Digital
Storytelling   235

Notes   245

Bibliography   275

Index   283

Acknowledgments

For stories and ideas: Bret Boessen, Thomas Burkdall, Annette S. L. Evans, Steven Kaye, Gail Matthews-DeNatale, Peter Naegele, Ruben Puentedura, Geoff Scranton, Mike Sellers, Ed Webb, and Middlebury College folk Jason Mittell and Hector Vila, the latter for inviting the Center for Digital Storytelling to teach a workshop and encouraging me to attend; this book owes much to that dual invitation.

Tobin Siebers for getting me to think about the uses of nonfiction stories.

The superb Twitter and Facebook hordes: pfanderson, rivenhomewood, KathrynTomasek, j_breitenbucher, and all.

Blog commentators Andy Havens, Steve Kaye, D'Arcy Norman, H. Pierce, and more. Infocult is in your debt.

For teaching inspiration: my two genius co-teachers Bret Olsen and Doug Reilly.

For every kind of collaboration, from coauthoring to teaching, inspiration to scheming: my wise and playful teachers Barbara Ganley and Alan Levine.

For all kinds of support and tolerance over many years: my NITLE colleagues. And especially the many NITLE workshop participants, in all their energy, creativity, and generosity.

For helping me through the process of writing the book: Raymond Yee. Howard Rheingold for endless inspiration and guidance.

For the second edition, many of these co-conspirators continue to give generously of their thoughts and practice.

I would like to thank the StoryCenter crew, led by the very great Joe Lambert, for not only kicking off their digital storytelling movement, but also for putting up with my questions and brooding.

My family has pointed out many new stories and movements which I might otherwise have missed.

Friends and blog commentators have been very helpful: Alan Levine, Sandy Brown Jensen, Sue Cornacchia, Doug Reilly, Chad Bergeron, Chris Lott, Barbara Ganley, Vanessa Vaile, and many more. Len Rowell has been a powerful force for good in trying to build an Addison County storytelling movement.

Introduction

I created my first digital story in 2003. Two brilliant teachers from Berkeley's Center for Digital Storytelling led a workshop at the Center for Educational Technology in Middlebury, Vermont. That latter center inhabited an old building, the former courthouse for Addison County. There, Joe Lambert and Emily Paulos met with a dozen of us, and we learned to turn new technologies to storytelling purposes between gleaming labs and refurbished court offices. We wrote voiceovers while watching the morning sun light up the Green Mountains' slopes, scanned photos under fluorescent lights, and shared our final films on DVD in a darkened, 19th-century courtroom.

In a sense, that experience was the genesis of this book. My quirky tale of experiencing *The War of the Worlds* convinced me of the power of blending personal life and digital technology. Through recorded voiceover, photos snagged through Google Images, audio tracks drawn from podcasts, and frantically typed subtitles, I remembered being terrified by a book when I was a child: H. G. Wells's novel of alien invasion, hauntingly illustrated by the late, great Edward Gorey (Looking Glass Library, 1960). I recalled how the memory of that terror returned to me as an adult when a copy crossed my desk at a used bookshop.[1] The Center for Digital Storytelling class helped me remix those memories with technology, drawing forth emotions I'd forgotten, eliciting new reflections. The experience was simultaneously a deep dive into my past, a fast yet effective grappling with multiple technologies, and an epiphany about the new nature of story.

In a different sense, though, I created my first digital stories back in the 1990s, as when I created a virtual haunted mansion for students in my gothic literature class. It was really just a series of Web pages, each holding some small piece of literary criticism or content. Very little media was involved beyond text, dark backgrounds, and some images. Those pages were hyperlinked together by logical steps, following a hypothetical yet recognizable building's interior layout. Pages were also connected through hidden pathways, puzzles, and mysteries, appropriately enough. My students had to navigate this monstrous architectural metaphor for a final exam: first to *find* the exam (hidden away in a secret chamber), then to use its form and content as a study guide for the rest of the test. The students were at first terrified (again, appropriately enough) and frantic, nearly delirious when finding the exam link, then simply energetic as they wrote.

I can rewind my digital storytelling life further back into the 20th century and try to recall writing computer games in BASIC during a very geekish adolescence.[2] From sixth grade into junior high, I typed laboriously onto dumb terminals yoked to distant, hidden mainframes by the early Internet. I snatched keyboard and monitor time from the local RadioShack, learning and experimenting as long as I could before getting kicked out. Space wars and Robert Frost poems, postnuclear adventures and quizzes, even very primitive animations emerged from cryptic alphanumeric lines. These games sometimes let players tell stories, or told stories themselves, back in the last decade of the Cold War.

There is nothing extraordinary in this autobiographic excursus, at least for an American lifetime. These technologies were not secret in 1979 when I was in New York and Michigan sixth grades, but known, and steadily growing in reach. Many people considered these "machines to think with" as tools of imagination, grounds for storytelling.[3] Their story is one of steady experimentation and two generations of creativity, culminating in our time—an extraordinary era for creating and experiencing stories.

Who Is This Book For?

The New Digital Storytelling is aimed at creators and would-be practitioners, first of all—people who want to tell stories with digital technologies for the first time, those who are already using digital tools and want to try new approaches, and storytellers using nondigital means (like voice or print) who seek to cross the analog–digital divide. We will cover a wide range of ground, as the field has opened up. You may be a storyteller working in another medium, wanting to explore the digital world. You may be a teacher, or a marketer, or a communications manager. Whatever your background, herein you will find examples to draw on, practical uses to learn from, principles to apply, and some creative inspiration.

You might be considering a full-scale project, such as a YouTube video series, a virtual reality experiment, a novel-length e-book, or a blog. Perhaps you are building a game space or virtual environment and expect users (players) to tell themselves the story of their adventures within it. Alternatively, a story may lurk within your conception of that world and will unfurl during the course of its creation. Or perhaps you have a story in mind, a full-length one, and are not sure upon which digital stage (or stages) it should play.

On the other hand, you might not have a full digital story in mind but are already using digital platforms and social media for various purposes and would like to add the "story factor" to improve your work.[4] Perhaps you do not think of your work as storytelling or yourself as a storyteller. This book is *especially* intended for you. Each chapter explores principles for better storytelling that can be applied to many situations and at any scale: how to make that PowerPoint presentation less of a death march and more of a compelling narrative; how to increase a blog readership's attention or better shape a podcast—to any such situation, storytelling proves a helpful advisor.

What this book is *not*: It is not a hands-on manual concerning the technical details of using certain digital media. It does not have the space to delve into the nitty-gritty minutiae of different video editors, wiki markup, and blog hosting options. Instead, this book is based on the mid-1990s Center for Digital Storytelling's subtle insight: that one can select just enough technology to be dangerous, an appropriate baseline amount to get the narrative going (see Chapter 2). The reader is not assumed to be a technologist, and the book's language is accordingly accessible.

It is also in the social media spirit to recognize that much information is provided by experts located elsewhere. I will outline many technologies in the pages that follow and point to communities and leading experts to connect with in order to find more information. It is my fond hope that readers will be inspired to contribute to various digital storytelling social networks in multiple ways, building still more resources for others.

This book is also not a literary theory-level study of digital storytelling. I will be drawing on literary criticism along with media studies, history, and other fields while avoiding jargon from those fields, much as technical terms are minimized. More literary and theoretical studies of digital storytelling are certainly needed, bringing to bear the formidable hermeneutic tools of contemporary literary criticism. There is already a good amount of work along these lines being done in several allied fields, including net.art and gaming studies. Those texts will play an important role in this book; this book, however, is not entirely of that sort. Instead, we will explore a wide variety of stories and strategies, applying basic literary and media criticism in order to inspire creators and their supporters while entering into texts at enough of a depth to start understanding them.

The New Digital Storytelling straddles the awkward yet practical divide between production and consumption, critique and project creation. Ultimately a single book cannot do full justice to both. Instead, it can at best connect one domain with the other, hopefully bringing a kind of stereoscopic vision to bear. Put another way, the core of this book surveys the current state of the technologically enabled art in a way grounded in both contemporary theory and practice.

Organization of the Book

I begin with a historical sketch in Part 1. The first chapter tries to untangle the Gordian knot of storytelling, teasing out the different models and modes we inherit in 2017. Chapters 2 and 3 then survey the digital storytelling ancestry, the two generations of computing and narrative practice preceding our time.

The second part of this book surveys the current state of the digital storytelling art. This part proceeds by increasing levels of scale, beginning with simpler and more accessible technologies (text- and image-based social media), advancing through richer media (audio and video), and climaxing with the most advanced forms (gaming small and large). These constitute a series of new platforms for narratives. Some are emergent ones in the sense of having recently appeared, yielding a good number of examples, and continuing to develop on multiple levels. Others are more mature, if still evolving.

It is important to emphasize the persistence of older, seemingly obsolete or outmoded technologies. As David Edgerton argues, multiple strata of technology continue functioning while and after new ones enter society. Older technologies and practices can maintain their purposes or become repurposed for new uses.[5] In this book, we examine interactive fiction, a form robust in the early 1980s, alongside augmented reality, an information ecosystem still being born as of this writing. Perhaps the most powerful metaphor for thinking through successive technologies is that of tile imbrications. As each new row of tiles partially obscures, yet partially exposes, already established rows, new technologies often overlap the old, partially but not entirely obscuring their predecessors.

In Part 3, we turn to new narrative forms emerging from combinations of the storytelling practices sketched out in the preceding chapters. Personal stories, gaming, and social media have each developed quite far in a short period of time, so it is unsurprising that they have begun to connect with each other and crossbreed. Perhaps we can think of the emergent swarm of projects and strategies under the header of "combinatorial storytelling."

Chapter 8 focuses on how storytelling redistributes itself across multiple platforms. Chapter 9 recognizes the sweeping, global transformation of cyberculture being wrought by mobile devices. New devices have elicited new storytelling designs. Indeed, mobile devices, especially phones, may be emerging as the world's primary digital storytelling devices.

In Chapter 10, we turn to alternate reality games (ARGs), which have grown into one of the most innovative approaches to multimedia storytelling. ARGs demonstrate new techniques for engaging audiences and collaboration. Out of a decade of ARG practice comes the concept of chaotic fiction or chaotic storytelling, which might be considered a good aegis to cover a multitude of narratives. ARGs remix and combine a variety of storytelling approaches covered in previous chapters, from personal stories to casual games.

Another synthesis comes from the intersection of mobile devices, distributed storytelling, gaming, and visualization. Augmented reality, the practice of connecting digital content to the physical world—virtual reality turned inside out—is the subject of Chapter 11. As we collectively build a digital laminate over the Earth, it is logical to expect storytelling to appear in this new "Worldboard." In Chapter 12, we explore the newest media synthesis, that found in the reemerging area of virtual reality. There we set aside the hype to understand VR's storytelling capacities.

The fourth part of this book delves into practical methods for building digital stories, including adding "story-ness" to nonstory projects. Chapter 13 describes the different ways a digital storytelling class works, then offers guidelines for creators not working in a workshop environment. The next chapter outlines ways to find new digital stories and storytellers, mapping out the relevant social media landscape. Chapter 15 dives into educational uses of digital storytelling, drawing on my experience in teaching workshops on the topic and helping grow a network of academic practitioners for nearly two decades.

The final chapter is a kind of hybrid, a coda that also evokes futurism. After spending the book discussing developments of the past and present, it makes sense to gesture toward what appears to be coming next. Chapter 16 extrapolates from what we have seen of media practice and digital storytelling old and new, seeing trends forward into the near future.

Each chapter of this book occupies a position on a digital storytelling continuum, stretching between theory and practice. Some chapters occupy positions farther toward one end than the other. However, every section is grounded in actual historical evidence, the fruits of research and networking, since digital storytelling is now old enough to provide a wealth of documentation.

Some of these chapters commence with very short stories as examples of the practices to be covered, a kind of extended narrative epigraph. Several describe real stories and the process of either consuming or producing them. Others are mildly fictionalized accounts of my experiences with digital storytelling workshops. Still others are instances of what Bruce Sterling and Julian Bleeker describe as "design fiction," stories that imagine the lived experience of a new object.[6] The purpose of these is partly to give the reader a sense of what the chapter will explore, but also to use a very small form of storytelling in the service of discussing that art.

At a meta level, some chapters address a somewhat dizzying phenomenon, the practices described being nested within stories presented in *other* media, like digital storytelling *matriochka* dolls. This means mobile device storytelling appears as a plot device within other stories, blogs are depicted in print science fiction, and classic interactive fiction is mimicked for political satire. It's a sign of how widespread or compelling these practices are that they can be taken up or reproduced elsewhere with hope of audience engagement. Indeed, we can probably identify a nascent metafiction subgenre, a body of stories *about* new digital stories.

A Note about the Writing of This Book

It is appropriate that a book about new forms of digital storytelling should partake of those new media platforms. I blogged about digital storytelling old and new in two different venues and also aggregated and tagged examples on a social bookmarking service.[7] Another way I "dogfooded" the book was by crowdsourcing topical discussion during the manuscript's penultimate month of preparation. I had been using Twitter to explore digital storytelling ever since joining the service. Then in August 2010, I ramped up the process. Every day, I tweeted at least one observation, note, or query to the world and read back as Twitterites (or "tweeple") returned their thoughts. This book owes much to them, to faithful correspondents and capable observers like riven home wood, dethe, and derekbruff. In a very real sense, our Twitter conversations through the course of writing this book constituted a digital story.

This book's social networks are not to blame for any errors or gaps in the text. In covering a broad, rapidly developing, multidomain world, I am certain to have committed some of these. I expect the distributed Argus eyes of social media to identify each one, both sins of omission and commission. All gaps, slips, gaffes, and errors are solely my own.

Introduction to the Second Edition

In 2017, we are very accustomed to the rapid pace of digital development. In the six years since this book first appeared, we have seen new forms of mobile devices appear, smartphones spread across the world, virtual reality return from its 1990s grave, and drones range from weapons of war to popular hobby devices. Social media has grown still further, shedding its old Web 2.0 monicker, spreading throughout daily life, and becoming an international political force. Computer gaming has leaped ahead from its already prominent position, going on to snare fortunes and Hollywood actors.

At the same time, storytelling has become a more visible cultural practice. Marketers vie with each to hook consumers with narratives. Voters assess political candidates based on their storytelling abilities. Job candidates, nonprofits, businesses, and government offices seek ways to best tell their stories. Storytelling workshops, books, classes, and experts proliferate. Old school oral story projects, like the Moth, have blossomed.

Readers of this book's first edition will be unsurprised to learn that these fresh story and technology developments have coincided, and digital storytelling has continued to grow. The Center for Digital Storytelling became StoryCenter and shared a rich trove of video stories on the Web. More story-making tools have appeared, especially for mobile devices, and media creation is both easier and more versatile. Amazon's Kindle marketplace has seen a boom in authors self-publishing e-books. Creepypasta tales have seized the popular imagination, even spawning the modern monster myth of Slenderman. We are just starting to explore the narrative potential of virtual reality.

Best of all, people continue to make and share digital stories. Podcasting had a second birth with the surprise success of *Serial* (2014–2016). YouTube carries stories from around the world. Indie gaming has pushed the edges of what kinds of stories games can tell. More teachers assign or create digital stories. Social media gurus instruct us on how to use story to make our use of those platforms compelling. Digital storytelling is, in short, becoming mainstreamed. It is more accessible, more widely used, and more versatile.

In this second edition, I have brought elements of the first up to speed. The historical sections stand, and the story theory remains applicable, but many chapters include subsequent technologies and projects, from blogging to mobile to podcasting. The sheer number of new forms and stories testifies to digital storytelling's ongoing vibrancy.

A new chapter introduces virtual reality storytelling, which is a necessary yet risky move: necessary, due to the enormous attention paid to this nascent medium, and for its sizable potential; risky, since that vast amount of attention is currently accompanied by a great deal of invention and investment, so that my 2017 observations risk becoming all too historical by 2018. To make the best of it I have done several things. I have extended concepts from the rest of the book into this new world, identifying ways VR stories can echo or draw upon previous media. I have also considered the small yet growing corpus of VR narratives in their diversity in order to tease out multiple directions their successors can take. Naturally, this account owes something to science fiction, which has been dreaming VR stories for decades.

This second edition owes its new form to conversations rippling across social media. Practitioners and scholars have generously shared their work and reflections through Twitter, YouTube, Facebook, the blogosphere, and podcasts. Leading lights such as Joe Lambert and Alan Levine have kindly responded to my ongoing probes into this developing world. They and others were also kind in addressing Youtube, my blog creations, published on Cowbird and elsewhere.

Face-to-face encounters have also been vital in my revisionary work. A fine conference hosted by Smith College surfaced many cutting-edge questions and ideas. Workshops and presentations at New Media Consortium, NERCOMP, and EDUCAUSE events kept me in close contact with the pedagogical uses of digital storytelling. Discussions with my local Vermont storytellers have been fruitful.

Across these conversations, the theme of digital storytelling as political avenue has risen, especially during the increasingly tense years of 2015 and 2016 and the impending cultural panic of 2017. Digital stories have given form to causes and driven some onward. It's hard to imagine Black Lives Matter without heartbreaking videos of callous inhumanity, shared through social networks. Members of communities afflicted by exclusion, threats, and violence turn to stories to share their experience, to strengthen themselves, and to bear witness.

We have always told and shared stories for political purposes; it only makes sense that we continue to do so with new, digital platforms. May they address our hearts and illuminate the way ahead.

PART 1

Storytelling: A Tale of Two Generations

CHAPTER ONE

Storytelling for the 21st Century

What is digital storytelling? Simply put, it is telling stories with digital technologies. Digital stories are narratives built from the stuff of cyberculture.

We can also conceive of digital storytelling through examples of it in action, such as:

- A very short story about growing food, made out of remixed archival photographs
- A podcast about medieval history, where each installment takes listeners through the extraordinary lives of Norman rulers
- A virtual reality environment where we follow workers ascending a dizzying height
- A blog novel about America in 1968, following two teenagers as they travel through political and personal landscapes
- An account of an alien invasion delivered through multiple Twitter accounts: an updated *War of the Worlds* hoax, tweet by tweet
- A video clip about a mother–daughter relationship over time
- A game of sorts seemingly about *The Matrix,* based on a Web site, but mysteriously extending across multiple platforms, including your e-mail inbox
- Novels read on mobile phones—and often written on mobile phones
- Hundreds of Vermont teenagers creating multimedia stories for each other
- A Holocaust victim's life retold by Facebook[1]

Digital stories are currently created using nearly every digital device in an ever-growing toolbox. They are experienced by a large population. Their creators are sometimes professionals, and also amateurs. They can be deeply personal or posthumanly otherwise, fiction and nonfiction, brief or epic, wrought from a single medium or sprawling across dozens. We are living in a time of immense creativity, with new opportunities for creators appearing nearly every day. Several decades of energetic digital experimentation have borne fruit, and yet, in the larger historical frame, still these are early days of innovation.

The phrase "digital storytelling" has several interesting resonances as this book is being written, and we can break out some assumptions from them. Pairing those two words can still elicit surprise or even shock for some if the listener expects the two domains to be fundamentally separate. "Storytelling" suggests the old storyteller, connected to a bardic or Homeric tradition, a speaker enrapturing an immediate audience. As Coleridge and Wordsworth imagined it:

> He holds him with his glittering eye—
> The Wedding-Guest stood still,
> And listens like a three years' child:
> The Mariner hath his will.

Stories are spoken and heard in this classic model. The story is a personal, intimate, analog thing. Therefore, cyberspace is a world apart, at its worst a cold domain of data. At best, since many of us now inhabit cyberspace to a degree, this view of story assigns to that vast domain functions that might assist, but not constitute, narrative: communication, database access, entertainment, socialization, document management.

When I teach digital storytelling workshops, as an initial discussion prompt I ask participants to describe what stories are *not*. Inevitably people are surprised, even wrong-footed, as they probably expect to speak to what stories *are* (which is also a fine prompt; see below). Usually the negative answers that emerge identify an item typically associated with the digital world: data, especially data without meaningful patterns. Data are cold, while stories are warm. Data lack intrinsic meaning, while stories are all about meaning. (If things get contentious at this point, I can show examples of storytelling through data, like Neil Halloran's "Data Visualizing WWII's Devastating Death Toll.")[2]

Other workshop participants see the gap between storytelling and the digital world as based upon a preference for analog media, namely, books, movies, TV, and music. Few will hedge this stance by noting that much seemingly analog content is already being produced and distributed through digital means. Instead, they focus on pre-Web devices such as the paperback novel, film stored on reels and projected into a peopled theater, live music, or vinyl records. These objects are more familiar than digital ones to many participants and have an additional aura of ever-increasing historical value. They may be spoken of with love, nostalgia, or pride.

Once brought into conversation, these apparently predigital media help workshop participants describe what makes good storytelling happen. Thinking of favorite TV shows or novels, workshops quickly summon up examples of appealing characters, solid plots, great scenes, and what makes a particular genre successful. A class can work with such details of either oral or "analog" storytelling and take them into less medium-bound, more generic territory. Conceptually, this abstraction then prepares the ground for reconnecting these concepts with digital platforms. Practically speaking, participants who start thinking about digital storytelling by bearing in mind narrative traditions in which they place value and comfort, tend to feel less anxiety about the newer, digital tools.

At a different level, pairing digital storytelling with other narrative traditions brings to mind the sheer scope and persistence of storytelling in the human condition. The historicity of storytelling tempts us to consider the narrative impulse to be a universal one. Every culture tells stories. Each epoch brims with tales insofar as records make them available.

For our purposes, it's vital to realize that people tell stories with nearly every new piece of communication technology we invent. Portable video recorders led to video art, starting in the 1960s with the Portapak and Nam June Paik's work. Long-playing vinyl records enabled concept albums, from Gordon Jenkins's *Manhattan Towers* (1958) to Jethro Tull's *Thick as a Brick* (1972) and Pink Floyd's *The Wall* (1979): a series of songs thematically unified and interrelated by content and/or formal features.[3] The motion picture camera elicited cinema. Radio spawned the "theater of the mind." The Lascaux caves either represented scenes of daily life or taught viewers hunting and other tasks. Indeed, no sooner do we invent a medium than do we try to tell stories with it.

What, then, are stories? It's often productive to see how people react when asked to answer that question themselves in conversation, in class, or as an audience. As a teacher and presenter, I have seen every single audience energized by the question. Their faces light up with memory of stories and storytellers; their heads tilt in forceful, almost physical recollection. Goofy smiles and critically engaged frowns appear and disappear in succession. Asking the question "What is a story?" is a more positive and productive exercise than asking the opposite, as answers come more quickly, tend to expressive positive emotions, and are often usefully diverse.

Answering this question, some will volunteer versions of the Freytag triangle, usually without naming it. This is the customary sequence of exposition or introduction, rising action, climax, falling action, and a denouement, first codified by the German writer Gustav Freytag (1816–1895) in the 19th century. Nearly every person will recognize this sequence on its own terms, perhaps rephrased in the ancient trinity of beginning, middle, and end, or through variations like inception through crisis and resolution. A story is simply a thing, any media object, which demonstrates this clear sequence. Some workshop participants will recognize this notion from either Robert McKee's influential screenwriting book, *Story*, or the 2002 film, *Adaptation*, both of which reference that approach explicitly. McKee also (and usefully) expands that three-step sequence to include five stages: inciting incident, progressive complications, crisis, climax, and then resolution.[4] The linear nature of stories is crucial to many definitions of *story*. Events arranged in time, or an event broken down into a temporal sequence: these make intuitive sense. Given that stories reassemble previously existing materials (language, media, audience, lives), perhaps we can go further and see stories as consisting of some selections from the set of available cultural practices, crafted to represent events chronologically. But focusing on the importance of time to stories risks being too obvious. How can a story exist outside of time, beyond the cliché of being timeless? If we emphasize time's role in the definition of storytelling, Will Eisner's definition of comics as "sequential art" could be translated and applied to any storytelling form or practice at all.[5]

Some story definitions appear to reflect a frustration with other media—hence the argument that stories are objects (books, movies, documents, etc.) with *meaning*. This definition opposes a story to a pile of data or a document that is difficult to parse or an experimental work that is challenging to grasp. Related to this sense of story as meaning–vehicle are definitions that place *engagement* in the foreground. In this model, stories are that which pull in the viewer/reader/listener; nonstories (or very bad stories) are things that do not attempt to engage us, or fail miserably at it. As Nick Montfort argues, a story "has a point. There's a reason for introducing it, there's a reason for bringing it up. If it means something to our situation, and to the way we talk to one other, *then* we're doing storytelling."[6] Documentarian Sheila Bernard places engagement at the root of storytelling: "A *story* is the narrative, or telling, of an event or series of events, crafted in a way to interest the audiences, whether they are readers, listeners, or viewers."[7]

The reason for a story—its point, its meaning—can be understood as a theme: "the general underlying subject of a specific story, a recurring idea that often illuminates an aspect of the human condition."[8] The full sweep of emotions and details ground that theme, making it accessible and engaging. Daniel Pink sees these as definitional: "Story exists where high concept and high touch intersect. Story is high concept because it sharpens our understanding of one thing by showing it in the context of something else. . . . Story is high touch because stories almost always pack an emotional response."[9] Radio artist Ira Glass considers a story's theme or meaning—"why the hell you're listening to this story"—as one of storytelling's two essential "building blocks."[10]

Another way of contrasting data with stories is to classify some short narratives as data points: too small to consider as whole stories, but useful as material out of which to *build* stories. The Cognitive Edge group calls these "microcontent anecdotes" and urges organizations to generate as many of them as possible. They can then be used later on:

> An anecdote is a naturally occurring story, as found in the "wild" of conversational discourse. Anecdotes are usually short and about a single incident or situation. Contrast this with a purposeful story, which is long and complex as well as deliberately constructed and told (usually many times).[11]

Here we see stories distinguished by scale, a kind of quantitative argument: anecdotes are short and focused, while stories are longer and focus on larger or multiple topics. Anecdotes are also concrete, while stories build toward abstract knowledge out of them. Put another way, Cognitive Edge makes a distinction between uncodified knowledge and knowledge codified through narrative. Stories decode and encode.[12] Glass offers a similar view using the same term, "anecdote," as one of the essential building blocks of stories.[13]

No writer offers a hard-and-fast rule for distinguishing small from large, anecdote from story. No precise measurement of clip length nor word count can be sustained (see the discussion of Hemingway's six-word story in Chapter 13). But the scale differential can work as a rule of thumb if applied to our consideration of small bits of multimedia such as images, sound effects, or maps. Stories are assemblages; storytelling is a kind of scaling up.

A related approach to understanding meaning in a story is to focus on a problem or crisis, especially a personal one. On the face of it, such a model seems obvious; what kind of story is there without some problem or struggle? It is, after all, easy to dislike a story for its lack of significant problem, which leaves an impression of dullness or emotional flatness.

Sheila Bernard notes: "If something is easy, there's no tension, and without tension, there's little incentive for an audience to keep watching."[14] We can readily dismiss a story in the mystery genre for having made the killer's identity too easy to solve or a romance where the lovers' obstacles are too quickly overcome. Stories seem to require a challenge at their heart, one for characters to work through and for readers or listeners to appreciate.

Problem-based storytelling is a popular model in the literature. For example, Jason Ohler calls his problem-based model the "story core" and breaks it down into three parts. First, a "central challenge" must be evident—"a question, a problem, an obstacle, an opportunity, or a goal." This "creates tension that gives the story its forward momentum, which in turn produces listener involvement." Second, characters change as they wrestle with the problem. "Either life or 'the old you' pushes back as new circumstances or 'a new you' struggles to emerge." Third, the problem receives closure: "solving a mystery, slaying a dragon, reaching a goal, applying new academic knowledge or learning processes, overcoming an obstacle. . . . Closure by no means implies a happy ending, just a resolution of events."[15]

Problems can be escalated in scale to a far greater level than the personal, according to the mythic school of story making. This stems from the early 20th century's anthropological boom, climaxing for storytelling purposes in Joseph Campbell's *The Hero with a Thousand Faces* (1949). Campbell claimed to have identified a monomyth of a hero's journey, an *ur*-tale or Jungian archetype with deep, regular underpinnings. The hero is summoned to extraordinary challenge, faces strenuous and even deadly obstacles, overcomes them, and then returns home victoriously. Campbell saw this pattern embodied in myths and ancient stories with local variations, from the lives of Buddha and Christ to Greek epics.

Campbell's monomyth is a staple of many storytelling approaches, having reached an acme of fame in its association with George Lucas and the (chronologically) first *Star Wars* movie. Some schools broaden the hero's journal into a set of myths or simply the strategy of crafting a story to draw on popular radical-appearing myths. This is the basis of James Bonnet's screenwriting work, connecting writers to mythic plots in order to create better scripts.[16] As another screenwriting guru, Robert McKee, argues: "An archetypal story creates settings and characters so rare that our eyes feast on every detail, while the telling illuminates conflicts so true to humankind that it journeys from culture to culture."[17]

The mythic school has garnered criticism over the decades, beginning with Campbell's focus on male characters to the all-too-frequent exclusion of women. The mythopoeic approach is also critiqued for the way it necessarily diminishes the importance of craft and media specificity. Further, it falls in and out of fashion, depending on the status of Carl Jung's reputation.

Perhaps the most important objection to the mythic approach for our digital storytelling purposes is the way myth sidesteps the materials of everyday life. Rather than looking for mythic substrata in the quotidian, we can respect the details and stories of our lives, letting them resonate on their own terms. That is part of the genius and appeal of the Center for Digital Storytelling methodology, which is built upon giving voice to every participant, regardless of his or her professional ambition or life experience. Or, as Annette Simmons argues: "Myths and fables are not the only timeless stories. There are stories of your life, from your family, in your work experience that if you told them, would activate a deep recognition in almost any human being in the world."[18]

In my workshop experience, both approaches—mythic and everyday—appeal strongly to participants engaged in the creative process. Both clearly appeal to us as media consumers, as even a casual glance at the media landscape reveals.

Engagement can also be understood as a kind of mystery, a story in whatever medium elicits the audience's curiosity and makes us want to experience more of it. Consider, for example, a famous opening line:

> The last man on Earth sat alone in a room. There was a knock on the door.
> (Fredric Brown, "Knock," 1948)

The first sentence immediately summons up a sense of vast catastrophe, a crisis already passed. The second then shocks our sense of the first, eliciting a frisson of wonder: who, *what* could it be? An alien? A robot? A woman, if "man" means "male"? A mere 17 words in and the reader is hooked, driven on toward the lines that follow. Compare that one with these famous openings:

- "It was a bright cold day in April, and the clocks were striking thirteen" (George Orwell, *Nineteen Eighty-Four,* 1949).

- "Last night, I dreamt I went to Manderley again" (Daphne du Maurier, *Rebecca,* 1938).

- "The sky above the port was the color of television, tuned to a dead channel" (William Gibson, *Neuromancer,* 1984).

- "As Gregor Samsa awoke one morning from uneasy dreams he found himself transformed in his bed into a gigantic insect" (Franz Kafka, *The Metamorphosis,* 1915).[19]

Each of these presents us with mysteries. How can a clock strike thirteen? (Answer: military time.) What is Manderley, why did the narrator go there before, and why once more? What does that kind of sky look like, and how did it get that way? How on Earth did this Gregor Samsa person become a bug, and what does it mean? These openers are mysterious enough to engage us without being so cryptic that we cannot quickly find meaning in them. They are puzzles we want to decode.

For creators, this kind of mystery making can seem wrongheaded and perverse, especially in nonfiction contexts. After all, we come to tell stories in order to *share* our material, not to *conceal* it. Yet, concealing the matter of a story in a way that pulls in attention can engage the audience enough that they will deliberately pay more attention to the story. As Bernard writes of documentary filmmaking, as a creator, "your goal is to create a film that's driven by a story, one that will motivate even general viewers to *want* to know more of those details that thrill you. They'll grow to care because those details will matter to the story unfolding on screen."[20] In Chapter 2, we will reference Espen Aarseth's idea of experiencing hypertext fiction and gaming as a "work path" where such stories are predicated on an audience's effort. But a good story wins its audience to efforts on its behalf even without the formal device of hypertext or games through careful use of mystery. This element of concealing and attraction is the root of interactivity, and of cocreation.

Compare such mysterious story elements to a bad PowerPoint presentation. The latter does not draw us in, failing to summon our willing efforts to see it advance. Instead, the poor PowerPoint depresses us with the prospect of its extension into the future. It is a spectacle of inertia, a kind of audience assassination. We do not want the presenter to advance the slides unless it is done quickly. We viewers and listeners come to expect that the next slide will appear monotonously through PowerPoint's sequential logic.[21]

A presentation that uses storytelling well, by contrast, makes the audience want the next slide to appear. Individual slides might seem incomplete, but in a way that elicits our desire to finish them ourselves. Two or more can seem to be a puzzle for which we can supply an answer. Alternatively, we may come to expect that the next slide, or one further along, will complete the puzzle for us; this sequence is a form of trust won by decent storytelling.[22] We will return to puzzles throughout this book, especially in gaming; for now, consider them another part of the story mystery of stories.

Another classic sense of story emphasizes representation of life to an audience, or *mimesis*. We find this theme as early as Plato and Aristotle, and mimesis persists as a storytelling theme throughout the subsequent history of aesthetics. Representation does not require a story to occur, as the nonnarrative arts attest. For a story to connect with an audience, however, it must represent something recognizable from life.

Simmons sees the skill of storytelling as "the unique capability to tap into *a complex situation we have all experienced and which we all recognize.*"[23] This recognition is a form of connection to the audience on par with the sense of engagement discussed earlier. But it is in the service of carrying one part of life (a situation) to another (the audience). Simmons recommends that creators develop skills with empathy and sensory detail in order to better connect with their readers or listeners, which aligns well with this definition from *Wikipedia*: "Storytelling is the conveying of events in words, images and sounds often by improvisation or embellishment." In this sense, stories are events conveyed to an audience through the skillful use of media.

Instead of reproducing events or situations through art, perhaps stories are essentially about representing people. My workshop participants inevitably deem personal content to be part of a story. They value highly stories that feature appealing characters but generally like stories with any characters at all. Charles Baxter, a leading teacher of writing, emphasizes characters as being essential to a story through their desires: "Without a mobilized desire or fear, characters in a story—or life—won't be willing to do much of anything in the service of their great longings."[24] The Center for Digital Storytelling (about which see Chapter 2) bases its curriculum upon personal stories, those about the creator's life or concerning the life of someone who deeply affected the creator. Jason Ohler, an educator who teaches with digital stories, argues that stories usually work when

> they have at their heart an effective story core: a central character . . . that undergoes a transformation in order to solve a problem, answer a question, meet a goal, resolve an issue, or realize the potential of an opportunity.[25]

Bernard agrees, referring to "the way or ways in which the events of a story transform your characters" as an arc. Sam Pollard, interviewed by Bernard, describes a character arc as "a transformation of a state of being."[26] A story without such an arc will often feel flat, its emotional range blunted. A character who does not change in a story is not a person but a trading card.

Put another way, we deem a character's story worthy through multiple, overlapping validations. Does a character seem convincing, realistic, human? (See a related note on gaming and consistency in Chapter 6.) Do we empathize with them, feel an emotional connection? These two assessments are widespread in the reception of nearly all fictions. A third evaluation reverses the terms and questions the storyteller's character: is he or she convincing? Do we feel hailed by or connected to that voice? Naturally, these criteria apply differently across cultures, times, and individual preferences, but the forms remain popular.

So far, we have not dealt with the distinction between fiction and nonfiction. The term *storytelling* often implies fiction, or even myth ("That's just a story they tell to explain . . ."). But every aspect of story definition we've discussed so far applies as well to nonfiction narratives: characters (people), extension in time, mystery and engagement, even Freytag's triangle. A good exercise for people who aren't narrative professionals is to think of nonfiction storytelling examples. As Alan Levine and I noted, these include "marketing used to sell a product's story; the mini-stories so essential to any discussion of ethics; the use of storytelling for surfacing implicit information in knowledge-management practice."[27]

In fact, nonfiction storytelling is widespread. Journalists often describe their work as "telling the story" of a present-day event, as "history's first draft." Historians, in turn, want to tell us the story of past events to the highest degree possible. A common therapeutic process has a patient learning to tell his or her own story of a threat, a trauma, or a relationship; Freud's case narratives are fine stories in themselves. Ethical discussions inevitably turn to parables or exemplary stories to illustrate a point or elicit thought. For instance, the classic runaway train problem—"If you had a choice between letting a runaway train kill ten people or murdering one yourself, what would you do?"—requires a short-short story to work.[28] Attorneys before a judge or jury assemble evidence, then knit it together into a performed narrative in order to persuade the court.

Businesses use storytelling in a variety of levels. Marketing sells products by telling persuasive stories about products. For example, Google accumulates and blogs positive stories about people using its search service. These short-short tales involve Google-based happiness around love, physical health, language learning, and, of course, finding information.[29] Companies like StoryQuest help company staff learn to create and share stories.[30] Public relations firms try to tell the most effective story of an enterprise in the face of sometimes oppositional narratives. Internally, a common knowledge-management practice involves employees narrating an operational process in order to surface tacit or hidden knowledge about how work gets done. Politicians combine all of these in campaigns, which mix current events, history, and persuasion. In fact, our daily lives are permeated by nonfiction stories coming at us from all media, competing with and complementing each other.

For our purposes, let us attempt a synthesis of these definitional attempts. For a given audience, a *story* is a sequence of content, anchored on a problem, which engages that audience with emotion and meaning. Breaking this down, *audience* is a crucial definitional component simply because what makes a story for one group might fail utterly for another.

Being able to determine a *sequence* or significant extension in time lets us distinguish a story from a data point or anecdote. The timeline of a story does not necessarily have to map directly onto the temporal sequence of what it describes. Flashbacks, for instance, or revisiting events can twist a straight timeline into retrograde orbits or curlicues.

Sequence is important for another reason, namely, the importance of stories' extension in time. A single image, object, or musical tone does not usually constitute a story. They are story pieces, media fodder awaiting use. Now, an audience can turn a single item into a story through the process of reception. Looking at a portrait of a weeping clown, one might envision reasons for such sadness or ways of alleviating it—and at that point the audience member is making a story, indeed beyond the extent of the original. Skillful creators can pause their narratives to facilitate precisely this form of engagement, drawing the audience into cocreation. Some digital tools make this explicit, as we'll see in Chapters 2 and 3.

Returning to our previous examples of famous opening lines, note how they get audiences thinking sequentially. For one thing, they put forth mysteries that require explanation. How did the sky get to be that color? What happened to poor Gregor? They therefore push us in two different time directions: back, to understand the reasons preceding the situation, and forward, into a plot which must surely follow (if the clocks ring thirteen, something bad is bound to happen next).

Emotional engagement and meaning, again, are something audiences must at least partially determine. But it's a good rule of thumb to bear in mind that some kind of struggle or problem, some source of friction, is usually required to generate both engagement and meaning. When audiences complain about a story being weak, slow, or uninviting, it's often from a lack of such struggle. Too easy a plot rapidly becomes dull. Think of poor PowerPoint presentations that proceed solely by inertia or, even worse, by the speaker merely describing what's on a slide. These lack a sense of urgency, some problem being wrestled with, a question asked and being replied to. Stories require at least a bit of struggle.

Character can survive a lack of plot if the character is interesting enough. A fascinating environment can take the place of a crisis in a story: hence the cliché of a city, building, or landscape being part of the dramatis personae. Yet these impersonal objects usually go through changes in stories where they appear significantly enough to merit characterization. The city of Baltimore in TV's *The Wire* (2002–2008) experiences major changes in policy and leadership while enduring crime waves. Algernon Blackwood characterizes one Danube River location as an entity in "The Willows" (1907), showing its response to a challenge (the arrival of two human visitors). Character grounds meaning for a story so long as it offers credibility and change.

If we can work with this template definition of *story,* then we can proceed to see how it helps us understand stories in the digital world. First, we can assess a given digital object against our definition to see how it performs. Second, we can explore how the digital story functions in ways emphasizing the unique affordances of cyberculture. How does being digital enable new aspects of storytelling?

One way of answering the second question is to start by recognizing that a greater proportion and number of people than ever before now have access to storytelling media—for both story production and consumption, united by myriad networks of critique, support, examples, and experimentation. This development is a profoundly democratic revolution in media usage and one whose outlines we are just starting to grasp.[31]

Perhaps the most striking example comes from the 2008 U.S. presidential campaign. If elections can be seen as storytelling contests where candidates battle to promulgate the most effective narratives about their programs, then the Obama campaign conducted the largest digital storytelling exercise to date. The then-candidate's strategy included many social media components, including Facebook and MySpace pages, Twitter feeds, public and password-protected Web sites, and YouTube channels. Fan-made content was published, shared, and spread widely through these networks along with blog posts and *Wikipedia* entries. Think, for example, of the many remixes of fan videos like the "Yes We Can" series. Mobile devices carried all of this still further with the additional features of smartphone apps and text messages purportedly from the candidate himself.[32] It is now commonplace to view Obama's successful campaign as a mythopoeic story where a heroic figure journeys through trials, ultimately arriving at triumph. As this book enters its second edition, the Trump administration offers a very different example of social media storytelling, as the new president continues his campaign practice of emitting rapid-fire, provocative tweets. That, too, has become a historical narrative.

If digital storytelling is so extensive in our culture, we can reverse the question into its negative: What *isn't* digital storytelling? This question, in some ways, is harder to answer. First, an increasing amount of "analog" storytelling is being delivered and/or experienced in digital form. Television is increasingly experienced through Web browsers (Netflix, YouTube,

Hulu) and mobile devices. E-books are finally beginning to be adopted beyond the cutting edge. Movies have followed TV into the home and are even digitally projected in theaters. Radio is played through satellite networks or from laptops. Music is consumed in mp3 format, playable through nearly every digital device we can use. Is watching a TV show on one's iPad a digital storytelling experience?

Second, a large amount of analog storytelling is built in digital formats. How many print books began life as Word documents? How few video productions emerge without digital editing, sometimes in multiple layers? Digital effects are widespread throughout the television world and are growing in the form of computer-generated imagery (CGI) within movies.

Rather than see the digital and storytelling domains overlap each other entirely, we can restrict ourselves to the exploration of digitally native stories, which means stories "born digital" and published in a digital format. Included are blogs, Web video, computer games, and mobile apps. How we tell stories with them, through the cybercultural matrix, is a question we begin answering in the next chapter.

CHAPTER TWO

The First Wave of Digital Storytelling

We've been telling stories with digital tools since the first computer networks linked nodes. This assertion is surprising in some contexts, especially if one does not associate narrative with computer hardware, much less digital information. It's even more startling to recognize just how far back digital storytelling goes historically and to grasp that it has a lineage, with all the implications that follow.

Yet, it is vital for practitioners and audiences alike to think historically on this topic rather than viewing digital storytelling as something utterly new, alien, or freshly emergent. A feel for the past helps explain some of the present's technological structures and practices. For creators, it opens up a broader field of examples to draw upon and to be inspired by. We may even elicit insights about currently emerging practices by analyzing long-term trends grounded in the historical record.

Just how far back we start that record is not immediately apparent and depends on our understanding of terms. We can start before the Internet if we choose. To the extent one considers games to contain stories, we could begin with a game called Spacewar, an early storytelling engine that dates back to the 1960s. If we think of world-building as storytelling, the first virtual worlds in the early Internet age—all text based!—appeared in the late 1970s with the first Multi-User Dimensions or Multi-User Dungeons (MUDs).

We are on firmer consensual ground by the 1980s, still prior to the World Wide Web, but when a mix of technologies had advanced. The Internet had grown immensely in hosts and users after two decades of growth, and there was even a popular movie about networked comput-ing, *WarGames* (1983). Personal computers (PCs) had stunned mainframe supporters by racing into the consumer market via Apple, Amiga, and others. The first virtual communities appeared and flourished, from e-mail lists to the Whole Earth 'Lectronic Link (WELL), as documented by Howard Rheingold.[1] Science fiction was growing skilled at depicting digital identities and virtual worlds: examples include Alice Sheldon's "The Girl Who Was Plugged In" (1973), Vernor Vinge's "True Names" (1981), William Gibson's *Neuromancer* (1984), and John Varley's "Press Enter []" (1984).

In that environment, the last decade of the Cold War, we see the rise of hypertext fiction based on such technologies as Apple's Hypercard (1987) and Eastgate Systems' Storyspace.[2] Hypertexts consisted of two elements: content items and their connections. Multiple readable chunks, or *lexia,* are positioned on a computer screen: "documents of any kind (images, text, charts, tables, video clips) . . . scrolling 'pages' (as they are on the World Wide Web) or screen-size 'cards' (as they are in a Hypercard stack)."[3] Read-ers (or users) traveled hyperlinks among lexia to experience (or develop) stories. Stories were published via floppy disk and discussed by a grow-ing community of practitioners such as Stuart Moulthrop, Shelley Jackson, Michael Joyce, Richard Holeton, and Sarah Smith. Scholarly investigation appeared in print with works like Jakob Nielson's *Hypertext and Hyperme-dia* (1990), George Landow's *Hypertext* (1992), and Michael Joyce's *Of Two Minds: Hypertext Pedagogy and Poetics* (1995).

Awareness grew of a predigital proto-hypertext tradition, including a galaxy of texts and practices that seemed to anticipate that combination of links with lexia: the accretion of commentary upon religious manu-scripts; the *I Ching;* Maya Deren's "An Anagram of Ideas on Art, Form and Film" (1945); Julio Cortazar's *Hopscotch* (1963); Milorad Pavic's *Dictionary of the Khazars* (1988); and the very popular Choose-Your-Own-Adventure children's book series (beginning in 1979). It eventually became common-place to recognize that Vannevar Bush had argued for hypertext even before the integrated circuit was invented in his extraordinary post-World War II essay, "As We May Think" (1946).

How do hypertexts work as digital stories? Users—readers—experience hypertext as an unusual storytelling platform. We navigate along lexia, picking and choosing links to follow. As with reading a novel, we assemble the story in our minds. Unlike a novel, we have no single, linear direction to follow. Instead, reading a hypertext is something like a hybrid of exploring a space (think: museum, park, city), solving puzzles (which path will be pro-ductive?), and reading an opera libretto or closet drama (staging it mentally).

From the production side, creators of hypertexts had several tools available. Hypercard was the first to allow easy, visually clear creation and linking of lexia. Storyspace offered a powerful writing platform, letting authors select from multiple organizational structures. In the following decade, once the World Wide Web appeared, every page-authoring tool from Notepad to Dreamweaver was a potential hypertext digital story tool as well.

While hypertext storytelling proceeded, digital gaming went through a simultaneous blossoming in the form of interactive fiction (IF). These stories were born from the generative matrix of MUDs and MOOs (MUD, Object Oriented), text-based virtual worlds first launched circa 1979. Users interacted with those environments via grammatically simple comments, entered via keyboard, such as "go north" or "take apple." In a MUD or MOO, users interacted with the environment and other players; in IF, with the environment and the story.

In retrospect, it seems logical to write stories in these environments. Much as users worked their way by clicking through hypertexts, they could—and did—explore textual spaces by typing. The foundational digital story in IF is *Adventure,* created by a programmer and spelunker to entertain his caving-happy children in 1975. Users entered simple commands to advance their way through the story, exploring spaces in a vast cave (initially named after the real-world Colossal Cave in Kentucky). There they encountered other characters, acquired objects, and solved puzzles. Harry Brown argues that *Adventure* marks a crucial shift in gaming: "It substitute[d] scoring with a quest, a narrative." Digits on the scoreboard were less important than the story unfolding.[4]

Other such IF story-games began to appear, and companies formed to support and profit by them: Adventure International, Sierra, and, most notably, Infocom.[5] A rapid product development cycle saw games released on disk, sometimes with physical objects as bonuses or tools.

Taken together, interactive fiction and hypertext fiction had—and have—much in common as digital storytelling platforms in our historical survey. They both relied heavily, if not exclusively, on text for content, although other media began to infiltrate as technologies improved. Both forms saw businesses arise, leading to the first digital storytelling market environments. Both combined stories and play, narrative with gaming. And both provided an unusually user-centered experience, requiring readers to choose their own pathways through, to contribute, to interact in a basic, if not radical sense. Stories were co-creations, partially determined by the audience. Indeed, Espen Aarseth coined the term *ergodic literature* to cover these new combinations and affordances, where *ergodic* is a neologism from the Greek words for "work" and "path."[6]

A third form of digital storytelling arose during the 1980s, one more popular than either IF or hypertext, yet not so well respected. This is the body of urban legends and demotic folklore, spread virally through e-mail messages and Usenet posts—Nigerian financial scams, the perpetual Mrs. Fields cookie recipe, horror stories involving street gangs or politicians. To those we can add countless quizzes, number puzzles, jokes, prayers, and inspirational texts. Some of these are quite readily understood as very short stories, like a news account (no matter how truth challenged) or a report of a life-changing experience. Like IF, some of this content depends on the reader's puzzle-solving abilities (Can this be true? Do those numbers really add up?).

Such e-mail stories became well known enough to serve as vehicles for satire, such as this one:

> Dear American:
>   I need to ask you to support an urgent secret business relationship with a transfer of funds of great magnitude.
>   I am Ministry of the Treasury of the Republic of America. My country has had crisis that has caused the need for large transfer of funds of 800 billion dollars US. If you would assist me in this transfer, it would be most profitable to you.
>   I am working with Mr. Phil Gram, lobbyist for UBS, who will be my replacement as Ministry of the Treasury in January. As a Senator, you may know him as the leader of the American banking deregulation movement in the 1990s. This transaction is 100% safe.[7]

These stories differ from hypertext and interactive fiction in some important ways that anticipate subsequent movements. Unlike ergodic literatures, these viral texts required little work on the part of readers beyond the occasional forwarding (compare with viewing a YouTube video). They required no extra platform for their creation beyond typing in a text window. Additionally, this sprawling body of content is deeply social, always spread and shared via formal and informal networks. A nested series of embedded e-mail message headers, for example, narrates one item's passage through people connected by school, work, or friendship.

All of this digital storytelling ferment occurred before Sir Tim Berners-Lee unleashed the World Wide Web, the world's largest hypertext project, in 1991.[8] These ergodic systems constitute a pre-Web digital storytelling history, its first generation.

Once the Web took off and its user base grew at a historic pace, hypertext storytelling techniques migrated there. Indeed, hypertext is enshrined in the basic URL naming syntax, where *http* stands for Hyper

Text Transfer Protocol and the page suffix, *html*, refers to Hyper Text Markup Language. The rapid penetration of the Web into daily life combined with the ever-increasing ease of creating Web pages meant a continually expanding arena for storytelling. The Web's second decade, that of "Web 2.0," accelerated possibilities and production still further. Some of these storytelling approaches took hypertext into new realms, while others focused on media-rich experiences, sometimes called "hypermedia."

Individual Web pages work well enough as hypertext lexia, chunks of content connected by easily recognized links. Nonfiction nonstories, such as the Internet Movie Database or any reference guide, are familiar examples of this quotidian hypertext. Working through them, ergodically, creates a stream of accessed content, a pathway without a tale, if you will.

Creative writing took to this format easily. One example is *Ted's Caving Journal,* a series of mock journal entries describing the exploration of an ominous underground structure. Like players of the 1970s *Adventure* game, the spelunker/narrator and associates encounter mysteries and challenging navigation in caverns. Formally, the story consists of ten static, relatively simple Web pages. Each one contains several paragraphs of text along with basic formatting and an ominous black background. Each page is dated, with months and days in 2000 and 2001. Some pages are preceded by a single photograph illustrating a point from the text while others contain links to further images ("Click to see a photo of the original opening. I put my glove in the hole for size reference"). Below the text is a simple navigational menu, leading forward and back in the story sequence, with directions often named ("Work Continues/Back to Cave page").

The tenth, final page alone has flawed navigation, as clicking "Next" leads to either a dead link or an endless loop fixed on that page itself. Evidently something terrible has happened to Ted, preventing him from completing the journal.[9] The link becomes more than a Vannevar Bush-style path and instead points to a spooky, open-ended absence. It is an abyss or unplumbable hole, aptly enough.

Other Web-based digital stories deployed richer, more complex media. A source of good examples is the long-running Dreaming Methods project (1993–).[10] That group has produced a series of multilinear stories that partake of the environmental strand of digital storytelling history, portraying spaces like an old building's mailbox or a decaying house. As with hypertext, each story includes numerous linked lexia. The user works through these tales ergodically, selecting pathways to follow. Dreaming Methods uses Flash to combine audio, text, images, and animation. Stories escape easy genre classification, brilliantly exploring often debilitated mental states along with intertwined lives of contemporary characters.

The first decade of the Web, approximately 1994–2004, saw a great deal of browser-based storytelling. Examples proliferated, such as the *Simpleton* series, "The Jew's Daughter," "Lexia to Perplexia," *GRAMMATRON*, and Zoeye.[11] Alan Sondheim has been exploring digital expression in an extraordinary series of forms, thoroughly blurring fiction and nonfiction, dating back to 1994.[12] His technologies are multiple: "I have used MUDS, MOOS, talkers, perl, d/html, qbasic, linux, emacs, vi, CuSeeMe, Visual Basic, etc. . . . ."

His formal structures are complex, as are the topics explored:

> Almost all of the text is in the form of short- or long-waves. The former are the individual sections, written in a variety of styles, at times referencing other writers/theorists. The sections are interrelated.
>
> The long-waves are fuzzy thematics bearing on such issues as death, sexuality, virtual embodiment, the "granularity of the real," physical reality, computer languages, and protocols. The waves weave throughout the text; the resulting splits and convergences owe something to phenomenology, programming, deconstruction, linguistics, philosophy and prehistory, as well as the domains of online worlds in relation to everyday realities. . . .
>
> I continue working on a cdrom of the last eight years of my work (Archive), as well as a series of 3d animation and other videos.

Perhaps what most clearly makes this a form of digital storytelling is the way Sondheim developed a series of complex, shifting, Blakean characters:

> On occasion emanations are used, avatars of philosophical or psychological import. These also create and problematize narrative substructures within the work as a whole. Such are Susan Graham, Julu, Alan, Jennifer, Azure, and Nikuko in particular.

In addition to this period's creative work, scholarly work also grew, sometimes under the aegis of the emergent field of "new media studies." An Electronic Literature Organization formed up in 1999. Retrospective anthologies have appeared in the years since.[13] A "net.art" movement developed.[14]

As the Web advanced and the 21st century dawned, the 1980s period became the subject of still another form of digital storytelling, a relatively esoteric one: digital memoirs of that period. For example, a former systems administrator carefully archived on the Web a series of very simple, text-only, nonhypertext accounts of hacking and technology. Alongside practical technological documents of historical value, there are humorous stories, musings on culture, and autobiographical reflections:

> I'm reading through these old textfiles, completely blown away. I was also in the 914 area code, with the absurd little handle King Kilroy. . . .
> Ever since I got started in computing in 1981, I was certainly aware of telecommunication services such as bulletin board systems (called "BBSs" or "boards"), commercial time sharing services (Compuserve, The Source, etc.) and even this mysterious thing called "Usenet". And of course, a modem on my very own personal computer would be really handy at college. . . . No more crowded computer labs at 3 A.M., just dial into the system from the comfort of the dorm![15]

These short, focused memoirs provide the basics of good nonfiction storytelling: personal presence, emotional content, clearly described information, a sense of why the subject matters. They are digital stories about Internet history from which we can learn about the situation out of which the first generation of digital storytelling sprang.

While Web storytelling appeared and developed during the first decade of the browser, another often offline form appeared and was the first to seize the name of "digital storytelling." A Berkeley area group anchored in community theater and social activism sought ways to capture digital video for use by everyday people. As with performance art and community organizing, the goal was to make tools widely available. After a great deal of invention and iteration, a curriculum was distilled: a three-day intensive class, during which participants learned at least just enough technical skills to create a short story in short video form.

A key move in what the creators dubbed "digital storytelling" was an emphasis on personal content. The power of this approach was discovered around 1990 during studio performances by an artist and video producer, Dana Atchley. Atchley's work, *Next Exit*, was autobiographical, covering "five decades of his life." That topical focus, combined with innovative use of video and projection, inspired Bay Area audiences: "Many people who watched the performance [said] yes, I have a story like this."[16] By 1993, Atchley and others had developed and led workshops at the American Film Institute wherein participants created personal stories, with topics including parents and a dying friend. Joe Lambert writes of the experience as the moment when digital storytelling started to appear:

> It was "like" many things, but it was also unlike anything I had ever seen before. The sense of transformation of the material, and of accomplishment, went well beyond the familiar forms of creative activity I could reference. . . .

I came to understand that the mix of digital photography and non-linear editing are a tremendous play space for people. They can experiment and realize transformations of those familiar objects, the photos, the movies, the artifacts, in a way that enlivens their relationship to the objects. Because this creative play is grounded in important stories the workshop participants want to tell, it can become a transcendent experience.[17]

That emphasis on transformation is key to understanding the power of the digital storytelling creative experience. Participants can feel that their relationship to media, technology, memory, and themselves has been revitalized or defamiliarized, made fresh again (if with some frustrations along the way). Note, too, the sense of play (play space, creative play) that pervades so much of the first generation of digital storytelling. It points forward as well to the gaming boom to come and the creative forces of two decades of the World Wide Web.

By 1994, digital storytelling workshops were being taught in San Francisco studios.[18] Participants developed stories about their lives or the lives of people close to them. Scripts were written to emphasize the creator's speech, what the Center for Digital Storytelling (CDS) came to refer to as the "gift of voice"—a heightened sense of personal presence resulting in the final video. This personal focus helped to decrease jitters about technology and to bring story content to the fore more rapidly, with greater emotional power.

The idea of storytelling brought workshop participants more rapidly into the creative spirit. While technology can seem geekish and video the province of audiovisual professionals, storytelling is, as we have seen, as close to a universal as human culture gets. Ask someone sitting before a powerful computer to think of stories and the intimidating nexus of tech before them becomes simply a tool, like a notebook to write upon or a tape recorder to capture voice or a canvas to paint.

Although technologies have developed rapidly, the CDS curriculum has remained relatively stable. Three days see participants, from start to finish, begin with only the idea of making a story and finish up with a (roughly) three-minute digital video. Participants learn to write a script, handle images (scanning and/or editing and/or obtaining from sources), record audio, edit multimedia within a video editor, and publish a video, either to DVD or the Web. Other technologies are brought in as needed based on the story's nature and the workshop schedule: digitizing analog materials, for example, or shooting video. (For a full description of these workshops, see Chapter 13.)

One of the most widely taught examples of the CDS approach shows how this approach is realized in the final product. "Momnotmom"

(Thenmozhi Soundarajan, 2000) is a reflection on a mother–daughter relationship from the daughter's perspective. The story isn't a plot-driven one, but a meditation on a human connection over time.

Images show Thenmozhi's mother Thiakavaly depicted over several stages of life. Animations draw our attention to each one, allowing separate emotional charges to be felt: apparent sadness, playfulness, frustration, seriousness. The voiceover—Thenmozhi's voice—organizes these images, not always directly describing their contents. The narration situates them in the mother–daughter relationship framework (e,g., Thiakavaly seen in marriage costume), while Thenmozhi describes a sense of loss. The speaker's voice is controlled but offers meaning through nuanced intonation as when it drops in pitch to express guilt ("But I also feel guilty, because I think my mom . . ."). A guitar track complements the narration, a solemn performance lending gravity to the words. Repeated rising tones create some energy, but never rapidly. It continues over the credits, carrying the mood past the voiceover's conclusion.[19]

"There's a picture of my mother that I always keep with me"—from its opening words, "Momnotmom" is concerned with mediation and separating layers. We see images and film of the mother but do not hear her voice, neither directly nor in someone else's reading. The mother poses not for nearby people or for herself, but for history ("for the future . . . searching for the past"). The narrator speaks of distances, either geographical ("across oceans and between cultures") or between herself and her mother. We learn from the closing titles that Thiakavaly received a degree, but nothing of its meaning to her nor of the process of achieving it. Degrees, photos, film, time, culture: "Momnotmom" packs in a tremendous subtle meditation on mediation in a very short time.

The success of stories like "Momnotmom" and of the curriculum enabling it led to the founding of CDS in 1998, whose work continues to this day. A growing cadre of CDS instructors offers workshops in the United States and beyond. For a decade, from 1995 to 2005, the CDS hosted a Digital Storytelling Festival, and "1999 . . . was the year people stopped asking what Digital Storytelling *was* and focused on *how* to apply it."[20]

The CDS approach has also been adopted by many individuals and organizations, helped in part by the openness of (lack of licensing for) the curriculum.[21] For example, the British Broadcasting Corporation sponsored two major digital storytelling projects: Telling Lives and Capture Wales.[22] Community-oriented and activist projects have found digital storytelling useful for eliciting and sharing local knowledge, combining organizing with outreach. One example is the Mountain Reporter Network, which develops stories about the Appalachian region.[23] Another is the Stories for

Change coalition, intended "to connect and extend the network of work-shop facilitators and organizations that have come together in community-based digital storytelling workshops."[24] Historical societies connect with local teenagers and children to build location-specific cultural stories—stories of memories—as in the town of Skowhegan, Maine.[25] Some uses have also emerged in health care where, for example, chronic care patients tell their stories in order to better communicate their experience.[26] Other offshoots include LifeBio ("Customers create an autobiography or the biography of a loved one by using LifeBio's carefully crafted questions") and TellOurLifeStories.[27]

Educational uses have grown steadily over time, ranging from digital storytelling course assignments to assessment to a master's program. Elementary, middle, and high school students have created stories in class. Streetside Stories, for instance, works with children in grades K–8, helping kids tell digital stories about their lives and adjusting the CDS curriculum to suit participants' needs. The videos are shorter than the CDS average, being roughly 90 seconds long, and often feature children's art. One, "The Truth Hurts," consists of a series of drawings voiced over by an outraged girl who described a rumor cycle among her friends and other girls. The voiceover narrator of "English of My Life by Lili" describes her experience learning a new language after emigrating from China; it also contains drawings, presumably by Lili.[28]

Colleges and universities such as the Ohio State University, University of Houston, Georgetown University, and the University of Minnesota offer a mix of classes, consultation, workshops, and online materials.

Others publicly share examples and case studies of classroom use, including Hamilton College, Williams College, Seton Hall University, Hunter College, and LaGuardia Community College.[29] Two campuses offer degrees in the subject, to date: a master of arts in telecommunications (digital storytelling emphasis) at Ball State University and a bachelor of science in digital arts and design–digital storytelling at Dakota State University.[30] Naturally, individual courses are also being offered, such as one at Queensland University of Technology.[31]

Although there are variations, the sense of digital storytelling remains remarkably stable, if open enough to allow iterations. For example, a California State University, Chico, class generated a five-part definition of digital stories, according to which, for assessment purposes, they should

- include a compelling narration of a story
- provide a meaningful context for understanding the story being told

- use images to capture and/or expand upon emotions found in the narrative
- employ music and other sound effects to reinforce ideas
- invite thoughtful reflection from their audience(s).[32]

The spread of digital storytelling interest has inspired variations and experiments. After all, the curriculum is based on powerful concepts that allow different implementations. It also rests on a set of technologies, which change frequently. For instance, digital video tools continue to proliferate and re-version. As a digital storytelling practitioner, I can describe two such variations I've helped develop, teach, and iterate. These variations were supported by the National Institute for Technology in Liberal Education (NITLE), a nonprofit organization that offered, among other things, professional development services to small colleges.[33] NITLE first hosted a CDS workshop in Middlebury, Vermont in 2003. It was brilliantly taught by Joe Lambert and Emily Paulos. After experiencing the curriculum's success and appreciating the tremendous enthusiasm shown by participants, we decided to launch a digital storytelling program, teaching such a class on our own.

After announcing our intentions to do so, an interesting criticism of the approach appeared in discussions with populations across numerous campuses. Some saw the personal, (auto)biographical essence of the CDS curriculum as inapplicable to many classrooms. First, some faculty argued that while they wanted to create a digital story, the content should not be personal in nature. Indeed, more than a few professors were adamant about removing themselves from narratives. "I care about teaching African politics," one told me, "not teaching about my own interest in the subject." Second, others evoked C. P. Snow's two cultures model, arguing that the CDS curriculum was really suited only to the humanities as the home of expressive art in academia; personal storytelling could not map well onto the hard, quantitatively based sciences. In response, we shifted our class focus slightly, welcoming "both personal and impersonal" stories to our "multimedia narrative" workshop. So far, the two coexist quite well, with stories of self-discovery appearing alongside explorations of molecular processes.[34]

A second concern about the CDS approach involved timing. Three days—intense, work-filled days—is a long time to allocate to a new practice, even an appealing one. Since the Great Recession began, this problem has sharpened, given constrictions in the labor market and professional development field.

We will explore further details of digital storytelling workshops in Chapter 12. For now, we should recognize that as the 21st century has progressed, the term *digital storytelling* has achieved some currency. Narrowly, it is usually understood to describe the CDS approach. Consider one *Wikipedia* definition: "Digital Storytelling is the use of digital tools to let ordinary people tell their own real-life stories."[35] That personal emphasis, that popular focus is very much in the CDS tradition. Construed more broadly, the use of digital tools for narrative purposes had grown into a broad field by the time the term "Web 2.0" started being used (and mocked). We can point to a generation of work, stretching from hypertext and hypermedia to browser-based fiction, from Web-based memoirs of Usenet to autobiographical videos.

With the advent of social media and the Web's second decade, a second generation of combining storytelling with technologies began. This is taken up in the next chapter.

CHAPTER THREE

The Next Wave of Digital Storytelling Platforms

The technological environment for digital storytelling advanced rapidly after the start of the 21st century.[1] Some technologies and platforms disappeared or were marginalized. A portion of digital content followed the same route as multiple forces compounded to deepen the still unsolved problem of digital preservation: device and format succession, link rot, ever richer media and session states. Other technologies and content survived, finding new niches or defending already held ones in the ever-emergent information ecosystem.[2] Web pages, Web browsers, desktops, and laptops continue to play key roles, even as their respective fields hold new arrivals.

The Second Web

A single year in Internet time can be like a decade in ordinary history, so a decade of Internet history implies a large catalogue of events. It is possibly with this historical perspective that Tim Oi Reilly coined the term *Web 2.0* in 2004.[3] The term has, in turn, lasted for nearly a decade, surviving a great deal of criticism and parody. Like "deconstruction," *Web 2.0* was often put in quotes, hedged, redefined, considered to be dead, and then used once more with resignation. Subsequently, *social media* has supplanted and superseded *Web 2.0*.[4] Throughout this book, we shall use both terms interchangeably, especially when discussing historical events.

How did the Web change so as to make a new name meaningful? We can describe the transformation by exploring three trends and their mutually reinforcing relationships: microcontent, social architecture, and new platforms.

The first feature, microcontent, rather obviously describes small forms and items of content. "Small" is a comparative term set in relation to the rest of the Web. Microcontent pieces are easier to produce and consume than full-scale Web sites in terms of information architecture. They can sometimes be reused in multiple ways and places, including syndication and remixing. Microcontent is often much smaller than Web sites in terms of the amount of storage that each chunk takes up: blog posts, wiki edits, YouTube comments, and Picasa images are usually only a few thousand bytes. Some types of microcontent, interestingly, can be quite large from a storage perspective but are so easily managed and self-contained as to fall into the microcontent category: for example, audio files (podcasts), .pdf files to SlideShare, or video (for Web platforms such as YouTube).

Getting microcontent, be it large or tiny in memory size, to the modern Web is also a relatively simple matter for the user, requiring little if anything in the way of Web design expertise. Such was not the case in the 1990s. That first iteration of the Web required multiple tools, phases, and reiterations. First, there was the creation of an HTML (Hyper Text Markup Language) document on a computer, which meant either entering the text by hand after learning the HTML syntax or obtaining and learning how to use an HTML editor such as Netscape Composer or Dreamweaver. Second, the would-be Web author required a Web server space, which entailed either locating and purchasing some, along with a domain, or obtaining permission to do so from a friendly institution. Third, HTML files had to be sent to that Web space, meaning using yet another tool, a file transfer protocol (FTP) application, and learning the ins and outs of directory management. Finally, once this third component enabled the transfer of the first to the second, the Web creator, gazing at his or her handiwork, then discovered the necessity of learning Web design—that fraught combination of visual aesthetics, style, accessibility, and information architecture.

In contrast, Web 2.0 services deliberately winnowed down the process to a single Web site, with a narrow selection of options, then authoring content to the Web. Templates were made available, obviating the need to study and practice detailed design. Design freedom was thereby curtailed, but production enormously eased. Hence the vast torrent of content appearing through blogs, modern wikis, and other social media services. Users can focus on content rather than form (or, in ignoring the former, cause grievous aesthetic harm).[5] One way of shaping content through these new channels is, of course, to tell stories.

Web 2.0 represents one of the strongest moves to mitigate the digital divide, and one of the least appreciated. The ability to create content for zero software cost is historically significant and now par for the course. Access to enabling hardware, once an issue, has dwindled in importance as the number of computers available has increased, especially through public schools and libraries.[6] Internet-enabled mobile phones have also increased access, offering still more ways for users to create through social media.[7]

The second piece of Web 2.0 is the social element, or social architecture. Before Facebook's rise, certain services—MySpace, Orkut, Friendster, LinkedIn—called themselves "social software," existing primarily to connect people with each other. Those represent a narrow instance of Web 2.0's general social approach. Compare any Web 2.0 site with a first-generation Web page. For the latter, the browsing experience was primarily one of reader and computer. The page's author was not openly present unless he or she had exposed an e-mail address and been drowned under resulting spam. A reader had few options for connecting with the author and fewer still for adding content to that page beyond the unlamented guest book function. Beyond the creator and consumer, a third party would have no way of knowing that the first two had even remotely connected.

Web 2.0 sites, in contrast, allow multiple channels of communication between site visitors, site creators, and other parties. They are fundamentally designed to encourage such connections through wiki editing, comment threads, media embedding, tagging, Facebook Liking, Digg and Reddit services, and more. A site's visitors can leave comments or add tags or link to it from their own site. Other visitors can see these comments and other connections, like a party guest entering a room where a conversation is in full swing. Multiple users can build objects and collections together, from an iterated wiki page to a shared Flickr photo pool to a co-drawn Gliffy image.

One side effect of re-architecting the Web along social connective lines is the acceleration of distributed conversations. Consider, for example, a single blog post. Its author shares her thoughts about a current event. A reader disagrees, and so he writes a comment appended to that post, arguing against the blogger's interpretation of, say, military policy. A third person then adds a following remark, agreeing with the original post and arguing against the critic's comment. A fourth writer decides to write a blog post about this whole exchange, seeing it as indicative of another idea in the present age. This fourth writer also adds an embedded media file, one which copies content from and points to an article hosting by Scribd. The original blogger sees all of this—from the comments on her post to the fourth writer's post—to which she was alerted by an automatic ping between their respective blog platforms. She then (1) writes a comment on her own blog, (2) adds a comment to the fourth writer's blog, and (3) tags that Scribd page to bring out her perspective.

Admittedly, this kind of conversation happened in Web 1.0 and on pre-Web platforms. Usenet, after all, was driven by distributed conversations. E-mail listservs also thrived on conversations distributed in time, if focused in space. What's significant about this Web 2.0 shift is that it redesigns the experience of Web content. Rather than assuming a default mode of reading, with rare and distanced exchanges, we now expect sociality to underpin most publication. Rather than a dyad of reader and written, we experience a tripod, where two people connect through a shared interest in an object. "Social software works in triangles," observed one early analyst.[8] "Object-oriented sociality" is the phrase applied by one social media designer.[9]

Based on this combination of easy Web content authoring and social architecture, Web 2.0 platforms continue to emerge. The number and variety of hosted services is now large enough to be difficult to track. Bookmarks: Delicious, Diigo, Amplify, CiteULike. Image sharing: Flickr, Google's Picasa, Facebook. Image creation and editing: Gliffy, Picnik. Blogging: Blogger, LiveJournal, WordPress. Collaborative writing through wikis: Mediwiki, PBWorks, Confluence; otherwise, Google Wave. Social networking: Facebook leads the planet, but others continue to function, such as Myspace, Orkut. LinkedIn leads the resume-sharing and job-seeking domain alongside smaller services like VisualCV. Presentation building and/or sharing: Slideshare, Google Spreadsheets. Pdf sharing: Scribd. Video editing and sharing: JumpCut, Google Search Stories. Microblogging or social status updates: Twitter, Facebook. By the time you read this paragraph, not only will more services have emerged and some disappeared, but new categories may have appeared as well.

Aggregation tools have grown, unsurprisingly, in the wake of such a services explosion. The RSS standard lets creators syndicate their content so that readers can collect it or update it with new material. RSS readers now include Digg Reader, Bloglines, Cooliris, FeedDemon, NetNews-Wire, along with plug-ins for the Firefox browser and Outlook e-mail. The iTunes application uses RSS to gather podcasts. Alongside RSS readers are user-built (or, more precisely, user-customized) Web portals, including PageFlakes, iGoogle, and MyYahoo!. Other sites function as distributed portals wherein users aggregate and rank stories and other Web content—Digg, Reddit, Memorandum, and Techmeme being some of the leading examples.

Some services encompass many of these functions. RSS readers consume updates from blogs, wikis, social image sites, podcasts, and even searches. Facebook lets users upload and share images, status updates, and social gaming. Various Google services include most of the preceding. Some blog platforms let users set up feeds for their images, Twitter and Facebook updates, and other blogs. An increasing number of Web services include connections to other services so that one can quickly tweet a blog post or send a new story to Digg.

The reader should not neglect "the old Web" or Web 1.0 in our exploration of new storytelling technologies. Traditional Web sites continue to produce content, including narratives, even as they partake of social media elements.

Perhaps the best know form of this practice is what some refer to as the Snowfall paradigm. This paradigm is essentially a multimedia Web page, a classic HTML document with text, images, video, audio, and animation smoothly integrated into a seamless artifact. The name comes from the title of a groundbreaking *New York Times* story about a skiing disaster, whose lead author was John Branch. "Snow Fall: The Avalanche at Tunnel Creek" is anchored on a textual narrative, which also appeared in the newspaper's print edition. That narrative explores in detail the complexity of the event, moving back and forth in time while trying to establish a clear chronology.

The Web page expands this story enormously by adding media. It begins with a title superimposed over what at first appears to be an image of a snowy landscape until the reader sees snow blowing, hears wind keening, and realizes that it is actually a video. Proceeding down "Snow Fall"'s page, the reader encounters video and audio interviews with participants, each carefully situated in logical points within the text. A large animated map of the setting takes over the browser window, letting the readers/ viewer explore the torturous mountain topography referenced at that point in the story. Historical photographs pop up when Branch reaches back in time to give more context to the present day.[10]

"Snow Fall" does not represent a paradigm shift in Web-based storytelling. Instead, it offers an elegant form for others to imitate, one based on incremental improvements in certain technologies (new browser standards, better multimedia plug-ins, gradual growth in bandwidth and user device specs, greater user comfort with complex digital artifacts). *The New York Times* has followed this pattern in subsequent works, and others have created their own "Snow Falls." "Unfathomable," for example, depicts the history of early British divers by smoothly integrating a textual narrative with historical images, diagrams, and contemporary photographs.[11]

Perhaps the most ambitious example of "Web 1.0 storytelling" is "Welcome to Pine Point," a memoir of a small Canadian town wrought in extensive and rich multimedia.[12] The user/reader/viewer/listener is confronted by a blizzard of images, organized through a familiar left-column vertical interface. Each entry plunges into a different aspect of the town, laid out in different styles, crammed with photographs, videos, music, text in varied fonts, and never structured by strict chronology. "Pine Point" is an immersive complement to virtual reality, giving us a very deep sense of history and place, as well as a multimedia story achievement worth aspiring to.

While Web 2.0/social media have swept the world, the old-fashioned web continues to develop its own storytelling capacity.

Cyberculture Ludens

While Web 2.0 grew explosively during the 21st century's first decade, another cybercultural development progressed in tandem. Computer gaming had grown enormously in diversity, size, and reach through the 1990s and the following decade after a crash in the 1980s. As of this writing, digital gaming rivals cinema and music as a global cultural force. In fact, it would be as foolish to consider contemporary storytelling without dwelling on gaming as to describe storytelling without movies, the spoken word, or print.[13]

Statistical research varies, but the trends and scope have been fairly clear for several years: "Almost all teens play games."[14] Thirty nine percent of the most frequent gamers play social games.[15] The stereotype of gamers being children and teens has been incorrect for some time, as the average age of a game player has risen, from 33 in 2007 to 34 in 2010, and "the most frequent game purchaser is 40—old enough to remember the early days of Atari."[16] In short, digital storytellers should assume that an increasing proportion of their audience, constituting a majority, has game experience.

As with any other significant media experience, this statistic has implications for an audience's expectations, worldview, and participatory practice. Oral storytellers have always paid attention to local listeners—their physical location, speech patterns, political situation, and so on. Films began by referencing print fiction, and fiction went on to return the favor. TV, books, movies, and oral traditions are audience touchstones for presenters, teachers, and other storytellers, offering points of personal connection and cultural resonance; we should now add games to that referential list.

Games are already being used as storytelling vehicles and are increasingly seen as such. In Chapter 6, we explore small-scale games in more detail, followed by large-scale games in Chapter 7. One especially interesting and unusual form of gaming is the focus of Chapter 10. A more practical or project-based approach to making stories in games is seen as parts of Chapters 12 and 13. Before reaching those points, though, we will first set the stage via a survey of the current gaming landscape.

The diversity of the gaming world is driven partly by the depth and difference of gaming platforms. Playing a computer game can not only require a substantial investment in time but also obtain to (access) multiple platforms, with combinations of often very separate hardware and software. Many of these platforms are deeply siloed or closed, not allowing interoperability. An Xbox 360 game, for example, cannot be played on a PC, phone, or Nintendo DS. When one game is recreated for another platform (a process known as "porting"), the game interface, the way it uses the new platform's hardware, and all of its content can be altered. For players, time is also needed to learn new devices (what each button does, where the keyboard is or isn't) and the social situation of that gaming platform (Xbox Live versus the *World of Warcraft* universe). In other words, an investment in one platform can mean playing more games there rather than elsewhere.

As a metaphor, compare playing games across platforms with learning world literature if translation were not possible. You would learn one language in order to read its writings but be unable to explore another's without making that investment in time. Once you learned Chinese, becoming fluent in French would let you read that language's novels, stories, poems, and plays. Those formal story structures will seem familiar, though their contents may profoundly differ based on the rich history of that language. Learning those two languages will make studying a third somewhat easier, but it will still require time before advancing into the new tongue's writings. Compare this with exploring social media, which is more like learning film with decent subtitles: images and sounds are generally understood, and the text is good enough to allow initial comprehension. Moving from wikis to blogs to social bookmarking requires far less effort than jumping from browser-based PC games to the Nintendo DS.

This platform-determined gaming in depth can be seen in the way some critics write about gaming in general, as they tend to remain focused on one hardware/software combination. It also points to gaming's diversity, which is wider than it often seems, given the sheer amount of time it takes to survey.

Console gaming is one of the more recognizable families of gaming platforms today. The term describes a hardware combination of base station (a small computer, including a hard drive) and handheld controllers, connected wirelessly. The base station is usually corded into a TV or monitor and can also be connected to the Internet. Games are either played from a compact disc inserted into the main unit or downloaded from the Internet. The controllers are designed to fit comfortably in one's hand, with buttons positioned to be pressed easily. Some contain tactile or haptic feedback mechanisms, such as vibration. For most, their buttons are the sole means of input; the Wii, however, added its physical orientation as an additional way for users to communicate with the game. Leading console game platforms include Wii (Nintendo), Xbox (Microsoft), and Play-Station (Sony).

Console game genres tend toward action, based on their interface's affordances. A Wii or Xbox controller makes it very easy to rapidly press buttons, get haptic feedback, or move the unit in space. Therefore sports, first-person shooter, and adventure games proliferate. Users may play by themselves, with players using the same unit, or with players across the network.

PC gaming contrasts with console games in several key ways. This term refers to any games played on laptops and desktops using inserted disks, the unit's hard drive, or a Web browser. Input mechanisms include the computer's keyboard and mouse and, less frequently, a microphone or camera.

The types of game content available to the PC are far broader than those for the console, due in part to the different interface. Action and sports games are present along with puzzle and strategy games. The latter do not require an especially responsive interface, so the relatively slow keyboard and mouse serve well enough. As with console games, PC users can play by themselves (against a game's artificial intelligence or AI) or with several networked fellows. In *Rome: Total War* (see Chapter 7), for example, one player can take on the role of the Julii family, trying to defeat the Claudii on a Gallic battlefield; the other family is played by a user located elsewhere in the real world or by the game's AI.

Massively multiplayer online games (MMOs) have been a particular success for PC gaming. These games are based on persistent virtual worlds, housed on servers elsewhere and populated by avatars, some of which are played by users located elsewhere. A game program is downloaded from the Internet or installed from disk, making available a game client through which to enter and interact with those worlds. Leading examples include *World of Warcraft, Eve Online, Lineage,* and *City of Heroes.* MMOs are social games, meaning that interpersonal relations are crucial to their play. Asking other players for information or goods, or fighting them, is a key component to interacting with the world. Players organize into guilds or raiding parties in order to accomplish tasks. These connections are maintained by both in-game means (text or audio chat) and the many out-of-game social media currently available, from Skype to wikis.

PC-played MMOs differ from multiplayer console games in terms of where complexity resides. The latter expend an enormous amount of processor power and memory to realize very sophisticated multimedia, while the former devotes development power to supporting millions of simultaneous users in a single game. PC MMOs can also require more PC-suited actions, such as using more input keys than a console allows.

At the other range of complexity and scale from PC MMOs are *casual games*, which are played from within a Web browser or a downloaded program. As the name implies, casual games are far easier to play than MMOs, requiring less memory, processor power, and learning time. Users can play them while doing other computing tasks, Minesweeper alongside Excel, for instance. As with other PC games, users can play casual games alone or across networks.

Perhaps the ideal casual game hardware platform is handheld devices, including but not limited to mobile phones. Phones constitute another platform entirely, with radically different interfaces as compared with consoles or PCs. The relatively small screen and input mechanisms (touchpad, basic buttons, numerical keypad, alphabetical keypad) challenge developers to maximize gameplay and content in a very small situation. Casual games often come preloaded or are available for download—card games, backgammon, and word puzzles being early successes. The iPhone App Store's growth has been partly driven by a very rapid creative boom for gaming on that platform. Bandwidth limitations have kept phone games largely asocial; they do support social play, however, in the context of augmented reality games (see Chapter 11).

Other mobile devices besides phones serve as gaming platforms. Handheld game consoles are portable, self-contained devices, combining a hard drive with console-like button inputs (and sometimes a stylus, touchscreen, or microphone) and multimedia outputs (screen and audio). Examples include the Nintendo DS and the PlayStation Portable (PSP). Games for these handhelds occupy a middle ground between PC and phone games, being more ambitious than the latter due to a focused design (phones serve other functions besides gaming), but less powerful and featured than the former. Genres accordingly include casual games, basic action games (racing), and adventure games in *Dungeons and Dragons* style.

Yet another handheld platform is available in the second-generation tablet computer, of which the most notable examples are the iPad and Android tablets.[17] While similar in interface to the Touch and iPhone, the iPad's increased size has yielded a very different computing experience, eliciting another creative rush in game development. Unlike the Tablet PC, the iPad uses a touchscreen interface, which drives changes in game design. Fingertip-based movable icons need to be larger, for example, than icons driven by a mouse pointer, with more of the background obscured thereby.

Even this rapid survey of the current game platform situation should give the reader a sense of its diversity and possibilities for depth. At the same time, we should also explore different genres or classes of games, at least in a big-picture, schematic view, because major divergences in game categories cut across hardware–software platforms. Those differences may point to distinct venues for storytelling.

A set of computer game genres has stabilized over the past decade, meaning players can expect certain things from such games. A 2008 Pew Internet and American Life study of teen gameplay offers a good catalog, including racing, puzzle, sports, action, rhythm, strategy, fighting, simulation, first-person shooter, role-playing, and horror.[18] Many of these are recognizable on their face—horror games involving monsters threatening the player, racing games providing vehicles on courses, and so forth. There is strategic overlap and hybridization between many of these, as with any domain marked by genre. *Bioshock* blends first-person shooter and horror along with a healthy number of puzzles. And, as with any genre classification scheme, each category can blend into others without seeming avant-garde. First-person shooters are fighting games, in a sense, unless we insist that fighting games must be third-person (in which case, the two combine into a new genre). Role-playing games often involve action, puzzles and some form of combat. Simulation and strategy overlap extensively, as do adventure and role-playing.

We can also break out subgenres within these. Platform games, or plat-formers, are a type of action game. Hunting games are a strand of the first-person shooter tapestry. Real-time strategy (RTS) and exploration games are part of the strategy genre. Simulation games have multiple instances of the same object being simulated: political problems, vehicles, physical processes. Point-and-click games are a subset of adventure games, and so on.

Other genres can be identified as well, such as exercise games or games as part of advertising, "advergames." Flight simulators, artificial life games (e.g., Tamagotchi), gambling games, mazes, and quizzes can be separated out.[19]

This process of game classification and reclassification can be pursued indefinitely, given the sheer scope of the gaming world and its continuing growth. But the purpose of this short survey is threefold. First, exploring the diversity of game platforms and genres provides some tools for getting more rapidly into understanding gaming. As friable as such categories may be, they can help organize a sprawling, heterogeneous mass. This exploration may prove especially useful for someone interested in storytelling, but new to considering gaming under that aegis. Second, these frameworks suggest possible avenues to explore for those interested in building a storytelling game. A creator should think through which platforms' affordances are best suited to the story he or she is developing; genres may give shape to stories in initial stages. Third, for creators interested in digital storytelling but not in developing a game, thinking through these categories may help in better understanding game-playing audiences.

We should also note two genres or design approaches with special relevance for storytelling. The *serious games* model appeared roughly around 2001 in an attempt to distinguish a certain style of game as being engaged with art or politics. Michigan State University's academic program on the field offers a representative description: "Serious games are games with purpose beyond just providing entertainment. Examples include, but are not limited to, games for learning, games for health, and games for policy and social change." From the creation side of gaming comes a different description: "Designing effective, engaging serious games requires theoretical understanding of learning, cognition, emotion, and play."[20] Serious games have also been associated with education, both as objects of study and as a way of thinking about educational gaming. While the term is sometimes contested, it has yet to be replaced, and the concept remains.[21] Games like *Oiligarchy* (Molle Industries) and *Jetset* (Persuasive Games) aim to make political points; the *Great Shakeout* (State of California) and *DimensionM* (Tabula Digita) are very different types of public educational games, each seeking to improve players' knowledge and skills in their areas of disaster response and mathematics, respectively.[22]

Another style of game is different enough to sometimes be considered not a game at all. *Virtual worlds* are digital environments that emphasize their nonstructured nature. They are spaces to explore, platforms to build upon, rather than games with clearly stated objectives. The leading example of this approach for some time has been *Second Life*, its epochal reputational crash and subsequent half-life notwithstanding. Like an MMO, *Second Life* consists of a large world populated by user-driven avatars. Unlike an MMO, however, there are no centrally determined quests, puzzles, organizations, or anything else suggesting a game. There are many games played within *Second Life,* but they are organized by and among players rather than by Linden Labs, provider of the service. Linden Labs maintains the service, but the content of *Second Life* in all its richness was created by participants.[23] Other virtual world services exist, such as *Activeworlds* and *Smallworld,* and open-source virtual worlds are also under development, including *OpenCroquet* and *OpenSim.*[24]

As with serious games, virtual worlds as a concept is an attempt to distinguish some work from the broader world of digital gaming. Perhaps building a castle in *Second Life* or creating a game to encourage citizens to vote are different enough experiences so as to represent something other than genre. The distinction opens up at another level, either strategic or ontological. The desire to create (or create within) such game-like entities mobilizes a set of expectations very separate from that summoned up by, say, a hunting or karate game. The experience of play should also be deeply other: being taught to find windup radios is fundamentally different from learning how to blow up barrels.

Yet, these two categories cannot remain entirely distinct. We can identify examples of projects that serve overlapping purposes. *Rome: Total War*, for example, can be considered a serious game in its extraordinary educational depth. The amount of historical documentation is vast, and play requires learning about various aspects of the Roman Republic: geography, politics, economics, warfare. *Rome: Total War* can also be played as a classic war game, with richly designed battles. *America's Army* is a first-person shooter, but also a serious game in the sense of persuading some Americans to join the military. Similarly, some games, especially ones with "sandbox" versions (allowing free, unstructured play), are both games and virtual worlds. One may explore the section of our galaxy imagined by *Mass Effect 2* for long periods of time before returning to its intricate plot. *Eve Online* does all three: as a political simulation, it offers very detailed models of trade and political organizations; as a game, great space battles; and as a virtual world, a large universe to explore.

For the purposes of digital storytelling, it can be useful to keep these categories in mind. Games still possess a negative reputation in many areas, which makes the serious games division potentially productive for audiences and outreach. Focusing on games under that header may also be a useful guide in researching games, especially for those new to digital gaming. Virtual worlds do not have as sober a reputation as do serious games,[25] but the ontological difference radically structures game design and play. As with serious games, the *virtual worlds* term still has impact with some audiences.

Storytelling Segments

In the following chapters, we explore the diverse landscape of new digital storytelling platforms, projects, and movements. We have seen several movements progress in parallel over the past generation: social media, gaming, and a range of digital storytelling efforts. In Part II, we see how they are starting to combine.

The term *digital storytelling* has often been used to describe the Center for Digital Storytelling curriculum specifically or, less often, to refer to the broader world of computer-mediated narrative. Since both realms of practice have advanced over the past two decades due to technological and storytelling developments, we can now prefer the broader sense of the term. *Digital Storytelling 2.0* is how marketing might label that idea, but "new digital storytelling" does the same semantic and historical work without the clichéd numerical sequence. From now on in this book, we shall simply use the term *digital storytelling*.[26]

The relationship between these three domains—social media, gaming, and storytelling—is complex. Given our focus on storytelling, we will emphasize the ways that domain overlaps the others, and when all three coincide.

The next four chapters of this book explore these overlaps in pairs: social media and storytelling, then gaming and storytelling. The four chapters after those, comprising part III, examine what happens when the binary overlaps become threefold ones through experiments and their extension into mobile devices.

As a way to knit these connections together, we can abstract out some storytelling themes from our discussion in Chapters 1 and 2, applied to these digital domains and platforms. Each of these will appear in every chapter, apropos of at least some of the styles and strategies described therein. Some will describe large portions of a story, as a biography is necessarily committed to personal presence; others will see these principles functioning at a lower intensity, as when a podcast series only lightly establishes a serial sequence. We will refer to all of them as we proceed in a critical or surveying way, then review them in a more practical, applied setting in Part 4.

Serial Structure

Many digital stories and storytelling approaches arrange content as separate iterations over time. This method can mean episodic style, or material issued in a series, or accepted positions for supplemental content.[27]

Scott McCloud argues passionately for a definition or renaming of comics as "sequential art,"[28] referring to a smaller scale, to the level of individual panels in a sequence. We can borrow the term, or at least be with it in spirit, and use it to emphasize the segmented nature of much digital storytelling.

Some of that segmentation is distributed in space. As McCloud observes: "Nothing is seen between the two [comic] panels, but *experience* tells you something *must* be there! Comics panels *fracture* both *time* and *space,* offering a *jagged, staccato rhythm* of *unconnected moments.* But closure allows us to *connect* these moments and *mentally construct* a *continuous, unified reality.*"[29] Perhaps we can refer to much digital storytelling as "segmented art," or segmented storytelling.

Personal Presence

Many digital stories depict one or more characters, either fictional or historical. These representations are often in the third or first person, biographical or autobiographical. A good number of games and some storytelling frameworks involve the audience as a second-person character through some mixture of address and presence. Every medium can be mobilized to support character. Establishing a personal sense is a powerful storytelling strategy.

Social Framework

In the social media age, every story is ultimately part of social media. Stories engage with social media directly through positioning content on the Web via platforms supporting linking, commenting, editing, sharing, and other audience co-creative activities. Story segments may well include content produced by other creators and hosted elsewhere. Indirectly, even the most asocial story can be discussed, remixed, shared, and otherwise amplified through the social Web. Moreover, we can build stories using content made available through that social Web.

This aspect of digital storytelling should seem familiar to most readers, whatever one's experience with social media Web 2.0. It echoes the ancient oral practice of transmitting tales from person to person, reflecting on stories, and talking before creators who eventually repurpose others' words for their own story. Current social media operations also recall print and electrical media practices of commentary, from critical reviewers to gossip columnists. What's different, simply put, is that these preexisting practices are now democratically accessible and capable of persisting far beyond the evanescence of verbal communication.

A related point about digital stories being necessarily included in social media is that story boundaries are often blurry. Once a story is launched directly into the Web, determining its beginning and end is not always an easy matter. A blog's termination, for example, is usually not clear, as it may be extended indefinitely until the site disappears (only to probably persist in the Internet Archive and a Google cache, not to mention locally saved copies). Supplemental content may appear in the form of Web video clips, a newly published podcast, or further wiki page edits. So much for story materials produced by creators; the boundaries of story content produced by others are even more difficult to pin down. Remixes, fan fiction, comments from involved or interested parties, wiki resources generated by friendly or hostile parties, game walkthroughs and cheats—stories can be surrounded by a halo or aura of secondary material.

Multiple Proscenia

Increasingly, there is no single point of story experience. If digital stories are distributed in space and time, this practice can necessitate multiple platforms for experiencing them. Henry Jenkins's model of transmedia storytelling means creators and audiences meet each other across multiple stages for the same story or world (see Chapter 8). Social media routinely cross locations, media, languages, and styles. The ease of copying and embedding media means echoes and versions of stories can be reflected across different hardware and software ecosystems. We may read a book in print, on a handheld device, or on printouts, or hear it read aloud (either automatically or by humans). TV content shifts from broadcast to cable to authorized video (Hulu) to unauthorized (bit torrent) to some gray zone in between (YouTube).

Time shifting is a key part of this "multiple proscenia" notion. Recording a TV program in order to experience it at another time is already commonplace and has transformed the social reception of television. Formerly inaccessible historical media may appear in digitized form on YouTube or as podcasts, from obscure TV commercials to Golden Age radio.[30] Stories are segmented in time, both because creators release them that way and because audiences choose to experience them on their own schedules.

Platform Affordances

Every digital story can take advantage of the unique affordances of each digital platform it uses. Games for the Xbox can vibrate controllers to indicate unusual stresses, bloggers categorize and allow comments upon posts, Flickr images are capable of being tagged and pooled, and interactive fiction supports replaying a game/story. Each segment of a story can push the unique nature of its digital housing to accentuate the story's power.

Janet Murray argued in 1997 that deeply exploring such affordances is a sign of a medium's evolution. When a new medium appears, we copy preexisting practices into it in what Murray dubs "additive art": theater staging for early films, for example. Creators next determine how to use the new platform on its own terms, "seizing on [its] unique physical properties," "exploring its own expressive power." Filmmakers, in this example, developed montage, new forms of lighting, and the moving camera point of view.[31] Digital storytelling sees both of these types of technology usage, additive and expressive, first and second stage. Their combinations, too, progress along that arc, as we shall see.

We now explore digital storytelling as it occurs in various platforms, seeing how the preceding principles play out in each.

PART 2

New Platforms for Tales and Telling

CHAPTER FOUR

Storytelling with the Technology Formerly Known as Web 2.0

Since social media, or what we once referred to as Web 2.0, has led to an explosion of user-generated content, we should expect to see some storytelling emerge out of all of that material, in its huge size and full diversity. If we use our working definition of storytelling, which combines sequence with meaning and engagement, we can find many examples of these.

Two cautions concerning fragility should be borne in mind as we proceed. First, social media evolve at a very rapid speed. It is likely that some of the platforms and styles we explore here will be outmoded or replaced by the time you read this. Some were outmoded or replaced between the two editions of this book. Consider this chapter, then, to be a historical snapshot of Web 2.0 storytelling in 2017. As with any historical content, some will persist through the reader's time, and some will not.

Second, some of this content may disappear. "Link rot" has been a persistent problem since the dawn of the Web, as URLs change syntax, hosts cease hosting, creators change their mind, or technologies become obsolete. Such evanescence is now essential to Web storytelling's nature: not as temporary as sand painting, but perhaps closer to television content in durability. The number of those rotted links will increase over time, doubtlessly. The Internet Archive's Wayback Machine is one of the best resources to check for backup copies of Web-based content.[1] In fact, astute readers will note that some references in this book point to Internet Archive versions of content now vanished from its original site. Google's habit of caching Web page copies can also be useful.

Blogs

Blogging may well be the most visible and accessible form of Web 2.0 storytelling. It is one of the oldest social media authoring platforms, allowing at least a decade of steady creation to provide a wealth of experiments and examples. From the first days of the form, its similarity to diaries provided a ready comparison to that classic narrative tool and easy ways to think about both production and consumption. The personal sense associated with diaries also enabled "blogger" to emerge as a category, even a professional identity, letting us think of blogs as character vehicles. This, too, situates blogs well for story thinking.

For example, on a personal note, I first taught with blogs in the spring of 2001, during a British literature class. Assigning students the task of creating their own blogs from the Blogger.com service (since purchased by Google), I (and they) was pleased at the ease of building Web content. As the semester progressed, I found myself thinking of each blog as the student's self-representation, far more than I had through such other digital teaching tools as discussion boards and Web 1.0-style Web pages. They felt like personae, the face of the student in my class, as opposed to their broader life. Even though this class's blogging was an experiment, it felt easy, even natural, very quickly.

The personal aspect of blogs has persisted over the past decade, simultaneously complemented by other interpretations: group blogs, community blogs, intranet blogs for corporate knowledge management, newspaper blogs, and so on. This historical diversity makes it imperative that we not consider blogging as a single, simple entity. As Steve Himmer argues, "Focusing exclusively on the material production of a weblog is akin to arguing that what allows individual novels to fit into a class of novels—or, indeed, for a class 'novels' to exist at all—is that they all consist of printed pages of prose fiction bound into a volume."[2] Accordingly, the category of blogs as storytelling devices is broken down for this chapter into a typology: diary, character exploration, time-based republication, and one-post stories. As noted in Chapter 1, these forms include both fiction and nonfiction.[3]

Blogs are diaries: This metaphor has been a powerful one, especially as a heuristic to explain the odd-sounding technology to newcomers. There is an obvious connection, since both forms consist of content chunks arranged in linear chronological order. There is also a strong appeal, since diaries are often associated with personal intimacy, sometimes from childhood. The metaphor breaks down rapidly, though, once one realizes that each form proceeds along opposed chronological directions and that so many blogs are nothing at all like diaries.

Yet the metaphor remains lively and sometimes describes projects. *She's a Flight Risk* (2003) narrates a woman's life as she travels around the world, escaping from an unhappy situation. Instead of eating, praying, and loving, Isabella v. describes encounters with private detectives and reporters. The first post began: "On March 2, 2003 at 4:12 PM, I disappeared. My name is isabella v., but it's not. I'm twentysomething and I am an international fugitive." The remaining posts narrate this adventure, alternating biographical details with claims to veracity. The story unfolds in sequence of blog time stamps, date by date, with some digressions back in time to present context.

A public diary, a social media journal—comments appeared on it to offer suggestions, criticisms, protestations of disbelief. John Richardson offers a good account of the skeptical range Isabella's storytelling induced, from disbelief to credulity. Richardson's ultimate face-to-face meeting with Isabella, or someone claiming to be her, echoes the shift from digital to physical we also see in alternate reality game storytelling (see Chapter 10). The *Flight Risk* blog acts as a public performance, with audience participation included. Its blurring of the boundary between fiction and nonfiction parallels its storytelling stance straddling content authorship and audience co-creation.[4] A similar fiction/nonfiction blur attended the *Belle de Jour* blog from its launch in 2003 until the author revealed her identity in 2009.[5]

Blog stories have continued to appeal as a narrative form ever since. One good example is *The Sick Land* (2013), which presents itself as the diary of a researcher investigating a mysterious and dangerous natural phenomenon. The physical location is never specified, adding to the setting's appeal. Alex Case narrates his work, focused on studying a peculiar disease or ontological crisis dubbed *the mal* (evil). Practical difficulties in doing the work challenge him, as do increasingly powerful dreams and mental breakdowns among his colleagues. Post by post, *The Sick Land* builds up through escalating violence into something approaching cosmic horror.

As exemplary blog storytelling it proceeds simply through *Flight Risk*'s posts-as-diary model. The tale proceeds chronologically, without any asynchronous foreshadowing or editing of earlier posts. It begins on a note of hope and positive anticipation:

> Tomorrow I leave!
> I'm excited to have the opportunity for field study; these positions are few and far between, and I'd like to thank my supervisor, Professor Grant Ramirez, for sponsoring my application.

There is also what seems to be obligatory in this form, a clear statement of how the blog narrative works:

> I've set up this blog as a diary come[sic] research log. I hope to update it as often as possible. I've been assured that the station has internet access . . .
> I'll also use the blog to talk about all things *mal*. I hope to bring together as many disparate strands of research as I can.
> Mainstream discussion of the Sick Land is hard to come by. I hope that, as a researcher in this area, I can help disseminate information pertaining to this fascinating area and its history.
> My next post will be sent from station Alpha!

There's an openness and self-awareness to blog-based storytelling, a performative way of staging the technology as narrative. It's a public way of explaining sharing a private discourse.

By the final post, Case's mental state has changed drastically:

> This is my last post.
> The facility is dark. Eviscerated bodies lie face down in the deepening water . . .
> I don't think many places will survive . . .

Sick Land traces Case's transformation in tandem with changes to the landscape and the entire research effort. There isn't much else. Comments are either deleted or blocked, so the posts stand alone. There are no other media besides text. No other social media enterprise extended or engaged with the story. *The Sick Land* may be the most basic, and one of the most effective, instances of using a blog to tell a story.[6]

The blog-as-diary concept became recognizable enough to appear as a device in fiction. Bruce Sterling used this approach to tell a short story about a hyperlocal, yet very mobile future, one taking place around the same time the second edition of this book appears. The blogger-narrator describes the rocky course of his engagement, while noting developments in net.art, social media, and general technology along the way. "Dispatches from the Hyperlocal Future" is not a blog, but it mimics one, consisting of serial, dated, and discrete posts. We don't see blog comments, but the narrator refers to them as well as to other social media effects fictionalized around his blog:

> 06.18.2017 | In transit
> . . . Thanks for the many supportive readers who wrote in with wise advice when I was so visibly losing it there.

05.22.2017 | Torino

I just egosurfed myself, and I discovered that a comical picture of me glaring at my misbehaving handheld is by far the most popular pic of me ever placed on the Internet. I was caught between expressions—it was one of those unlucky shots—but it appeared overnight in the commentary of Janis' blog. An instant worldwide explosion followed, lavishly tagged with "hilarious" captions by Janis' legions of fans:

I CAN HAZ LIMELIGHT NOW? . . .

and hundreds of others even more puerile.[7]

Nothing restricts a diary-style blog story to a single blog save authorial decision. Multiple blogs, each hosted on a different site, can combine their individual voices into a polyphonic, hyperlinked whole. The *World without Oil* alternate reality game (2007) consisted of a half dozen bloggers, each describing his or her life as an oil shock rapidly unravels civilization. Each blogger's biography offered the person's perspective on events, grounded in personality, socioeconomic status, and geographical location. Readers/ players could post comments on each blog, offering advice, asking questions, and participating in the unfolding story.[8]

Dionaea House (2004) follows a similar pattern. This haunted house story is concerned with seduction and psychological dislocation; aptly, its components are character studies. One part consists of a young man's e-mails and text messages, putatively edited and copied into single Web pages in blog style. Mark Chondry's story, as related to Eric Heisserer, traces the identification and pursuit of a sort of monster, an architectural analogue to the Venus fly trap (and hence the title): "Here are copies of the correspondence I received from Mark over the course of the last month. For the most part, I have merely copied and pasted them from my e-mail application."[9] Each entry consists of a sparse Web page, each one with an addressable URL, and a very basic navigation tool.

Once we finish Mark's story, which climaxes on an effectively spooky note (texting and explaining, by doing so, that "THE DOOR IS OPEN"), we are led back to Eric's editorial voice and his apparent destruction by the same malign force. This occurs not on serial pages, but in two different sites: first, a single HTML document, titled "Updates and Other Resources," with diary entries arranged in chronological order; second, a personal blog, *A Quiet Place*, linked from the first page.[10] The content in both describes Eric's research into the haunting force and his truncated exploration of a scary house. The Updates page consists of e-mails to another character, while the blog is written in (presumably) Eric's own voice. Like *Ted's Caving Journal*, Eric's narrative breaks off at the moment of a final-sounding plunge, followed by no further content: "Here we go."

"Updates and Other Resources" includes links to several other story sites. This is where we first find *A Quiet Place*, along with a babysitter's Live Journal.[11] Dani describes caring for a child in one of the haunted houses we now recognize. Her perspective, that of a teenager utterly unaware of the plot, is both sad and clichéd, recalling the past generation of teen slasher movies. After describing ever-increasing terror, the blog ends on a destabilized note. The last entry, evidently written by Dani, indicates mental breakdown or possession, consisting of two nursery rhymes without explanation. Next follows a single-line post, reading only "found you" and linked to Eric's *A Quiet Place* blog. The monster has claimed another victim—and perhaps a fourth, as we learn nothing of the fate of Dani's charge.

The Updates page links to still another blog, maintained by one Loreen Mathers.[12] This stands as a sequel to the others, dated as starting one year later (2005, continued into 2006). Loreen describes an attack by the haunted house in more detail than we've read so far, and in a very different voice. She portrays herself as very worldly, cynical, and practical, and also as a murderer.

Blog comments also contain what seems to be some additional authorial content. One "JennyLevin" comments on one of Eric's posts:

> Hey . . . Hang in there, Eric . . . I know what you mean, and I'm having the same feelings and thoughts just like you wrote here . . . Let me tell you how far I have gone, so you won't feel so alone in this.[13]

Two comments are attached to Eric's final post, one from ally Jenny, and the next from an apparently possessed (or imitated) Dani:

> **JennyLevin** said . . .
> Please. . . . PLEASE answer your phone . . .
> This waiting is killing me . . . . . .
> 12:28 PM
> **ohdanigirl** said . . .
> jenny levin where are you
> the boys are all inside now
> come and find us
> the door is open[14]

Also included within the overall Dionaea project, linked from "Updates and Other Resources," is an instant message conversation, archived and published as a single, plain text-only page.[15]

Taken together, the several voices of Dionaea House comprise a single interlinked story. Characters refer to each other by addressing them, describing their actions to a third party, or linking to their Web content. This process is dialogic, as each of our readings connects with and reshapes the others. Dani's naiveté throws Loreen's cynicism into relief, and Loreen's detailed descriptions of the terrible place fill out Mark's sketches.

Readers can enter into dialogue with the story through blog comments. After Eric posts about the ominous-seeming Sweatsuit Man, comments appear wishing him well and offering helpful advice.[16] After his final post, with its ominous comments, readers weigh in with assessments about the story's veracity and craft. A first-time reader encounters each blog with that combination of content and commentary.

Dionaea is not as interactive as *World without Oil* and some other blogs in that commenting is not available for two sections of it, Mark's tale and Eric's single-page account. Readers can create social media content elsewhere and link to Dionaea but not interact through this classic blog feature. Not all blogs allow comments, but the practice is general enough to shape blog reading.[17] In a sense, this combination of blogs, bloglike pages, and flat HTML constitutes an anthology of Web strategies for the time of its creation. Perhaps we should consider Dionaea as a transitional text, crossing between Web 1.0 and 2.0 storytelling styles. We can hear that historical arc here: "These emails are becoming more of a journal for me, to help me [b]log my progress."[18]

Project 1968 is a better example of what Angela Thomas calls "blog fiction": "fiction which is produced where an author or authors have used a blog as a *writing* device, using all of the features afforded by the blogging or journaling software, such as hyperlinks, graphics, and the commenting system."[19] Read for the first time, *Project 1968* appears to be a two-person group blog out of time, each author writing as if she were participating in the 1968 Democratic Party national convention in Chicago. Its front page offers several ways to proceed. We can read the entire blog chronologically, either backward or forward, with Amy and Janine together as a dyad or separately, thanks to the author function of the blog platform.[20] We can look for the "About" page and there find an explanation of the project, along with supporting documents and hyperlinked resources[21]—going behind the scenes, as it were, sidestepping the blog's presentation as historical fiction. Along those lines, we can read an explanation of Amy and Janine's characters.[22] Leading away from the *Project 1968* blog is a link to a MySpace site that provides a kind of parallel story content base as well as an example of cross-platform, transmedia storytelling (see Chapter 8).[23]

Focusing in on the main blog content, we find it presented as a diary or newscast. Read chronologically forward, *Project 1968*'s notes about current events yield a serial account of historical unfolding. Unlike a single diary or a newscast purporting to speak with a single voice, Amy and Janine write (or speak) with similar yet complementary voices, offering parallel perspectives. For example:

August 28, 1968
by Amy
12:10 A.M.—Lincoln Park
    They were beaten. We watched them from afar. They beat the priests who gathered to protect us. Coleman asked Glasses if the priests knew what was about to happen. Glasses assured him that they did. They sent him away, and they stayed.[24]

Such a post immediately launches itself at the reader's emotions through the combination of violence and mystery. For the latter, this is clearly an entry lacking context, at least, which sends us into the blog archives to search for explanations or to wait for the next entry. Perhaps we will investigate the MySpace page or search the open Web for other platforms. Some readers will want to respond, either in fictional or objective modes.

But this is a putatively coauthored blog, and we have been trained to expect a complementary view. On the same date (August 28, 1968), Janine posts from a different location, observing another set of events:

Unstoppable . . .
5 P.M.
    Craig is gone. He yelled at Ron that he was going to burn his convention pass in the park. It's horrible. She told him that it was important not to give up, but he just kept saying over and over again that it was all a set-up. The entire convention was a big fake, phony exercise and that the whole thing was rigged.
    I have to admit, it looks like he's right. It doesn't matter what the people want. We have no say in our own government. "IT'S A SHAM! THE WHOLE GODDAMN THING IS A SHAM! WE'VE WASTED OUR TIME!"[25]

Janine is inside the convention. In other words, her attention is divided between party maneuvers within the building (and, metaphorically, within the party itself) and protestor–police interactions outside (also outside of the party as well).

The post veers back and forth between the two, touching on numerous characters, framing out the historical moment. Later in that same post, we read:

10:30 P.M.
> We can't get enough organized quickly enough to get it through. The Humphrey/Daley people are ramming it through.
> We can't stop them.

And yet, again in the same post, Janine perceives the events in which Amy is acting:

7 P.M.
> . . . I'm angry at Becca. And I'm also afraid for her. What if she gets arrested? She hit that policeman in Madison. What if she does it again?
> 9:30 P.M.
> We're standing by a television watching what is happening outside. I can't believe it. No one can. Mrs. Stoutmiller says that some delegates are planning to protest inside the convention. I certainly don't want to be on the floor when that happens.
> Ron keeps trying not to stare at the television. He's talking with people, chatting up The Senator's aides. We wonder how The Senator will get to the Amphitheatre. What kind of security precautions are there?
> I just saw a cop hit a demonstrator across the legs. It was a blonde girl. He broke his baton.
> Disgusting.

Project 1968 brings into play all of the storytelling principles we discussed in Chapter 3. The blog structure breaks up the flow of content into a serial sequence. The two main characters are the ground of the story, each going through personal transformations. The social framework is made available through these blog posts' comment features along with similar interaction elements over in MySpace. That MySpace site offers another proscenium for action, while *Project 1968* takes advantage of various blog affordances on the main site: an About page and serial and social presentation.

This history–story blog offers a readily accessible version of blog-based storytelling. The events portrayed are recent enough to evoke memories in some readers while remaining formally comprehensible to many American audiences. The vivid personal presence of the two women demonstrates blogging characters, while the documentary evidence shows a way of integrating multiple documents.

Temporally Structured Archival Blogging

Some predigital content was published in chronologically marked forms. The epistolary novel, for example, usually includes letters identified by date. Diary, or journal-based stories, of course, must do this, and readers expect as much. These stories can violate that expectation to make a point, such as establishing that the narrator has gone insane. Some rare examples of fiction rely on a detailed chronological structure, like Bram Stoker's *Dracula* (1896), which consists entirely of dated content items: letters, diary entries, telegrams, receipts, audio recordings, and newspaper clippings.

We've seen this storytelling style in other venues besides print. *Time-code* (directed by Michael Figgis, 2000) features four parallel plot lines, each visible on screen (depending on which version or performance) and occurring at precisely the same moment. More famously, *24* (Fox-TV, 2001–2010) attempts to follow a single day, with each episode pinned to an individual hour.

The point of identifying such examples is to give background for similar digital storytelling cases using blogs, sometimes with the same material. The first well-known example of this is the *Pepys Diary* blog (2003), which posts from Samuel Pepys's journals on the same date as the original entry. The "10 February 1665/66" entry, for example, appeared on February 10, 2009.[26] The source material is available in the public domain and is republished using the popular WordPress blogging platform.

A series of other projects have followed suit. *WW1: Experiences of an English Soldier* republishes letters, other personal documents, and contextual information related to one Western Front soldier and his biography. Dated content is associated roughly or precisely with the date of each post.[27] *The Orwell Diaries* offers a similar, if more narrowly focused project, blogging George Orwell's 1937–1942 journal entries "70 years to the day since each entry was originally written. The diaries start as Orwell heads to Morocco (with his wife Eileen) to recuperate from injury and illness, and end in 1942 (or 2012) as the Second World War rages."[28] That war is the subject of another blog–history project, *World War II Today*.[29]

News from 1930 posts selections from each day's *Wall Street Journal* during the early years of the Great Depression.[30] For example, the May 1, 2010 entry draws on material from the Friday, May 1, 1931 *WSJ* issue ("Dow 151.19. +7.58 [5.3%]"), including editorials, letters, macroeconomic news, miscellaneous news, stories about individual businesses, movies reviews, and jokes:

> *Editorial:* Businessmen should be responsible and stop joining "college economists" and "maverick politicians" in their talk of "failure of the capitalist system" and "challenge to the existing order." . . .
>
> *Trained monkeys* are now used by Chicago burglars to squeeze through transoms . . . and open locked doors from the inside, thus demonstrating the uplifting power of evolution.[31]

News from 1930 has several avowed purposes. As with other time-based republication blogs, the format defamiliarizes the document: "I do think you get a different feel for history seeing it day-by-day like this—less tidy, but more real." The blog reading revises the blogger's sense of the time:

> In histories of the Depression the leaders of the time are commonly portrayed as oblivious to what was going on, do-nothing, and stupidly optimistic. . . . [Yet] It appears that the people in charge at the time were well aware of what was happening, and did most of the things that we're doing now to alleviate it (with a couple of notable exceptions). And as for unjustified optimism, we will see that at least in mid-1930 there was a fair amount of good news coming out about the economy.

This leads to a political aim, both in viewing the past as well as the Great Recession present: "And it just might give you a useful skepticism for some of the more Panglossian commentary we're seeing today when you see that similar things were said back then—and probably with more reason!"[32]

Shifting ground from history to fiction, I can share the story of having blogged *Dracula* for several years.[33] My motivations for launching the project were to reread the novel from a different perspective, to win more readers for the book, and to further explore the blog storytelling platform. The logistics for doing so were quite simple. I was preparing an edition of the book for print, and so had an annotated digital copy on hand. I already had a blog platform that allowed me to spin off secondary blogs. It was an easy matter to simply copy and paste content from Word to Web browser once I set up a basic schedule. I did nothing for publicity and collaborated with no institution.

Readers began to arrive, based on Typepad's blog statistics, which put daily hits in the hundreds, then some thousands. Readers also began leaving comments on individual posts. As with the *Pepys Diary*, comments ranged from reader response to scholars sharing their research. For example, following Dr. Seward's first post (a fascinating technological artifact, purportedly a transcription of a wax cylinder audio recording), the first commentator shared his thoughts about the characters. David40 then asked, "Why is Jack drawn to Renfield during his period of pining for Lucy?" Babyjinx offered an explanation, then David40 responded. Next Elizabeth Miller, one of the world's leading Dracula scholars, commented about Renfield's name: "The name 'Renfield' never appears in Stoker's Notes. The character is there from the outset, but he is referred to as either the Mad Patient or the Flyman." More discussion ensued.[34]

After the first year ended with Van Helsing and the other survivors contemplating victory in November, I reran the novel several times, each time beginning in May with Jonathan Harker's first bemused journal entry. I revised the presentation slightly, splitting up some entries into two posts, due to clearly marked internal timeline breaks, and more precisely timing several posts according to their own description (midnight, etc.). Each year, a new commentary layer appeared, gradually lower in number, but still interesting. One reader, Andrew Connell, created a set of Google maps to illustrate several voyages in the novel (Dracula's trips from Romania to Britain and back, for instance). Repeat readers offered reflections on their experience now that they'd finished it. In a sense, the Dracula blog offered—and still offers—a distributed, collaborative reading of the novel, "an online reading group," in Angela Thomas's account.[35] As a teacher and scholar of the novel, I learned a great deal about its temporality and the skillful way it creates suspense.

These temporal blog-publishing projects partake of many social media qualities. First, they often trigger active audience contributions. *Pepys Diary* readers post comments (called "annotations") exploring each entry in detail: inquiring about mental states, London locations, British politics, and so on. They reflect on the day's description:

> "He was coldly received by us, and he went away before we rose also, to make himself appear yet a man less necessary." The tension in this scene must have been enormous and Sir Thomas obviously reacts in a way that further discounts him in the eyes of Pepys and crew. This would be harsh for any man to endure, but for a Gentleman, it would have been a humiliation. Still, I have to give it to Pepys for this superb line ". . . yet a man less necessary." The concision of the image is brilliant.[36]

We can see these temporally based republication blogs as doing the work of storytelling in two ways. First, they reproduce a text that has already been received as a story. Fiction (*Dracula*) and nonfiction (Pepys) alike, the source material clearly tells a story and has a reception history as such. The blog format heightens the temporal nature of these stories, marking it more clearly than otherwise, blog post structure being more clearly dated than the same content nicely formatted in a paperback book. Blogging also makes the time structure more vivid by mapping it onto the reader's time schedule. There remains a gap between the two timelines, which we will see plays a role in gaming (see Chapter 6), as few can afford to read each blog post on precisely the date it appears. Nonetheless, a blog structure makes such a temporally distributed reading more possible, and even likely.

Second, blogging a preexisting work adds a social layer to the texts. As Thomas observes, "What is unique is the quick and easy blog commenting mechanism for relatively instant feedback and critique."[37] In this sense, blog republication is social publication, embedding the source material in the full Web 2.0 world. Thomas is correct to note the ease and speed of commenting and linking; we should also add a long tail effect insofar as a blog remains on the Web. The source material can be accessed after posting, and the comments around it constitute an already present discussion. Other blogs and other social media venues can then serve as guides to these republication projects, functioning as "post-filters" to their stories, in Chris Anderson's term.[38]

Character Blogging

Revisiting the theme of blog as diary, we can pause to observe what should now be a truism. Bloggers are characters. Each blogger demonstrates a persona, to whatever degree of fiction. These personalities are shown over time, according to the serial nature of digital storytelling. As Steve Himmer puts it:

> As one day's posts build on points raised or refuted in a previous day's, readers must actively engage the process of "discovering" the author, and of parsing from fragment after fragment who is speaking to them, and why, and from where whether geographically, mentally, politically, or otherwise.[39]

In this consideration, blogs tell stories through the presentation of characters. *Project 1968* and *WW1: Experiences of an English Soldier* each depend on the exploration of a character engaged in historical events. Their experiences and reactions proceed, and through them we can grasp the larger situation.

But even nonfictional blogs present themselves as characters. The practice of taking pseudonyms is rarely for actual anonymity, cases like *She's a Flight Risk* notwithstanding. Political bloggers often use names as a kind of character designation, branding exercise, or approach to shaping the reader's experience of the site's content: *The Volokh Conspiracy* and *Insta-pundit* each have resonances of self-deprecation.[40] In contrast, *Informed Comment* suggests competence and seriousness ("Thoughts on the Middle East, History and Religion").[41] Consider Hobart and William Smith College professor Michael Tinkler's blog title: *The Cranky Professor.* Its subtitle completes the misanthropic picture: "You type, and I tell you why 4,500 years of written history shows you're wrong."[42] Swarthmore College professor Tim Burke calls his blog *Easily Distracted*, and once more we see a self-parodic subtitle: "Culture, Politics, Academia and Other Shiny Objects."[43] The content of blog posts over time obviously grows a character presentation. What isn't necessarily obvious are the implications of content choices. Blogging about politics triggers expectations of character type based in that milieu: activist, cynic, party loyalist, and so on. Gender implications also appear, as Justine Musk observes, drawing on gender discourse theory: "The attitude seems to be that personal, confessional blogging ('female' blogging) is narcissistic, and authority blogging ('male' blogging) is not." Musk also makes an intriguing argument about a blogger's authority and implied commercialism:

> Authority blogging establishes the blogger as an "authority" in some particular niche, and relates information that (theoretically) solves a problem the reader might have or teaches something that the reader wants to know. An authority blogger usually has a product or service to sell you.[44]

Blogs reveal authors' personae through posts, but also through other content contained on the blog site. Blogrolls, for example, show intended affiliations and interests. "About" pages can contain small (or large) autobiographies. Departments or categories offer a snapshot of blogger interests. Feeds from other content sources broaden the portrait: photos from Flickr, Twitter updates, and so forth. Without necessarily setting out to tell a story, bloggers present themselves as characters.

Some ways of blogging cut across these different modes and apply elsewhere. No matter the content or format, blogs lack a clear boundary for their storytelling activity. They can always extend via posting or comments, while being included in another story is always possible. They differ from other, more concretely delineated story forms in what Himmer refers to as an "absence of a discrete, 'completed' product."[45]

Related to character blogging is what I call "one-post stories." These are a version of short-short stories taking place on a single self-contained blog post. They may include images or other media embedded or consist solely of text. Over time, a blog publishing many of these develops a kind of character, as in the preceding category.

For example, *Small Town Noir* blogs about historically true crime in western Pennsylvania. Each post offers police photography accompanied by research into what crime led to that photo. "The mug shots on this site date from the 1930s to the 1950s—from the temporary slump of the great depression to the terminal slump that followed Korea."[46]

For example, one post—"Martin Fobes, 'intox driver,' January 8 1948"—begins with a white man's face, seen in two different views, head-on and profile. The post's text describes Fobes's arrest for drunkenness and then explores a likely second connected crime of either attempted assault or rape, ending in a woman's death. Pieces of evidence are presented to establish the second crime, including statements and a mapping exercise about Anna Grace's death. The whole is presented as a series of mysteries or mistaken explanations:

> The file card that accompanied the mug shot listed the charge as "intox driver", but Martin Fobes was suspected of something much worse. . . .
>
> It was a mystery to the police, which isn't unusual, but it also seemed to be a mystery to the man who was arrested in connection with the death. Or so he claimed. . . .
>
> The case appears to have been dropped. The *New Castle News* doesn't mention it, or Anna Grace, after that day. Fobes wasn't charged with a serious crime.
>
> No one seems to have been certain what happened in those missing 20 minutes.[47]

Reading post after post, *Small Town Noir* offers a composite character of personal extremity and frequent desperation. This is obviously due to the accumulation of crime stories and criminals, but the overall effect is also colored by the editor–writer's sense of historical melancholy, combined with historiographical mission:

> Small Town Noir is dedicated to recovering the life stories behind mug shots from the vanished golden age of one American town.
>
> The men and women in these mug shots are nobody special, but they saw things that none of us will ever see. . . . It was once one of the most industrially productive cities in America, but all that's gone now.[48]

That sense of gloom is accentuated by the site's black background. Even its material nature seems grim, as per this note emphasized on every page by a sidebar item:

> The mug shots on this site were all taken in New Castle, Pennsylvania, between 1930 and 1959, and were rescued from the trash when the towns police department threw them out. The information that has been used to

reconstruct the stories behind the pictures comes mostly from old copies of the local paper, the *New Castle News*.

Twitter

Twitter might appear to be the least likely storytelling platform of all. Despite the enormous size of its user base and diversity of content, its reputation as a site for trivial pseudo-conversation should preclude meaning and narrative. Twitter's own self-presentation suggests self-abnegation, from its language ("tweeting," even "Twitter" itself) to goofy imagery (the chirping bird, the notorious fail whale). Yet its sheer simplicity and ease of use have enabled tremendous creativity.

As with blogs, Twitter storytelling can be divided into modes. First, Twitter's immediacy lends itself to live, staged stories. Each tweet is written to the moment, a quick snapshot of a rapidly unfolding fiction which users pretend to be a current event. The *War of the Worlds* reenactment referenced in Chapter 1, for example, portrayed an alien invasion through multiple Twitter writers describing their local experience. The organizer issued writing prompts while promulgating a timeline and hashtag ("@wotw2") to coordinate things:

> The alien invasion occurs. Follow @wotw2 to keep in sync with the progress of the invasion. This Twitter feed will automatically update, in general terms, the unfolding of the alien invasion like clockwork throughout the world. Coordinate with Tweeters in your area to tell local stories.
>
> 1. cylinders fall from the sky. Tweet about where you are. Ask your friends where they are. Form posses. Skip town or take a closer look.
> 2. tripods emerge. Flee, get stuck in traffic, or take refuge and tell us what you see.
> 3. Martians begin obliterating every Terran metropolitan area with heat rays. Don't call them heat-rays; that would be a dead giveaway. Describe what they do and come up with your own name! Do you work in a public service like hospitals or fire? What's your job and what do you do? Do you organize your coworkers and flee? Do you head for the hills with your go-bag?[49]

Participants tweeted accordingly: "The freeways are packed! I've heard from a few stuck on 252 and 94, they are sitting ducks."[50]

A similar, if narrower story was told by the inevitable *Zombie Attack*. This first-person narration is a very fast-paced, almost stream-of-consciousness narration of a "zompocalypse":

We ran as fast as we could up the stairs Matt slipped and cut his leg, i helped him up and continued to run. Just then we bump into guards.

The guards grab us and ask us if we are okay, we say yes and they continue on by, we walk over to the bench and sit down. What now?

We go to the offices, and are greeted by a guy different from the one we had the first time around, he says he cant help us and grabs my arm

He looks at it for a second, and asks me to come with him, he pulls me into a side office, i turn and Matt is away . . . did he abandon me?[51]

A related project narrates a thousand years of history while trying for this kind of immediacy. CryforByzantium narrates the Eastern Roman Empire's long career. "Usually the 'person' speaking will be the Emperor. He (and occasionally she) will explain in brief terms what's going on. When there's a change of emperor, the Twitter feed will update with 'New Emperor' and the name of the new ruler."[52]

25 December 820. Going to traditional Christmas hymns at the Chapel of St. Stephen. Still mad about @Michael_the_Amorian.

25 December 820. New emperor: Michael II (Michael the Amorian).

First orders: throw Leo's body into the latrine. Clean up all the blood on the floor. And get somebody to break these manacles off me!

Merry Christmas, Byzantium! You've got a new emperor! I warn you, don't mess with me! *holds up Leo's severed arm*

Spring 821. Whit Sunday. I'm crowning my son Theophilus co-emperor so he will succeed me. We've had 7 emperors in the last 25 years![53]

These are creative and entertaining paraphrases of historical moments, drawing from fuller historical works. A narrower historical focus can be seen in *Kennedy 1960,* which tweets details of that president's election campaign: excerpts from speeches, travel itinerary notes, and links to larger documents.[54]

A second type of Twitter storytelling uses single tweets to tell very short stories, really micronarratives. One such story republishes selections from Felix Feneon's *Novels in Three Lines.* This 1906 experimental novel excerpted or remixed true crime stories from popular newspapers. The Twitter account then tweets these extremely condensed stories, alternating between pathos, daily life, and black comedy:

On Bécu, 28, who arrived at Beaujon hospital with a gunshot wound, they counted 28 scars. His nickname in the underworld: The Target.

The Anti-Rabies Institute of Lyons had cured Mlle. Lobrichon, but as the dog had been rabid she died all the same.

In Méréville, a hunter from Estampes, thinking he saw game afoot, killed a child and with the same bullet wounded the father.

Amiens will crown its muse on September 16. Forty beauties were vying for the role. It has gone to Marie Mahiou, a velvet weaver.

Misses Cabriet and Rivelle, of Plaine-Saint-Denis and Bagnolet, and M. Goudon of Saint-Denis, all drank: he cyanide, they laudanum.[55]

Tweeji's biographical snippets ("Follow Dead People on Twitter") are closely allied to this approach.[56] Virginia Heffernan suggests that this might be one way for Twitter and Facebook users to consider posting by carefully reshaping their thoughts about immediate, daily life: "You take a tiny story, which seemingly concerns only you and in which you play the role of hapless, bumbling protagonist, and you turn it into a haiku version of universal truth."[57]

Other Twitter accounts follow this historical microstorytelling strategy. Medieval Death Bot publishes one-tweet accounts of how some individuals died in the Middle Ages:

Nicholas de Byterle, died 1320 after an altercation with some clerks, receiving mortal head and belly wounds.

Robert Denys, died in 1321 after his hand was feloniously cut off in a quarrel with John de Pastone.

Entertainingly, if another Twitter user tweets @ Medieval Death Bot, the Bot will reply with a tweet inserting the other user into a medieval death. Medieval Death Bot has murdered me several times.[58]

Witch Court Reporter complements Medieval Death Bot nicely. The Reporter presents snippets of witch trials. "All the accusations, all the time. Modern English, period sources." Hashtags chain together a series of tweets from the same trial:

After dinner, the bewitched girl had a fit & saw the witch dressed in a white sheet with a black child on her shoulders.
#warboys1593

The woman was floating on a plank, not walking on water. Even so, she moved with such ease & skill it must have been witchcraft.
#newbury1643

To stop the Earl conceiving, the witches mixed his gloves & some mattress wool with warm water & blood & rubbed it on the cat.
#lincoln1618

Witch Court Reporter occasionally adds a period image or contemporary art.[59]

Magic Realism Bot follows a similar approach to these Twitter accounts, but not by repurposing historical records. Instead, it emits very, very short and surreal stories, or story ideas, or summaries:

> In a marble rainforest there is a glass library.

> An HR manager is found murdered in a hospital. Beside her is a trampoline and a dead succubus. Can you explain what happened?

> A sociologist is murdered. The murderer is revealed to be an emerald.

> An astronaut blinks her eye. In that time, she lives a whole other life as a sentient pun.[60]

MicroSFF offers another example of microstorytelling. At least once a day, O. Westin tweets a complete science fiction or fantasy story, or at least a setting, in a single tweet.

Here are some recent examples:

> The autot.5axi stopped outside his house.
> "No charge," it said.
> "Thanks! Why not?"
> "Streaming video of you and your friend has paid your fee."

> "Begone!" the ghost said, sword aloft.
> "Or what?" he laughed.
> He didn't feel a thing when it struck. Or when he went to work. Or ever again.

> In Mexico City is a rhinoceros who swallowed a star. It wanders shining, searching kin.
> Finding none, the star offers to swallow it in turn.[61]

These are all microepisodes, usually unique in terms of characters and setting. Rarely does one of these microstorytelling feeds follow the same story across tweets.

A third Twitter storytelling category is related to this one and draws on the long history of short, pithy observations. Twitter, indeed, seems well suited to aphorisms. Jenny Holzer tweets her own, a mixture of exhortations and warnings:

> SIN IS A MEANS OF SOCIAL CONTROL

> TECHNOLOGY WILL MAKE OR BREAK US
> YOU ARE RESPONSIBLE FOR CONSTITUTING THE MEANING OF THINGS

THERE'S NOTHING EXCEPT WHAT YOU SENSE
SOMETIMES THINGS SEEM TO HAPPEN OF THEIR OWN ACCORD
PUSH YOURSELF TO THE LIMIT AS OFTEN AS POSSIBLE[62]

Another project republishes aphorisms from the most famous English-language creator of them, Oscar Wilde:

Public opinion exists only where there are no ideas.

Education is an admirable thing. But it is well to remember from time to time that nothing that is worth knowing can be taught.

To love oneself is the beginning of a life-long romance.

Occasionally this feed will break the one-tweet limit and yoke two together:

The only thing that the artist cannot see is the obvious. The only thing that the public can see is the obvious. . . .
    The result is the Criticism of the Journalist.[63]

The extremely short nature of Twitter seems to lend itself well to the aphorism. These may not be stories, like the Feneon republication, but they certainly establish a character over time. They may also take advantage of the very short form to attempt other, preexisting short forms, such as the haiku.[64] Excerpts from longer poems can also benefit from Twitter's focusing of readers' attention down to the single line.[65] To the extent that argument is a form of narrative or partakes of storytelling, tweets can partake.

A fourth mode heightens the human while, perversely, abstracting it out. Twitter's success is due partly to the ease by which creators can build programs using the public Twitter feed, pulling out shared tweets and remixing them in new ways. For example, TwitterVision and TwittEarth extract public tweets, then republish them on a world map using individual geo-locations.[66] A type of storytelling remix comes from Twistori, which searches the public Twitter mass of feeds for key verbs: love, hate, think, believe, feel, wish. It then republishes all current tweets containing those words. The result is a stream of story stuff, emotive shards of daily life.[67] *We Feel Fine* does something similar with "a large number of blogs":

We Feel Fine scans blog posts for occurrences of the phrases "I feel" and "I am feeling". This is an approach that was inspired by techniques used in Listening Post, a wonderful project by Ben Rubin and Mark Hansen.
    Once a sentence containing "I feel" or "I am feeling" is found, the system looks backward to the beginning of the sentence, and forward to the end of the sentence, and then saves the full sentence in a database.

Once saved, the sentence is scanned to see if it includes one of about 5,000 pre-identified "feelings".[68]

The result is a kind of posthuman story material abstraction. The experience of reading these flows may inspire one to remix them once more, or to create something new.

Since the first edition of this book appeared, a fifth mode of Twitter-based storytelling has emerged. A leading use of the platform has been, and remains, sharing and commenting on news. Indeed, many news organizations and journalists use Twitter to expand and engage with their audience and as a tool for gathering and assessing information. Nonjournalists also witness events and tweet about them. Perhaps the most famous early example of this involved passengers and eyewitnesses tweeting the spectacular landing of US Airways Flight 1549 on the Hudson River. These tweets offer a first draft of history, in the famous phrase formerly applied to journalism.

A somewhat more startling example occurred in 2011 when a Pakistani man tweeted the U.S. raid on Osama bin Laden's compound that ended with the Al Qaeda leader's death and the team's exfiltration. Sohaib Athar's Twitter updates describe a helicopter overhead, followed by more sights and sounds as they occurred:

Helicopter hovering above Abbottabad at 1 AM (is a rare event)
Go away helicopter—before I take out my giant swatter . . .
Huge windows shaking bang . . .
Uh oh, there goes the neighborhood.

Eventually he concluded, "Uh oh, now I'm the guy who liveblogged the Osama raid without knowing it." Athar's tweets are a historical document, a story from a time, much like a war diary or a cache of letters.

Subsequently, in a sign that tweeting history has become an accepted narrative form, the CIA staged a Twitter story of that bin Laden raid on its fifth anniversary: " 'live' tweet[ing] the details as if they were happening again . . . Over the course of six hours, the tweets laid out the events that ultimately ended what had been a nearly decade-long search . . ."[69]

Still another Twitter-based storytelling form has surfaced over the past half-decade: Twitter as a site for reading another story, a tweet-based cross between book club and seminar. Users post comments and reactions to other Twitter readers, linked to each other and rendered accessible to others through a shared hashtag. In 2015, one group read Charles Dickens' *Our Mutual Friend*, relying on the hashtag #omftweets.[70]

During the winter of 2016, I instigated a reading of *We Make the Road by Walking*, a kind of mutual interview between legendary educators Myles Horton and Paulo Freire, using the tag #HortonFreire.

These collective tweets take a narrative shape in two ways. To the extent they reflect readers working their way through a text in linear order, their tweets will follow as a kind of chronological commentary. Then, taken as a whole, the aggregated tweets constitute a linear record of the reading discussion, something like informal minutes or an organization's internal history.

A seventh Twitter storytelling mode has also appeared, and it lacks a widely used name. This mode involves a sequence of tweets, either numbered or not, constituting a serial narrative. Some refer to this as a tweetstorm, although that title may be too dramatic for some tales. A story about visiting an extraordinary museum offers a good example of this mode wherein the writer describes his adventure by giving some personal background, setting, institutional context, spatial exploration, and photographs.[71]

Wikis

One of the most powerful and effective digital collaboration tools is also one of the oldest. Wikis first appeared in the mid-1990s, created by Ward Cunningham to help programmers share code more easily.[72] Wikis are Web pages that users can edit directly in the browser, without going through Web markup (HTML) or sending files to Web servers. Their ease of use explains their steady growth, seen most notably in the *Wikipedia* project. Many different wiki platforms and approaches have been developed, with variations ranging from editing formats to authentication. Google now supports a wiki-style service, Google Docs, integrated into that company's broad sweep of services.

How can wikis be used in the service of storytelling? We can now identify several levels of wiki-based storytelling, depending on type collaboration.

First, authors can collaborate on stories through wikis as a form of document hosting. Any number can take turns editing a text, adding, deleting, or modifying words. The results can be read on wiki pages directly or exported to other formats. In this level, wikis serve a very basic function. This function could be served by other technologies as well, such as coauthored blogs or spaces supported by groupware (e.g., SharePoint); wikis are simply more focused on this feature.

Collaborative writing through wikis can be attached to other media in the form of response writing or prompts. A three-dimensional visualization of a new building, for example, could be projected on a screen or viewed in a Web browser; viewers could then write together in wikis about that digital object.

Second, people can take turns advancing a story through a wiki, round-robin style. One editor (which can be a single person or a group clustered around one computer) writes something and then hands off the URL to another creator. The second editor adds to the story, but cannot subtract. Instead, he or she takes the story forward, perhaps in a new direction. This editor then passes the amended tale to a third party, and so on.

There are storytelling benefits to this wiki approach. The challenge of adding your vision to another's can elicit creativity. It can also build relationships, as round-robins provoke challenges, one-upmanship, parody, and creative competition. I can speak to the buzz of excitement such "wiki-robin" exercises elicit. Participants laugh, protest, and plot against each other, pointing to the playful nature of wikis (and a partial explanation of their popularity). Additionally, wiki-robin storytelling helps participants learn one of the most practical lessons of social media: that other people will use your content beyond your ability to control it.

A different spin on the wiki-robin uses the Exquisite Corpse method. This method refers to a French surrealist game where players write sentences or phrases in round-robin style. However, each successive writer cannot see the previous writer's words. A third person receives the two-handed composition and reads it aloud. The results are, predictably, surreal. The game's name comes from one such paired snippet: "The exquisite corpse drinks the new wine." Wikis can be used to play the game or to ramp up its scale to paragraph levels. A group of American liberal arts colleges have used this approach with multimedia, each creator responding to a hidden creation from another campus's student.[73]

A parallel form of wiki storytelling is available through one subtype of wiki software. MediaWiki, the wiki instance used by Wikipedia, and several wiki platforms all provide a supplemental discussion page alongside each wiki content page. For example, a *Wikipedia* entry on French bread describes the composition and history of baguettes, while a discussion page is also accessible from that page via a top-menu tab. Clicking on that tab reveals a kind of shadow page where we read the history of the main page's creation and editing over the years. Furious debates about syntax and French culinary law ricochet down the screen, all built through a wiki format. This feature opens up a space for two different storytelling functions. First, two parallel stories can be told, each responding to the other, perhaps in dialogue. Second, the discussion tab allows a creator and audience to communicate in a separate but closely linked area, similar to a blog post's comment thread. Such a pairing also resembles the well-known DVD combination of movie with director's commentary. The first, dual wiki use, is actually storytelling, while the second is in support of that purpose.[74]

Can wikis be used for storytelling beyond this level? Penguin Publishers launched an experiment in 2007, opening up a wiki platform to allow the entire Web-reading world to write a novel together. The conceit or ambit of *Million Penguins* ran thusly:

> Can a collective create a believable fictional voice? How does a plot find any sort of coherent trajectory when different people have a different idea about how a story should end—or even begin? And, perhaps most importantly, can writers really leave their egos at the door?[75]

A single page was launched, empty of content but for a Bronte line: "There was no possibility of taking a walk that day." Contributions and edits rapidly appeared, then grew. An editorial apparatus emerged in order to keep server load manageable while dealing with spam and other attacks. Several times the wiki "forked," as the project split into two parallel projects, then more. The text grew and won public attention. Eventually the wikis were locked, preventing them from further editing.

Several storytelling themes emerged, which appeal to social media and digital storytelling more generally. First, characters became major figures— not only fictional ones, but editors and contributors whose work won attention both positive and negative, such as Nostrum19, YellowBanana, and Sentinel68. Pabruce, a particularly energetic participant, won an honor of sorts in being rendered within the text as "just another wiki character."

Second, content forking indicates a latent possibility within social media, based on remix culture. The term *fork* is drawn from open-source coding and refers to a single body of text copied into two different locations, then each developed separately. Within the *Million Penguins* wiki, several forks appeared, including nine choose-your-own-adventure stories and an unusual parallel novel caused by a participant's ruthless insistence on writing bananas into every wiki page.

Third, at least some observers consider the *Million Penguins* project to have forked our understanding of wikis. Bruce Mason and Sue Thomas see the experiment as challenging the "garden" model.[76] Popularized by such authors as Stuart Mader, and drawing on ecological metaphors from works like Bonnie Nardi and Vicki O'Dea's, this understanding sees wikis as requiring nurturing in dynamic systems.[77] Wikis require feeding, pruning, fertilizer, time to grow, transplantation, healthy competition, and so on. Good wiki organizers are gardeners, users with a healthy horticultural approach to these organic texts. *Million Penguins* did feature gardeners, and Mason and Thomas were able to divide them into subtypes. For example, they consider light editors to be "garden gnomes," even "Wiki-Gnomes": "Unlike gardeners, WikiGnomes rarely make major changes to the structure of the wiki [and] consequently their actions are often not noticed."[78]

But the garden paradigm was balanced, or even outmatched, by a "carnival" one. Some contributors fought each other for wiki page dominance rather than collaborating to care for the novel. Some of those battles resulted in the numerous forks mentioned earlier, where a unified text broke into a divergent pair, then each branch divided again. Moreover, a surprisingly large number of pages were created outside of a hyperlink network. "Approximately 75% of all these pages do not link to any other pages in the site. In addition, there are 150 content pages [30%] that are not linked to by any other page." At best, Mason and Thomas deem these "walled gardens," while at worst they call them "wastelands, undeveloped, unlinked fragments of content." The characters mentioned earlier seemed to oppose the gardener idea from a different level. They attracted attention as performers, not as cultivators. "Content may have been generated by many people yet, with occasional exceptions, the users rarely actively collaborated."[79]

Taken together, Mason and Thomas see these strands combining in terms of Mikhail Bakhtin's carnival concept. In this model, social rules are not transplanted to new soil, but are upended in creative riot. Voices do not collaborate, but struggle dialogically. "There was no community built around 'A Million Penguins' because it was not a setting in which community could form":

> Like a carnival, the wiki was bounded in space and time and provided an opportunity for "ordinary folk" to hold a barely controllable party. . . . A carnival is a moment of excess featuring multiple competing voices and performances _____The wiki novel was in no way a neat, orderly wiki . . . [and] many of the norms of wiki behavior and aesthetics were turned on their head.[80]

If the full wiki collaboration approach doesn't seize our imagination, perhaps a more structured Web writing approach using the wiki philosophy will. A browser-based social media version of Choose Your Own Adventure launched in 2010. Unknown Tales presents readers with the usual format of short prose sections, followed by limited choices (leave the building or wait for the timer to go off?). What's different about its approach is letting users add more content. Registered users can add new choices to a chapter, add new chapters, or launch entirely new stories. In wiki fashion, we can anneal already existing content—expanding what's already present, filling in gaps, or helping finish stories published in incomplete states.[81]

Another ambitious and perhaps more successful wiki storytelling project is the SCP Foundation site. It purports to be the records of a secret organization devoted to securing, containing, and protecting (hence the initials) mysterious anomalies, such as ghosts, demons, temporal rifts, living mannequins, or stranger things. Individual pages are usually records of single entities, listed by Item #, Object Class, Special Containment Procedures, and a narrative Description. Some have images attached and/or extra documents, such as Experiment Logs.

SCP appears as an impersonal, objective set of roughly 3000 records, powerfully shaped by cryptic authorities. Entries' prose, shaped by multiple hands in wiki fashion, is coldly bureaucratic. Sentences describe emotionally fraught events scientifically, even to the point of depicting horror and death. Some words or phrases are redacted. Many entries describe meticulous and severely enforced security protocols:

> Due to the results of the final exploration (see Document 087-IV), no personnel are permitted access to SCP-087.
> The object cannot move while within a direct line of sight. Line of sight must not be broken at any time with SCP-173. Personnel assigned to enter container are instructed to alert one another before blinking. Object is reported to attack by snapping the neck at the base of the skull, or by strangulation. In the event of an attack, personnel are to observe Class 4 hazardous object containment procedures.

Around this careful presentation, the fourth wall is breached by classic wiki structures and practices. Users can find entries through the random page function, search by keyword, or look through lists. Readers can also follow a given entry's growth over time by looking at the discussion tab, which reveals a critical workshopping process. Authors are nearly invisible from entries, but have their own pages. There is a large discussion forum, a news hub, guides for writers, and many other ways in for readers and writers.

The results are uneven, but the best entries are quite effective. Honed by the SCP community, entries can provide effective chills, humor, and feelings of sheer weirdness. At another level, users have linked stories to each other and have built additional narratives ("Tales"). SCP is ultimately an anthology of strange, short tales. Its collective nature, enormous productivity, and iterated development may mean it is the most advanced achievement of wiki storytelling.[82]

Social Images

The field of visual literacy is based on the power of images to influence viewers. Images communicate information, share moods, persuade audiences—in short, they partake of storytelling capabilities. This is not controversial; it is, in fact, the stuff of clichés: "A picture is worth a thousand words." Images provoke stories:

> Our easiest direction to anyone thinking about making a digital story is to look around his or her house and find images that provoke memories and stories that are meaningful. Then, see if there are other images around the house that are part of that story. And in the end, you will try to connect the memories that link all of these images together.[83]

Images have played a key role in multimedia since the cave paintings at Lascaux, and probably earlier, if we think of early humans scratching images in sand. More recently, digital multimedia has relied heavily on image content, adding static visuals to other media. The Center for Digital Storytelling curriculum, for example, works closely with images, turning them into video content alongside audio tracks. For this section, we will focus on image-centric storytelling; subsequent chapters will deal with images as integrated more evenly into other stories.

The leading social media site for images, Flickr, offers many examples of the different ways social images can tell stories.[84] For example, a Flickr group called "Tell a story in 5 frames (Visual story telling)" aggregates narratives built along strict guidelines.[85] Each story consists solely of five images in a linear sequence. A title is the only bit of text allowed and hence serves as the only explanation of what the images reveal, although creators sometimes sneak in several words within the description field.[86] This framework determines a good range of projects, from the humorous to the historical.

Depicted events tend to follow a progressive sequence. "Gender Miscommunication" (nightingaile, 2006) traces a man and a woman's experience on a date, where she tries and fails to get him to cuddle. We see the non-couple seated, then her looking at a snuggling couple, her wordless request to her seatmate, his response, then their respective reactions.[87] "The Chase" (Benjamin!, 2009) shows a shot of some birds (chaser or chased?), a hunter (ah, the birds are prey), two shots of the chase, then the hunter having returned to his mother.[88]

A very different type of five-image story is "Farm to Food," which remixes a series of Library of Congress archival photographs from the Great Depression.[89] Again, we see only five images representing a linear sequence, accompanied by that explanatory title. Each photo may be unconnected to the others in its source, but the combination is quite coherent. Each image offers various historical markers to help us guess at a time period (roughly the 1930s). We begin with a potato field, then proceed to two boys unloading potatoes into a barrel. Next, we see barrels awaiting transport, presumably filled with produce, followed by a grocery storefront where fruits and vegetables are visibly for sale. The fifth concluding photo shows a family eating a meal; clothing suggests the adults and children may be farmers.

Fiction or nonfiction is blurred by the act of arranging this quintet, and further still by our act of viewing and reading it. We imagine and infer connections between the items, but the set is silent on details. Our social and historical faculties are roused by the content, shaped by the title, and honed by the archival background. At a different level, we recognize the skills required to assemble such a coherent series: visual literacy, to comprehend each image; remixing, to arrange these images; archival competence, at least at the level of knowledgeable user. The result is an accessible, emotionally affective, and thought-provoking story.

What is Web 2.0 about regarding these five-photo tales? Surely, we could experience each story as a static Web page. We could even view these outside of a browser if they were forwarded to us in an e-mail or even printed out on paper. But on Flickr, as with the rest of the social Web, we see two major differences: microcontent and social media. As microcontent, it is simply easier to publish photos through Flickr than by making a Web page (or site): fewer skills to learn, fewer resources to marshal. This doesn't change our experience as consumers, save to remind us that there is more content being published:

> The social aspect of social image sites is more transformative. Each five-image story can be commented upon, and usually is. A casual survey of comment threads reveals something like a Web-based writers' workshop, with feedback about craft and interpretation. The three examples we have examined elicited praise, mostly, along with different emphases (some taking the woman's side in "Gender" and others the man's). A fourth example, the sinister and comic "If You Go Out to the Barn Tonight . . . ," caused one viewer to brood: "I feel like the rabbit so often, the observer, appalled at the downward spiral and the rush of speed as we fling ourselves toward disaster, the driven, not the driver."[90]

Another piece, "A War Story" (Zafiris S., 2010), received this criticism:

Beautiful pictures, buuut:
>   they look like a mosaic of a battle, not a tale of a battle.
>   It doesn't mean that your piece is not good (it's, indeed, superb), but I would like to see an alternative sequence.[91]

Compare those comments with these more concrete critiques of another story:

Now, consider the same photos, in this order: 1, 5, 2, 3, 4.
>   A completely different story. (GustavoG)
>   Or even, 2, 3, 5, 4, 1. (Violet Danger)[92]

As a social media platform, Flickr opens up stories for feedback to the entire world, especially the millions of registered users. It's like a classic workshop, but a global one. The creator therefore benefits from greater exposure and feedback; viewers see not only the stories but also others' responses. Unlike e-mail, unlike Web 1.0, social image storytelling exists in a social framework, which alters both creation and consumption. As with blogging, an individual work may not win comments or annotations nor links from other sites, but that social assumption as a default reshapes our expectations and experience of the work.

An alternative to Flickr emerged in 2010 and has since challenged the older platform for social image dominance. Instagram lets users quickly share square-shaped photos with each other. Users can also lightly edit images, notably through filters, and add some text to each. While not as fully featured as Flickr, Instagram does allow the creation and sharing of stories. For example, the Center for Investigative Reporting has published a series of narratives through Instagram, posting images with text to carry the multimedia story along.[93]

An alternate form of social image sharing shifts the hosting ground to Web 2.0 presentation services. The best known of these (so far) is Slide-Share, which lets users upload, present, and view PowerPoint files in a very YouTube-like fashion: large media file on the left side of the screen, embeds and comments allowed, connections to other social media services, and so on. It is not that removed from social image hosting sites, conceptually, which helps explain how Barbara Ganley was able to use SlideShare to host "Into the Storm."[94] This series of images is actually presentation slides, combinations of visual and textual content. "Into the Storm" describes a physically and emotionally challenging trip where images and captions oscillate between the two realms. Like the Flickr five-image stories, we read/view the work in sequence, then have the possibility of commenting. Like YouTube, we can also embed the code for "Into the Storm" in a blog post or wherever else on the Web one's host allows.

Facebook

"Facebook is the novel we are all writing."[95] Given the history of story-telling where each new medium becomes a vehicle for narrative, we should expect to see narratives on the world's largest social media platform. With more than 1.23 billion registered users as of this writing,[96] the combination of platform size with sheer diversity is certainly appealing. So far, Facebook stories draw on other social media and digital storytelling practices while beginning to surface new forms.

Facebook as character study draws on the personal nature of some blogging practices (see previous discussions). At its simplest level, a single Facebook account houses a process of personal presentation. As with blogging, the boundary between fiction and nonfiction is blurry and often contextual. Blogging provides another comparative aspect in that each Facebook account or site offers many different ways in for reading and writing. While blogs present a current or promoted post, an archive, a search box, comments, and an About page, a Facebook profile offers a wall, a status update, a friends listing, events, discussion, "Information," and even a microlevel option to "like" the whole person or small bits of their content.[97] Multiple media folders or channels are also present, including images, audio, and video. A character emerges from the intersection and accumulation of these, extended over time.

One such single-character Facebook project is the archival biography of a Holocaust victim, Henio Zytomirski, created by the Brama Grodzka Cultural Center.[98] Like the Flickr "Farm to Food" remixed story, this one is based on preexisting archival materials, repurposed and represented. His (or the Center's) site presents us most forcefully with two items: a black-and-white photograph of a young boy and a string of multilingual comments on Henio's Facebook wall. The image suggests an older origin than the Web's, both with its color scheme and clothing style; any historical context or research immediately brings this to bear. The gap between that historicized image and the up-to-date visitor comments presents itself as a space of historical difference, an attempt at memory, or the reach of archives.

Exploring the site yields more components for this character. His Information tab reads simply: "Location: Lublin, Poland/Birthday: March 25,

1933," quietly informing us of the historical nature of this characterization. Under images, we find three categories—two with few photos, but one offering a broader mix, "Henio Zytomirski Family & Others." Here we see a variety of people, along with photos of documents, letters, and tables. One photo of German soldiers marching through a town points quietly, terribly, to Henio's fate, and the end of the story.

Status updates mark positions along the story's arc. Like Twitter tweets, each microcontent item can sketch out thoughts or impressions of surroundings:

> Winter has arrived. Every Jew must wear the Star of David with his last name. A lot has changed. German troops walk the streets. Mama says that I shouldn't be frightened, and always that everything is just fine. Always?
>
> Grandpa says that the war will soon be over. He says that soldiers also have families. How is that possible? They have a family, but they kill families.

These updates initially appear as ventriloquism, content authored by someone writing from an imaginary Henio's position. It is through the direct documentary context and a reader's reflection that the historical situation emerges. These offer another example of the power of social media storytelling to elicit readerly engagement.

While Facebook maintains a strict policy against fictional identities, more projects like Henio's can be found, and more may appear. For example, a marketing project for the film 9 (2009) presented one of that story's characters as a Facebook page. "9 Scientist" portrays itself with and without the fourth wall.[99] An upper level of social engagement reads like marketing language, with contest winners celebrated and timelines announced. Another level is that of fiction, where a character known only as "Scientist" broods on his life, treating Facebook status updates as a kind of public journal:

> I am alone, consumed by the ringing in my ears. It's so quiet out there. My body is cold and fatigued, vision blurry.
>
> I haven't heard from anyone in days. Maybe they had to reroute after the strike? But as a pragmatist, I can only assume the more likely outcome and continue on my path.
>
> I am sorry everyone. This world was a place of tarnished beauty, but a place worth fixing nonetheless. And all I ever wanted to do was give my part in fixing it.

He hints at a new project, which a viewer of the film will recognize as the titular nine cloth robots:

> For whatever it's worth, these are my new gifts to the world . . .
>   It is time.
>   Our world is ending, but life must go on.
>
> —The Scientist[100]

Years after the 9 movie appeared, the Facebook story signaled the arrival of a sequel movie with another post:

The light has faintly flickered on again beneath the ashes and I have begun the long-awaited search for hope . . . I must find 9

His brooding, terrified face greets us from the classic upper-left corner on the Facebook page. Elsewhere on the page are other signs of this two-level approach. An embedded game, "A.I. Challenge," is clickable from the main navigation menu. The Discussion tab leads to open talk of merchandising. But the Photos tab brings up content from the movie without qualification—diagrams of robots, as if we were clicking on an inventor's actual site.

Also linked from this page is another "proscenium," one allied to the Scientist's Facebook page. It is a more traditional movie site, www.9exper iment.com. This site contains a clickable, navigable image, which appears to be a study. Numerous objects cover a desk and table behind which loom bookshelves and walls. Fans of the film will recognize items associated with the Scientist, while others will be confused or unexcited by the textless, caption-free presentation of objects. A 1930s-style radio plays music and speeches from the film, a music box contains a journal, a puzzle game opens in a new window, and so on.

The site presents itself as a mystery, in contrast to the far more accessible Facebook component. In a sense, the Facebook page is a supplemental, explanatory, even documentary resource for 9experiment.com. Taken together, viewers can shift between the two, seeking an appropriate level of story consumption. Put another way, the social media piece extends the reach of a more traditional, 1990s-style Flash-driven Hollywood marketing site.

A Facebook profile can serve as one component of a complex multiplatform story, as Dionaea House used several blogs, bloglike Web pages, and other Web content, as described earlier in this chapter. For example, *My Darklyng* (2010) posts a novel's worth of content into 33 Web pages, allied to one character's Facebook profile.[101]

Natalie Pollock's Facebook site gives no immediate indication of belonging to someone who doesn't exist, but it soon points to fiction. Its leading photo is unremarkable, resembling any current teenager. The status page is rich in content from both Natalie and visitors. Digging into it, one metafictional update points to a *New York Times* article about the project (the metafictional level is unclear from the update text itself).

The information tab first yields basic information about Natalie's birthday, supporting the front-page photo's teen age ("Founded: April 15, 1994 . . . Mission: To survive 10th grade in one piece!;)"). The next lines give the game away by pointing to story content: "Website: http://www.slate.com/mydarklyng/ / http://www.twitter.com/eternalnat." The latter is a Twitter feed that seems to generally echo Natalie's Facebook status, but the first is Slate's directory of *My Darklyng* chapters.

Pollock's Facebook story, the story within *My Darklyng*, advances partly by content contributed by other parties. As Slate's promotional introduction page describes the process: "Over time, mysterious pictures begin to appear on her Facebook page—'70s album covers, sheet music, photos of old Hollywood starlets—all clues to the shattering truth."[102] Natalie responds to each addition to her wall with increasing anxiety:

Anyone have any idea what this weird image means? Somebody put it on my wall. Not that it isn't pretty:)

Okay whats up with THIS weird photo popping up on my wall? Last time I checked I was not religious.

Eeeeeeeeeeeeeew! Way to scare me to death, creep.

My Darklyng adds Twitter content to the Facebook material. Jenna Stecklow is one of Natalie's friends according to the Slate introduction page. Her tweets focus on shopping (as does her avatar image), eating, friends, homework, and other staples of urban teen life.[103] "Fictional best-selling vampire writer Fiona St. Claire" posts about writing vampire fiction, appropriately, and her Twitter profile (photo, bio blurb) reflects this:

Was just approached about launching a fragrance in Sweden. They'd rather smell like blood than meatballs?

Just reread my chapbook of Poe's ghost stories. Edgar Allen Poe: sexiest writer alive. Even if hes dead.

RT @lilithsaintcrow From WIP: "It was the first good sleep I'd had since I'd come up out of the grave, and it wasn't nearly long enough."

That last tweet retweets content from another Twitter account and in so doing displays the fuzzy boundary around social media fiction—for lilithsaintcrow is Lilith Saintcrow, an actual author, with two series of books in print. Saintcrow does not appear in the Slate introductory material. We have no evidence linking her to the *My Darklyng* production process. It's reasonable to assume that this is a case of the story using social media to bolster itself, yielding material (retweet) and perhaps a greater sense of realism.

This strategy is paralleled by a nominal connection to the story's nature as fiction. St. Claire's Twitter profile displays a home page URL, which returns us to the fictional layer, pointing directly and right back to Slate's *My Darklyng* introduction. St. Claire naturally enough has a Facebook account, which links to Pollock's. The small set of personae interlink neatly.[104]

Other media platforms have also hosted parodies of Facebook's story-telling ability through the device of portraying hypothetical accounts. For example, a short Warp Zone video imagines Facebook accounts operated by comic book superheroes.[105]

This discussion of social media storytelling has focused on those plat-forms driven by text and images. Because these are more accessible to most creators than other, more complex media, we should expect to see more in the near future in the way of this creative ferment. For the more daunt-ing media in Web 2.0, we proceed to the next chapter.

CHAPTER FIVE

Social Media Storytelling

Blogs, wikis, social images, and Twitter represent some of the most popular swaths of social media. They are also the least media intensive. Text and images take up less memory, are easier to create and edit, and are faster to upload than other types of digital media. Audio and video are more demanding media in terms of complexity, memory size, and hardware and software requirements. They have also evolved different storytelling practices.

For this stage of our exploration, we should assume a somewhat artificial degree of story isolation. Social media is already a deeply intermixed field where each platform connects with others: podcasts recommended via Twitter, YouTube videos embedded in blogs, everything streaming into an RSS reader. We will return to that kind of recombinatorial mixing in later chapters; here we will focus on audio and video on their own terms in order to identify their unique storytelling properties.

Podcasts

To a new listener, storytelling by podcast appears familiar, which can be either disconcerting or comforting. Listening to a voice or voices tell a story without other media is an ancient human experience, hearkening back to the oral tradition. It is a personally radical one as well, echoing memories of parental or scholastic storytelling. In addition, the podcaster's voice resembles other speaking voices familiar to audiences of different ages and media experience: the radio announcer, the newsreel narrator, the TV anchor, even the ham radio operator. Further, we may also know that telling voice from audiobooks (formerly "books on tape"). We already knew aural performance before downloading the first mp3 into RSS or iTunes. In this way, podcasts are deeply historical, even nostalgic.

The term *podcast* is something of a misnomer. The two sources of this portmanteau term, *iPod* and *broadcast,* do not actually describe reality very closely. iPods are not necessary for consuming what are usually simple audio files capable of being played through any device that can play mp3s: laptop computers, desktops, and phones, along with the multitude of mp3 players not sold by Apple. Similarly, broadcasting is not a good description of a media platform often involving small audiences. Nonetheless, the term has persisted without replacement since its 2004 coinage.[1]

We can define podcasts as digital audio files that are downloadable (not streamed) and organized in a sequence. An individual audio file can be a podcast, but it is presumed to be part of a series. While there are music-only podcasts, our focus here is on those anchored by the human voice, which powers the steady appeal of podcasting. In Gardner Campbell's words:

> There is magic in the human voice, the magic of shared awareness. Consciousness is most persuasively and intimately communicated via voice. The voice is literally inspired language, language full of breath, breath as language. Consider the phrase "thinking aloud." . . . Photographs are undeniably powerful, and perhaps a picture is worth a thousand words, but a few words uttered by a dear voice may be worth the most of all.[2]

Or, as Rudolph Arnheim mused on radio in 1936:

> Radio drama, in spite of the undeniable features of an abstract and unearthly character, is capable of creating an entire world complete in itself out of the sensory materials at its disposal—a world of its very own which does not seem defective or to need the supplement of something external such as the visual.[3]

Podcasts tell stories in a range of ways, best arranged on a continuum ranging from oral storytelling to the classic radio theater model. On the one end is the lone narrator, simply speaking for a length of time until the audio file ends. On the other is a complex production with multiple voices, effects, and music. Across this podcasting range stretch a variety of possibilities and combinations, including diverse senses of professional and amateur, budget, and expected audience.

A New York high school teacher produces good examples of the oral storytelling podcast model. Lars Brownworth published a history of the thousand-year Byzantine empire through a series of biographical accounts, called *12 Byzantine Rulers*.[4] He followed this with a similarly structured medieval history, *Norman Centuries*.[5] The content of each is straightforward. Brownworth begins each podcast with his own voice, without music, sound effects, or anyone else's voice. He quickly introduces the series, then the specific podcast episode; similarly, each episode ends with a pointer to the subsequent one in terms of the overall series—for example: "*12 Byzantine Rulers*, by Lars Brownworth. Episode 14: Alexius. [pause] Welcome back. Last time, we talked about the reign of the emperor Basil II. . . ." In between, Brownworth tells the story of a Byzantine or Norman ruler, speaking carefully yet with evident love for the subject. His voice is assured, as one expects from a subject area expert, but without evident hubris: narratives are qualified by reference to primary and secondary sources, with uncertainties highlighted.

We encounter these nonfiction podcasts through several different venues (compare Chapter 3's "multiple proscenia"). Each one is located on the Web and can be played directly from a browser. They can also be downloaded from those sites and time shifted to another day. The podcasts also appear in the iTunes podcast directory and can be stored there or similarly played or downloaded from that application. Since both programs publish an RSS feed, individual podcasts can also be found and downloaded from an RSS reader. The audio files can be played from any mp3 playing device: phone, laptop, mp3 player, Kindle.

Each venue provides a slightly different experience. Listening to the story of Alexius I (1081–1118) from a laptop allows us to Google terms or maps, whereas listening from an mp3 player while walking down a city street does not allow such contextual research (at least, not easily). If played from the Web page, we see this introductory text, which shapes our understanding of this part of Byzantine history: "When the 24 year old Alexius Comnenus came to the throne, the glories of the Empire seemed long gone. Its 'invincible' army had been smashed at the battle of Manzikert. . . ." The story remains essentially the same, and the audio track unchanged; each proscenium, or venue, allows the context to shift, if only slightly.

In Our Time offers a similar podcast template to Brownworth's, but with two useful differences.[6] It is an interview program featuring interviewer Melvyn Bragg along with interviewees, usually academics expert in each podcast's topic. As with *12 Byzantine Rulers*, each podcast begins with a quickly spoken mention of the overall series plus a pointer to its URL and a copyright policy, followed by an introduction to the topic. Bragg next introduces his interlocutors, and a furious discussion results for the next half hour. No sound effects nor music is played, like Brownworth's podcasts.

Each speaker's voice is distinct, rapidly establishing a sense of different personalities before topical differences manifest themselves. Without visual or textual cues, that aural characterization gives listeners a sense of each expert's presence, even when the speaker is silent for a time. We may anticipate the silent person's thoughts, extrapolating from what we've heard so far, bringing us a little further into the program. Although the program's topic and dramatis personae are established, each podcast has an energetic, improvisational air, as Bragg rapidly reframes questions, academics politely disagree, and discussion perhaps wanders off course from the topic's initial framing.

In Our Time is published in a way similar to *Norman Centuries* and *12 Byzantine Rulers*. Each podcast may be downloaded or played from the browser, time shifted, or listened to in the full range of Web research possibilities.[7] The BBC Radio 4 site is far larger than Brownworth's single-purpose sites, of course, giving the former a cultural cachet and reputational boost the latter does not provide.

These differences and similarities between *In Our Time* and the Byzantine/Norman podcasts are fairly obvious, but are important to identify for storytelling purposes at one end of the oral-radio theater continuum we mentioned earlier. First, they open up a range of production options: one or many speakers, prewritten versus improvisational speech, subject matter expert versus enabling speaker. Second, each lacks a way for listeners to directly and publicly contribute. The social media aspect is therefore to occur elsewhere. Third, both programs demonstrate the power of the human voice to tell stories without any additional sound or other media.

We can contrast these storytelling strategies with those of several other podcasts clustered toward the oral storytelling end of the podcast spectrum. *The Standards of Creation* (2008) is a novel-length story consisting of 24 podcast episodes, or "volumes," each including several chapters. James Campanella wrote and reads the entire work, much as Brownworth did in his historical podcasts. The story's text sounds very much like a print novel's, with chapter subdivisions, character directions, and clear differences between dialogue and description. Unlike Brownworth, Campanella provides distinguishable voices for each character, relying on ethnic and gender differences. There are some musical tracks, most notably a poignant opening instrumental that suffuses each podcast with melancholy. Each volume ends with many open questions—not necessarily cliffhangers, just mysteries that lead us toward the next volume.[8]

We can see many similarities between this story and *Playing for Keeps* (2007–2008), another novel-length podcast story.[9] Mur Lafferty both wrote and recorded this 15-episode series. Each episode ends without closure, encouraging listeners to return for the next. The world's unusual nature (one with two generations of superheroes) also intrigues us, as each podcast episode develops the premise step by step, from history to practical implications. She narrates the podcasts in a calm, bemused tone, capable of shifting mood from outrage or sadness to exhilaration—a good example of the Center for Digital Storytelling/StoryCenter "gift of voice." Lafferty also published the text in multiple formats: as a downloadable pdf, print book, and Kindle e-book.[10]

In contrast, *Radio Open Source* is, like *In Our Time,* an interview podcast featuring a professional host speaking with topical experts.[11] It rarely tells a story as such, since each interview tends toward the discursive. But *Radio Open Source* offers an interesting example of segmented storytelling with podcasts. In August 2006, Christopher Lydon started work on a podcast about literature concerning the September 11, 2001 terrorist attacks. After assembling some materials via a blog post, he recorded a discussion and released the mp3 on September 11 of that year:

> We've all internalized September 11th in our own way—what can writers improve on that we haven't already figured out and experienced for ourselves? What are the challenges for writers in crafting a post 9/11 story with authenticity when this is an event that is so clearly etched in our collective consciousness? Can post 9/11 literature compete with the exemplary journalism, commentary and synthesis that followed the attacks?[12]

Radio Open Source followed this with supplemental podcasts: extra audio that didn't make it into the main podcast along with a blog post rejoinder to another blog's response to the original podcast. A recognizable story doesn't unfold along these segmented lines, although the discussion does flow across them.[13] More to the point, this serial podcast structure, different from the self-contained one seen in the *Standards of Creation* and *Playing for Keeps* examples, can be used by others, both for fiction and nonfiction.

Individual podcast audio files are usually the work of an individual creator, either a team or a single person. An interesting exception is *The Yellow Sheet,* created by some of the LibriVox team in 2007.[14] LibriVox is an international Web-organized audiobook podcast production collaborative. Participants select public domain texts, record readings of them, then publish the results as mp3 files. It is one of the most exciting and useful podcast and audiobook sources (also see Chapter 13).

The Yellow Sheet differs from the normal LibriVox project in that 14 readers-turned-writers collaborated to create their own fiction. A round-robin story, each LibriVox volunteer wrote and then read a chapter, picking up from where their predecessor had left off. Alan Drake began with a somewhat mysterious heroine leaving home for a walk, describing natural and psychological details. Drake's chapter ends on a sudden cliff-hanger, which msirois used in his chapter to drive an action sequence, wherein characters flee from an atomic explosion. In Chapter 3, gesine shifts the story to a hospital and recovery from Chapter 2's trauma, introducing more characters.

Each *Yellow Sheet* chapter is read by a different reader, with only a few repeat voices. This technique gives each item a distinct style, although the format is identical (LibriVox introduction, project name, then chapter in full). No characters are voiced directly, as the entire novel is written in the third person. No sound effects or music are present.

Other podcasts exist on the other end of our productive continuum. *The Memory Palace* is very short, but uses music more often than many others in a few minutes.[15] Each podcast tells the story of a person's life or historical event, building up to an emotional climax: a feeling of triumph, despair, endurance. The writing is careful not to spoil those climaxes, leaving us in suspense not only to the story's outcome but also to its overall feel, even its genre. It establishes main characters, even if the tale turns out not to be biographical in nature: an ex-slave, a Nazi commander, an atomic bomb's babysitter. Instrumental music tracks appear, heighten a mood (tension, levity), then fade, to be succeeded by another playing a similar function. Narrator Nick DiMeo is the sole reader and voice, speaking rapidly but precisely, swinging his tone across emotional registers. DiMeo's voice and the musical track sometimes parallel each other, as a duet.

An even more ambitious use of sound can be heard in the *Radiolab* podcasts.[16] These are also nonfiction, consisting of short stories centered on a scientific topic: phantom limb syndrome, the sentience of animals, the statistical distribution of abilities across populations. Some of these stories are less narrative and more discussion, but so many stories are told throughout *Radiolab*'s ongoing run that they merit our inclusion of it here. The two narrators and hosts, Jad Abumrad and Robert Krulwich, are accomplished vocal performers. They establish themselves as characters in depth, playing off each other, toying with clichés of age difference, but with sometimes unpredictable moments of passion toward topics and events. They also play off of other people's voices during the course of a show, which ends up well populated by characters.

But *Radiolab*'s audio range also includes a complex mix of music and sound effects. In any given podcast, these can include ambient noise, musical excerpts, human voices (for effect, not content), orchestral riffs, and more. They are smartly layered onto the spoken track to establish a location, impress us with an emotional pull, build a sense of mystery, or remind us of an object or living thing (animal or tool noises). These individual tracks are occasionally mixed into others for transitions or synthetic effects. In one episode, Abumrad asks a scientist about how her experiment surprised her. We hear their initial conversation, underscored by sounds from the scientist's office: door closing, chair squeaking, window closing. As the scientist relates her memory, we hear travel noises (plane), environmental sounds from the field (wind, sea, gulls), sudden jazz routines to emphasize shock, and a calming tone to make us pause as the narrator, Abumrad, and we reflect. This podcast creates a rich soundscape in depth, a richly layered story experience.

Individual *Radiolab* podcasts are fairly self-contained. They are capable of varying widely in length, from 10 minutes to an hour, in order to encompass their topic and associated stories. They rarely end in cliff-hangers. As serial art, these audio tracks are only lightly connected by some themes and references (a persistent concern with William James, for instance) and by the two hosts, with whom our familiarity deepens during each podcast. It is not necessary to listen to the podcasts in order as it is for more sequential works, such as *Playing for Keeps*.

After initial years of creation and experimentation, the podcast world experienced a renaissance, starting in 2014 with the launch of *Serial*.[17] This story explored a true crime story, a murder and conviction, by steadily accumulating challenges about the latter. *Serial*, as befits its name, structured itself in linked episodes, with each one acting as a self-contained unit. Each episode built on the next, gradually growing a cumulative arc. That arc completed in a single formal container, as with much classic serial storytelling. While not breaking new formal ground, this podcast won a massive audience—in this case, a season, akin to TV and radio serials.

There is no simple explanation for *Serial*'s success. After all, podcasting had been thrumming along for more than a decade before this one began. It may be that its primary characters—teenagers in high school—connected podcasting with younger millennials and rising Homeland Generation youth for the first time in their lives. Connections to National Public Radio conceivably boosted the listener base. Whatever the causes, *Serial*'s popularity triggered a second wave of digital audio storytelling.

Nonfiction storytelling has played a key role in this new podcasting era. Inspired by *Serial*, a swarm of stories have appeared, some taking the cue of true. *Crimetown* takes a season of episodes to narrate one American city's organized crime experience. *Unresolved* and *Unsolved* are two projects probing criminal histories lacking closure, as their titles suggest. *Criminal* examines a wide range of perpetrators, from murderers to too enthusiastic bibliophiles. *Lore* explores urban legends, disturbing crimes, and creepy stories, narrating their real-world origins as well as their creative sequels.[18]

Other nonfiction topics have burgeoned in the podcast field. *The History of English* narrates this language's development over millennia, each episode (out of an impressive 89, as of this writing) selecting one particular linguistic feature, then tracing it out over time. *Stuff You Missed in History Class* narrates historical events and personages, with subjects sometimes suggested by the audience. Dan Carlin's *Hardcore History* narrates military and political history, such as the course of World War I and the Mongol conquests. *Revolutions* similarly tells several long stories in a string of podcasts, each sequence concerning the unfolding of a historical uprising.[19]

Autobiography appears in many podcasts, such as *Risk!*, as people narrate stories from their lives in ways related to the Center for Digital Storytelling/StoryCenter project, although more narrowly themed toward experiences of personal extremity. *The Story Collider* focuses on autobiographies by scientists and other people working closely with scientific topics, each podcast episode a single story spoken aloud and recorded. *Rumble Strip* is closely related to these, offering biographical stories of interesting people in Vermont.[20]

Some podcasts blend fact and fiction. For example, *Flash Forward* is a futurist program. Each installment begins with a short story about that episode's theme, turning to fiction to dramatize technological and social issues. We might listen to a future museum docent explaining the automation of labor in the distant past of the mid-21st century.[21]

Fiction in general has seen a boom in the podcast. *Welcome to Nightvale* is the signal success story of the post-*Serial* new wave. It purports to be a community radio program based in a small town on the edge of an American city, where things are surreal, if not actively strange. Over dozens of episodes, *Nightvale* has realized this fictional world, complete with an ominous dog park, perpetually threatened interns, dimensional portals, the ubiquitous town secret police, and a multiheaded dragon running for mayor against similarly fantastic characters. Each episode takes us through a short story, a crisis in the strange town proceeding from inception to some kind of resolution. The podcast has, like *Serial*, become enormously popular and crossed into multiple proscenia, spawning fan art, successor podcasts, a novel, and a string of live performances.[22]

Indeed, fantastic or genre fiction is having a podcast heyday as of this writing. A series of podcasts perform stories from fantasy, horror, science fiction, and mystery fields such as: Clarkesworld, Escape Pod, Podcastle, Pseudopod, the Drabblecast, Tales to Terrify, Crime City Central, and

Starship Sofa, the last three gathered into an omnibus media platform, the District of Wonders. Others perform original fiction as staged readings, such as the science fiction comedy *Wolf 359*.[23]

TANIS and *The Black Tapes*, sister and interrelated podcasts, head further into the territory where digital audio meets radio theater. They offer original stories, the former about a quest for a mysterious myth, the latter a paranormal investigation led by a public radio host and a very skeptical experimenter. Each episode carries the story arc along, returning to recurring characters, and often ending on mysterious notes or open cliff-hangers. *TANIS* and *The Black Tapes* have increasingly drawn on radio theater's traditions and tricks, from atmospheric and incidental music to sound effects and getting referential about the medium. A running gag in both programs is that nobody besides a handful of main characters knows what a podcast actually is. The physical properties of digital audio appear frequently and openly, as characters discuss mp3 files, digital recorders, bandwidth problems, and the ethics of recording people in challenging situations.[24]

Other dramatic podcasts carry on this rich production tradition. *LifeAfter* and *The Message*, produced by the same team, present densely layered sound files, with multiple tracks working simultaneously. The results are very powerful soundscapes and audio textures. The plot of *Archive 81* centers on a problematic audio recordings archive and not only faithfully renders the recordings in their complexity, but layers on top of them modern technical challenges. That podcast team went on to produce *The Deep Vault*, a postapocalyptic action thriller drenched in more sound effects than any other podcast I've encountered, representing a claustrophobic and suspenseful setting very well.[25]

One of the most powerful podcast fictions is *Limetown*. It begins as a self-described podcast/radio program investigating a historical (if fictional) incident. As the reporter and narrator probes the past, her personal connections to the event emerge and start to struggle for control of the narrative. Mysteries around the incident ramify, especially as our protagonist winkles out semireliable sources. *Limetown* takes time with each episode, letting excellent voice actors unfold their characters and the story's overarching mystery before tugging the narrative in surprising directions. By the end of season 1, the plot has burst its formal bounds, threatening the existence of an NPR analog.[26]

Clearly, the second wave of podcasts represents a powerful dimension for digital storytelling. It is useful to know that while some are professionally produced, many are made by a handful of amateurs on do-it-yourself budgets. Podcast narratives are an important form for storytellers to consider.

Web Video

If podcasting connects deeply with audiences, establishing a rich relationship through the medium of time-shifted sound, Web video has reached one of the largest audiences in human history. According to YouTube:

> YouTube has over a billion users—almost one-third of all people on the Internet—and every day people watch hundreds of millions of hours on YouTube and generate billions of views.
>
> YouTube overall, and even YouTube on mobile alone, reaches more 18–34 and 18–49-year-olds than any cable network in the U.S.[27]

In five years, YouTube and, to a lesser degree, other Web video services have amassed an astonishingly diverse realm of content. The storytelling practices in play there are similarly diverse, ranging from oral storytelling delivered via Webcam, to rich multimedia presentations, political appeals, raucous stunts, gameplay captures, to archival republications.

While some proportion of those stories simply represent professional content from elsewhere—TV shows, movie clips, music videos—other material is created for Web video by an array of creators ranging from amateurs to professionals.[28] The entire swarm of YouTube's channels and comments, clip arrangements, and tag clusters is driven by a large audience—but that word is no longer correct. "Audience" no longer describes this complex mix of many watchers, a large number of arrangers and commentators, uploaders and creators, with amateur and professional roles cutting across all strata. "The People Formerly Known as the Audience" is Clay Shirky's suggested replacement term.[29]

Given the scope of Web video, what we can best accomplish in this section is to identify several types of storytelling that both embody and extend the kind of narrative principles we've seen at play in other social media so far. We will focus on social, serial storytelling projects and minimize single-shot, unconnected work like the brilliant Fewdio horror channel.[30]

One of the most innovative uses of Web video for storytelling was the lonelygirl15 project (2006–2008).[31] This was, at root, a YouTube serial. Its primary content was roughly 153 short video clips, released at a steady pace, and lasting from under one minute to as much as four. These clips began by describing a seemingly ordinary high school girl's daily life, initially through basic Webcam footage. Bree discoursed on classes at her new high school, excitement over developments in her religious life, relationships with her parents, and her relationship with a friend, Daniel, who was *not* a boyfriend (although perhaps . . .). These clips were not presented as fiction, but as actual Webcam footage from a typical teenager.

As the episodes proceeded, however, things rapidly became darker and more complex. Her family's church was revealed to be some kind of sacrificial cult. Daniel became a romantic interest, in part because of his desire to save Bree. As the story deepened, the video content grew more formally complex. Each clip showed increasing editing skill, multiple cameras, more complex soundtracks. Ultimately the latter undid the story's premise, as the video quality implied a production team beyond just Bree (or Daniel, who contributed content after Bree was kidnapped).

While the premise held, lonelygirl15 won a significant fan base. Fans wrote comments on each video clip's YouTube page, offering advice and cautions to Bree. Fans also made their own videos, usually Webcam footage, like Bree's earliest clips along similar lines. This fan-made content formed a kind of aura or penumbra around the core footage, not only signifying a high level of popularity but also adding a documentary feel to the would-be realistic plot. Viewers experienced a dual level of content: Bree-and-friends-made and fan-built.

Eventually the plot's basis was uncovered, thanks to the efforts of dedicated fans, including bloggers and a clever MySpace Java code hack.[32] Bree was not a teenager, but an older actress, and her entire life was a fiction. A production team created the entire story. Its success with viewers led to spinoffs, including a second story. But let us emphasize two features of this initial project. First, the viewer and fan response was distributed. Comments appeared attached to each lonelygirl15 post, but also on blogs. Fan videos appeared elsewhere in the vast YouTube realm. The story itself was anchored in that series of video clips, but its boundaries blurred across the Internet, thanks to fans' use of social media. Once again, we find that the edges of new digital stories are often unclear.

A second key feature of Bree's tale is that it was a hoax. The video clips combined to purport a certain reality. The pretense was thin, collapsing under the weight of its verisimilitude; indeed, one lesson for creating such a narrative is to keep a lid on rising technical skills. Yet it held long enough to win an audience. Arguably, pricking the illusion's balloon represents another type of audience engagement, based on viewers willing to pay close attention and analyze the stories. That kind of attention is encouraged in other areas, including alternate reality games (see Chapter 10) and, arguably, both media and information literacy. The ways people trust the Web too much and also our long-standing wariness of digital technology both come into play. Credulity and skepticism: two types of audience postures that a competent hoax evokes.

Lonelygirl15 stands as an odd kind of representative Web video story. Its generic nature, being a faux realistic tale, is fairly unusual. Its large audience and reputation are also extraordinary. But we can learn and borrow from it nonetheless. First, its intensive emotional appeal is worth studying. Note how much time Bree's face is on screen, reflecting her moods as they slide from excitement to trepidation. Her voice is heard for longer still, the words carrying as much information as the tones in which they are spoken, another good example of the CDS gift of voice. As creators, we don't have to go as far as pretending to be someone else to realize how important it is to shade our inflections with emotions and subtext.

That emotional appeal helps explain the story's social media penumbra. The contributions of others can add to the content a storyteller provides, much as the experience of an oral storyteller is enhanced by audience reactions (laughter, boos, cross talk, rapt silence). Social media content is a form of audience feedback, which can be analyzed and responded to digitally, much as any performer in a more traditional venue listens and watches the audience.

Watching lonelygirl15 over time reveals a solid use of the serial form. Some videos end with cliff-hangers, like Bree's disappearance, which classically win back return audiences. Others end more obscurely, which is perhaps a more effective strategy in the social media age, with final scenes simply hard to grasp, sounds muffled, resolution uncertain. This strategy mobilizes the skeptical mind, the critical approach, the investigator rather than the consumer, especially if such formal muddiness appears deliberate or genuine, not accidental. A related strategy applies to the beginning of episodes, which lack any formal framing. Instead, we plunge right into Bree's or Daniel's narration. The overall effect is a kind of *in media res*, placing the viewers inside the story without gently leading them through an intermediary stage.

A different sort of audience placement appears in the less well-known Web video story *Connect with I*.[33] This story consists of a series of short video clips, each showing a scene from the life of a harassed narrator. Not only is he suffering from depression, but he is also being stalked by some surveilling force, perhaps the viewer or an agency unwittingly representing us. This intruder cheerfully asks the hero about his activities, comments on his replies in a somewhat friendly fashion, and offers suggestions. The stalker/surveillant uses multiple devices to accomplish this, including several cameras located throughout the hero's apartment and mobile phones slid under the front door. *Connect with I* follows the narrator's gradual descent into torpor, unhelped by roommates and friends.

It's another serial story, as with lonelygirl15, dividing up content into chunks, but without much introductory or concluding material in any of them. Instead, the viewer must turn to the framing Web site or Google for more information. Like a sitcom, *Connect with I*'s situation is quickly grasped by a returning viewer, due to its simplicity. Unlike all sitcoms and lonely-girl15, *Connect* is something of a second-person narrative. While the main character occupies the center of visual and narrative space, he focuses largely on us, or the surveilling power acting for us. He addresses this "us," responds to our activities, and hails us grumpily. "We" are part of the story. Therefore, as with lonelygirl15, this project emphasized the social media aspects surrounding the video clips. Comments were incorporated into the story with such importance that the *Connect* intellectual property holders claimed them as creative properties.[34] This combination of serial video stories, elicited fan content, occasional physical content, unsettled reality status, and immersion in daily life has no widely used label, but it had certainly emerged as a uniquely Web video-based form of digital storytelling.

The most effective recent example (and evidence of a persistent trend) is perhaps *Marble Hornets* (2009–2010).[35] As with lonelygirl15, *Marble Hornets* began with a single video clip and a premise for extending it. The "Introduction" clip simply narrates a backstory: the clip maker is exploring a video archive left behind by a friend, Alex Kralie, who has disappeared. Alex was making his first film, the eponymous *Marble Hornets,* but abandoned work on it. His friend, Jay, plans to share content of interest through a YouTube channel.

What transpires is an exercise in quiet horror, much in the brooding, suggestive tradition of Algernon Blackwood, M. R. James, or preslasher pregore horror films. Alex was apparently distracted from his film by encounters with a mysterious well-dressed man. We see very little of this threatening figure on screen; instead most of the videos are taken up with the quiet construction of tension and unease. What glimpses we see are unsettling, very fast, and suggestive of monstrous distortions. Alex is progressively unhinged by the ominous "slender man," his work and personal life falling apart in clip after clip.

As Jay works his way through Alex's materials, something related to Slenderman begins to impinge on his life. The YouTube channel videos now alternate between Jay and Alex, comparing and connecting disturbances. Jay records a visit to a strangely abandoned house, where he is attacked by a masked figure. He sleepwalks and cannot account for missing hours. The masked figure appears in his room, addressing the camera.

While Jay's life crumbles, another YouTube channel, "totheark," appears, which seems directed at him.[36] Totheark's contents are as abstract as Jay's and Alex's are straightforward, mixes of distorted sound, hand-drawn signs, and cryptic visuals. Whereas Jay's clips are labeled in a clear-cut sequence, totheark's have resonant, sometimes sinister titles: Attention,

Return, Signal, Exit, Impurity, Deluge, Regards. Some of his/their clips use a YouTube uploading setting to connect them with the *Marble Hornets* videos, as: "This video is a response to Entry #9." Perhaps totheark is the masked figure or is allied with him? *Marble Hornets* concludes with Alex's return, and perhaps Slenderman's last move.

While the first YouTube channel was the primary channel for *Marble Hornets* content, story creators supplemented those videos with a Twitter feed. That story content openly addressed the YouTube channel, referring to uploads and technical issues. It also added new content, describing Jay's fears and plans:

> Considering boarding up my windows. Still feeling incredibly unsafe here.
>   Looking through some surveillance footage. Not sure what I'll find. I feel like I just have know one more time what's been going on.
>   Typo earlier. Still looking through the footage.
>   Entry #24: http://www.youtube.com/watch?v=B_rA7gQl95w
>   Feeling like I'm being watched constantly
>   Checked the latest surveillance footage again last night. Nothing unusual. Maybe Entry #24 was a camera glitch?
>   I did not post Entry ######. http://www.youtube.com/watch?v=N7QX QZ jp5XM.[37]

As with our previous examples, *Marble Hornets* elicited a significant social media response. Fans made video responses, from documentation of reactions to clip edits to parodies.[38] One group set up a wiki to aggregate information about the story, including introductions, a timeline, and a list of items for wiki editors to investigate.[39] The *TVTropes* wiki site developed a different resource for the story, extensively linking to previous *TVTropes* pages and themes, incorporating *Marble Hornets* in its analysis.[40] A Facebook fan site appeared, aggregating discussion and resources.[41] The Unfiction forums, home of alternate reality game discussion (see Chapter 10), hosted a series of topical investigations.[42] Each of these serves a different function or style of audience response: general introduction, cultural criticism, investigate gameplay. Fan art appeared.[43] One fan even mocked up a *Marble Hornets* location in 3-D, using the Half-Life game engine, in order to better understand events there; naturally, he turned the results into a YouTube video.[44] A first-time viewer and reader of *Marble Hornets* would find the YouTube and Twitter channels embedded in an aura of social participation.

Additionally, *Marble Hornets* may represent a second-order social media story. The source of the Slenderman is a social media discussion thread.

The character first appears on Something Awful, within a thread where participants sought to create urban legends and spooky stories, emphasizing convincing documentary evidence.[45] While lonelygirl15 and *Connect with I* produced content, then elicited social media participation, *Marble Hornets* began with some preexisting social media content, worked it into a new story, then was followed by social media responses. In other words, this storytelling approach presupposes social media, draws from it, and contributes to that world. *Marble Hornets* is the next stage, or a second order, of social media storytelling and YouTube video narrative in particular.

VoiceThread

One Web service combines nearly all of this chapter's media into one interface, and does so with an astonishing ease of use. It has produced far less content than podcasts or Web video, yet remains a vital platform for story exploration. VoiceThread is a unique Web service, seemingly based on multimedia annotation of media documents.[46] Users upload images, text, or video clips, which other users can then comment on with text, audio, or video. Built in Flash, VoiceThread presents all of these functions with simplicity and playfulness.

Where VoiceThread changes from an annotation focus is in its ability to combine media in a sequence. One user could, for example, upload a series of photos and then allow the world to comment on each. Like Flickr, this becomes an example of image-based social media. Unlike Flickr, however, users can comment through media other than text. And the original uploader can also add media other than images, leading to results more like multimedia dialogues or assembled sequences thereof. Like Seesmic or a YouTube "in response to" sequence, the results can be a video-based dialogue; once again, the multiplicity of media and the option to create a group of these makes for a different experience.

For the creator, VoiceThread offers another advantage. Since it identifies with no single medium, it opens up a free space to explore. A storyteller with plot in mind but uncertain of its eventual housing can quickly try out different forms in VoiceThread: audio, images, video. After exploring in VoiceThread, a creator may well decide that one medium is the right platform for the story and then shift to a more powerful, more focused tool along those lines (see Chapters 12 and 13 for some options). In this way, VoiceThread is a kind of practice floor or multimedia storytelling dojo, a place to nudge a story into media and see where it wants to go.

CHAPTER SIX

Gaming: Storytelling on a Small Scale

What role do computer games play in present-day digital storytelling? As with the broader question of how we use digital platforms to tell stories, this question can surprise some audiences. Either games are considered to be *games*—how does chess reveal a narrative?—or else video games are seen as too primitive, perhaps too childish, to be capable of creating the space required for a convincing tale. Looking for storytelling in gaming makes too much of too little, an exercise in apophenia. Alternatively, story simply isn't that important to the real functions of games. John Carmack, creator of *Doom*, put it this way: "Story in a game is like a story in a porn movie. It's expected to be there, but it's not that important."[1]

This is the moment in any modern gaming discussion where one can expect a narratology-versus-ludology gesture. Perhaps the reader expects a rehearsal of that old divide between those who see games primarily as mechanisms for narrative delivery and those emphasizing gaining mechanical operations beyond stories. Such a reiteration is not especially necessary for our purposes.[2] Our focus is storytelling, so the reader should expect discussion to focus on the various degrees to which different games and platforms support stories. The point here is not to settle the ontological status of games, but to focus on their storytelling functions—not to decide what proportion of gaming is storytelling, but to identify how games tell stories. If we can respond to Carmack, this chapter is about romance, not pornography.

At the same time, the purpose of this chapter is to identify how gaming expands the realm of digital storytelling, which requires attention to its differences from social media, Center for Digital Storytelling-style video, and the other forms we've covered so far. This is why the present chapter's opening passage begins with attention to a game's characters as well as to the vibration of the Xbox controller. The approach is not a balanced synthesis, since storytelling is the point, but it is materially grounded in game play.

How, then, do computer games tell stories, and what does this process mean for digital storytelling? We will proceed by exploring a series of practices, drawing on several recently published and widely played games. Each of these practices can be found throughout other digital media as of this writing, which should be considered as proof of applicability as well as a challenge to remember gaming's specific deployments.

In this chapter, we focus on "small" games. This rather arbitrary definition is a catchall aimed to capture scale and storytelling: games smaller than massively multiplayer online (MMO) games, games that don't require a computer's full processing power, and games that are capable of being created by a small team or individual. These include casual games, interactive fiction, and browser-based games. All of these can be used for storytelling; many draw on storytelling elements.

By selecting these types of games, we may also be violating the expectation of many game discussions, which use large-scale games as exemplars: *World of Warcraft*, *Grand Theft Auto*, *Eve Online*. Those large-scale games do win large amounts of attention through their mix of sales, craft, and fan bases. But their players are sometimes dwarfed by the numbers of those playing casual games. As the Pew Internet and American Life Project showed recently, MMOs and major console games are played less often by teens than are puzzle games, racing games, and other lighter fare.[3] Perhaps the field of Tetris is where gaming discussions should now begin rather than on the streets of Liberty City.[4]

Elements of Story

One key aspect of game-based storytelling is the immersion of a player in the story's environment. This immersion is especially true for large-scale games, as we see in the next chapter, but it plays a vital role in smaller ones as well. In 1997, Janet Murray argued for the importance of immersion when she described computer-mediated communication as inviting users to cross a boundary into a different realm. Games, virtual worlds, and even discussion boards appear to us first as transition sites, supporters of liminal states, an avenue of enchantment.[5] Once we agree to enter the airlock provided (to add another metaphor), an environment creates a sense of immersion through specific strategies: "Immersive stories invite our participation by offering us many things to keep track of and by rewarding our attention with a consistency of imagination."[6] For instance, if we manipulate objects, they react reasonably, and the world changes in accordance with our actions: immersive world as feedback loop. Digital platforms are akin to participatory theater, with the imaginative engagement the stage creates. Compare this with Rudolf Arnheim's 1935 meditation on radio, which we first noted in the previous chapter:

> Radio drama, in spite of the undeniable features of an abstract and unearthly character, is capable of creating an entire world complete in itself out of the sensory materials at its disposal—a world of its very own which does not seem defective or to need the supplement of something external such as the visual.[7]

Don Carson echoed this approach in 2000 when he argued for the importance of creating a sense of immersive story for theme park rides. That immersion is, first, conceptual: "I am talking about an all encompassing notion, a 'big picture' idea of the world that is being created." Second, it must be consistent, as per Murray's observations:

> A set of rules that will guide, the design and the project team to a common goal If you break any of the rules [of a pirate theme], more often than not your team will argue, "we can't put that in there, that's not at all 'piratey'!" . . . Once you have created this story, or the rules by which your imagined universe exists, you do not break them![8]

The act of play is then a form of moving through space in such an environment. Murray emphasizes navigation in new media; Harry Brown sees this as central to understanding stories in games: "Whether we adopt choreography, architecture, or cartography as a model, the ascendance of videogames as a literary form, it seems, will rely on the understanding of gameplay as a form of navigation. . . . Our aesthetic response to games like *Oblivion* comes from our sense of presence in the virtual world."[9]

A consistent world combined with a consistent set of rules doesn't mean an integrated immersion. Jesper Juul argues for the opposite, seeing that ultimately the user's experience of the game world becomes felt as imperfect, which causes the player to fall back on the operations of game rules to explain the world. "If the effort required to fill in a blank in the game world becomes too big, we have to resort to a rule-oriented explanation, . . . an *incoherent world,* meaning that there are many events in the fictional world that we cannot explain without discussing the game rules."[10] Seen from an after-play vantage point, this dual track remains: "For a given game, is it possible to describe *what really happened* in the game without resorting to describing the rules, propos, or the real-world situation where the game was played?" A dual consciousness of this "incoherent world" results: "By *game conventions,* the player is aware that it is optional to imagine the fictional world of the game. . . . We can agree to believe in the fiction, and we can agree not to."[11]

Further, immersion is sensual and multimedia in nature. As Carson wrote of his pirate theme: "Every texture you use, every sound you play, every turn in the road should reinforce the concept of 'pirates!' "[12]

One can readily think of examples by which large-scale media projects, such as console games or Hollywood movies, enact these rules. Small-scale games follow these as well—simply with lower media and computational quantities. *Plants vs Zombies* (2009), for instance, carefully establishes a suburban yard as its physical environment. Although the visual textures are not lushly mapped, they are cartoonishly convincing. In each level, the game's point of view pans horizontally along the lawn, establishing its extent for that scene's action. Sod rolls forth, deepening our awareness of the lawn's presence. Ominous theme music plays. When zombies attack, their various moans and shambling footsteps build and echo. Your defensive plants emit equally present sounds (popping, squishing, crunching). Their physical presence persists: once planted, they remain and fulfill their various functions. This sense of spatial immersion may be one of the most powerful contributions gaming offers to digital storytelling.[13]

Immersion must also persist over time, iteratively. A mastered and unchanging game becomes a mere exercise, and an explored space bears little further exploration. Characters that do not change are often derided as flat and undeveloped; the desire for character development assumes an iterative arc. Therefore, successful immersion must progress over time, repeatedly establishing Murray's sense of enchantment and engagement.

Game designers painstakingly calibrate ever-increasing play challenges with an eye toward presenting an attractive succession of ratcheted up challenges. In doing so, creators can recall Carson's admonition to maintain an "all encompassing notion." In our *Plants vs Zombies* example, the game continually fleshes out the gardening defensive metaphor. After we begin by being able to plant peashooters and capture sunlight for growing reinforcements, we're next allowed to plan a different kind of foliage, which arrives in a seed packet. After that, we are rewarded with explosive fruit, then a defensive nut, a shovel, and so on. At the same time that these defensives build up, the number of zombies increases, consonant with that horror subgenre's rules. Their variety ramps up as well, with some sporting new clothes, accessories, weapons, or headgear (beware the football helmet!). The humor of these enemies and weapons, the goofy puns (a "cherry bomb" is literally cherries, a "wall-nut" is a temporary wall) are part of the world-building, since our ability to groan at the jokes requires our recognition of the game's communicative abilities. This humor and the working out of the game's metaphor persist through all levels of *Plants vs Zombies*, keeping alive a small but engaging sense of environment.

Sound is a critical element in enabling casual games to invite us into their worlds. Musical scores can be symphonic in large-scale games, but even a simple MIDI track lets us listen to a game's sense of world. Such thematic or ambient sound can signal genre or mood on its own or by referencing other media (martial music does both). Sound effects elicit a sense of the game's object world by adding a signifying layer to actions. These effects are important both for establishing the world's material nature as well as for grounding a user's actions in immediate feedback—a ball whizzes as it comes toward the player's paddle, then makes a satisfying *thwack!* when the paddle hits it. The voices of characters represent still another level of sound generating game immersion; we have already introduced this theme in Chapter 2, under the header of the "gift of voice." Here we should note the object nature of sound for characters in establishing their physical presence. Like physical objects or tangible events, characters' aural trace deepens the most casual world.

A game's text is also crucial in shaping the user's experience of play and story. Text tags are sometimes the only names attached to objects and events, especially in a small or crowded screen common to casual games and mobile devices. As we saw with the Flickr stories in Chapter 4, a title can decisively determine the shape of nontext stories. Juul notes, "The title of the game sometimes creates expectation about the fictional world."[14] Katie Salen and Eric Zimmerman point out that text-based "narrative descriptors" not only "fram[e] the elements inside and outside of a game as objects that communicate a story" but also can carry a large amount of story content in a small space.[15]

On a noninteractive level, many games pause play to offer "cut scenes." These short video clips can be quite rich in large-scale games, enough so to be termed *cinematics* (see Chapter 7). They still play an important role in casual games, even with far smaller resources involved. Consider the opening animations, even the ones with "skip intro" button options. They quickly establish the game's grounds: story details, theme, tone, setting, characters. These are Twitter-like pieces of narrative brevity. At their most effective, they help "create the feeling that the player is participating instead of merely interacting."[16]

In the game itself, cut scenes can serve as connective tissue between levels. They bridge the story, such as by explaining the passage of time, changes of setting, or the introduction of new characters and important objects. Cut scenes also reward successful play, offering small celebrations for user achievements. They can be brisk, quick, formal acknowledgments of the completion of a game segment. Alternatively, cut scene rewards can be energetic, lyrical, and "excessive" in Juul's account. This can "seemingly enhanc[e] the experience of feeling competent, or clever." This excess or "juiciness" constitutes an emotional appeal to the user as a second-person character, almost breaking the fourth wall by "address[ing] the player in player space."[17]

The emotional impact of casual games' minicinematics is partially driven by the psychology of the immediately preceding gameplay, which invests players more deeply in the video that follows. "A cut-scene in a game, viewed by a player who has just spent two hours of active involvement with the world and characters, will be more emotively powerful than an identical scene viewed as part of two hours of passively watched film."[18] Finally, a cut scene can conclude a small game, wrapping up the story, closing out events.

It is useful here to reference Salen and Zimmerman's dual-track model of game-based storytelling. They acknowledge the value of cut scenes, placing them in parallel with emergent gameplay. On the one hand, games present story content in predetermined, almost static ways, including cut scenes: "Players can experience a game narrative as a crafted story interactively told." On the other, players win different story experiences from each game, based on the operations of play: "Players can engage with narrative as an emergent experience that happens while the game is played."[19] In *Plants vs Zombies*, the enemy always charges from right to left during the backyard pool level, but my decision to focus defenses on the upper tier one time led to a different story than the time I allocated resources across all three tiers, in depth.

In James Paul Gee's powerful account of learning to play *Rise of Nations*, that game's tutorial contains the same basic narrative arc for every player, but each player's experience of learning the moderately complex interface differs with each attempt. As a pedagogical tool, Gee finds these differences allow a great deal of player experimentation along with a healthy balance between comfort and stretching beyond the comfort zone. The player, in other words, can afford to fail, then try again, mixing up a different approach while being able to count on the game world's consistency.[20] The balance of these two tracks, crafted and emergent, changes from game to game, but the concept remains broadly applicable.

All of these components—cut scenes, sound, immersion (spatial and progressive)—will not necessarily constitute a story, although they certainly can enhance one. These elements can contribute to realizing our Chapter 1 definition of story, including engaging an audience emotionally, progressing in time, and building a sense of meaning for certain audiences. Yet small games also need characters to achieve a story, to embody a plot and deeper emotional charge. We can become emotionally invested in play by frustration and excitement, without the game constituting a story. It is quite easy to generate examples of characterless, storyless small games, such as Solitaire or Minesweeper.

Indeed, in at least one case, a story-based game uses another game's lack of story to set up a plot. *Chain Factor* is a Tetris-like game where the player arranges numerically assigned spheres, trying to clear a small board. While it appears to be a stand-alone (and very addictive) diversion, *Chain Factor* is actually the front end to an alternate reality game associated with the TV show *Numb3rs*, a game telling the story of a plot to use game players to crash the global economy. Understanding that story imbues the innocent-seeming *Chain Factor* game with ironic ominous overtones. For example, the innocuous About page is, upon review, fairly sinister:

> Why Chain Factor?
> The games industry is poised on the brink of a profound transformation. Games have the potential to be the most powerful art form ever invented, an unparalleled medium for the exploration of dynamic interactive systems and the expression of complex emotional, social, and political ideas.[21]

The fact that *Chain Factor* conceals additional content, revealing it only through sustained play, points to another storytelling element within small or casual games. The subgenre of point-and-click adventure games is predicated on that dynamic of hiding content within a visual display. Gameplay involves visually scanning a screen to discern clickable items. Discoveries then enter the play's inventory or alter the screen's contents in some way. A sword barely noticeable within a rock disappears into your inventory; pulling a candle down opens a hidden door. It is a truism that stories require a setting; point-and-click games sink more deeply into that sense of locale.

Hunting a screen to find obscure pixels is not inherently storytelling, obviously. It can be less Middle Earth and more Whac-A-Mole. A quick press of the tab key can sometimes reveal all clickable items, sapping even that bit of suspense. Yet we can find two storytelling elements in play when a game forces players to carefully scan and interact with a space.

First, the game establishes some sense of setting. The more deeply a player plumbs a static or limited space and the more time invested in checking individual pixels, the greater the presence that space can evoke. Escape-the-room games are a good example. This subgenre traps a player in a small space containing linked puzzles; solving those puzzles ultimately yields an exit. Escape-the-rooms are variously decorated, but they all share a common sense of situating the player.

Second, drawing a player into "spot the hidden object" behavior can be an exercise in building mystery. After all, what is desired is concealed, and the player expects some reward for successfully revealing it. As we saw back in Chapter 1, creating a sense of mystery that draws an audience into trying to solve it is a classic way of increasing audience engagement. It is not coincidental that some casual games are described as addictive, given the allure of mystery.

In traditional storytelling terms, casual games sometimes feature characters of a sort. One-dimensional third-person people and anthropomorphic creatures (animals, robots, aliens) sometimes appear as targets, enemies, or bystanders. Their visual and aural features can elicit our engagement: "The smallest dash of empathy, like fairy dust, transforms bitmaps into characters."[22] We also know these microcharacters by their effects on each other, on the environment, and upon our plans: "Spiders *eat* mushrooms, for example, whereas scorpions *poison* them. When shot, the deadly centipede's segments *transform* into mushrooms, an evolutionary action that changes the state of the creature from insect to landscape."[23] Recall Charles Baxter's emphasis on desire: "Without a mobilized desire or fear, characters in a story—or life—won't be willing to do much of anything in the service of their great longings."[24] Even tiny characters and their small, radical longings can foment the stuff of stories.

Appearance and action combine in these small entities to elicit our partial storytelling response of character recognition. For example, in our *Plants vs Zombies* example, one Crazy Dave appears from time to time, offering mumbled assistance rendered legible by comic-style word balloons. Newspaper Zombie is an old man who initially strolls slowly through the scrum, reading his newspaper like he presumably did when alive. When your plants destroy his reading materials, Newspaper goes berserk (eyes redden, head turns upward, snarling is heard) and charges ahead at a fast clip. As another example, airport security games like *Jetset* include multiple passengers and security officers.[25] Such characters are, at best, what the role-playing tradition refers to as non-player characters (NPCs). Below the player level of power, these aren't really characters in any meaningful way, simply counters.

The most effective casual-game character is probably the player. If we consider small games as second-person stories, such games narrate the conditions for your actions: setting, timeline, objects, characters. There is, of course, a long tradition of second-person storytelling wherein texts address the reader, albeit without gaming's level of interactivity. For example, Theodore Sturgeon's "The Man Who Lost the Sea" (1959) places you in the position of a disoriented man who gradually, heartbreakingly comes to understand his extraordinary circumstances. Every other chapter of Italo Calvino's *If on a Winter's Night a Traveler* (1979) describes your reading a novel of the same title. The 1976 film *Mohammad: Messenger of God* uses the second-person mode to avoid Islam's prohibition against depicting its prophet. In it, your portrayal is silent, or rather you have no lines; other characters address you out loud, but only hear your unspoken dialogue internally. An earlier film, *The Lady in the Lake* (1947), places you in the protagonist's position as a detective solving a mystery. In this case, unlike *Mohammad*, your lines are spoken by an actor. One episode of the M*A*S*H TV series, "Point of View" (1978), is presented from a wounded soldier's perspective. He/you are silent due to a throat wound, as with *Mohammad*, until the very end, when surgery allows you to croak, "Thank you."

Some of the power of these works lies in the ease by which we can slip into that second-person character's position. As Jill Walker writes:

> You assume that you're the "you", for an instant at least. You turn because the word YOU is empty in itself. The vacuum inside it sucks you in, filling itself with you, and it will take a moment before you realise that you may not belong there.
>
> The word "you" is ready to be filled by anyone. It is empty: it doesn't refer outside of the situation in which it is uttered. There's a word for this emptiness: deixis. Deictic words like "you", "I", "she", "this", "that", "there" have no meaning except in relation to other words and to a context. Their power lies in this emptiness. Filling the empty space of a "you" can be "wonderfully stirring" . . . for a reader, as writers and rhetoricians have known since ancient times.[26]

Roger Caillois observes that taking up another's position can be a delightful experience. Children discover this at an early age, in make-believe. For all ages, "the pleasure lies in being or passing for another," especially if that other is powerful, successful, or otherwise interesting.[27]

Children also learn a deep secret about art, which is that the less detailed the representation of a character, the easier it is for us to identify with him or her. Scott McCloud explains this phenomenon in exploring the great popularity of very simply drawn cartoon characters, such as Mickey Mouse or Hello Kitty: "When you look at a photo or realistic drawing of a face— you see it as the face of *another*. But when you enter the world of the cartoon—you see *yourself*." That mimetic strategy does not have to extend to the entire work of art, be it a comic book or a storytelling game, since "readers [can] *mask* themselves in a character and safely enter a sensually stimulating world. One set of lines to see, another set of lines to *be*." McCloud labels that character mask an *icon* and assigns to it as great a participatory audience power as does Caillois. What McCloud's comics icon does, small games do with second-person play.[28]

Further storytelling power lies in the tension between the constraints second-person addresses place on the reader/viewer and the open world of detail-grounded possibility opened up through the rest of the story. Our full range of movement is utterly constrained, then thrown into relief by the apparent flexibility of other characters. A gap between our desire and that of the character opens and closes, forming a sort of dialogue across psychological states. A dual narrative results: given a sense of "our" progress as protagonist, we also construct a sense of our own embedded reactions. This construction can give rise to friction between the narratives. Think of an extreme example in *Blade Runner*'s opening scene (1982), when one character narrates another's action against the latter's will and to his increasing (and homicidal) dismay. Tester: "You're not helping." Leon: "What do you mean, I'm not helping?!" "I mean *you're not helping.*"

In this sense, we play the role of second-person narrator in small games. On the one hand, we are deeply constrained in our actions, being pinned at the bottom of a screen, forced to use two paddles, incapable of leaving the letter-flinging turret, only leaving a level when the game is satisfied that we've perfectly met its conditions. On the other hand, we—you— experience an inner sense of linear development, at least in terms of incremental gameplay progress. You react to objects and minicharacters, celebrate triumphs, and curse errors. You are free to pay no more attention to world details or whatever subjectivity might be gleaned from game entities as a pinball player cares about the scene depicted on that arcade machine's cabinet. In a structurally similar sense, you exist in dual-track time as well: that of what the game represents (night falling after a zombie attack) and that of real-world play (mouse clicking, pause button selected then released).[29] Those dual consciousnesses, that character development arc, happen largely offscreen in the player's body and mind. The most accomplished storytelling effect of casual gaming is therefore invisible.

More evident than that is the social connection between players afforded by social gaming, which is not unique to small games, as LAN parties, massively multiplayer online gaming, and other forms of large-scale gaming demonstrate. But casual games have been social for some time, and are increasingly so. Web versions of predigital games, from chess to mahjongg, have been played between live opponents since the 1990s. More recently, social gaming has exploded on Facebook, most notably with the homestead simulation *Farmville.* On average, 17,764,662 people play this game each day, and 61,744,252 each month, according to Facebook's statistics.[30] Social gaming companies like Playdom and Playfish have been acquired by game giants Disney and Electronic Arts.

Several points are significant about social casual gaming in storytelling terms. The first reinforces the general observation about social media and audience transformation: To the extent that social games tell stories, their audience is increasingly collaborative. This collaboration can involve direct play or the indirect following of another player's gaming through social media—as through screen captures shared through Picasa, Twitter updates about rising on a leaderboard, or blog posts about new games.

The second point is the establishment of social media resources for small games. *Wikipedia* is obviously one such source, but so are widely read blogs such as *Jay Is Games* or developer blogs. These provide hints, walk-throughs, play-throughs, background information, gaming analysis, and so on. Gamers can connect not only with each other's play but also with supplementary game content. We pick up a version of this second point with the "networked book" discussion in Chapter 8; for now, it is worth noting that small gaming is often a form of social gaming—social interaction mediated through that very thin, yet productive connector. It is social representation through small worlds: "Masks are the true social bond," notes Caillois.[31]

Little Mysteries

Complementing the rise of social small games is the development of art games at the casual game level. This has been enabled in part by the independent games movement and the availability of relatively powerful, low-cost, accessible technology. Unlike large, industrial-scale games like *Halo* or *Guitar Hero*, casual games can be created by small groups or individuals. Adobe Flash has established itself as a stable, widely used multimedia editing tool, a kind of remix and production studio in the way video editors serve for classic digital storytelling (see Chapter 12). Recent battles between the Adobe and Apple corporations, combined with the possible supplanting of Flash by the HTML5 standard, point the way to a successor platform, but none has emerged as of this writing at anything like the Flash scale.

A ferment of creativity has been bubbling on the edges of the large-scale gaming industry for some time in the domain of small, creative games. Examples are plentiful once we sift out major studio projects. Ferry Halim has been creating small, charming, and sweet casual games for his Orisinal project since 2000.[32] In 2004, Michael Clague created *AOOA,* a mysterious puzzle game where the nature of each stage is unclear until its completion. It begins with a fearsome-looking rotary phone ringing on screen, while a weird red light plays over a grim soundtrack. Each successive level shifts to a different tone, genre, and style of game: hidden object, memory recall, and so forth.[33]

"There is too much noise" is the single line beginning David Shute's *Small Worlds* (2009).[34] That bit of text is heavily pixilated, signaling the very low-resolution graphics to come. We begin play with a crudely depicted avatar, utterly lacking in characteristics but responsive to our basic motions. The entire world around our simple representative is dark, with the exception of the immediate vicinity. Those grounds (flooring?) are as undistinguished as our avatar. No gameplay statistics, such as health bar, skills, map location, or items carried, are presented. Instead, we move left or right, with the options of falling harmlessly or leaping upward slightly. As with *Second Life*'s default setting, our avatar apparently cannot be injured.

And yet the moment we move a few steps (yards?) away from our initial location, the game screen's viewpoint pulls back, revealing a larger world: more passageways and further floors. More movement yields further reveals and a correspondingly greater worldview. As we poke around what seems to be an abandoned military (scientific?) complex, the world fills out. An orchestral score broods—the only soundtrack, as the game lacks both voiceover and sound effects.

At the bottom of the world shines a tube of light. Stepped into, it flicks our perspective straight into a new world, the musical track cut off and a new one begun. That perspective has restarted to *Small Worlds*'s opening position of a narrow focus surrounded by darkness. Once again we explore, and again the world progressively scrolls back in staged reveals. With each progression (or regression, really), our avatar shrinks correspondingly. Once a titan on the screen, we are a dwarfed handful of pixels at the end of each world expansion. *Small Worlds* consists entirely of exploring a handful of worlds, each environment strongly hued by a distinct musical track. No other characters appear. The avatar cannot die or lose in any fashion. Once the worlds have been completed, the game ends on a quiet coda: the word "Silence" emblazoned over deep space, above a sun.

The narrative effect resembles that of a tone poem. We experience washes of emotion, if the music succeeds. A long series of detailed imaginations are revealed: waterfalls, rocky chambers, a captive sun, winking instrument panels, ruined missiles, spills of blood, snowbanks, shadows spreading behind rocks. The pleasure of exploring these is married to a sense of progression. Somehow the avatar, the player, is advancing. We overcome a continuous stream of platform challenges, which are all doable. That is all that *Small Worlds* has for a plot. The result is a meditative narrative, an unfolding, abstract contemplation.

Compare this with *Machinarium* (2009). Its aesthetics are very different. Amanita Design creates a whimsical and grim world, a postindustrial alien landscape populated by robots, wastelands, and mysterious machinery. Unlike the heavily pixilated art in *Small Worlds*, *Machinariums* visuals are hand-drawn, from objects to backgrounds, even to the menu options. Our representational avatar is a resigned-looking robot, which arrives in a junk drop from some alien spacecraft. We explore one screen, a refuse pile, in order to assemble "our" parts to make a functioning (and stretchable) robot protagonist. This unnamed, unspeaking avatar then voyages through a series of screens, each depicting another whimsical yet ominous world scene, every one structured as a puzzle to solve. The alien world is gradually populated and given a politics. The robot hero is in a relationship with another robot.

Puzzle-solving advances levels of the game, as many casual games do, but here each level adds story content. Cut scenes appear, the player is posed puzzles out of the narrative (how to neutralize the villain), and each solution advances the plot a step. *Machinarium* is a storytelling game, alternating content delivery with gameplay like a much larger game such as *Halo*. The differences with *Small Worlds* seem vast.

The two games do share some art-game storytelling approaches. First, each explores a world, adding levels of detail through gameplay. This technique remains a useful way of distinguishing games from most Web 2.0 storytelling—a Flickr image sequence requires a world but does not usually explore it in this sense. Second, both games offer an antithesis to the popular image of hyperfast, media-saturated gaming in that each presents vistas for contemplation rather than action. *Small Worlds* and *Machinarium* build in pauses, where intricate landscapes are paired with powerful music and held in suspension. Our avatars remain unchallenged, invited to stall. This strategy is akin to what McCloud sees as a non-Western graphic narrative style, which presents some static vistas between bouts of action.[35]

Third, these casual art games require us to frame, then solve, mysteries. *Machinarium* doesn't always make each puzzle's parameters clear, as we don't necessarily know what we're trying to accomplish. *Small Worlds* doesn't proclaim that exiting a world is our goal in that space; we derive this knowledge over time. But neither game allows our avatar to advance without successfully solving their mysteries. "Mystery" describes the formal operation of gameplay (finding the teleport, figuring out how to open a door), but also names the atmosphere of confusion each game presents. We are thrown into each story and only understand that in *media res* through play. The visual and sonic art in both heightens a sense of mystery, of awe, wonder, intrigue. It may be that mysteries, grounded in the form of puzzles, are necessary to casual art games. Many point-and-click adventures explicitly connect themselves to the mystery genre through detective characters, with murder and theft narratives; perhaps they will prove a ground for more storytelling games in the near future.

The Shock of the Old: Interactive Fiction

One of the oldest digital storytelling forms remains very much alive in 2010 and offers yet another route for game-based narrative. Interactive fiction (IF) was a business and creative concern in the 1980s, as we saw in Chapter 2. Text-based game-stories, where players entered commands to manipulate a world displayed entirely in text, emerged as a computer-mediated art form. After Infocom failed and other media-rich games began their rise to global prominence, IF persisted quietly as an artistic movement. Even in the age of *Gears of War* and *Eve Online*, these text-based games continue to appear, and the field continues to develop. Not unlike modern poetry, IF is made and consumed by devotees without a great deal of public attention or economic profit. "Like poetry, interactive fiction does not need to be lucrative to become a form that helps us gain new realizations about our world, a form that is relevant to our lives."[36]

The functions of early text adventure games—virtual worlds, user-generated content, hypertext, multilinear storytelling—have migrated to other platforms, making IF a new media ancestor. Interactive fiction has also worked its way into cyberculture deeply enough that it can be repurposed to serve other functions. Anthony Clarvo used classic IF as a metaphorical basis for his play *PICK UP AX* (1990).[37] Or consider this political satire, "Iraqi Invasion: A Text Misadventure":[38]

> Oval Office
>   You are standing inside a White House, having just been elected to the presidency of the United States. You knew Scalia would pull through for you.

There is a large desk here, along with a few chairs and couches. The presidential seal is in the middle of the room and there is a full-length mirror upon the wall.

What do you want to do now?

>INVADE IRAQ

You are not able to do that, yet.

>LOOK MIRROR

Self-reflection is not your strong suit. . . .

>EXAMINE CHAIRS

They are several chairs arranged around the center of the room, along with two couches. Under one couch you find Clinton's shoes.

>FILL SHOES

You are unable to fill Clinton's shoes. . . .

>INVADE IRAQ

You are not able to do that, yet.

>INVADE IRAQ

You are not able to do that, yet.

Note how the author, Matthew Baldwin, uses IF game mechanics for effective puns, mapping political ideology shorthand onto digital navigation prompts:

>GO RIGHT

Far-Right

You are on the far right of the political spectrum.

Jesse Helms is here.

John Ashcroft is here.

>GO RIGHT

Radical Right

You are on the extreme right of the political spectrum.

Dick Cheney is here.

Pat Robertson is here.

As with casual games, we—you—are placed in an uncomfortable second-person position, caught between your desire to act and the text's constraints. This example is extreme and perhaps unfair, since interactive fiction actually allows freedom of movement, but it does recall that dual subjectivity and remind us of a similarity between casual games and IF.

Interactive fiction offers several additional similarities to casual games. Both present players with virtual worlds to explore, spaces and narratives awaiting the user's actions. As stories, they present "potential narratives" requiring our traversal.[39] They are often perceived as solitary games, player versus program, but are often social, given a tradition of cooperative play and the nature of the IF community.[40]

Adventures in Browsers

Web-based social games blossomed and boomed starting around 2009, and remain a significant part of the gaming landscape thanks in large part to the success of *Farmville* and *Mafia Wars*. *Farmville* lightly simulates farm life, including animals and crops. *Mafia Wars* represents schematically competing family hierarchies. Both games have succeeded by leveraging social interaction, as players show off their farms to friends or try assassinating other friends. They have also succeeded in creating cash markets for their virtual goods.

Echo Bazaar offers an intriguing counterexample to this trend. It is a browser game, but one based on storytelling, card play, the steampunk genre, and social media. Play is based on a series of actions you take (and it is certainly you, as you log in through Twitter or Facebook), charting a strange course of biographical events through the parallel universe of Fallen London.[41]

As with a role-playing game, several quantitative levels reflect your skills and attributes (shadowy, persuasive, dangerous). You may equip your character with clothing, tools, money, and props as the game progresses. As with a card game, events appear in a random yet structured sequence. Players can pick or pass over some cards. Like storytelling games, each card's event unfolds a narrative, which can be attached to other cards. For example, a "storylet" offers this ministory sketch:

> Avenge a struggling artist's broken heart
> The rejection has driven him into an artistic frenzy. He needs a thimble of blood from the one who betrayed him to complete his work. "The colour!" he explains, red-eyed. "The colour must be true!"

You are then faced with several options in response: either "Teach the heartbreaker a lesson/He's holding court in the Singing Mandrake, trading tales of the artist's private affairs for drinks" or "Blood is blood / No need for a confrontation. He just needs some blood. Yours will do." Picking one option leads to more events along this story's path, such as:

> You must suffer for art
> You give the struggling artist a cup of your own blood and a satisfying tale of revenge. He finishes the work quickly, but seems disappointed. "It hasn't the quality I'd hoped," he tells you. But artists are their own worst critics. A surface collector snaps the painting up regardless, and the artist grants you part of the proceeds.

As befits a social browser game, some game functions directly connect with other players, as when you invite a friend to share a secret or play a game (within the game). Like a social media platform, *Echo Bazaar*'s Web interface contains a supplementary feed, a "snippet" of background information about the story-game's world ("Are the Clay Men really clay? That's a very personal question. They don't ask you if you're really meat."). And like many games of any size, a minigame can be played—"Mysteries," which is a quiz game.

Echo Bazaar feels like an energetic experiment, remixing multiple gaming and storytelling traditions and trying them out on the new platform of browser-based social casual games. It offers a representative sampling of the creativity small games sometimes evince at this time, especially when combined with storytelling attributes.

How large-scale games tell stories is the subject of our next chapter.

CHAPTER SEVEN

Gaming: Storytelling on a Large Scale

The man on the radio is talking, but you don't know who he really is. You don't know who you are, either, but the bathysphere continues to travel through the deep.

Your plane crashed into the ocean surface above a few minutes ago. Struggling free of the burning, bobbing, or sinking wreckage, you swam to a lighthouse. Remarkable stroke of good fortune, a haven appearing right then. The lighthouse wasn't what it seemed, however, as its doors opened into an art deco staircase, brass-on-black figures stretching up to herald a staircase winding downwards. A huge banner vaguely reminiscent of Ayn Rand, proclaiming "NO GODS OR KINGS. /ONLY MAN." loomed overhead as you made your way down, lights snapping on to light the way.

The golden bathysphere was a beautiful surprise, a delicate engineering bagatelle resting at the descent's end. Its door opened wide, and a bright, cozy-looking interior beckoned. Seeing no other way to go, you stepped inside. Seeing nothing else to do within, you pulled a single lever.

The chamber plummeted quickly, into the dark (and your controller shook, then froze). Seen through the single port more art deco work sped past, then an ad-prefaced short filmstrip plays on a screen: one Andrew Ryan outlining his views of private property, followed by his vision of a utopian city called Rapture. Ryan's voice continues as the screen rolls up, and the open undersea world is revealed. After cresting a fish-swarmed ridge, you beheld, music swelling . . . a sprawling 1950s-style American city, resting miraculously on the seafloor. Unable to control anything, you passively watch as the city draws near, then slides by on either side: tall buildings, statues, neon signs, billboards, squids and whales. The radio crackles and two men can barely be heard discussing your plane crash.

The voices continue, mentioning a crisis and strange words—splicers?—as the bathysphere turns, and a kind of tunnel mouth appears. Into the tunnel you helplessly proceed, as neon phrases pass overhead: "ALL GOOD THINGS / OF THIS EARTH / FLOW / INTO THE CITY." Your small vessel bumps to a stop, then rises in a shaft lined with lights and more ads. After a pause, you see a man backing towards your port, apparently in a dry space, and pleading with someone. That someone appears, laughing horribly, before doing something bloody to the first man.

You cannot move. And now the killer has seen you, is mocking you, coming closer. You cannot move.

How do games tell stories? So far, our discussion has focused on stories produced by individuals or small groups, from Twitter to small games. At this point, we increase the scope of storytelling forms, ramping up to large-scale computer games. These games—massively multiplayer online (MMO) games, most console games, large-scale PC games—require significantly more memory, processing power, multimedia support, and user time than casual games. They are the kind of computer game commonly cited when the art form or industry is discussed, titles like *World of Warcraft* or *Grand Theft Auto*.

In this chapter, we apply our storytelling models to them for several reasons: first, to test those concepts against a different body of work; second, to see what platform-specific storytelling approaches are being used in this field. Third, if readers are not currently capable of producing games to this scale, they may draw inspiration from such storytelling. Moreover, as digital authoring tools continue to improve, ever-increasing realms of game design are accessible.

While various titles will be referred to, three main, popular, and well-regarded works will serve as exemplars: *Bioshock*, *Fallout 3*, and *Rome: Total War*. *Bioshock* is a science-fiction game, a hybrid of first-person shooter with horror structured around a satirical dystopia. The protagonist is hurled into an underwater city in an alternate-history 1960, where cutting-edge science has transformed inhabitants into monsters. *Fallout 3* is a postnuclear adventure story where the protagonist explores a desolated Washington, D.C. area in the near future. It is also a first-person shooter featuring bouts of meticulously detailed combat. *Rome: Total War* is a strategy game where players take the roles of major Roman families during the Republic, seeking to expand their influence in preparation for the inevitable civil war.

In Chapter 1, we defined stories thus: "For a given audience, a story is a sequence of content existing in one medium or more, which engages that audience with emotion and meaning." Obviously, games like the *Call of Duty* or *Mass Effect* series fulfill this very broad definition. They proffer vast amounts of content in various sequences. Their emotional pull is significant and multileveled. The kind of meaning they provide is often criticized for being shallow or dangerous, but clearly manages to win players for large amounts of time.

Our discussion of storytelling can go beyond this axiomatic test. We went further in Chapter 3, identifying a set of digital storytelling principles. In Chapters 4 and 5, we expanded on those by seeing their expression through social media. Small games (casual games, interactive fiction, browser games) took these storytelling ideas onward into a different field of interactivity. Our question then should not be "Do large-scale games tell stories?" but "By what similar and different ways do they do so?"

Elements of Story

Games produce story in multiple levels of sequence, manipulating time in ways now considered commonplace, but reflecting some sophistication. One of the earliest notions of game-based storytelling was the "story on rails," a narrative that users would play through. Like being on a railroad car, we would see scenery (events, characters) pass by. We could change our vantage point, slow down the car a bit to linger, even get out to enjoy a particularly interesting station, but could never really alter the train's course. In this concept, we are free to choose another train running on another line, which is a different story.

That strictly controlled linear sequence has remained popular in part because of its simplicity and easy recognition. It maps onto the Freytag triangle, at least in a basic way (see Chapter 1). It fits our real-world experience of storytelling where we personally progress forward in real time while watching a movie, listening to an oral story, reading a book. And this basic train line metaphor simplifies game creation. As legendary game designer Greg Costikyan puts it, "A story is best envisioned as 'beads on a string,' a linear narrative."[1] Ubisoft designer Clint Hocking approvingly reviews one major recent game, *Call of Duty 4*, as

> a rigidly authored narrative game that has a fairly good story. It pushes some of your buttons and manipulates you and makes you feel stuff. And yet the story you experienced is exactly the same as the one I experienced, with very minor variations that are probably no more different from the minor variations you and I have in our subjective experience of reading a novel. . . . The best story *Call of Duty* can ever have is something either very close to or marginally better than the best war movie ever made.[2]

We can see this borne out in our exemplary games. *Bioshock* follows a strict chronological sequence, from the narrator's crash landing into Rapture through his defeat of Fontaine. *Fallout 3* is bound closely to the hours of the day, with fatigue building up without rest, night following day. The player's exploration of the Capital Wasteland unfolds in a daily sequence. Our knowledge, possessions, and reputation accrue steadily. And in *Rome: Total War*, the tale of our family's progress is pinned to each half-year turn.

But each of these games allows divergent timelines. As with most games, we can replay selections of the overall game, rerunning a story to attempt a different outcome. This element is predicated on user control, of course and not driven by the game's internal logic. Fontaine doesn't send *Bioshock*'s hero back in time to refight Peach Wilkins nor does the Scipio family invite the Julii to try invading Carthage by reloading a saved game. This replay is a user movement through time, not unrelated to rewinding a videotape or rereading a book's passage. What changes from those media is selecting a different story through selecting a different timeline, much like returning to an earlier Choose Your Own Adventure's page in order to avoid one of the dreaded defeat pages. The game experience enables that reiteration through various and popular mechanisms: save points, check points, and loading saved sessions. Games also restrict our temporal mobility through cut scenes (see later) and limiting save points, so our ability to replay and reiterate is not unlimited. Indeed, we should see those limitations as strategic ways for games to trammel user behavior, story-shaping constraints like chapters.

These games break with the string-of-beads model in another, more classical fashion: through flashbacks, conversation, and documents. The narrator in *Bioshock* will sometimes experience a memory that intrudes into the present, akin to a post-traumatic flashback. The game depicts these in altered sound and black-and-white visuals, the images nearly blotting out the present's imagery. Other *Fallout 3* characters will inform you about your father's past, the mysterious Project Purity, or backstories for the myriad hamlets dotting that postnuclear landscape. Historical and personal documents appear in both games: audiotapes, computer text files, old posters revealing information about the past.

Indeed, in the contemporary game *Halo: ODST* (2009), audio documents constitute a minigame within the overall game, complete with puzzles and rewards. The *Penumbra* game series did something similar, which its designers refer to as "fragmented storytelling":[3]

> It is about having a certain background story (or similar) spread out over the world. The player must then find these fragments and piece them together. These fragments usually come as notes or character dialogs, each giving a piece of the "puzzle."

An unusual storytelling approach lies behind this, one combining an open structure with some attempts to guide discovery:

> Fragmented storytelling allows for much more freedom as it is possible for the player to pick up fragments in different order and even to miss certain fragments without ruining the story. [Some kind of order is usually wanted] . . . and normally it is solved by not having all fragments available from starts, each level/section of the game containing certain fragments. It is also possible to solve by procedural generation of fragments.[4]

Taken together, large-scale games can be seen as progressing backward and forward in time within the same experience. The past is very present, filled in as play moves forward.

Rome: Total War is an exception to this, a historical game without internal history. Its rich documentation, providing information about contemporary cultural developments, is always in the present. Communications from diplomats and other players appear in the present. When we encounter previously hidden peoples and terrain, we cannot explore their histories. Physical sites prohibit archaeology, Egypt being the land only of Seleucids, not pharaohs. Perhaps this is unexplored minigame territory for future games.

Since storytelling requires personal content, we should not be surprised to find large-scale games well stocked with characters. PC and console games market themselves through characters, prominently featuring protagonists on box covers, Web sites, trailers, and merchandising. Master Chief (the *Halo* series) and Marcus Fenix (*Gears of War*) feature in fan-made videos. Within the games, characters are presented in significant detail. Professional actors speak voiceovers. High-end graphics represent faces and bodies. Characters sometimes change and develop over time.

Fallout 3 is an especially ambitious example of game characterization. It takes place in a heavily depopulated land, but is well stocked with minor characters. We are able to interact with a sheriff, a general store manager and part-time amateur scientist, a priest to a very disturbing god, a childhood friend, a militia leader, and a mad scientist, to describe a few. The main character's father dominates the game's tutorial prologue, then retains a lurking presence for the main plot. Radio announcer Threedog is capable of speaking throughout most of the game; we can meet him face-to-face and work through several plots in which he is a player.

Rome: Total War contains characters in a small but significant way. Historical simulations are not often described in characters' terms, but *Rome* insists on presenting individuals throughout the game. As player, you lead one of three major families, and the game maintains your family tree by names, relationships, and short biographies. Your "faction leader," or patriarch, plays an active role in some situations, and his death changes your family's fortunes. Marriages between characters, children being born and coming of age, and deaths all matter to the complex dynamics of power politics. Additionally, you control other named characters: assassins, diplomats, and spies, each associated with a biography and active set of attributes. You may recruit or otherwise have access to new ones, and all eventually die.

Perhaps it is likely that players will not invest themselves emotionally in this swarm of historical figures who populate the game world like a stereotypical Russian novel's cast. And yet it is noteworthy that a simulation should decide to expend resources on creating so many persons, then mandating player interactions with them. Maybe this design strategy echoes the history pedagogy of humanizing complex situations by embodying processes in individual human form, by giving us something more intimate with which to connect. Regardless, this insistence on representing individual human characters occurs throughout the popular *Total War* series and is echoed by other strategy games to differing degrees. To the extent that even these large-scale games covering the destinies of nations choose to represent individuals, they possess the stuff of storytelling.

These games also rely on characters beyond their worlds. We saw social connections as important to many casual games in Chapter 6, and we can find a similar aspect to large-scale gaming. As with most digital storytelling, these games are embedded in a world shaped in part by social media. First, multiplayer play remains a highly valued feature for many games. *Halo, Gears of War*, the *Call of Duty* series, and others owe some of their popularity to interplayer combat options. Game reviews often assess multiplayer functionality as one of a game's most important aspects. Like Soylent Green, much of large-scale gaming is made of people.

Second, social media production around gaming is very large. Players and game professionals contribute gaming content to the social Web. As a casual Google search reveals, game guides and walk-throughs are available for most games, published in multiple formats: text only, images combined with text, video captures, and screencasts. Some are satirical and critical, such as the "Let's Play" genre; some creators can develop a series of these, building up their own characters.[5] Others are helpful, even encyclopedically so. Game wikis provide a mix of information at the level of a world rather than a single play-through. For example, the *Bioshock* wiki has material enough to be categorized under the following headers: Characters, Enemies, Weapons, Plasmids (a science-fiction technology), Gene

Topics (same), Levels, Audio Diaries, Trophies and Achievements, and Downloadable Content. Alongside those is a separate set of commentary on Rapture, the undersea dystopian metropolis where the game is set, including general information, "storyline," and timeline (an interesting sub-division).[6] A similarly large wiki resource exists for *Fallout* as well.[7] This kind of secondary material is often compared to *Cliff's Notes* for literature, but the comparison isn't apt: too much of the content is apparently uncompensated, the quality uneven rather than uniform, and the depth sometimes exhaustive.

The diversity of this secondary material brings us to another storytelling principle, that of multiple proscenia (see Chapter 3). Large-scale games tend to be deeply anchored in single platforms, often developed for one particular hardware/software stack. Our experience of them would seem to argue for a singular proscenium, as it were. Several factors complicate this view, however. As we just noted, each game tends to be surrounded by a secondary wave of content published through social media. Alongside supplemental material designed to assist other players, there is also a different stratum of fan productions where players share their triumphs and experiences of games. Here we find photo and video documentation of *Bioshock* and *Fallout* cosplay costumes, for example, or video clips of exciting scenes. This level of social media production leads us to the professional social media gaming world of reviewers, workers in the game industry, game studies scholars, and reporters at large. Games are marketed much as movies are, with attention to audience response. In this way, large-scale games appear to us out of a social media matrix, at the very least contextualized by commentary and documentation. As players, we may contribute to this matrix with as small a step as commenting on a nasty blog post about our favorite game. Our gaming experience cannot be reduced to player versus console, at least not for long. To the extent that we experience games as stories, that experience tends to be distributed across multiple sites, if focused on one.

Within those primary sources, how does one of these large-scale games take advantage of its platform's unique affordances for storytelling? *Bioshock* and *Fallout 3* were both released as console games, and each uses a different set of that device's abilities. For example, *Bioshock* signals physical impacts by vibrating the controller. At a basic level, this vibration jars the player, emphasizing a shock from the story's action (a plane crash, a Big Daddy hurled against you); at a meta level, it shifts the game's ground from the screen to your hand, at least for players unaccustomed to the effect. It is a form of dramatic punctuation, like the sound of a thunderclap or a screen going dark, an unusually intense signal to the player.

Fallout, too, addresses the player, but through a nonphysical, slightly ironical move. Your character carries a Pip-Boy, a kind of personal digital assistant providing information about your health and skills, a map, a radio (through which you can listen to Threedog), and an inventory of your belongings. Its design follows the game's hybrid of 1950s consumerism and 1980s computers, with a monochrome display and thick buttons—while also resembling in size, shape, and importance the handheld controller through which you play the game. The Pip-Boy is a kind of game controller within the game, a multitool for interacting with its world. Although it's indestructible, at least one character mocks it for being out of date.

Since the Xbox controller does not include a keyboard, both games minimize the amount of input the player can offer. Interaction with the story is therefore narrower in options. For combat, this level of interaction is traditional. For social situations, the games diverge: *Fallout* presents conversation menus with several choices available at a time (answering affirmatively to a question, answering negatively, changing the subject, ending the talk), and *Bioshock* leaves discussion out of your hands entirely. Both strategies map well onto the different nature of each story, as *Fallout* emphasizes exploration of a complex interconnected world that can be understood and navigated in part through human communication. In contrast, *Bioshock*'s protagonist is a cipher, an artificially grown creature without much in the way of social skills; fortunately, the world of the game is a collapsed dystopia without much opportunity for conversation. In one story world, you navigate limited option menus to incrementally explore a deeply networked environment, while in the other, you listen passively to human speech as the container for information you turn out to be. Each game's use of the console controller reflects the nature of the story.

PC gaming offers a very different set of storytelling tools. The full keyboard lends itself to richer player interaction options. In *Rome: Total War*, players have a large number of choices during a given turn. The game presents these through the screen, while the keyboard supports the full variety through hotkeys and other keyboard shortcuts. During the strategic game, a player can move troops, shift funds from city to city, marry off a relative, urge research in the social sciences, construct ships, attempt an assassination, or restart peace talks. The tactical game offers a similarly broad range of choices for the battlefield: many different types of units, each capable of different configurations and actions; terrain to explore; the enemy to scout.

In the previous chapter, we observed that games can be seen as immersive environments or digital objects producing that effect. Large-scale computer games have been known to provide immersion for some time, due in no small part to the larger production and display resources used in their creation. A PC screen and speakers are simply quantitatively more powerful than a smartphone's. A television projects more information than a handheld device. A deeper, broader game world is thereby supported. This depth can extend into multigame franchises, as the series of sinister, gorgeous *Assassin's Creed* historical cities, or simply be encyclopedically rich in one game: the cyberpunk city of *Mirror's Edge*, for example.

Each of this chapter's exemplary games seeks to immerse players in its world, be it preimperial Rome or a fictional undersea dystopia. They do so progressively, but in very different fashions. *Bioshock's* complexity increases with each story phase: more enemies, more plasmids, additional spaces to explore and characters to learn. The backstory also grows as we learn about Ryan's regime, the scientific experiments, and the Fontaine–Atlas arc. The game actively layers itself, in other words, through its sequential narrative. *Fallout 3* leaves that progressive layering to the player. We must explore the Capital Wasteland ourselves, meeting new characters, finding sites, learning of new groups and plots. We can refrain from exploration at our discretion or focus on a particular area.

The Roman world lies in between these two cases. No determinative narrative drives us forward, and we can explore Europe, North Africa, and the Near East as we see fit. However, other nations and Roman factions, controlled by the game, will impinge upon us, each according to its design. The Scythians are not likely to harass the Scipii in Italy, for example, but the Carthaginians will quickly do so. Eventually one Roman family faction will declare war against the Senate, which automatically alters the status of the others. And, of course, one's success or failure with other factions can drive them to act against your own on a new timeline.

In the case of Rapture, progressive immersion follows Costikyan's string-of-beads paradigm, each new item strung into place after the one before it. The postnuclear world, in contrast, scatters those beads through space, letting the player pick and choose the string order. If we see the Roman Republic between these two, a continuum of progressive world immersion is apparent. The story each game tells us, then, and the story we create by playing through assume a gradual depth through each.

Two particular kinds of multimedia effects enhance that immersion still further: sounds and cut scenes. As we saw in Chapter 6, these each add story content and atmosphere. Sound is especially important for large games. Spoken dialogue, for example, strongly shapes our sense of each character's personality. Accents, tone, and rhythm of speech all play a role in building these personae. In *Bioshock*, the character of Andrew Ryan first appears as a confident authoritarian. As voiced by Armin Shimerman for the first third of the game, Ryan snarls defiantly at your character, a presumed saboteur, then calmly meditates on the exercise of power in audio recordings. As the game progresses and Ryan's power is revealed to be a sham, Shimerman's voice changes, shifting to ranting or abstraction. His final scene, where he orders the player to kill him, is delivered with a quiet, resigned mixture of pride and understatement. We could read these lines as text alone, but Ryan's character is immensely more powerful through this "gift of voice." Similarly, we first hear two different voices for characters we assume are separate people, Atlas and Fontaine, which maintains that illusion for plot purposes. The remix of the two into one, showing us the nature of that plotline, is a terrifying moment.

Beyond the voice-acting aspect of game audio is ambient sound. In *Bioshock*, the decaying city is made apparent by continuous sound effects: groaning metal, footsteps that change depending on what surface they tread, different types of rushing water sounds, the hissing of broken electrical lines, burbling lava, crumbling rock. *Fallout* offers a similarly rich soundscape where we are sonically alerted to the presence of animals and people or, left alone, allowed to hear the quiet sounds of desolation. Battle scenes are accompanied by a rich stew of audio violence: shouts, shots, grunts, thuds, screams.

Cinematics or cut scenes in these games can be quite impressive and provide key pieces to stories. We learn, for example, about the horrible nature of *Bioshock*'s Big Daddies and Little Sisters from a cinematic. Our first view of Rapture is footage glimpsed from a bathysphere porthole. The death of Ryan is one we witness without being able to act. *Bioshock* offers an unusual approach to cinematics, taking narrative advantage of the player's powerlessness. We watch a friendly scientist get killed by Ryan, for example, and that death is more poignant, more humiliating to us, because we cannot intervene. The game's protagonist murders Ryan without player input, although the controller trembles with each sickening blow. The passivity of Jack is a crucial plot point, and one against which we can chafe. When our ability to act is returned to us after a cut scene, as when we first see a Big Daddy kill, it isn't always a chance for us to exercise power. The game takes advantage of cinematics' negative side effects. What some call "ludonarrative dissonance," the sharp gap between cut scenes and normal play, is repurposed to show cognitive dissonance for a character with a troubled mind, ratcheting up nerve-tautening tension for a suspenseful game.

Rome: Total War creates a mix of mimetic and diegetic soundscapes. We receive verbal acknowledgments from commanders when we send them about the strategic map. Tactical maps are rich in sound, as each type of unit makes its presence known with separate audio tracks: twangs of archers' bows, snorts of cavalry horses, heavy infantry's stomping and shouting. But things shift in the strategic map, where the representational sounds are less prominent. Instead, *Rome* assigns each player action a specific and distinct sound: clicks, slides, snaps, and whirs, indicating the game's responses. *Fallout* also emits sounds in response to our use of menus, but blends the diegetic and mimetic layers when we interact with the Pip-Boy. It is both an interface layer to the game and an object within it. The sounds the game plays for it help establish its boundary nature.

Lastly, all three of these games rely on creating a sense of mystery. As we saw in Chapter 1, stories can elicit audience engagement by concealing some content in a way that drives the audience to curiosity and investigation. Large-scale games can use their full range of immersive media to structure the playing experience along these lines. *Fallout 3* offers a clear example. After the game's prologue, you are expelled into the Capital Wasteland with barely any information about the area at all. Your Pip-Boy's map is nearly blank. In a sense, the rest of the game consists of filling in that map, both the physical and the human terrain. Many social encounters give rise to new mysteries, which pull you in other directions. In the town of Megaton, for example, one bar patron mentions Tenpenny Tower. Your Pip-Boy has nothing to say on that score, so perhaps your curiosity is aroused. Without a library or Internet to research, heading out to the Wasteland for investigative purposes is the best option. In Tenpenny Tower, you meet more characters and learn of still more mysterious locales, such as the ghouls' city. Each discovery draws the player further into the game world; few stories are as recognizable as the story of exploration.

Bioshock is more blatant in its use of mystery, as it evokes a whole series of tropes and strategies from the start, recalling the intertwined literary historical roots of mystery and horror. Your character has amnesia or at least lacks any memory. Rapture is visually dark and shadowy at its brightest. Each sector contains hidden rooms, traps, and ambushes. The identities of main characters—Ryan, Atlas, yourself—are continually revised and cast into doubt. The overall shape of the plot changes course several times, offering pauses of confusion. Early on, one scene exemplifies this mystery-rich game: while exiting an elevator, you hear a woman's voice singing a kind of lullaby. Scanning the area, you can just make out a shadow cast on a wall from an obscured room, the silhouette of a woman and baby carriage. The lullaby changes, becoming a plaintive adult song before breaking down, then restarting. The visuals and audio track are mystifying, pulling us forward. When we turn the corner to look upon the scene directly, the woman's back is to us, and we cannot see the carriage's contents. Again, our curiosity is stoked, and we want to act to learn more.

Rome: Total War is a very different type of game, but is nonetheless steeped in mystery. When the game begins, we are equipped with a map of Europe, North Africa, and part of the Near East. Geographical details are plainly visible, but the political landscape is almost entirely invisible. Your family's handful of holdings is visible, as is the Roman capital and details of your immediate neighbors. In order to progress, you need to explore. Who rules Gaul beyond northern Italy? Did the Nubians raise an army, hidden in the desert, or are they actually defenseless? How powerful is the economy of that kingdom just encountered east of Greece? Moreover, as years pass, political fortunes change, and what you once knew about a region may no longer be accurate. The Parthians ruled Cilicia, but could the Claudians have seized it back? Exploration requires reiteration, as the game restores mystery over each move of resolution.

The World Is Not Enough

Given such a rich set of storytelling tools, we should expect them to be used for other purposes, especially in the Web 2.0 age. Digital media lend themselves to remixing, as we've seen. Large-scale computer games produce rich media content, from audio to video, which can be captured. Some of that captured content becomes material for the various social media game-related content noted previously: play-throughs, tutorials, screencasts.

Games can also be repurposed as storytelling content production platforms. *Machinima* is the portmanteau term describing the creation of videos using game engines (as opposed to shooting video, creating animations, or editing images). A machinima creator can play a game for a time, recording the action. That record can then be imported into a video editor, where voiceover can be mixed in. Other content can be added, including subtitles, animation, music, audio, and video effects. One of the most famous examples of this technique is *Red vs. Blue*, a comedy series using *Halo* franchise games to create video.[8] The *Second Life* virtual world service offers another machinima production venue even though it is not a game, strictly speaking.[9] There are annual machinima contests and a growing body of work.[10]

What does machinima contribute to digital storytelling? It can enable a serious cost savings for video production, since a copy of a computer game can be less expensive than hiring actors and staging videography. It also draws on the current status of major games: advanced enough to provide three-dimensional visualizations, yet distinct enough from live humans to offer a very different appearance, something between animation and live action. The growing body of machinima work, too, offers yet another strand of digital storytelling practice to learn from.

Machinima-style game production work can also be built into projects that are not primarily video. *Alice and Kev* (2009) is a hybrid form: social media storytelling combined with gaming and machinima. Its creator, Robin Burkinshaw, uses *Sims 3*, combined with blogging, to tell the story of a homeless couple. Alice and Kev, along with other characters, inhabit the world of the Sims, which can pass for our own (hence the game's sustained appeal). They are created by a mix of Burkinshaw's manipulations of them, along with the game's automatic responses:

> Kev is mean-spirited, quick to anger, and inappropriate. He also dislikes children, and he's insane. He's basically the worst Dad in the world. . . .
>
> His daughter Alice has a kind heart, but suffers from clumsiness and low self-esteem. With those traits, that Dad, and no money, she's going to have a hard life.[11]

They try to survive, meet their emotional needs, and get along with each other (or not). We experience this story as a series of images linked by text, each set constituting a blog post. Comments are plentiful, as *Alice and Kev* has won a large following. Users can also download the two main characters as game content, then run them within a local version of *Sims 3*.[12] Burkinshaw connected his work with homeless advocacy, adding yet another hybridization to the project: a persuasive game, or one played for us.[13]

As Jesse Walker and others observe, we are witnessing the increasing democratization of creative tools through decreased costs, new technologies, and the spread of creative practices. "When the cost of filmmaking falls and more people, in more places, from more social backgrounds, learn to shoot and edit, the results may include an increase in crap, but there will also be an increase in creativity, variety, and verve."[14] Games with large production costs like *Bioshock* or *Rome: Total War* are, as of this writing, beyond the budgets of everyday creators. Their storytelling achievements, however, can perhaps be learned from, while the games themselves can be repurposed for other creative ends.

PART 3

Combinatorial Storytelling; or, The Dawn of New Narrative Forms

CHAPTER EIGHT

No Story Is a Single Thing; or, The Networked Book

Horatio thinks he saw a ghost. His friend Hamlet is annoyed by his family's recent behavior; the king returns the favor. Laertes considers Ophelia's choice of mate, out loud, while Hamlet's father has, curiously, become a zombie. The king and queen exchange pokes. Hamlet becomes a fan of Daggers, a Sports/Athletics group with 129,374 other fans. This is *Hamlet* via Facebook.[1]

At this point, we return to the definitional problem from Chapter 1: What is a story? Or rather: What is *a* story? What separates it from the world? It's the boundary question to which we now turn. The social media world has made the outer frontier of stories porous. Where a story begins and ends, what the container is that holds a narrative: these questions are more difficult to answer than before.

In a sense, this subject is not controversial, nor one driven by technology. Literary criticism has established many ways of understanding connections between a story's interior and its surrounding world. Intertextuality, manuscript and publication history, historicism, cultural studies, structuralism, and deconstruction have all broken down the story world barrier in multiple ways.

On the other hand, as a culture, we simultaneously maintain the opposite view of story composition. In policy terms, copyright law is premised on creative works being carefully demarcated from the rest of culture and closely assigned to their creators (or subsequent intellectual property owners). Despite the growth of remix culture and the Creative Commons licensing project, this form of traditional, even Romantic copyright shows little sign of declining.

On a practical level, we consume a great deal of story content in clearly defined boxes: the DVD, the theatrical release of movies or plays, the boxed set of TV show episodes, the printed book, individual songs downloaded from iTunes or Amazon, and e-books ultimately housed in a bookseller's servers.

The technological and cybercultural transformation of the past generation, partially sketched in Chapters 1–4, has increased the salience of this problematic situation. Defining the boundaries of one's story has increasingly become not only a theoretical chestnut, but a matter of urgent pragmatism. As Ben Vershbow observes, "How to design these sorts of layered documents so that they are not overwhelming or hopelessly muddled for the reader is a pressing issue."[2] Boundary determination is not only a formal issue, but a material and strategic one. Given a cultural milieu of ever-increasing media networking, story creators are now faced with three compositional stances:

1. *Actively embrace networking.* Internally, arrange story content in multiple, inter-linked items. Externally, point to other media, sources, and stories, and expect that the audience will do so on their own.

2. *Accept the networked environment.* Expect social media connections, but without devoting energies to solicit them.

3. *Secede from networks.* Select a format that actively sets up a discrete boundary around story content. As Barbara Ganley says, "If you're not thinking about social media for digital storytelling, you're basically creating something that is analog."[3]

The third option is meant to sound shocking in order to emphasize the unusual nature of not participating in social media. If multiple social media trend lines continue—the amount of such content, the number of users—social settings should become recognized as the default for cultural activity, and not engaging them would be unusual. And yet, we still produce and consume stories that exist in networked isolation. Cinema and drama in theaters, books in print, games played and podcasts listened to offline—the entire offline digital experience all occurs in a separate space from digital comments, updates, and tweets.

We will return to this separate strategy in subsequent chapters. We have already referred to instances, most notably the single video clip created through the Center for Digital Storytelling's approach. In this chapter, we focus instead on current versions of the first option—the active embrace of the social—with some engagement with the second strategy of acceptance.

One model for understanding storytelling in a social media world, one where content and audience interaction is distributed over multiple sites and across time, is that of the networked book. The term is evocative, hybridizing the two forms of digital networks and printed codex. Unpacking the phrase reveals several subsidiary elements. To begin with, hyperlinking is assumed, both internal and external. Internal linking draws on the history of hypertext (see Chapter 2), with multiple content items (*lexia*) navigable by hyperlinks. In social media terms, a networked book's contents can be multiple blog posts, wiki pages, a series of podcast files, YouTube clips, and more. They may be organized by departments, categories, or tags, each of which is clickable.

The networked book depends as well on external linkings, both inbound and outgoing. The latter are commonplace enough for us to assume, but worth noting for several reasons. First, outbound links have various rhetorical effects: building credibility by linking to evidence, affiliation with favored sources, and a sense of openness and sociability. Second, while Internet-connected PCs can hyperlink easily, and the open Web assumes this behavior, various platforms and strategies mitigate against external linking: policies against "deep" or direct links, mobile devices where apps are self-contained, and links requiring authentication or payment. Third, a broader stance can be taken with external links, namely, that of portal. A networked book style of Web engagement can cast itself as an authoritative guide to parts of the Web. This is not the same as a generic or broad-based Web, but a way of framing links as curation and authority. A set of links on microbiology resources, for example, can be presented as a disciplinary act of connection, mediating professionally for the viewer/ reader.[4]

Networked book connections can also take the form of user contributions. The *Wikipedia* is the most famous case of this, as are blog comments. Joseph Esposito recommends that we think of a networked book as a platform whereupon visitors build materials in a collaborative space. Vershbow suggests the annotation concept instead, emphasizing a primary source upon which visitors reflect. Both models expand the classic form of the isolated book to include a social aura or stratum. User contributions also require some form of editorial strategy. The networked book's creator or creative team becomes something like an editor or archivist, depending on the levels of control exerted: how frequent the content survey is; what the requirements for contribution are; and policies about appropriate content, automatic systems (CATPCHA, login), and types of sanction (banning, deletion, "disenvowelment"). The *Wikipedia* version of a distributed team of content minders checking on registered users' contributions is one model, as is open blog commenting or blog comment approval.

Nonfiction networked book examples have been available for some time and continue to appear. Some are attached to and may offer Web 2.0 versions of print books. Robert Frenay's *Pulse* (2006), a work of natural history and philosophy, was accompanied by a blog version, which republished content from the novel not in a single unit, but in many pieces of microcontent released sequentially: blog posts. Also in blog style, the site allowed comments, reformed posts into departments, offered a blogroll, and linked to related blog carnivals. These last did not merely allow readers to venture forth into the Web, but even encouraged them to do so: "This is a visitor's guide to rest of the Net, to the people who are laying the groundwork for our cultural transformation into the 'new biology.'" These selected, curated routes to the Web represent a very outward-facing story form, diametrically opposed to single-device or single-app books. Put another way, the *Pulse* network is heterogeneous, blending its own content with user contributions and external content.[5]

Other book blogging projects are not necessarily based on their source materials' full content, but either expand on that content or help develop it. For example, Siva Vaidhyanathan blogged his book, *The Googlization of Everything*, in progress. This meant sharing passages from the book's early drafts, noting relevant news stories, offering book-related analyses of those news stories, updating readers on its progress, and so on. As Vaidhyanathan is a public intellectual, often publishing articles and being featured in interviews, his book blog links to those external venues, knitting together his broader discussions in one site.[6]

Similarly, Howard Rheingold blogged his book, *Smart Mobs*. As Joanne Jacobs describes it, this book blogging began during the writing process: "The blog contributed toward the final copy of the 2002 book, but also expanded on the theories propounded in the text." Next, the smartmobs .com site persisted after the book's publication, "continuing . . . to be regarded by its readership as a growing knowledge and critical discussion vase, where posts may well be adapted or copied whole into future editions of the printed edition." Again, we see social production appear: "Blog readers of *Smart Mobs* tend to carefully post suggestions and content in the hope that their analysis may contribute to the future canon of the printed edition, thus obtaining a kind of added credibility to their words."[7]

A deeper level of book blogging-based social production involves distributed editing. This mode publishes drafts of book content to blog posts, then relies on critiques in attached comments to improve the material. One example is Dan Gillmor's crowdsourced editing of his 2004 work, *We the Media*, which, in Jacobs's account, "allowed for correction of minor errors and, perhaps more important, expansion on ideas with relevant examples and feedback on content." Jacobs notes the risks involved: Gillmor "was placing a degree of trust in his regular readership."[8]

From another angle, Juan Cole offers a complementary approach. After publishing *Napoleon's Egypt* in print form (2007), the Middle Eastern scholar blogged extra materials that did not make that book's editorial cut. Some 227 posts over two years published primary documents from that late 18th-century event, such as letters, official documents, and journal entries. This practice can be considered analogous to the deleted or alternative movie scenes contained in many DVD releases.[9]

Some book blogs and book wikis are created by groups external to the author as a kind of fan response or critique. The Thomas Pynchon wiki contains extensive annotations to that writer's complex, allusive books. Each page of Pynchon's novel has been associated with multiple wiki entries, covering everything from translation to pun explication to topical references tracked down and sourced.[10] For example, the Pynchon wiki entry for page 128 of *Against the Day* (2007) contains eight separate items. A five-word phrase—"drawn into another, toroidal dispensation"—is explained in terms of theology, math, natural history, history of science, a reference within the novel, and the 9/11 attacks.[11] This ambitious form of generative textuality is wholly in keeping with Pynchon's own sprawling, encyclopedic, and digressive style. The Pynchon wiki also represents a kind of maximum realization of the book wiki, a very rich instance of a networked book anchored to a book.

In a similarly playful and devotional way, *Node* magazine is not actually a magazine, but a node or set of nodes. It is in fact a group blog/wiki resource for readers of William Gibson's later novels: *Pattern Recognition* (2003) and *Spook Country* (2007).[12] Readers built annotations (echoes of the *Pepys Diary*) and comments attached to individual paragraphs and even sentences in Gibson's allusive text. For example, part of one entry for August 2, 2007, under the header "Chapter 1. WHITE LOGO pages 1–8," begins with a quotation: " 'Rausch,' said the voice in Hollis Henry's cell. 'Node,' it said." Then it moves on to a mix of summary and commentary:[13]

> Shortly after 3AM on a Wednesday morning in the Mondrian in LA, Hollis Henry awakes to a call from Philip Rausch, editor of Wired-wannabe Node. "They're ready to show you his best piece," Rausch says.
>
> Careful to not step on Odile Richard's white lego robot (apparently "collecting data with an onboard GPS unit"), Hollis ventures out to meet Odile ("the least chic Frenchwoman Hollis could recall having met") and Alberto Corrales (a "broad young Latino with shaven head and retro-ethnic burgundy Pendleton") at the Standard.

The commentator, Memetic Engineer, muses: "Presumably a 'retro-ethnic burgundy Pendleton' is a plaid woollen shirt made by Pendleton Woolen Mills." The pattern of summary/commentary/commentary mixture repeats:

> Alberto, a historian of internalized space, hands Hollis a VR visor tethered to a laptop with which she sees a memory from August 1993, released from time but frozen in space, of a dead celebrity outside the Viper Room.

Memetic Engineer: "Presumably this dead celebrity was not River Phoenix who died on 31st October 1993 outside of Johnny Depp's Viper Room." And so on. As with the Pynchon wiki, we see (and perhaps contribute to) a loving, or at least detailed attention to story details.

How does this sort of project combine social media with storytelling? While not being a story on its own terms, it's a networked book-style approach to commentary on a story. The text is discussed, linked, and processed, all distributed over space and time. John Sutherland argues that "what this means, at the basic level, is a new kind of annotation." Multimedia content is added, from photos to maps. The annotations are contributed by multiple participants, distributed over space and time. Then a social media editor has a role. Unlike most wikis, or "the usual website-based 'everybody pitch in' mess," Sutherland continues, the unknown Node-maestro has:

> channelled the raw material supplied by his volunteers into a sign-posted route through *Spook Country*. . . . Clearly, you need the Googleised data. But then, it needs to be shaped. Not definitively shaped—no reading or interpretation is ever final—but formed into a critical route.[14]

Author Gibson himself observes a different implication: "I have this sense when I write now that the text doesn't stop at the end of the page. . . . Everything is bending towards hypertext now." Tellingly, Gibson goes on to describe social media storytelling and alternate reality gaming: "I suppose I could create web pages somewhere and lead people to them through the text which is an interesting concept. I actually played with doing that in *Spook Country* but I didn't know enough about it."[15]

The networked book model is a mixed form, aggregating created and discovered content. Aggregation is distributed, socially determined, and emergent.

Another model for apprehending distributed storytelling in the social media environment is transmedia storytelling. Henry Jenkins develops this term in *Convergence Culture* (2006), using the *Matrix* movies/world as an exemplary case.[16] In that example, story content is distributed across multiple sites and media: the movie trilogy, an anthology of animated short films, comics, computer games, a massively multiplayer online game, Web content, and additional DVD content. In addition to this material, which was produced by studies and allied teams, *Matrix* fans created their own work. The work included live action performances, an alternate reality game (see Chapter 10), fan fiction, and a swarm of Web-based commentary.

The combination of so many story pieces across that diversity of venues helps build an immersive experience. As one creator explains in Jenkins's account, "People are going to want to go deeper into stuff they care about rather than sampling a lot of stuff." One experiences the *Matrix* stories as individual stories, but can also enter into the broader world from which they apparently draw by experiencing them together, building connections across them. It's a question of distributed worldmaking.[17] J. R. R. Tolkien explained this in terms of what he referred to as "subcreation," the careful construction of a world different from ours in some ways, yet connected to our own closely enough to be taken seriously by readers.[18] Obviously, Tolkien's own Middle Earth series is an example here, being spread out across multiple books, short stories, and one of the world's most committed fan cultures, all before the Internet and recent films expanded it still further. Not all distributed stories allow for this scale of world-building, but the immersive experience occupies one end of a storytelling spectrum.

For the creator of stories, how does this distributed concept affect the composition process? What does it mean to build a narrative in a universe shaped by transmedia and the networked book? We return to this chapter's trio of choices: openly embracing the energetic social world, coping with it, or seceding from it, even temporarily. Each of these has ramifications for practice. The first option requires a creator to learn multiple platforms and to rethink media strategy across these (e.g., What works best in audio, and what in video? How are Facebook's unique affordances maximized?). This choice may mean creating more content than intended in order to address audiences who might not perceive all proscenia upon which the networked book's story unfolds. It means deliberate navigation strategies, requiring some level of human–computer interaction analysis, to shape a reader's possibilities well. Coping with the variety of what the Internet has to offer in terms of social content means forming an editorial/curation policy and practice. An attitude of recognizing some degree of loss of control is recommended—a very different mind-set than that usually assumed for a single book's author (see Chapters 12–14).

If the networked book creator prefers instead to accept rather than actively participate in the social media context, all of the preceding strategies are still activated, but in milder forms. If, for example, a creator recognizes that comments will appear, but does not plan on actively soliciting them or engaging in discussions through comments, an editorial policy is nonetheless important in the face of potential spam and other abuse.

Actively refusing the social media requires a different set of strategy and tactics. A blogger or Web video creator can choose to turn off commenting on posts and uploads. A wiki author can "lock" a page against future edits. A podcast author can publish solely through iTunes, meaning no direct social connection attaches to the work (podcasters seeking social feedback often post to blogs or set up discussion forums). A game designer will not enable social play, such as online multiplayer or multiple inputs to the same device. Selecting mobile devices may be a good option, as non-Web apps and content can be self-contained, linking only internally. Alternatively, physical publication may be preferable, keeping the self-networked story to CD or DVD disks. In all of these cases, the socially minded audience may choose to add other tools and services, but that is their affair. For example, reading a book on Kindle or iPad does not immediately allow access to the open Web for information or reflection. The reader needs to physically turn from those devices to others, such as a laptop or mobile phone's browser.

One intractable question persists in discussions of such modern, distributed hypertext: Where does a story end? If there is no physical story container (book, DVD) nor formal file limitation (a single pdf or mp3), then digital stories appear to have ragged edges, at least from the consumer's perspective. Readers/viewers/listeners may stop before exhausting all content. They might instead navigate away, leaving your Flickr sequence in order to chase down more images from one of its more interesting tags, or Googling a topic your podcast mentions while the pause command winds down to stop. The former is a classic issue for hypertext reading (i.e., How do I finish a branching narrative?), and the latter a perennial issue for Web designers and marketers (hence mobile device apps that don't lead to the Web).

Game studies offers one solution to this consumer-side problem. A game might not be exhausted by a single play session. That is, a round or hand might be completed, but the combinatorial possibilities of the game remain (can one ever finish chess?). The nature of gaming is such that players can exit from it. Play "is 'played out' within certain limits of time and place. It contains its own course and meaning."[19]

From the creation side, we might find new meaning in Paul Valery's famous line about works of art never being finished, only abandoned.

Vershbow observes: "Without the permanence of print, a work is never really finished. Remember those little 'under construction' animations people used to put on their Web sites? A networked book is always under construction, always a work in progress."[20]

The Endless War on Mary Sue

Within this complex domain of networked stories sprawling across diverse platforms and media, certain storytelling forms have surfaced that provide a way to organize content and its social connections. Fan fiction, another Henry Jenkins focus topic, has existed for decades in its modern form.[21] Its attachment to preexisting stories yields recognizable patterns and flows, neatly arranging narratives and materials in a rich social environment. The networked books we've just examined also do this, arguably, but often through different types of source texts.

Modern fan fiction is often seen as dating back to the 1960s and nascent *Star Trek* fandom. Fans famously created stories that reiterated or extended events and details of that TV show's universe, using mimeographed or Xeroxed paper to create "zines." Female authors dominated *Trek* fan fiction, creating new stories with the show's characters. This vibrant fan community helped save the program from cancellation, then laid the groundwork for successive films and further TV series in that world. We can also see fan fiction as dating back to the 1890s, with the advent of British amateur press associations (APAs)—small, self-organized, distributed groups that produced and shared creative work centered on a specific topic. Science-fiction and fantasy fandom started forming its own APAs in the 1930s, such as the Fantasy Amateur Press Association. Those groups resembled modern social media in some startling, microcosmic ways:

> The content of these zines, instead of consisting of the full formal apparatus of editorials and articles and colophons and letter columns, became a much more informal thing, typically entailing some loose personal natter and then a lot of "mailing comments," which is to say, remarks directed to the content of other members' zines in the previous mailing. In fact, as fannish APAs developed, the tendency was for "mailing comments"—which is to say, ongoing conversation—to become the dominant content. This is why some of us whose fannish memories extend back to this era now refer to APAs as the "Very Slow Internet."[22]

Fan fiction took up new communications technologies as they appeared, in order to continue their work: mimeograph to Xerox, Usenet and e-mail, the World Wide Web and Web 2.0.

Currently, Fanfiction.net is the leading exemplar of this storytelling movement.[23] Founded in 1998, Fanfiction.net (FFN) offers readers vast amounts of stories written in preexisting story worlds, from *Jesus Christ Superstar* to *Battlestar Galactica*. The entire body of work is broken down by medium and form: Anime/Manga, Books, Cartoons, Comics, Games, Movies, Plays/Musicals, TV Shows. It's broken down twice, in fact: once for stories in those worlds, and once again for "crossovers" between them. The site is meticulously well organized in terms of content, with multiple categories (genres, age appropriateness, stories, characters) and quick searching. Each work of "fanfic" is cleanly presented, usually as text.

What is the network status of fan fiction? By its nature, any of these stories is embedded in a larger network of original stories. A Mulder–Scully romance, for example, depends on the *X-Files* series and draws on details from that world: characters, events, themes. Stories can also reference, respond to, follow, or iterate other fanfic from the same world. The FFN site facilitates these interstory communications by adding light social media layers to the stories: commenting, linking, aggregation. An individual fanfic is a node in a visible network.

Fan fiction can also partake of remixing and writing across networks, forming sequences of stories and versions. For example, in August 2010, Megan Argo published a short story in the universe of *Doctor Who*, a long-running British science-fiction TV show. "Doctor Who and the Silver Spiral" describes a visit paid by the Doctor and a companion to a spectacular stellar event. "Where, a moment ago, there had been a fairly ordinary-looking large red star, there was now such a bright light that it hurt to look at it. Peering down she saw a jet of material shooting away from the site of the explosion."[24] The story is a basic travel narrative and includes a rather pedagogical discussion of stellar dynamics, using the star named 2007gr as an exemplum.

That pedagogy reflects the story's secondary nature. It is based on a primary text or experience, namely, Dr. Argo's actual astronomical research. Argo was part of the Jodrell Bank team that actually discovered 2007gr's supernova activity. She coauthored a scholarly article on it, but wanted to reach a broader audience as well:

> Megan, 28, a keen fan of British scifi favourite Doctor Who decided to write it up as a fan-fiction adventure to bring home the excitement of the team's finding to ordinary people. . . . The official paper in *Nature* is entitled "A mildly relativistic radio jet from the normal Type Ic Supernova 2007gr" by Paragi et al.[25]

There is a third term in this series after the paper and the fan fiction. The Darker Projects audio production group turned Argo's second text into an audio version, available as a podcast. This remix featured two audio actors voicing the two characters, David Ault and Sieiro Garcia, along with Argo as narrator.[26] This is then a remix of a work of fan fiction, itself a version of a different document. Needless to say, this chain of creation operates across multiple media: text, TV, and audio.

Reading Nodes

Much of the preceding discussion has emphasized the production end of distributed, networked storytelling. We now shift emphasis to consuming networked stories. Since social media interleave production and consumption, this should be understood not as passing from one binary to another, but as a tactical selection of some aspects of the overall problem.

First, finding networked stories occurs in a social framework of discovery and collaboration. As Alan Levine and I note, people do not search by Google (or Bing) alone. We often query our social networks, looking for trusted (or known) sources of information. As we expand the universe of content and population within social media, social search and curation is likely to continue to grow.[27] A friend praises a story on his or her Facebook update or tweets an interesting criticism, and we follow through. A podcaster we admire describes a fine narrative, either out loud or in related digital materials, and perhaps we check it out. Our consumption of networked stories sometimes begins in other networks.

Second, as many proscenia for publishing stories as there are, so there are avenues for consuming them, each with a distinct set of affordances. Taking the example of podcasts, downloading one through iTunes means: a commercial framework; the playlist model; and no immediate social context. We discern the mp3 file in a kind of isolation or in the historical milieu of a record store. If we play the track as an embedded audio file within a Web page, in contrast, the rest of that page's content can influence our listening. Downloading a new podcast through an RSS reader adds a radically different context layer, the set of feeds curated by the reader/ listener/viewer. Time shifting the track leads to yet another context, one driven by the physical environment selected by the listener.

Third, the story's software situation offers multileveled implications for audience experience. Consider the e-book as an example. To begin with, it presents itself in a curious combination of cutting-edge newness—witness the media frenzy over each new hardware reader—and a lack of historicity, although the e-book project dates back to the 1970s and the creation of Project Gutenberg. To create or consume an e-book is to potentially activate both of these temporalities, the shocks of the new and the old, respectively, experimental and sustained. Moreover, e-book file formats are deeply divided. Unlike the universally consumed mp3 for audio, e-books can appear as plain text (.txt), Web page (.html), .pdf, .epub, Kindle (.azw), or Microsoft Reader (.lit). Some e-book software readers only play one of these, such as Microsoft Reader or the Firefox EPUBReader plugin. Additionally, e-book providers are separate and, at times, economically and politically distinct. Project Gutenberg makes books available in the most widely used open formats currently used, namely, .txt and .html. Apple's App Store sells books only for iOS readers. Google's eBookstore and book scanning project offer downloads and streams.

Distributed socially embedded stories draw on the multiple strands of digital storytelling practice, extending and recombining strategies. Multimedia, multivenue digital storytelling may become more prevalent, even normative, as projects are produced and online contributing audiences grow. Consider the involvement of professional writers with recent networked stories like *Shadow Unit* or *The Mongoliad*.[28] These could point the way toward mainstreaming the approach, and they certainly offer interesting stories. Or consider the 2008–2009 novel *Playing for Keeps*. It entered the world through a series of blog posts (with comments), spoken word podcasts (each blogged, with those posts commentable), pdf chapter downloads, and a MySpace background page, not to mention additional blog posts from various content contributors, with these posts housed at their own locations.[29] In this vein, perhaps no book will ever be a single thing again.

CHAPTER NINE

Mobile Devices: The Birth of New Designs for Small Screens

Olga is reading her Bible on the train. As she rides the Metro past Dostoevkskaya station, she thinks again about that troubled writer, never one she liked, and shudders. She thumbs her phone to another New Testament passage. Revelations, she thinks, is better suited to her mood. She also checks to see if Father Piotr has issued any new commentary, but his next podcast is still apparently being revised.

Across the humming Lyublinskaya Line car from Olga, Vladimir continues writing. His story about the bitterness of Russian urban life just keeps growing under his fingers, every hour suggesting another scene, more characters, and somehow a persistent idea for comic interactions. The number of people populating "Notes from the New Underground" is getting hard to manage, and the concept mapping software on this old, flat handheld might be hitting its limit. But something about the sprawling combination of people feels right, somehow suited to Moscow and Petersburg. Vladimir chuckles to himself: yet another Russian tablet novel in the works.

Mobile devices may become the ultimate digital storytelling device. So far, we have addressed stories built and consumed on a variety of devices, including laptops, game consoles, and desktop computers. For this chapter, we focus on the most popular computing platform in the world—the mobile phone—and other related devices.

The mobile phone is a global computing platform used across all nations, languages, and ages. We should expect, if trend lines hold steady, "over five billion mobile subscriptions by the end of 2010."[1] To put that in context, the number of living humans is around 6.8 billion. By 2001, more people owned mobile phones than televisions, with East Asia and northern

Europe taking the initial lead.[2] Personal communication, media consumption, and news spreading have been translated to this popular platform. Social impacts have appeared, and some persisted enough to no longer be called emergent: smartmobs, flashmobs, rumor spreading, and mobile commerce, to name a few.[3] For some, the phone *is* the computer; others may prefer using the phone, with its easier size and apparent simplicity.[4]

Given a combination of mobile connectivity, portable multimedia, steady innovation, and popular usage, it is unsurprising that digital storytelling is already beginning to migrate to the mobile phone universe. Older forms and content are being ported, while new items are appearing.

Everyware

Defining the mobile world requires revisiting some classic frameworks. To begin with, *mobile* is a popular, if ultimately unclear term. Strictly speaking, it should describe both connected and unconnected devices, such as cell phones and mp3 players. Increasingly we assume *mobile* to mean "also wirelessly connected," and rely on *portable* for "not usually connected." *Wireless* itself is a curious term, a negative one, stating what it is not rather than what it is, like *atheist* or *postmodern*. After all, *wireless* simply means not using a wired connection, which can describe a PlayStation Portable without its radio on or an old Discman. *Wireless* really denotes a radio connection, but *radio* is a term usually omitted from discussions.

In the United States, mobile phones are referred to as "cell phones," based on the name of this nation's network structure. The Japanese name is *keitai*, often translated as "personal handyphone." Britain prefers *mobile* as a noun, and the name is sometimes used by other countries as well. *Mobile* seems to be the collapsed term left behind by the others and is the one we will rely on for our discussion.

We can reframe the mobile question by shifting the focus from devices to environment. *Ubiquitous computing* describes a much broader world— one where digital networked devices are not only widespread but blended into the world. The term was coined by the late Mark Weiser, who foresaw our time from the early 1990s with remarkable prescience:

> Hundreds of computers in a room could seem intimidating at first, just as hundreds of volts coursing through wires in the walls did at one time. But like the wires in the walls, these hundreds of computers will come to be invisible to common awareness. People will simply use them unconsciously to accomplish everyday tasks. . . .
>
> The technology required for ubiquitous computing comes in three parts: cheap, low-power computers that include equally convenient displays, a

network that ties them all together, and software systems implementing
ubiquitous applications. Current trends suggest that the first requirement
will easily be met.[5]

Ubiquitous computing (sometimes shortened to "ubicomp") emphasizes
the broader ecosystem aspect of mobile technologies, the combination of
diverse hardware with networks, and digital content moving across them.
It reminds us of the multiple networks and protocols for connecting devices:
Bluetooth, mobile phone, and WiFi, each being developed still further. The
emphasis is placed on multiplicity and interconnections, the matrix or
background against which digital storytelling now occurs.

Given this framework we can appreciate other recent developments,
such as the Internet of things. It is now commonplace to see nontraditional
devices located on networks, like printers and projectors. Assigning Internet Protocol (IP) addresses to objects is no longer remarkable; indeed, the
most salient upper bound to the practice is the current cap on the total
number of allowed IP addresses. Geolocation provides another way to
index physical objects, either through embedded GPS or by manually
assigning latitude and longitude, perhaps with a connection to a mapping
service like Google or Bing Maps. We are rapidly adding a digital layer to
the Earth's surface, a kind of inside-out virtual reality known as augmented
reality (see Chapter 11). Adam Greenfield dubs this emergent digital information order "everyware" and is not alone in pointing out that civilization
is only beginning to grapple with its multitudinous implications for daily
life, policy, business, and culture.[6]

Phone Stories

In such an environment, how do we tell stories?

If we consider a classic mobile phone, with its small screen and keyboard, we might determine that mobile storytelling has a shrunken, if not
dim world of possibilities. "We cannot do much with such a keyboard,"
runs the intuitive response, "nor see more than a little through that screen."
The reality, however, is quite the opposite. Every major topic we have
addressed so far in this book—social media, gaming, the framework of
digital storytelling—becomes accelerated, amplified, and somewhat
mutated by the onset of ubiquitous computing.

The amount of content we generate and consume is accelerated by the
presence of mobile phones. The devices represent an additional point of
Internet contact for those with access to laptops and desktops, and they
allow first-time connectivity for those without. This means more opportunities to contribute content to the social Web through taking and uploading

photos, audio, or video; commenting on or editing sites; writing posts; and updating status through Twitter or Facebook. The social Web is amplified by adding physical information through various means, including social service check-ins, geocoding captured photos and video. The reverse is also true, as connected participants can bring social media content into formerly offline social events. Political meetings, classrooms, and medical clinics are not the same now that those present can hit the Web for fact checking or peer support. All of these behaviors shape gaming as well, starting with increased opportunities to play games.

We can add to games from new locations, too, which brings us to media mutation. The mobile phone is a very different gaming platform than a console, PC, or even a handheld player. This difference means new ways of engaging with games, from touchscreen swiping to geolocation (what do I encounter *here?*) to texting and speech. Social media, too, become warped by the mobile phone experience. Large Web pages have to be rebuilt to fit the far narrower screens of even the biggest phones. Menus need to be reduced and sometimes nested in greater depth. Alternatively, applications are built to offer a different way into a site's content. More mobile phones means more and different social media.

For example, the Choose Your Own Adventure stories we discussed in Chapter 2 have been resurrected and reimagined as iPhone apps. It's a natural combination of gaming with digital storytelling:

> Instead of turning to a particular page to make a choice, the U-Ventures apps allow the reader to tap the screen and enjoy, with sound, light and other special effects—music and alien voices, for example—added to the titles, as well as new variations and endings dreamed up by [author Edward] Packard. Enhancements include readers having to remember codewords and type them in to affect the course of the story.

Interestingly, these stories may change tempo, given the different creative flexibility the mobile phone offers over print: "Packard is particularly excited about 'very fast-paced segments,' which would have taken up too much space in a printed book. 'There's no such problem in cyberland, and we take advantage of that.'"[7]

At a less technologically sophisticated level, but a commercially successful one, are Japanese text novels. These are meant to be read on keitai and consist entirely of text. Short sentences and paragraphs are the norm:

> The novels are . . . easy to read—most would pose no challenge to a ten-year-old—with short lines, simple words, and a repetitive vocabulary. Much

of the writing is hiragana, and there is ample blank space to give the eyes a rest. . . . Quick and slangy, and filled with emoticons and dialogue, the stories have a tossed-off, spoken feel.

Given that the medium is text-only, some formal design innovations are already the norm:

> "You're not trying to pack the screen," a cell-phone novelist named Rin told me "You're changing the line in the middle of sentences, so where you cut the sentence is an essential part. If you've got a very quiet scene, you use a lot more of those returns and spaces. When a couple is fighting, you'll cram the words together and make the screen very crowded."[8]

These text novels have become commercially successful enough to appear in print. More impressive for a non-Japanese audience is the fact that some are not only readable on a phone, but were *written* on them. Mobile phones can be used in the interstices of daily life, in between activities demanding our attention, freeing up minutes for access. If, according to Dana Goodyear, "The cell-phone novel, or *keitai shosetsu*, is the first literary genre to emerge from the cellular age," then we should expect more developments like this.[9]

Beyond these mutated story forms, mobile phones also increase the number of opportunities for us to view, read, or listen to traditional forms, be they Center for Digital Storytelling (CDS)-style videos, Flickr image sequences, podcasts, or text. Joseph Esposito suggests a different form of storytelling may surface via mobile phones during a certain kind of reader's time

> spent waiting for a plane, a doctor, or for a meeting to begin. That's a huge number of minutes in any day; a good portion of our lives is wasted while we are waiting for the main course to arrive. . . . How about the 10-minute crack? Five minutes? Think of your own day: How often are you simply waiting, doing nothing?

Esposito calls this "interstitial writing" and explores its possible form in some detail. How to organize the kind of material readable in such micro-bursts of time? Not long, sustained stories:

> More likely short items will be strung together in an anthology; the thesis of the anthology ("brief bursts about the new administration"; "101 short poems about transistors and current") will suffuse each item with a sense of being part of a whole.

Esposito is skeptical that a serial strategy would work to link together such small bits of text:

> it is improbable that item A will lead serially to item B, to item C, and so forth. It would simply be hard to gather the narrative in our minds if it were written in this way. More likely each episode will have a beginning and an end—and then cut to another episode, which may be built around a different time or place or another character. All the pieces get assembled in our minds, five minutes at a time.[10]

App World

When mobile phones approach the Internet, they have two ways to connect, broadly speaking. One is to use a specially designed Web browser, perhaps a mobile version of an already established one, such as Fennec for Firefox.[11] This approach presents challenges, though, as we've noted, since a phone's screen can display only a piece of most Web pages, which are designed with laptops and desktops in mind. Web content owners can opt to produce parallel versions of their materials, but that requires substantial redesign and rethinking.

The other option is a mobile-specific application, or "app."[12] Such programs are very narrowly focused on specific tasks or services, such as displaying the weather, giving access to a reference work, or playing a game. The launch of Apple's App Store triggered a huge creative boom, as developers sought to outdesign each other for market and mindshare. Two hundred thousand apps have passed the store's approval process as of this writing. Google and Research in Motion followed suit with app centers for their Android platform and BlackBerry smartphones, respectively.[13]

Storytelling through mobile apps has taken several forms. One is the e-book-as-app format, where a book or group of books is simply made available as a downloadable app. This format differs from importing an e-book file in its publication system, as well as formatting. Another app style uses the unique affordances of a mobile phone to influence a story's dynamics. *Ruben and Lullaby* is a good example of this style, where the story concerns an argument between two lovers.[14] The user advances the story by touching the screen to alter a character's stance, or by shaking the entire phone, which activates its accelerometer, changing a character's mood. Both of these changes are shown by different drawings of each person's face. A musical track plays, changing to reflect different stages of the conversation. The reader/listener/ audience/player can thereby drive the discussion's outcome.

Apps can also blur the classic divide between game and story by integrating game mechanics into chunks of story. The *Gamebook Adventures* and *Fighting Fantasy* series, for example, represent a synthesis that uses Choose Your Own Adventure-style pages (or screens) connected by reader choice or random event outcomes.[15]

Apps also combine game, story, and the social. For example, *Hitchery* begins by letting users represent themselves by quickly creating and shaping low-resolution avatars. Next, a second user downloads that cartoonish representation to their smartphone. That device then superimposes the first user's avatar on the camera view display, displaying it on whatever the camera sees. In *Hitchery* terms, the first user's avatar has now "hitched a ride" on the second user's phone, which the app renames a "bus." Game mechanics kick in as player two can win game points by conveying player one's avatar to different locations. Social mechanics appear as the second player receives reactions from the first based on where the former conveys the latter's representation.

Hitchery's structure offers a useful sampling of mobile technology affordances, especially as they represent key changes from flip phones or single-function, disconnected cameras. For example, using a mobile phone's geolocation service (through GPS) enables easy and quick geotagging of "bus" visits. The phone's ability to connect content to social media lets users rapidly share location photos with superimposed avatars. Combining these over time yields a sequence of geographically identified photo-visits, carrying the avatar character through space—in short, creating a basic narrative.

Put another way, players collaborate in sending their characters on voyages. These are characters in at least a minimal sense, shaped by association with their creators, the visual details of the avatars, and a sense of reacting to a series of different settings. This is where the app as game adds another feature, the insertion of non-player characters (NPCs). Player characters appear alongside "robot hitchers," allowing the possibility of imaginative social interaction between these avatars.[16]

Games are, unsurprisingly, a reliable area for apps creativity. Puzzle, role-playing, and point-and-click games have been steadily appearing, from *iBlast Moki* to *Zen Bound*. Games from other platforms have been ported over to phones, starting with older ones, like *Monkey Island* and *Beneath a Steel Sky*. Board games, card games, dice games, sports, and other predigital game types have been translated to the handheld. At least one interactive fiction platform, *Frotz*, has been ported. Role-playing games have been created, narrowed down in focus to fit the interface, including *Chaos Rings*, *Ravensword*, *Xenonia*, and *Hybrid: Eternal Whisper*.

Such games show ingenuity in maximizing the affordances of phone interfaces, much as we saw large-scale games doing with very different interfaces. *The Secret of Spyder Manor*, for example, creates a very touch-oriented system of gameplay. The user is represented by a spider and flicks the semi-eponymous hero from point to point.

Alternatively, the mobile Web might persist alongside the world of apps. Mobile Web sites—versions of desktop sites optimized for mobile devices' smaller window and reduced functionality—already exist. Accordingly, stories told through mobile sites tend to use narrowed-down presentations. For example, PortableQuest lets users replay classic interactive fictions in a screen barely 100 pixels wide.

As we saw with Twitter in Chapter 4, these focused forms drive readers (or players) to zero in on content, heightening the value of word choice and some layout details.[17]

Dedicated storytelling apps have begun to appear. StoryCorps has released one, for example, that emphasizes content delivery. Sonic Pix, in contrast, lets users build slideshows out of images and other media.[18]

Readers and E-readers

An alternative approach to reading stories on mobile devices was reborn when Amazon launched the Kindle e-reader. Portable digital readers, such as the Rocket and various Sony devices, had been marketed from the 1990s on without achieving significant market penetration. The Kindle, however, resurrected the e-reader market from its launch in 2007. Its apparent success has triggered a series of hardware competitors, such as the Nook and Que.

Reasons for the Kindle's success are largely based on its ecosystem. Unlike many earlier devices, which required a cable connection, the Kindle connects wirelessly to the world. This wireless connectivity allows users to access the specially designed mobile Amazon bookstore and quickly download content from it. As the mobile phone opens up more opportunities for owners to consume and create content, so this single connection increases a Kindle user's chances of buying books. Additionally, the device hooked into the preexisting Amazon online store, meaning users could work within a system they were already likely to know. Moreover, Amazon next released a Kindle application for many other devices and platforms, from the desktop PC to the iPhone. This app is synched at Amazon's servers, meaning a user can continue reading the same book across several devices, picking up on an Android phone from where they left off on a laptop.

Why read a story on such a device? What affordances does the Kindle or succeeding platforms offer? A series of benefits have appeared over the past few years. First, e-books tend to cost less than their physical counterparts, leading to a cost savings over time. As one American political group put it, "While the upfront hardware cost of providing a Kindle-like device to every child would necessitate a high front-end investment, costs for eText-books themselves would quickly produce a savings compared with print textbooks."[19] Most books have free sample downloads, and more than a few books are actually free, often because the text is in the public domain.[20] Second, e-readers offer a physical benefit by digital storage. Being able to carry dozens, even hundreds of books with the weight of a thin plastic wedge appeals to travelers, among others. Institutions as well as individuals can benefit from this space saving.[21] Third, the Kindle's wireless connection means automatic subscription updates are pushed to the device, along with book errata. These subscription updates include magazines and journals along with Web news sources and blogs, without the necessity of WiFi or a direct connection. All of these factors appeal to people wanting less paper in their lives and have combined to apparently boost Amazon's e-book sales past its hardcovers'.[22]

The visual experience is also worth noting. The e-ink display differs from a typical computer or phone LCD screen, presenting a muted color palette (grayscale) without glare. This display means the device can be read under both bright sunlight and artificial illumination. Amazon also claims, and apparently at least some buyers agree, that the experience is closer to that of reading print than is currently available through digital screens. Moreover, the physical e-reader makes e-books "flowable," capable of being rapidly resized or having the font changed. The benefits for readers with eye problems are obvious, but artistic uses have yet to be made.

On the other hand, the Kindle also serves as a good example of the many limitations of e-readers. Its physical interface is unusual, the first version receiving criticism for being awkward in some hands. The display can be problematic, since e-ink resolves more slowly than content does on an LCD screen and does not display color. The hardware cost was substantial for several years, in the hundreds of dollars; while lower-cost handsets have appeared recently, fancier models still require significant investment. Annotation of texts is difficult, involving several menus and lacking interlinear writing.[23] Another Kindle strength also has problems, as many of its cataloged books have digital rights management (DRM) code attached, limiting their usage. The Kindle platform is closed to outside intervention, not allowing new creative work to be imposed without editorial permission, much like a console game or peer-reviewed journal.

Do e-readers let us read digital stories? So far, they only let us read stories in a specific digital format, which isn't the same thing. The Kindle's success and the subsequent rebirth of the e-reader market suggest that these might well be new venues for reading digital stories. One unusual feature might appeal to the creator: the e-reader isolates the reading experience from the rest of the world. Neither the Kindle nor other similar devices support multitasking. The reader has to physically turn to another device to, say, browse the Web for information about a setting. While this digital isolation has some drawbacks, it could well facilitate a classic model of reading, where the story and its audience connect by themselves, contextualized only by the imagination.

The New Tablets

Another mobile device area has recently opened up, offering still more options for storytelling. Tablet computing has been imagined since Alan Kay first conceived of a "dynabook" two generations ago.[24] Weiser imagined a lightweight tablet in his ubiquitous computing work. Microsoft launched a Tablet PC laptop variant in 2002, letting users interact with a PC through a stylus. Several hardware makers produced Tablet devices, which won market niches. The appeal of this concept is intuitive, recollecting our experiences with paper and books, while also resonating with slates, Etch-a-Sketches, and various devices in science-fiction stories (the newspad in *2001: A Space Odyssey*, for instance). The Tablet PC platform is old enough now that Gartner Research can refer to it as the "traditional tablet."[25]

In 2010, Apple released its iPad, a touchscreen-based computer based on the iOS operating system, popularized by the iPhone and Touch. A commercial success, the iPad elicited more app development along the lines already established by the iOS series. Some apps were revised and made available for the new platform ("ported"), while other new ones were built from scratch to take advantage of the iPad's nature. Penguin and Moving Tales have created interactive children's books, for example, which allow readers to animate creatures with a fingertip.[26]

Ever since 2010, iPad apps and content have steadily appeared. Other tablets, notably based on Google's Android operating system, have also built up a content ecosystem. Tablets are now serious rivals for mobile phones and laptops as digital storytelling platforms. As digital storyteller and instructor Doug Reilly anticipates: "I can imagine a student or group of students spending a morning scripting and shooting raw material for a digital story onsite, spending the afternoon in a cafe putting the digital story together on an iPad, and showing it in the evening at a group session."[27]

Living in Science Fiction

Many of the technologies and practices we've described in this book have already been depicted within stories and in other media. Mobile devices are a fine example of this, having been a staple for movies, TV, and science fiction for some time. In visual media, they date back to the first *Star Trek* series, with its "tricorders" and communicators now realized with handheld devices. Mobile computing imagining appeared even earlier in print science fiction. By now film, TV, and print audiences are probably accustomed to plots turning on characters losing connectivity (a horror movie trope), agents or criminals tracking someone through mobile devices (mysteries and crime stories), love affairs carried on by phone, and so on.

While science fiction sometimes leads the charge in imagining mobile devices that the world eventually builds, it can fall behind. For example, in Chapter 4 we noted Bruce Sterling's blog story, "Dispatches from a Hyperlocal Future." It ends with a celebration of a historical shift in device usage:

> 07.10.2017 | Washington, DC
> I finally dumped my last laptop today. That big LCD. The full-size keyboard. Like a ball and chain, brother!
> From now on, Harvey Feldspar's Geoblog will emerge from a gizmo the size and shape of a Moleskine notebook. My new Senseo-Transicast 3000 is everything palmtops and cell phones have been struggling to become. I can already feel this device completely changing my life.[28]

Yet this shift had already begun happening in 2010 with the explosion in larger-screen smartphones. Indeed, Feldspar's triumphant device switch already appears antiquarian in the actual year 2017.

CHAPTER TEN

Chaotic Fictions; or, Alternate Reality Games

You are surfing the Web late at night, letting work and entertainment take turns with your attention, when a video clip makes you sit up in surprise. It's a commercial for an upcoming game, the next in a series you know. The characters are familiar, the setting interesting, and the plot, well, the kind of exuberant fighting you expect.

It's the trailer's finale that causes you to rub your eyes, blink hard, and replay the video. When the game's hero stands triumphantly upon a pile of rubble, clouds looming majestically above him and Wagnerian music soaring aloft, the studio's URL appears on the bottom of the image—then twitches. The URL looks fuzzy, appears again, but as the wrong address. It twitches once more, then returns to the current corporate HTTP://.

You watch for a third time and carefully pause when the anomaly returns. The twitch-fuzz-replace-return motion takes almost exactly one second, and you can write down the phantom address. It seems to point to a Web site about . . . bees? Was the trailer hacked?

Expecting not, you type in the rogue address, thinking that you've come across a production in-joke, maybe, and find, after all, a Web site about bee raising. The design smacks of the late 1990s, with thickly drawn menus, an animated .gif in one header, and an honest-to-God MIDI file playing a buzzing in the background. This makes no sense. What happened to the Halo game?

Suddenly the screen jumps and a black box appears, seemingly stamped over the apiary page. White typewriter characters appear in all caps: METASTASIS COUNTDOWN, and a string of numbers.

Welcome to the rabbit hole.[1]

This book has so far embraced both fiction and nonfiction as storytelling modes. Most of the examples we've chosen have clearly fallen into one category or the other. In this chapter, we turn to a storytelling form that makes its home right on the boundary between fiction and non-: the alternate reality game, or ARG.

An ARG is a combination of story and game. Its contents are distributed throughout the world, usually online, perhaps with physical locations as well. Users play the game by discovering bits of content and discerning the story to which those items belong, while comparing notes with other players. Collaboratively, collectively, players hunt for new pieces of the story, sometimes solving puzzles to do so. The pieces are usually not formally identified as part of a game but have been quietly inserted into the world without fanfare or label. Eventually, the game ends, often by a formal announcement from the game designers, known as "puppet masters."

The first major ARG was nicknamed "The Beast" and was created as marketing for the movie *A.I.* (2001). There was no formal announcement of the game's launch. Instead, a design team worked to create a large science-fiction story based on the movie. Much of this story appeared in the form of Web pages. Gameplay began with the release of *A.I.*'s first trailer, which featured a credit for one Jeanine Salla, "artificial intelligence consultant." Googling her name led to an academic home page for a university—which didn't actually exist. There were a series of pages for both Professor Salla and Bangalore World University ("one of the finest institutions of higher learning in the solar system"), none of which identified itself as part of a game or in any way affiliated with the *A.I.* film. Pages contained e-mail addresses, from which, if contacted, replies would come. Phone numbers were also published, connecting to voice mail.[2] The pages appeared to be real, in other words.

People (not "players" yet) interested in this odd bit of Web content began to share their thoughts online. Another trailer appeared with a different clue based on highlighted letters. As the movie's release approached, more clues surfaced, and the interested investigators formed the Cloudmakers group to pool their intelligence. The various pieces of Web content, e-mail conversation, and phone messages formed a story about murder and politics, turning on fundamental questions of human nature. The game designers finally came forward from "behind the curtain" to explain what they'd created and to reveal the game's identity at last. Players looked for new games, other creators were inspired to try their own "collective detective" stories, and the ARG genre commenced in earnest.

ARGs continue to be created, discovered, played, and evaluated. Many are tied to businesses, including Hollywood films and automotive companies, while some are independently created. Major themes, issues, clichés, and design approaches have been established. The principle of a game not appearing to be one, the famous "This Is Not a Game" concept, is one such chestnut of debate. The Web-based community Unfiction anchors a great deal of discussion.[3] Other social media are routinely used, including wikis to aggregate game information, blogs to share thoughts about the form, and an ARGNetcast for news and reflections.[4] Web 2.0 technologies are also used to provide game content, such as blogs or MySpace pages that establish characters. Several companies have formed to provide ARGs, notably 42entertainment and Universe Creation 101.[5] Since the run of *The Beast*, ARGs have grown in visibility, if still remaining marginal or quirky in the larger gaming and digital storytelling worlds. As a kind of high-water mark of respectability, Jane McGonigal, one of the leading ARG designers, recently gave a TED talk about the political implications of ARGs.[6]

This cursory review of the field should make it clear that ARGs exist on the boundary of games and social media, telling stories across those two domains of technology and practice. They don't appear out of nowhere, however. We noted in Chapter 2 that game-like literature has been created for some time, brought to greater prominence by innovative late 20th-century print and digital work. Several scholars ground digital gaming and storytelling in a far more distant past: the medieval and classical heritage of riddle games and tales. Nick Montfort, for one, starts with Babylon and India, then works forward through Anglo-Saxon literature to Freud and Tolkien.[7]

Once we are alerted to the presence of stories playing on the fiction/nonfiction boundary ("this is not a game"), we can find many antecedents from the long history of stories.[8] Literature includes a share of hoaxes, fictional authors, stunts, and guessing games (e.g., the *roman a clef*). A recent American presidency was satirized by a pseudonymous author, who was subsequently outed, as a major reporter: *Primary Colors* (1996). Edgar Allan Poe perpetrated several hoaxes, most ambitiously the *Narrative of Arthur Gordon Pym of Nantucket* (1838), which claimed on its face to be a real, true-to-life story of exploration (this is not a game). Horace Walpole published *The Castle of Otranto* in 1765 without his name, instead offering the splendidly Gothic name Onuphrio Muralto; the text begins with documents asserting its realism.

More recent examples include *The Report from Iron Mountain* (1967), Alan Sokal's 1996 *Social Text* hoax, and *The Codex Seraphinianus*, an illustrated tome without clear provenance. The latter includes a running text written in an alphabet never seen elsewhere, which provoked cryptanalysis. Its images are unusual, a mixture of the eccentric, the macabre, and the surreal. The *Codex* appeared without provenance from its first printing (1981), like a document from a parallel world or a lost story. After years of attempted explanations, the book's creator was ultimately unmasked as Italian designer Luigi Serafini. Embedding such a creative work in an atmosphere of investigation turned a bagatelle into a mystery, boosting its likely audience.

Film history includes its own share of hoaxes, from movies purporting to be snuff films (*Faces of Death*) to the mondo series of quasi-documentaries. *The Blair Witch Project* (1999) won fame and notoriety in part by its meticulously staged documentary materials.

Proto-ARG and ARG-style plots have appeared *within* fiction as well, constituting something of a very small, quiet subgenre. In 1905, G. K. Chesterton published "The Tremendous Adventures of Major Brown," wherein a retired military man unwittingly plays an adventure game staged to make him feel alive once more. A century-old fictional ancestor to 42entertainment, the Adventure and Romance Agency, Ltd., stages events, hires actors to play villains and endangered good folk, and gives secret clues and messages, all without revealing the thing to be a game or play until the end.

This plot was echoed in a 1997 film, *The Game* (directed by David Fincher). Again, we see an unhappy man (although he doesn't think he is, in this case) who plays a game staged into his life. Nicholas Van Orton receives secret messages, has his house vandalized, finds and loses people, is chased and exiled, all in the service of exploring a story, which turns out to be the tale of him becoming a better person. No clear boundaries to the game are ever established; part of the movie's pleasure involves trying to determine what is part of the fiction and what is part of the *other* fiction.

More such fictions succeeded Chesterton's. In the 1930s, H. P. Lovecraft delighted in giving his characters a bibliography mixing real with unreal books. The fearsome *Necronomicon* appears alongside Margaret Alice Murray's (fairly innocent) *The Witch Cult in Western Europe* (1921). In "Tlon, Uqbar, Orbis Tertius" (1940), Jorge Luis Borges describes how a group of academics create a mock encyclopedia for a fictional world and then, as a prank, sneak parts of it into the real world.

The ARG antecedent with the highest reputation today is probably John Fowles's *The Magus* (1965, revised 1977). As with Van Orton and Brown, the life of the main character, Urfe, is problematic. He is lifted out of it by what one character refers to as a "godgame." His reality is revised as people appear, change identity, and win his emotional attachment. If the game shapes Urfe's world, its god, the magician of the title, is not seen as consistently in charge. The design and rule of the game is unclear until the end, and perhaps not even then. As a player, Urfe investigates the boundaries of his game, researching, questioning, invading properties, and trying to take an active role in what he sees as a kind of theater. Like *The Game*'s Van Orton, *The Magus*'s hero endures emotional and physical extremity, climaxing in a series of magical rites. The final scenes turn on the extent to which Urfe has developed as a character in the game, as a human being in the novel.

Hiding a Story

If alternate reality games are currently being played and we can find a storytelling prehistory to them, how do they function in practice? We can begin with a small-scale example and then explore two different games more fully.

Consider the Bad Wolf Web site.[9] It appears to be a fan site for the British TV series *Doctor Who*. Against a blue background, a Flash animation gradually displays a fierce-looking wolf drawing, while an eerie music track plays. There is little else to this page apart from a short menu of options: "BAD WOLF" (apparently that page, since unlinked) | CLUES | THEORIES | REVELATIONS | UNSOLVED | DISCLAIMER | DOCTOR WHO. An ARG player would investigate this page for clues, looking at the HTML source code, for example. Finding nothing extra to go on, this player would click to the other pages indicated on the menu.

Clues, Theories, Revelations, and Unsolved each offer tidbits of content from the relevant *Doctor Who* story arc (2005). The *Doctor Who* link leads to the franchise's official BBC page. None of these offers any clues to additional layers of story. The Disclaimer page is where an ARG player succeeds. On the face of it an ordinary legal disclaimer, this one has some unusual content.[10] After a description of the site and a jab at corporate influence over the Internet comes a humorous coda:

> Please don't email us to ask what Bad Wolf means. We honestly don't know.
> If you're concerned by the thought that the universe has been irrevocably altered by an enormous experiment in neuro-linguistic programming, then just tell yourself "The Bad Wolf is not real. The Bad Wolf is not real. The Bad Wolf is not real."

The casual Web user probably will not read this far. The exceptions, and the determined ARG players, will possibly appreciate the humor and also wonder if "neuro-linguistic programming" is a plot point for the TV series: an example of transmedia storytelling. The ARG player may also wonder if said programming means the opening page's background audio had some ulterior motive, and return to analyze it.

Farther down the Disclaimer page, and higher up on any index of suspicious Web browsing, we might notice a line of invisible text. The font color has been changed to that of the background (blue, #000066), hiding the words in plain sight. Highlighting the entire page's text with a cursor or viewing the HTML source code reveals this line, very different from the preceding: "Rose—Are you there? Are you getting this? You've got the point, haven't you? Rose . . . ?" Viewers of the show could well interpret this as a message from the Doctor aimed at his companion for that season, Rose. Novices might be intrigued, confused, or startled. Either way, the page content has changed before the viewer's eyes, shifting in tone and implication. A rabbit hole has perhaps opened up beneath our feet.

Not all ARG clues are hidden texts, but the background principle of careful attention to content is fairly general. The next step in our example would be for the player to consult with others to see if they had noticed the same text; if it had changed; if it was, in fact, part of a game and not something other. That practical, social connection is a key part to ARG play. One may well decide not to partake, but the Unfiction forums will be busy, a wiki may be live, and somebody is probably blogging about it. That undefined sense of the game boundary, too—is this a game, or something else?—is another key part to experiencing an ARG story.

What does an ARG look like in its full life cycle? Let's examine one example, often called the "Metacortechs game" or *Project MU*. It ran in the fall of 2003 and features a good number of ARG elements. It is often cited as one of the more significant games, yet was created without a large budget.[11] What follows is a narrative of experiencing it fairly closely.

"Metacortex: Serving you into the 21st Century." This legend greeted visitors to an innocuous-seeming corporate Web site, supposedly for the Metacortex Company.[12] The URL had appeared on some discussion boards devoted to the *Matrix* franchise, then circulated in the ARG community. Metacortex was the name of the company "Thomas Anderson" worked for in the first (and best) film (1999). An initial survey of the site revealed what could have been either a marketing ploy created by the studios or an ambitious piece of fan art. A news tab showed the latest in Metacortex's operations, products focused on a gaming/VR rig, a mission statement, contact information,[13] and so on. Searching for Neo's character in the employee database yielded a wry line about him being on extended leave. Signing up to be a beta tester for the Metacortex virtual reality hardware quickly yielded an acknowledgment, showing someone or a program to be functioning behind the scenes.

Once the ARG community began its collaborative detection work, however, things began to get interesting, as characters and other organizations were discovered through it. The company page prominently featured as employee-of-the-month one Beth McConnell, who maintained her own personal/research site. This site documented her interest in the paranormal; it did not resemble the company's site in any way, nor did it mark its game nature in any way. The Metacortex site also proclaimed that it published a personal productivity/knowledge management product, *Metadex*. Digging through the Web for that fictional product revealed several sample sites. They were protected by passwords, which ARG players eventually guessed. As with McConnell's pages, these sites also lacked any similarity to the Metacortex one and showed no signs of being part of a game.

One cracked *Metadex* site included links to two missing persons sites: "he is missing" and "she is missing." Each of those sites demonstrated yet another design style. Coincidentally, "he" and "she" were both built by the MetaOffice Suites Web authoring tool, as discovered by looking through their source codes (content="MetaCortex MetaPage V1.0.3 for Windows"). Other projects turned out to be part of the Metacortex Web: an undersea hotel construction project, Aquapolis; Underscore Web Hosting; the Cascade Vortex. Still another site, PaintOver, portrayed no entity but a puzzle, encouraging visitors to solve it. Once solved, PaintOver congratulated winners, then added a new one. PaintOver came close to breaking the ARG's fourth wall, somewhat openly engaging with players through codes and the occasional chat.

As the Metacortex world grew—or rather, as players' understanding of it expanded—characters began to develop. McConnell pursued her occult interests, finding out ominous news about her employer, being betrayed by a friend, then learning startling truths about the world thanks to a mysterious visitor. Said betrayer gloated, then suffered a horrible death. Dina and Ethan Nekodas saw their lives rapidly fall apart, as their memories began to be revealed for something other than what they were. Their son, who had tried to help them by hacking, suffered a catastrophic sense of failure and withdrew from the story, perhaps suicidally.

Players experienced these events in several ways:

- First, by repeatedly checking on Web content for updates—new blog posts, changes to Web pages
- Second, by learning about developments from other players, either at Unfiction or elsewhere

- Third, by discovering new spaces and exploring them for backstories
- Fourth, by occasionally interacting with characters. When Beth McConnell learns the truth about the world—that she is living in a simulation—she chatted online with players for a period, answering questions. This breaking of the fourth wall was well suited to the character's shattered sense of reality.

On November 22, players who had signed up for the Metacortex beta testing were e-mailed that things were ready to go and given a URL to proceed. Players clicked on the link, only to find it a credits page, signaling the game's end. Afterward, the puppet masters gradually spoke about the game creation process.[14]

It is difficult to summarize the *Project MU* game and story in a short space, given its levels of plot, technology, and social media environment complexity. It is less challenging to explain the emotional engagement it elicited from myself, as a player. I greeted the closing link with a mixture of surprise, sadness at the end of a pleasing story, and respect at the elegance of closure. Characters were well written and represented across multimedia, summoning the sense of personal investment we've come to expect from good characterization: realistic persons, an emotional charge, and transformation over time. The timing of the story also played a role in winning player investment. As with successful serial-form stories, we learned to keep checking back for changes and new directions in the story. The complexity of the world established a rich and credible setting. At each step, mysteries appeared to lure us onward. Revelations were rewarding. I can still recall the shiver I felt when I first saw the image series depicting the fate of Metacortex's CEO, brought to ground by an Agent.

Fans of the *Matrix* series also enjoyed this game as a work of fan fiction. The Metacortex site and some subsequent content have all the hallmarks of fanfic: attention to details, key characters addressed (Agents), and extrapolation into new directions. The game also provides corporate satire through this channel whereby boilerplate business and technology language becomes sinister in the story context:

> The MetaVR system breaks new ground in providing absolutely immersive, lifelike, convincing gaming like nothing ever seen before.
>
> "Our new MetaVR system will take gaming a quantum leap beyond anything that our competitors have been able to create so far," stated Steven Walsh, CEO of MetaCortex. "We're on the cutting edge of the gaming marketplace. We're very excited about the worldwide anticipation for this new system, and we've put a lot of effort into putting more of what players want into the MetaVR. Already, we are building substantial inventories in anticipation of consumer demand."

"Absolutely lifelike" for "worldwide anticipation" indeed.

This game ran in late 2003 and marks a step in alternate reality gaming's rise. The technologies it used were light, yet effective: blogs, images, relatively simple Web pages, and sound files. The *Project MU* team publicly documented its work in the *Metaurchins* e-book, addressing project management, timing issues, workflow, writing, and what they hoped to achieve.[15] Since then, a small ARG industry has continued to grow, with some games tied to major media events, such as *The Dark Knight, Lost* and *Heroes*. Two political games have been run, *World without Oil* (2007) and *Evoke* (2010),[16] each seeking to inform players and to cause them to become politically active.[17] Business models have been experimented with, including selling cards with extra clues (*Perplex City*) and making a clothing line (Edoc Laundry).

The ARG movement continues to debate design and strategy issues. How much of the genre will be driven by marketing games that rely on businesses for significant funding? Should games become more accessible to a wider audience, using less challenging puzzles than those requiring steganography or advanced digital audio analysis? The odd-sounding awkward acronym has also been questioned.

Sean Stacey offers a new approach to thinking about ARGs, which can be applied to other digital storytelling forms. Stacey views "chaotic fiction" materials as arranged along three axes: authorship, coherence, and ruleset. Game practice can then be positioned along these lines, between extreme poles. *Authorship* refers to content creation: what proportion of gameplay content is created by puppet masters versus how much players provide. *Coherence* describes how clear the boundaries of game materials are. *Ruleset* ranges from strongly determined player options, like a Choose Your Own Adventure, at one extreme, to free play and creativity.[18]

We can apply this three-dimensional model to many other forms of social media storytelling. Social media narratives, for example, depend on some proportional mix of content authorship. The Penguin wiki novel situates itself toward one pole, with nearly all story material generated by users. Podcasts, considered as the audio files alone, occupy a position on the other end of the axis, being produced by the podcaster or production team. A blog story like the *Pepys Diary* is positioned near the middle, depending on how much value a reader assigns to comments, which tend to outnumber post contents by word count.

Coherence applies to boundary determinations: Just where does a social media story end? Do we include blog commentaries beyond an original site or a *Wikipedia* entry? Does an embedded video clip extend the story?

Ruleset offers another way of applying game thinking to non-game-based stories in social media. We can glimpse rules in the operation of community norms within a Web 2.0 story. Some of these are practical, following the established practices of virtual community facilitation dating back to the 1980s—norms of respectful behavior, disallowed language, allowing links, and anonymity.[19] Some norms are specific to discussions of story, such as how to handle spoilers or story-specific terms. Others apply to story performance: Should a blog commentator adopt a role within the story or write as an observant spectator?

With this kind of analytical approach, we can discern ARG-like elements in other digital stories. The *Dionaea House* story, which we discussed in Chapter 4, begins with what looks like a rabbit hole, from the ARG perspective, with multiple points of possible investigation:

> Jennifer, friends and family of Mark,
>
> As promised, here are copies of the correspondence I received from Mark over the course of the last month. For the most part, I have merely copied and pasted them from my email application.
>
> As you'll read, he requested this, in hopes that you'll better understand why he did what he did.
>
> I made this site because it's the most efficient way to share Mark's emails with all of you. I'm not advertising this to anyone. But I do think it would be wise to pass this URL along to anyone who may help with the investigation. As I collect more information, from various sources, I'll update this site to keep it an accurate record. I'll have that link at the end of the series as well.
>
> If you need to speak with me, Jen has my number. Thank you for your patience, and again, I am profoundly sorry.
>
> —Eric[20]

It opens with a call to characters both named and unnamed ("friends *and* family"). ARG history leads us to search for Web content about them. Eric says he edited the content, copying it "for the most part"—is there something we should be looking for, like Eric's e-mails partially copied in Mark Chondry's, or the openly redacted phone number from September 12?[21] ARG practice follows the rest of social media in nudging us to check for preexisting commentary on this story and its mysteries.

Out of the Rabbit Hole

What can storytellers and audiences learn from ARGs that could be applicable to other types of stories? ARGs clearly reveal new techniques for engaging audiences and collaboration.

First, creating a sense of mystery is powerful for mobilizing audience interest. Reading through the opening posts on Unfiction for any ARG or potential game shows a nearly kinetic level of excitement, as the energy of discovery triggers brainstorming and multiple explorations. The "rabbit hole" reference is an apt one, as it suggests not only mystery but also accelerating pace. That excitement leads to social media contributions, too—from wiki resources to players entering game fictions through comments and phone calls.

Second, there is power in creative invisibility. Hiding a production team as puppet masters, acting only from behind the scenes, removes them from discussion as part of the story. The story becomes the main focus, not its tellers. The act of creators revealing themselves then serves a different narrative purpose, as a kind of coda or reward to players.

Third, while we experience an ARG serially, most of a game's content is produced in parallel, as it were: preloaded before release. Much of the media production, from writing to videography to Web design, needs to be completed before the rabbit hole is opened to the world. This sequence is very sane project management, freeing up the creative team for improvisation and interaction during the game. Speaking as the *Dracula* novel blogger, I can testify to the importance of having blog materials ready before the story's main run.

Fourth, ARGs remind us as storytellers to learn the art of lack of control. ARG players energetically explore their game's dimensions, and not always in the ways intended. Clues can be missed and, if so, need to be reiterated or to have their failure compensated for. The audience can take a narrative at a faster speed than creators planned on. User-generated content can astonish or appall. ARGs teach creators when to hold onto a game as puppet masters, and also when to let go of the strings.

CHAPTER ELEVEN

Augmented Reality: Telling Stories on the Worldboard

Maxine walks slowly through downtown Burlington, hunting for invisible fragments of a story.

She started her quest at the head of Church Street, holding her smartphone before her, stepping carefully so as not to trip on cobbles and steps. As Maxine approaches a large fountain, her iPhone chimes quietly, displaying a photo associated with the now dry fountain. The image is of a worried-looking man. Aha, she thinks: maybe this is Godwin's last known location. Perhaps he met his killer here, or it's a visual pun: here's where the source ran dry.

Last week Maxine downloaded the story's instructions from her home in Quebec City, before beginning her trip. It's the sixth story in AR Suspense Anthology 2011, a collection of noir stories set in several North American towns and cities. Each story consists of pieces distributed throughout a limited area. Readers, or players, or "explorers," as the Anthology calls them, start from online instructions, then assemble the pieces as they walk through the storyspace. AR Suspense Anthology calls this a "derive" in order to emphasize the sense of drifting through a story. Maxine has derived her way through Ottawa, Portland (Maine), and Concord (New Hampshire) before heading to Vermont.

Maxine thinks of what she's doing as not deriving but deriving a story, pulling its pieces out of the air, then synthesizing or integrating the whole in her mind. She does much of this online, sharing questions and results with the Anthology community. But now she spots a QR code on the corner of Church and Cherry Streets. Scanning it from her iPhone's QR reader app, she finds a text file, background on Godwin's shady business deals. One of those deals involved a boating operation on Lake Champlain. I can take a hint, Maxine thinks, and turns right, heading down to the lake. She takes a photo of the vista before her, adds a quick *comment about who she thinks killed Godwin, and uploads it to her blog. Her iPhone held ahead of her, she probes the air for more story.**

Building the Worldboard

Augmented reality (AR) refers to linking digital content to the physical world, especially by location. The term was coined in the 1990s as an alternative to *virtual reality,* which sought to represent the physical world in digital terms. AR brings the digital back to the analog or offline world.

The 2010 Horizon Report helpfully described augmented reality as constituting a spectrum of technologies, differentiated by complexity and ambition.[1] "Light AR," for example, can be seen in geolocated Web-based media, as with the Hurricane Digital Memory Project from George Mason University's Center for History and New Media. This archive aggregates personal stories in different media (text, photo, video, audio) about Hurricane Katrina's onslaught, then pins each one to a map drawn from Google Maps.[2] Flickr similarly allows photos and short videos to be geolocated.

Further along the spectrum are "superimposed visualizations," which use a combination of printed page, Webcam, and Web page to produce three-dimensional animations. For example, a Web site maintained by General Electric creates an image of a wind farm next to solar collectors. The sun moves across the sky, while human figures wave. All of this is displayed on a computer screen while the user holds an appropriately printed sheet of paper in front of a Webcam lens.[3]

At the far end of the AR spectrum we find visualizations superimposed on the real world. The Wikitude service lets users hold up certain smartphones in front of selected city locations, then see digital information appear over buildings: *Wikipedia*-style basic information, housing values, street addresses, and so on.[4]

In this chapter, we explore further AR examples, bringing them into the storytelling "real." But first, it is worth pausing to recognize the historical moment of AR's leap into the mainstream, for AR has been marginal for more than a decade. Older projects were often awkward to use and never hit commercial markets.[5] When J. D. Spohrer described medium- and large-scale AR projects in 1999, it read like science fiction:

> Imagine being able to enter an airport and see a virtual red carpet leading you right to your gate, look at the ground and see property lines or

---

* This vignette is the author's, meant as a bit of illustrative speculative fiction. See Chapter 14.

underground buried cables, walk along a nature trail and see virtual signs near plants and rocks, or simply look at the night sky and see the outlines of the constellations.[6]

Spohrer saw a mix of servers, wireless access, mobile devices, and software that clients combined to let users find digital content that was linked to their physical location.

As Howard Rheingold described it:

> It is not hard to imagine a server computer storing information associated with every cubic meter of the earth's surface; computer memory is cheap. Geographic positioning systems could make handheld or wearable devices location-aware. Wireless Internet access would mean that a user could access the server computer and add or receive information about specific geographic locations.[7]

A user could stroll along a garden and check every meter for information about plants growing there. Office workers could "leave" (post to server) documents for colleagues in the same office, and the coworkers could download those materials while striding through their locations: office doors, hallways, meeting rooms. Once the infrastructure was in place, users could download and upload to the system, writing to or reading from the network. Spohrer saw this model as very extensible, capable of global realization, and so called his concept the Worldboard.

During the 11 years since Spohrer and others envisioned such a system, augmented reality has progressed into commerce and the mainstream. Companies like Wikitude and Layar sell AR content for mobile phones. Google has experimented with Goggles, a service enabling users to derive digital information from objects studied through an Android-platform smartphone. In the fall of 2009, Bruce Sterling gave a speech to the Layar staff in which he argued that AR was in its "dawn" phase; by June 2010, he advanced the AR clock to 9 a.m.[8] With the rest of that day presumably looming before us, AR remains strange and its uses uncertain. We have not settled the language for it, and the variety of terms suggest different ways of imagining the platform's open possibilities: magic window, mixed reality, reading the environment, annotating the world, laminating the physical world, a "looking glass" into an invisible world.

The mythic and poetic nature of the language we use to understand AR may reflect a folkloric ancestry. The Worldboard and Layar could be a digital reimagining of ancient practices, which have associated stories, information, and place. For millennia, Australian Aborigines maintained epic songs that were tied to that continent's geography. Mountains, rivers, cliffs, and waterholes were sung in a precise sequence, marking out a physical path via song. Writes Bruce Chatwin:

> In theory, at least, the whole of Australia could be a read as a musical score. There was hardly a rock or creek in the country that could not or had not been sung. One should perhaps visualize the Songlines as a spaghetti of *Iliads* and *Odysseys,* writing this way and that, in which every "episode" was readable in terms of geology.[9]

The songs cross linguistic boundaries. "The mystery was how a man of Tribe A, living up one end of a Songline, could hear a few bars sung by Tribe Q and, without knowing a word of Q's language, would know exactly what land was being sung."[10] We can think of Spohrer's Worldboard as a distant, digital echo, an attempt to build a platform for globally shared singing.

AR in Play

What augmented reality looks like in 2017 is a complex yet accessible mixture of hardware and software components knitted together by persistent networks. Mobile devices are crucial to contemporary AR. Smartphones are especially useful, as they combine a camera for capturing input, a significant screen to display directly seen and superimposed information, attitude awareness (an accelerometer), a compass, and radios capable of handling rich multimedia traffic.[11] These devices run software either locally, as apps, or through a browser to Web services. Devices are connected to services through one of several networks, including WiFi, various phone nets (3G, 4G, etc.), Bluetooth for short range, and GPS for location awareness. This quick component catalog should indicate how much recent innovation lies behind operational AR and how all of it is now available on the consumer market.

If we allow for geolocation to be considered as a light form of augmented reality, GPS navigation might be its most popular form. Ever since President Bill Clinton ordered the GPS military satellite network to be opened up for civilian use, consumer navigation tools have become widespread. Hardware makers like Garmin equip car owners and renters with real-time location and mapping information. Smartphones and featurephones also have navigation tools, provided by AT&T and others.

Following this successful implementation of digital geolocation is a growing host of mobile phone location-based services. BrightKite and Loopt let users search their local area for other users, games, events, and an increasing array of sites.[12] Some services add a social component. For example, Yelp points users toward local establishments, appending crowd-sourced reviews to each listing. Yelp users upload comments to these reports, growing a social overview of the local landscape.

Another light form of augmented reality is marker oriented, or perhaps object oriented. Rather than using GPS coordinates, these AR implementations use a physical information tag to locate the digital content. This concept is not new if we think of the long history of space-based mnemonics and landmarks. A more recent, pre-Web instance is the Universal Product Code (UPC), or bar code, which dates back to the 1970s. This physical impression allows computer readers to obtain encoded information by simply passing the bar codes object over a scanner. Over decades, UPC became ubiquitous enough for a consumer reader, the CueCat, to be launched in 2000. Although the CueCat failed dismally in the marketplace, UPC codes continued to proliferate into everyday life, and there are now downloadable smartphone UPC reader apps. Customer-driven UPC scanning has been mainstreamed in grocery stores and libraries.

Marker-oriented AR technologies have begun cropping up as the mobile device revolution continues. Quick Response, Quick Read, or simply QR tags are some of the simplest. Appearing in the 1990s, QR codes consist of a block of black and white squares. That block encodes information, which can be rapidly decoded and displayed by a QR reader, either a dedicated hardware device or a smartphone QR application. These text blocks have been used in advertising and art, from music and film.[13] Google launched a "Favorite Places" QR service in 2009, through which businesses can share information via tags, such as coupons or shop history.[14]

Microsoft released a competing standard, High Capacity Color Barcode (HCCB), or simply Tag, in 2007. Tag uses four to eight colors, rather than QR's two, allowing more information to be compressed into a smaller space.[15] The General Electric AR example mentioned earlier is another example of marker-oriented AR, requiring the physical indicator on a sheet of paper. Whichever standard is used, these codes are small enough to be largely unobtrusive and easily attached to objects. This size can allow users to effectively tag much of the physical environment.

Within the environment, we can track objects. Radio Frequency Identifier (RFID) chips are small devices that include two elements: a bit of memory and a tiny radio. Attached to or included within an object, they allow a user in the area to find them with a hardware reader. RFID chips can be affixed to products in a warehouse, for example, allowing a clerk to ping the space to inventory items. They can be added to library books and used to hold information about an item. Going further with this approach, Sterling has proposed associating not just present location information but also historical content about an object. A used book, for example, could carry an RFID chip or Microsoft Tag offering a sketch of, or by, previous owners. Sterling imagines such historically tagged objects as growing stories over time and refers to them as "spimes."[16]

While Sterling is known as a science-fiction writer, he also writes about current design, and spimes have recently shifted from the former to the latter. Projects like *Tale of Things* let owners of an object add digital content to an item, then hand it off to a new owner, who can track the thing's story (spime) up until the present: "Wouldn't it be great to link any object directly to a 'video memory' or an article of text describing its history or background?" *Tale of Things* hosts content created by users about an object and automatically generates linked QR code. You can pick up a coffee table from a flea market, find the QR code taped to a leg, scan it, and then read what the previous owner(s) had to say.[17]

Without using hardware chips, like RFID, such light AR projects depend on Web services for hosting and linking. Google has shown itself to be very interested in providing such services. We noted its Favorite Places QR service; far more ambitious is the Google Goggles project. This is a visual analogue to Google's signature Web search service. Users download the Goggles app, point their phone at an object, and wait for Google to recognize what it is. Not all items are recognizable by this occasionally uncanny service—the more well known, the more likely to succeed—but the amount of visual recognition data is steadily increasing.[18]

That combination of mobile phone, connection with object, and Web service leads us to what we might call deeper, markerless, or superimposed AR. This involves the superimposition of relevant digital data onto local imagery, as seen through a phone or other device. You can point your phone at a city street, for example, and see real estate prices floating above buildings for sale. An icon appears on top of one site; clicked, it reveals *Wikipedia-style* background text about that historical spot. Running a subway or restaurant app shows arrows in certain directions, pointing to the nearest locations.

Through a Glass, Sparkly

The reasons for mounting an AR project are manifold, as revealed by historical ambition and present practice. They will certainly multiply as more services are offered and experiments occur. Each of these reasons yields a storytelling purpose, either in terms of direct storytelling or indirect partial support.

The simplest and perhaps most appreciable use of augmented reality is to add information to a place. It may be to add practical information for immediate use, as the Wimbledon Seer app showed shops and facilities near that tennis tournament.[19] It may involve visualizing a future event to better understand its impact upon a present site, as with Layar's Rotterdam Market Hall AR layer. This application allowed users to see how a new building would appear upon that city's landscape. Architectural visualizations have done this for years via models, but Layar's app let users see how this would appear from multiple vantage points, both within and outside the prospective hall.[20] AR content may be historical, letting us view past objects and events superimposed upon present successors. The iTacitus project associated architectural plans and contextual information with a series of European sites, including an Italian villa and a British castle. AR content arrived in multiple media, including images, text, and audio.[21]

Those visualizations rely on preexisting professionally created content. As we saw with Yelp in a lighter form of AR, that does not have to be the case. Wikitude is attempting to enable the social creation of a *Wikipedia-like* AR content layer upon the world, perhaps the closest thing we have to Spohrer's Worldboard. At its most effective, Wikitude presents a series of data tags hovering over different points on a landscape, such as historical information about a building or a current event occurring at one street corner. Users can annotate the world and see each other's accumulating work.[22] For stories, these kinds of projects are at the very least useful for creators, offering ideas and information where they might not otherwise be available.

They could also host content for an audience to experience on the go. As in our chapter's introduction, a user could click on a series of Wikitude files in a row, unfolding a nonfiction tale: a biographical narrative, a political march's progress, or the growth of a town over time. Or a work of fiction would be downloaded and experienced as an AR layer, to be peered at as we move through the landscape, as with Maxine's story. Layar already offers several examples of materials for a superimposed story in its creative arts layers. One offers a series of Mondrian paintings set against the sky. Another positions cartoons of the Beatles crossing Abbey Road.[23]

A long-running Los Angeles project piloted how such a story can work. *34 North 118 West* told historical stories through content items accessed by audiences walking through several city blocks. Audience members carried a Tablet PC to display text, images, and sound, with a handheld GPS to identify their location and headphones to improve sound listening. The story objects concerned the intersection of persons and history, short narratives about people who used to work in that location before postindustrialism supplanted rail. Access was triggered by the physical motion of audience members, who literally strode through the stories' multiple spaces.[24] One of *34 North's* creators offers a provocative phrase to describe the work, one that emphasizes storytelling: "narrative archaeology."[25] This term is more precise than "locative media," which does not require story.

One Canadian project demonstrates a similar narrative archaeology approach: [murmur] makes audio files available to urban explorers, accessible through static or mobile phones. As with *34 North*, the goal is partly historical:

> "History" acquires a multitude of new voices. The physical experience of hearing a story in its actual setting—of hearing the walls talk—brings uncommon knowledge to common space, and brings people closer to the real histories that make up their world.[26]

[murmur]'s approach differs from *34 North*'s in being more concerned with the personal. As with the Center for Digital Storytelling (CDS) curriculum, the emphasis is on biographical content:

> By engaging with [murmur], people develop a new intimacy with places. . . .
> The stories are as personal as the relationship people have with the spaces they inhabit. Secret histories are unearthed, private truths unveiled and tales as diverse as the city itself are discovered and shared. All members of a community are encouraged to participate and contribute, so that the "voice" of [murmur] reflects the diverse voices of the neighbourhood. These are the stories that make up the city's identity, but they're kept inside of the heads of the people who live here. [murmur] brings that important archive out onto the streets, for all to hear and experience, and is always looking for new stories to add to its existing locations.[27]

Unlike the CDS, this content is spatially grounded. Rather than video, [murmur]'s format is audio only, emphasizing the gift of voice.

A similar project is under way in Biddeford, Maine where a downtown revival project helps residents identify "heart spots"—especially meaningful locations in the town. Residents then record audio stories about those spots, which can be accessed by future residents and visitors.[28]

A different use of AR involves visualizing neither historical events nor places, but focusing more radically on present-day people. Some services are now exploring connecting our mobile phones with our friends. Twitter360 adds visual indicators of a friend's most recent Twitter activity over the landscape where they tweeted from if they have enabled geolocation and are in the same area. In the "Locate my Friends" mode:

> the location of each of your friends is calculated with the "location" field data on the Twitter account. When a friend is selected, a blue arrow is

displayed to show the direction and the distance to the location of that friend. The selected friend is highlighted in blue. The distance is updated in real time as you walk in the streets.[29]

A more advanced application applies facial recognition to a user's social graph. Recognizr, developed by the Astonishing Tribe, tries to identify a person through your phone, then adds to the image their various public social media identities: Facebook, Twitter, and MySpace profiles.[30]

How could that kind of intimate, possibly creepy functionality be applied to storytelling? To the extent that a story uses social media, a social–facial AR link might facilitate audience interaction. For example, if a fan group is physically collocated, Recognizr or Twitter360 might speed their mutual identification and collaboration. If live actors are involved in a story, then they might be identified that much more quickly.

Storytelling games have already combined players with their environments. *Mad City Mystery*, for example, staged a murder mystery across a Midwestern city. Players had to investigate evidence, which led to an environmental danger, which had in turn driven a political scandal. At least one character was represented by an actor:

> Students must provide the police examiner (played by a real person) enough data to open an investigation into the causes of the death. In the process players use their handhelds to talk with virtual characters to learn life histories, access documents describing chemicals, conduct simulated tests for PCBs, TCE, and mercury, and must piece together an argument about the cause of the death.

These students think Ivan may have been poisoned. Are they right?[31]

Moreover, a history of site-specific gameplay and art dates back for decades. The game *Assassin* may date back to the 1960s. Without any necessary digital technologies, *Assassin* (also known as *Killer*) features players stalking each other with murderous intent across a local field of play: a town, city, or, more often, a college campus. Players can hide behind real-world objects, follow their putative prey down actual streets, and leave (play) booby traps in (real) kitchens. Live-action role-playing games, or LARPs, first appeared in the 1980s and combine *Assassin*'s use of the real world with role-playing games' detailed character mechanics. If we extend our genealogy to include treasure hunts, which are also games played across real-world locations, then predigital AR-like games can be seen extending even further into our cultural past.[32] As they appeared and evolved, digital technologies first played an enabling role in supporting these sorts of games (document management, Internet research, etc.). As AR develops, a rich node of site-based gaming and storytelling becomes available.

"Pervasive games inhabit a game world that is present within the ordinary world, taking the magic circle wherever they go."[33]

"Narrative archaeologies" might dig into the present or into a fictive version of the recent past. We read their stories by walking through them, summoning digital media by reaching their physical anchors.

Emerging Layers

Augmented reality is experiencing a sudden growth spurt as this chapter is being revised.

For example, Whereigo links a form of interactive fiction to geolocated smartphones to the physical world. A Whereigo story frames itself by displaying initial multimedia content, followed by a task to accomplish—walk to a certain location, for example. Once done, the next multimedia piece of the story displays, advancing the plot, along with a prompt for the following action. Virtual items accumulate in the classic adventure game inventory; players can obtain or use them by moving in the offline world or by in-game actions.[34] Stories, or "cartridges" in the Whereigo scheme, are open to genre and content. The Whereigo site suggests these categories: "Walking tour of city sights. Neighborhood scavenger hunt. Innovative marketing proposal. Pub crawl for your friends. Interactive fictional adventure. Alternate reality game."[35] Whereigo lets stories add to the world, in a sense augmenting reality.

Looking ahead, new projects and services appear frequently, with work being done around the world. By the time you read this, still more platforms will probably have emerged. For instance, Google and Microsoft are each developing AR layers for the visible universe. We can imagine a variety of stories based on those resources when they appear: science fiction, astronomy, or the history of science, for instance. We might also expect sky-based effects added to other stories, such as storm clouds added to threaten a sunny landscape or a night scene pulled over daytime.[36]

It is reasonable as well to expect further development in AR gaming. We have already seen AR games in play and should expect more, given the vast size and creative energies in the gaming industry:

> Games using marker technology often include a flat game board or map which becomes a 3D setting when viewed with a mobile device or a webcam. This kind of game could easily be applied to a range of disciplines, including archaeology, history, anthropology, or geography, to name a few.[37]

The practical challenges faced by AR are numerous, ranging from the technological to the personal, which helps explain why it has taken years for AR to reach its current level of development. First, superimposed or "strong" AR requires huge amounts of data crunching. While processing power continues to follow Moore's law, bandwidth increases are slower and the demands remain large. Continually positioning one geolocated point in relation to another, as one or both move unpredictably, is a complex task.

Second, social and personal comfort levels may repel AR deployment. No AR interface has yet won design plaudits, or even satisfied adoption. AR does not seem to have found as workable an arrangement as the Windows desktop or iPod wheel. This leads to usage problems, from the awkwardness of walking with a phone in one's face to small smartphone displays getting overcrowded by successfully filled-out AR content. Design problems are complemented by economic ones, as the AR business model remains unclear. Location-based advertising is attractive to marketers, but could trigger resistance to a *Minority Report* (2002)-style milieu of invasive commercialism. Privacy concerns represent still another hurdle. Although privacy remains a complex and shifting issue, with individuals capable of maintaining conflicting mind-sets simultaneously, especially in the digital world, augmented reality offers many ways to trigger public resistance.[38]

Third, AR has yet to trigger intellectual property (IP) struggles, but it certainly will, if the history of digital media can serve as a guide. Many businesses scrutinize digital media for misuse of logo and likeness, but it is from copyright that many IP problems are likely to emerge. How will an enterprise respond to an AR layer's use of its name? How much reuse and remixing will copyright holders stand before filing suits? On a related note, if adding AR content is a social, unregulated practice, we should also anticipate defamation charges—consider, for example, what all inhabitants of a city might say about its mayor or major industries.

Digital storytellers may face a conflicted AR landscape in the near future, as the burgeoning industry struggles with these challenges while experimenting with new approaches and content. The opportunities are fascinating for adding geolocated content and functions to stories. How best to organize one's story-creation process in this and other domains is the subject of our next chapter.

CHAPTER TWELVE

Storytelling through Virtual Reality

"This is the last medium"

—Chris Milk[1]

At long last virtual reality has become a real thing, where creators can compose stories and audiences can enjoy them. After the 1990s VR boom and bust, the medium fell out of favor and attention, but the success of Oculus Rift and subsequent platforms has finally brought the technology to the mainstream.

Earlier in this book I asserted that humans always are creating new forms of story whenever we invent new communications media. If my thesis is correct, we should see storytelling experiments proliferating through virtual reality as it develops and wins audiences. So far, this proliferation has been occurring.

The New York Times is a key player in VR nonfiction storytelling and may be the most exemplary to date, given their quality and range. They have invested significantly in the technology, creating a series of short VR stories for Google Cardboard's low-cost viewer. Most are strongly focused on carefully representing a location, such as the upper reaches of 1 World Trade Center ("Man on Spire"), the US–Mexico border ("10 Shots Across the Border"), and rural Somalia ("The Food Drop"). These stories take advantage of VR's immersive capabilities to bring home the feeling of being elsewhere. Some of these stories display a very short narrative in time, such as part of a battle ("The Fight for Falluja") or a journey ("Pilgrimage"). Others in contrast make an argument ("How Bees Explain the Future of

Business," "The Click Effect").[2] Naturally all of these overlap, as narrative and argument can blend into each other, and both use the power of place to enhance their ideas.

We can see these *New York Times* VR storytelling patterns in many other early VR projects. "6 × 9" immerses us in solitary confinement, carefully representing a location. That act, and the sounds (sometimes echoed in text) included in the space, make a powerful argument about penal strategies and human rights.[3] "Doom Room" takes the viewer on a first-person journey through death and a Buddhist rebirth cycle, using VR to make the process as personal and arresting as possible.[4] "The Turning Forest" (BBC, 2016) turns the titular forest into a surreal fairy-tale landscape where the users can produce sounds and new visuals by interacting with objects. "360° Camera In Haunted House" (2016) offers glimpses of potential story starters situated in a scary house.[5]

What can we learn from these examples about potential storytelling in virtual reality? What have we learned about digital storytelling's history that might help forecast or inspire new narrative work in this emerging medium?

To begin with, VR storytelling is deeply invested in setting. Presenting a space and time is the medium's most powerful effect. When people speak approvingly of VR's immersive powers, it is usually the setting, rather than plot or characters, that they refer to. Setting is and should be for some time the grounding of VR narratives. As Heston L'Abbé observes:

> The types of stories that will work best in VR—at least in the early days—will be those that emphasize a sense of place: Really doubling down on setting and environment to convey emotion. Hence why I like the term storyscape. The setting isn't just decor to hang off the story, the setting is the story.[6]

We could see stories based on extended examinations of space, less like action thrillers and more like gardens. As one VR creator describes their work:

> "[I]n VR, we feel an urge to slow down, to land and really explore the moment." . . . Lajeunesse and Raphaël want viewers to stay focused on a moment for five, six, even ten minutes. "For us, it's not just about the content itself," Lajeunesse told me. "It's also about creating the right conditions for the viewer to feel a part of it."[7]

This perspective could point the way toward a contemplative storytelling school, perhaps aimed at mindfulness practitioners, building on design principles seen in art galleries and public installations.

And yet, the embodied presence of the viewer/participant is crucial, with implications beyond such slowed-down setting perceptions. As Katy Newton and Karin Soukup argue, the VR audience member is very conscious of being on stage, being embedded within the narrative space, unlike the experience of a reader in a novel or a spectator at a film or play. The VR user might feel that every visible item is of importance, entering "detective mode" to turn objects into narrative clues, like escape the room games. Further, without clear cues for engagement, such as being hailed by characters or framed into a role, the viewer/participant may feel awkward. As another creator put it:

> Last summer, Strassburger told me, he ported to the Rift a photorealistic 3-D model of a bikini-clad Budweiser girl he'd rendered for a demo, so he could look at the work up close. Too close, it turned out. "I had this immediate feeling of, like, 'I'm invading her space!'" he said. "Being in somebody else's presence is a huge thing."[8]

VR stories will have to take this central position into account, building interactivity in the way games do.

Because of this embodiment, there are additional technical demands on the VR creator. Newton and Soukup again: "If something doesn't jive with their expectations, it takes them out of the experience. It sends them into detective mode, investigating the scene from a distance." If the history of movie and game graphics is any guide, VR creators will compete to constantly improve their representational fidelity. That will be a baseline for VR storytelling, grounding interacting users in an immersive, nondisruptive setting.[9]

We can go further with that user position. Jesse Damiani breaks open audience embodiment into two levels. On one, the viewer/participant observes the VR setting actively by moving her or his head and/or location. To realize 360 degrees of immersion, the viewer/participant must do some work. On another level, the viewer/participant interacts with the story in game terms, acting upon objects and spaces, which advance or even fork the narrative.[10] Addressing the first mobilizes the power of setting and spectacle, such as what film has historically offered, while engaging the second draws on interactivity, best seen in recent years through gaming. If Damiani is right about the nature of the VR user, VR storytelling maybe emerge from the interconnecting, overlapping zone between film and gaming.

One underappreciated element might come to the fore, addressing all of these principles. Sound design can transform the experience of a space, while grounding presentation of characters and kicking off stories. Think of the use of sound in scary stories, like "House Guest."[11] Audio content draws our attention to points on the screen that the only visible character doesn't notice, building up tension. The sudden stopping of water makes us realize there are two possible threats or extra characters. Music escalates a sense of dread. Beyond suspenseful stories, sound shapes our awareness of setting. Music, audio effects, and dialog deepen our immersion.

Most VR, however, has downplayed one crucial aspect of storytelling. Few VR stories have characters. They seem more interested in exploring setting than personality. Yet our embodiment as viewers/users/spectators brings us much closer to characters than many other media allow. Storytellers can bring us deeply into the minds of others through this intimacy. Character study is the next frontier for VR to explore. Perhaps when costs fall further, digital storytellers will start composing autobiographical narratives, literally foregrounding the self as well as its setting.

We should also expert VR to engage with other media. As the history of digital storytelling has shown, creators tend to link across storytelling platforms. VR can do this through offering supplementary or complementary content in social media or gaming. We have already seen this development in a basic way with VR shorts produced as marketing materials for films, and 2D videos released on YouTube as outreach for 3D VR. Looking ahead, imagine combinations of podcasts with VR, wikis supporting VR stories, and blogs accessible only in a VR setting. Virtual reality will join other media in the storytelling realm of multiple proscenia.

Missing from most discussions of virtual reality is serial storytelling. The clear majority of projects are isolated works, one-off narratives without connection to others. Since we know from the history of social media storytelling that serial structures are very effective and accessible to both creators and audiences, we should expect at least some serial storytelling from virtual reality. In the near future, creating a sequence of VR installments in a row may appeal to those investing significant amounts in that work, since production costs are still high. In other words, if a group commits to VR storytelling, they might prefer to turn out a sequence rather than a singleton in order to maximize audience and returns. As production costs decline in the medium- and long-term future, following the established economics of digital technology, we may see people creating serial VR narratives because it is no longer difficult to do so.

There have been some quiet signs of serial VR work as of this writing. One creative team spoke along these lines:

> "The majority of VR non-gaming content currently comprises of short films and videos. There are few things to keep you coming back. We would watch

something amazing in VR like [animated film] 'Allumette' from Penrose Studios and then go hunting for something else," chief creative director Abhi Kumar told CNBC, explaining why his team chose to focus on episodes, instead of one-off experiences.[12]

Computer games may offer another inspiration here. While many are one-offs, a good number develop into series, such as *Call of Duty*, *Mass Effect*, *BioShock*, *Total War*, and so on. Moreover, many games offer continuing storylines through downloadable content (DLC) modules. Perhaps we could see both of these structures form new VR content. The first popular breakout VR hits should yield sequels and spin-offs, while also giving rise to short DLC expansions. The present popularity of podcasts and YouTube series should prove inspirational to creators.

To sum up, virtual reality storytelling is in its earliest stages. We can anticipate ways it may recapitulate current and historical digital storytelling practices, such as the importance of sound, serial structure, game-like interaction, and expansion to multiple proscenia. As a new medium, VR storytelling also presents its own affordances, which so far appear to be powerful settings and audience presence. The combination of these elements helps us glimpse the contours of this new storytelling form.

PART 4

Building Your Story

CHAPTER THIRTEEN

Story Flow: Practical Lessons on Brainstorming, Planning, and Development

Fifteen people are gathered in a darkened room, getting ready to watch movies. Most look tired, bleary-eyed with signs of long work, but also excited.

Chatter builds into a buzz, which drops to attentive silence as the first movie flickers into being on the screen. It's a story about a childhood dream that has haunted the creator into adulthood. The dreamer reviews his life in its terms, seeing it underpin his worldview. It's over in a few minutes, and astonished applause ripples across the dark room. The moviemaker smiles shyly.

Another movie lights the room, with a very different appearance. It describes a joyous trip that turned terrifying when one trusted person was revealed to be something quite different. The audience savors the last line, some repeating it out loud.

A third film is projected, and a fourth. One by one the audience members switch from viewer to creator, then back. Each movie ratchets up the collective sense of accomplishment, a building sense of ambitious work done in an audaciously short time period.

How does one create a digital story? What are the practices and strategies a creator should bear in mind in order to build the best possible narrative with new tools?

This chapter's opening narrative describes the penultimate session from a digital storytelling workshop, when each participant's video was being screened for the whole group. It's a powerful moment, one not simply reached over time but built up to through an intense, challenging set of classes.

We begin this chapter by describing such a way of teaching digital storytelling.[1] Next, we explore the story flow of a person or small group creating on their own, outside of a class framework.

The Digital Storytelling Workshop

What is involved in a digital storytelling workshop? This curriculum is both rich and historically significant to require a detailed exploration.

The classic Center for Digital Storytelling (CDS) workshop model takes three full days. There is no slack time, as each hour is crammed with practice and the final goal looms ahead (see later). Since that goal is a viewable short video, participants[2] often stay late on the first and second days, arriving earlier on the second and third. The heft of this time commitment is well worth being communicated to potential participants.

Organizationally, teaching the workshop usually requires two instructors due to participants' sometimes intensive and overlapping needs. Two instructors can also complement each other's skill sets, such as one being expert in digital video minutiae while the other excels at writing instruction. The number of students varies, but tends to number in the teens. This number is partly due to scaling issues inherent in group discussions and group formation. It is also a function of how many students, all working on complex multimedia projects at the same time, a single instructor can handle.

Workshops have spatial as well as human and temporal needs. At least one technology-rich room is mandatory, such as a computer lab, with one computer per participant. Each machine should be well stocked with the appropriate tools, including enough horsepower (memory and speed) to handle video editing simultaneously with multiple other applications (see the discussion later under "Software"). Overhead projection for a networking computer is required for showing examples and software. A flatbed scanner should be available for the dwindling number of participants who bring physical photographs.

A second space, not dominated by technology, is also recommended. This space is intended for sometimes emotionally intense discussion and needs to be free from distractions. It could be a space within the technology-rich lab, if appropriate, or a separate room. A third space should be set aside for audio recording as well—a room, a closet, a ballroom—anyplace will do so long as it offers quiet.

Before the workshop begins, during the weeks or even months before the participants arrive on site, we contact students via e-mail or whatever other digital means they prefer. We encourage participants, first of all, to prepare story ideas: concepts, nascent stories, topics that feel "story-able." We also recommend they bring media files for those stories because that may save time during the workshop. There's a potential feedback loop there, as the process of selecting media also can further story ideas. In addition, any advance feedback from participants can be useful for instructors, offering a sense of their personalities and interests and hints of their technological familiarity. Moreover, if the workshop will use any Web services requiring registration, such as Flickr or Jaycut, then having people create accounts early will save time on site.

Day One

Once the group is gathered in place, the first workshop day covers a lot of ground. We introduce the digital storytelling movement and show examples. We focus on the idea of storytelling, asking participants to share their thoughts about either what that practice is or what it is not (see Chapter 1). We then shift away from presentation and into small group discussion, where participants describe their incipient projects and motivations for being there. This small group discussion, called a "story circle" by the CDS, serves several functions: starting community and peer learning, making the digital story idea more evident, and helping instructors better understand participants. At this point, each person should commit to trying out a story.

While some participants will be racing ahead by this time, others will be stymied by the idea of writing a narrative. "A person's initial efforts at story making can be frustrating."[3] They may have concepts, topics, or themes to address, but no way of realizing them in a short narrative form. Others have a single point of story, yet are not sure how to unfold it in time and media. These participants can be nudged forward by questions, such as:

- *What is the nature of the concept: a person, problem, or object?* If a person, the participant can turn to biographies and autobiographical stories for models. If a problem, then the issue needs to be developed in context and course of action. Where does the problem stem from, and where is it tending? If an object, such as a location or an artifact, what is its biography? For all of these, participants need to be reminded to find sources of challenge or friction because the tendency is often to see persons, problems, and things as static, realized, or finished. Recall Sheila Bernard's advice we noted in Chapter 1: "If something is easy, there's no tension, and without tension, there's little incentive for an audience to keep watching."[4]

- *What media do you have in mind?* Living in a media-rich age means that many participants start stories with images, sounds, or other media already in play.

Old photographs are common prompts to autobiography, for instance. Barbara Ganley points out that a wealth of archival material exists in nondigital forms, such as home movies, photos, or tape recordings. They may be stored in homes or located in public spaces: library, museum, or historical society.[5] If participants already have something to consider, urge them to speak to what they see (or hear) in it. This directive can surface story material.

- *Who is the audience for this story?* This prompt is essential for most creative practice, historically. In the digital storytelling setting, asking it can clarify a series of issues. Different audiences have different expectations of media, especially digital media, so mapping a story onto the right one then suggests a media strategy, giving the nascent story some parameters. How much awareness a targeted audience has about a given topic drives how to present context, which starts filling in the story automatically.

- *How much can you say in three minutes?* Realizing a temporal limit can be a terrifying—but often beneficial—shock, as it drives home a sense of scale. If the story idea is too big, what can it be cut down to, and how? The time limit of three minutes is a rough one—a rule of thumb often violated, but nevertheless very useful. A three-minute video is doable by any participant in these workshops and offers enough room for a good amount of audio and visual work. Other time limits can be set instead: a shorter one (say, one minute) to get started more quickly, or a longer one (eight or ten minutes) to support more work over time. But the three-days/three-minutes combination is a very effective one for most participants.

Once each participant settles on a story idea, the next step follows immediately: voiceover writing and recording. Participants write their scripts using whatever technology and format they feel most comfortable with. Some prefer isolation and head off to other spaces to write; others insist on being around people. Instructors move from participant to participant, helping them with the specific nature of voiceovers.

How do participants write good voiceovers? For some, writing for video is more challenging than any other experience in the workshop, as many people are not used to writing for visual media. Some may also be uncomfortable with writing to spec. Conversely, writers accustomed to generating extended chunks of prose can be stymied by the requirement to draft something concisely in roughly 150 words.[6] That number is a placeholder, a rule of thumb—again, nothing we enforce strictly, but a target that serves a clarifying purpose. It shocks some participants into an awareness of just how few words video can support. It drives home, too, the importance of brevity. It reminds creators of the importance of other media in a multimedia story.

For some participants who experience writer's block or simply fear, a formal prompt or exercise can help them proceed. The CDS recommends an interview process, either involving two people or one interviewing herself. The CDS also offers a typology of personal stories, with prompts under each, in order to help participants find accessible forms for awkward autobiographical materials. For example, Memorial Stories:

> Honoring and remembering people who have passed is an essential part of the grieving process. These stories are often the most difficult and painful to produce, but the results can be the most powerful.

- What is, or had been, your relationship to this person?
- How would you describe this person (physical appearance, character, etc.)?
- Is there an event/incident that best captures their character?
- What about the person do/did you most enjoy?
- What about the person drives/drove you crazy?
- What lesson did the person give to you that you feel is most important?
- If you had something to say to the person but they never had a chance to hear you say it, what would it be?

Other personal story categories include The Story About Someone Important (Character Stories), The Story About an Event in My Life (Adventure Stories, Accomplishment Stories), The Story About a Place in My Life, The Story About What I Do, Recovery Stories, Love Stories, and Discovery Stories.[7] Similar sets of story categories and prompts can be created for different settings. Annette Simmons generates six for "influencing others": Who I Am, Why I Am Here, The Vision, Teaching, Values-in-Action, and I Know What You Are Thinking.[8]

The contents of this voiceover are primarily the words participants will speak aloud. The process of writing often brings to mind ideas for using nontextual media appropriately, so the voiceover becomes a script, with notes for images, sounds, and more. We don't mandate a particular format for this writing process, leaving it up to participants to select one with which they feel most comfortable. This format could be a classic script, a two-column table (one for words, one for everything else), or a flow of words interrupted by other media marked out in capital letters or some font style. People write on paper, in word processors, using a wiki—again, we leave the question of medium open in order to get writing going.

Storyboarding is a more powerful writing tool than these. It helps some, especially participants focused on images, but is too cumbersome for others. Storyboarding practice involves sketching out a story's visuals in a sequence, along with attached media items. For example, a writer can assemble 20 digital photos that speak to her project, arrange them in a reasonable timeline, and then write text under each one. A voiceover emerges from this. Other media effects and content become apparent during this image sequencing process, including soundtrack(s), image effects (close-up, zoom, etc.), title text, and image timing (how long to dwell on each one). The CDS's *Digital Storytelling Cookbook* includes a sample storyboard, including a list of potential media attachments for each visual: effects, transitions, voiceover, and soundtrack.[9] For the CDS, a storyboard

> is a place to plan out a visual story in two dimensions. The first dimension is time: what happens first, next, and last. The second is interaction: how does the audio information—the voice-over narrative of your story and music—interact with the images or video.[10]

At a more conceptual level, concept mapping can press out hidden details and levels of a story. Concept mapping builds a schematic analysis of an idea, literally drawing components out and tracing connections between them. Many tools are now available to support this process, although a chalkboard, whiteboard, or paper will serve well. A story can be mapped out directly using concept map techniques, too, with details broken out and connected both by narrative sequence and content relations.[11] Focusing on various mapping tools can allow a workshop to explore visual literacy, from the first day on.[12]

Providing a template can nudge some creators forward. Whatever the layout, while working one up, participants also have a choice of storyboard location: hung on a wall (good for social interaction), flat on a desk (reduced socialization), or on a computer screen (private). These choices can be determined by personal preference as well as by instructors' sense of social dynamics.

The CDS curriculum also condenses down the screenwriting world into a manageable approach. Its Seven Principles, while aimed at personal stories, work very well for nonpersonal ones as well. Creators look to these points during their morning writing, seeking to apply them to their stories. The Seven Principles are as follows:

1. *Point (of view)*. This is understood as a combination of overall meaning along with the narrator's perspective. The former can range from a moral or ethical message to a biographical statement ("I learned this from the crisis . . .").[13] Sheila Bernard is emphatic on this score when speaking of documentary creation, which "involves the communicator in making choices. It's therefore unavoidably subjective, no matter how balanced or neutral the presentation seeks to be. Which stories are being told, why, and by whom?"[14] Annette Simmons adds: "Narration simultaneously chooses and communicates a particular point of view. When you want someone to 'see' something they are obviously not seeing, then a story can take them on a route of their choices/behaviors/inactivity from another perspective."[15]

2. *Dramatic question.* This keeps open the point, building concern before its resolution. It might appear as an actual question within the voiceover ("How did I survive Katrina?") or as a force driving the writing without being explicitly stated. "Sophisticated story making distinguishes itself by burying the presentation of the dramatic question, like the realization, in ways that do not call attention to the underlying structure."[16]

3. *Emotional content.* We've discussed the importance of emotional engagement in Chapter 1; the CDS emphasizes this and offers some specific ways of building emotional content. One is autobiographical intensity, "a truthful approach to emotional material." Another is to trace a downward arc toward failure, then to lift up afterward ("A character must know a negation of their desire in order to finally achieve that desire"). It's important to draw this out from different points of a story's arc: challenge, frustration, exhilaration, resignation.

4. *Gift of voice.* The act of speaking one's story can summon up emotional depth as well as information for a narrative. Thinking through that experience, or practicing it, adds to script/voiceover writing.

5. *Soundtrack.* This includes both music and sound effects. The CDS project considers most workshop participants to be conditioned to expect musical soundtracks, based on their lifetime immersion in audio media. The process of choosing the right music can deepen one's sense of a story, especially as so many examples are increasingly accessible on demand via networked sources, such as YouTube, Pandora, or iTunes (some of these are streaming services, requiring recording to use). Sound effects serve a related function in the voiceover process; thinking through which story elements should receive sonic accompaniments, and what kinds of sounds to add, can expand one's sense of the story—what is most important, what might be hidden and need accentuation.

6. *Economy.* The CDS deems economy "the largest problem when telling a story." Visual media—images and video—require time for the viewer to process, reducing the amount available for hearing a voiceover. In addition, many first-time readers often speak too quickly, overestimating the pace at which most listeners can parse the voiceover. As a result, scriptwriters need to trim down their word count (see "Writing" later).[17]

7. *Pacing.* "Good timing encourages your listener to dance with you."[18] Some writers (and speakers) maintain a consistent pacing throughout a story (or presentation). This can rapidly deaden audience interest: "Good stories breathe. They move along generally at an even pace, but once in a while they stop. They take a deep breath and proceed. Or if the story calls for it they walk a little faster, and faster until they are running. . . . Anything that does not allow for that pause, to let us consider what the story has revealed, soon loses our interest."[19]

    I have found that most participants have a ready grasp of pacing effects once they are prompted to think about it. They can describe pacing examples, both good and bad, from movies, music, TV, or computer games. In that mind-set, they can add speed effects to the script, either in notes to themselves for their voiceover ("Be sure to pause here") or in points for media to be added shortly ("Several images in rapid succession here"; "Hold on that photo for a while").

Too fast a story tempo is a common problem. First-time digital story creators often choose too fast a tempo, based on their excitement and familiarity with the material. Others are accustomed to fast media editing styles from some movies, TV, or gaming. Addressing this in workshop presentation is good, but providing evidence is better. For example, playing drafts to other participants helps give a sense of just how long it takes someone else to grasp the story. Drawing attention to timing in oral communication also works, especially if examples can be drawn from workshop conversations. As Simmons notes, "There are times when you can communicate more in silence than when your mouth is running. Pauses give your listener time to participate, to think, and to process your story."[20]

For a good example consider "Boy" from "Shawnee, Ohio", where the narrator poses questions to his grandmother, yet she doesn't answer. Brief silences instead of replies force our attention to images and film clips instead, which we gradually infer are the actual answers. It's a powerful move, engaging the audience in the co-creation of story.[21]

After a half hour of furious brainstorming, writing, and confabulation, the first participant is ready to record. Recording voiceovers often occurs in overlap—that is, the first person to complete his or her script starts recording while others are still finishing theirs. In many ways, this is the most technically and personally challenging section of the workshop. Many people are nervous about sounding bad, as most of us are familiar with feeling embarrassed at the recorded sound of our own voices, perhaps on voicemail. The technological details can be strange to first-time recorders. Participants often want to re-record their speech or to slice it into segments.

We have learned to address these fears by emphasizing several points. First, the logistical problems of the latter desire to re-record or cut up audio are not usually apparent to participants. Describing the ramifying chaos of multiple audio pieces is usually convincing, because cutting up a single audio track into pieces leads to many, many headaches in the video-editing stage. Noting that repeated recordings of the same track rarely result in improvements—in fact, subsequent retakes sometimes lack the energy of the first—can also reduce the number of times creators turn to that practice.

Second, we explain a view of the audio track as the *spine* of a story. It is a unitary piece of content, emotionally powerful and extended in time about as far as the story will run. Once in place, creators attach other media to it, extending or fleshing it out, arranging pieces around that central structure, depending on how far one wants to take the metaphor. In a related context, Bernard refers to the *train* of a story, "the element of story that drives your film forward, from the beginning to the end. Get a good train going, and you can make detours as needed."[22] Such a unifying, unitary conception can help participants focus when overwhelmed by technological complexity and media proliferation or simply stressed by the workshop's tight timeline. "The recorded voice of the storyteller telling their story is what makes what we call a 'digital story' a digital story—not a music video or narrated slideshow."[23]

These audio recordings are then saved in mp3 or .wav file formats, stored on each participant's computer. Ideally participants are able to record and save on their own, but we find that some need help with practical details, like distance to the microphone or finding a quiet place to record. Some also need moral support, either to get started and overcome awkward feelings or to stop re-recording and move on.

To give a sense of the workshop's intensity, we try to have all voiceover recordings done by the lunch break on that first day. Sometimes several participants haven't reached that point and need help either over the break or after it, or both, but that half-day point is a key milestone.

The second half of that first day then moves on to adding images. If time allows, another story circle is held first so that participants can reflect on the audio/voice experience as well as share thoughts and feelings about their stories' further development. The same benefits from the morning story circle session apply: nurturing a sense of community and learning about participants. Images are then introduced under the header of multimedia.

We discuss two modes of adding images to voice: expressive and complementary. In the first, images extend the voiceover's meaning, illustrating a described scene, showing an example of a topic, or perhaps offering multiple visualizations of a single spoken term. Expressive media can heighten the voiceover's impact at certain points, as the CDS observes:

> When considering the use of sound, we help storytellers by asking: "Beyond the recorded voiceover, would the story and the scenes within it be enhanced by the use of additional layers of sound? Would the use of ambient sound or music highlight the turning point in your story?"[24]

The image does not have to directly express the audio content aligned with it. For example, a personal statement of happiness can work well with an impersonal photograph, such as a sunrise. Conversely, a creator can select images to add a second layer of meaning, where the visual is different from the aural. The image may supplement or even oppose the voiceover. For example, the speaker may describe a precise fact, while the image supplies its general context (a house and its surrounding city, a worker and her workplace). An object may be depicted while the subject is spoken of (a baseball and a player). In contrast, the two media can comment on each other ironically, as a grim image undercuts a cheerful narration (an optimistic economic report read over a photo of a rundown district). This last form of multimedia complementarity is also a form of critique, opposing content in one medium to that in another.

Given this basic exploration of combining images with sound, participants start building up an image directory on their computers. Instructors supply some basic image manipulation instruction, depending on participant needs: introductory Photoshop or iPhoto, Web image editing services (Picnik, Aviary), or quick scanning. We remind them that bigger is better for images before editing them and signal the importance of the 4:3 aspect ratio, which will soon become important. We point to several sources for images that aren't problematic for copyright reasons, such as the Internet Archive, Flickr's Creative Commons, and perhaps some local resources; we delay a copyright lesson until later (see below).[25] File-naming conventions are strongly emphasized for the purpose of sane file management—this point has become even more important as smartphones provide more photos to workshops and often have generic file names.

This afternoon image session also allows for some image capture. First, some photo scanning is done, although the amount of scanning has declined steadily with the rise of all-digital photography. Second, some participants will want to take photos as their stories evolve. For instance, the workshop site's environment might offer settings or objects germane to story details.

Third, some will want to shoot video. We don't require this from workshops due to the already crowded nature of the curriculum, since introductory videography requires significant time to process. Moreover, as a baseline, participants will assemble a rich enough multimedia project by workshop's end without the addition of still more media content. Some participants will arrive with videographic prerequisites, either some basic shooting skills and experience or a video-suited, compelling short story element. In that case, one instructor detaches from the rest of the class to assist. Results are saved to the participant's drive.

Once a healthy number of images have accumulated on participants' directories, we introduce the digital video-editing environment (for which tools to use, see "Software" later). Digital video editors are the most complex technology we teach, so we break up lessons across all three workshop days. In this first video session, we introduce the idea of nonlinear video editing, demonstrating the software interface with some very easy examples: adding a couple of images and one soundtrack. Participants then start exploring the video editor, briefly, to get used to its basic concepts.

We conclude the first day with a story circle, allowing enough time for each person to gather his or her thoughts and express them. At this point, the group has grown into some form of learning community, with at least a basic level of shared experience. Instructors encourage links between projects and creators based on similar content and common technological challenges; this helps develop a peer learning sensibility.

Day Two

The second day is spent in the digital video-editing application. It serves as a multimedia aggregation studio, a remixing center. The morning sees one technology-free story circle, either at the day's start or just before the lunch break. This one continues the previous day's practice of storytelling reflection and can press more deeply into technical matters. Participants can identify areas where they need help, either from instructors or peers (we encourage the latter). We instructors then outline the day: plunging into video work far enough that every participant will have a viewable video by day's end.

The day's instruction alternates between full class presentations and individual consulting. We explain basic video processes: importing media, synchronizing multiple bits of content along a timeline, adjusting audio levels, some animation and transitions—all depending on software limitations and participant ambitions. These explanations are spread across the day, alternating with work sessions where each participant drives the story forward. Video work is quite immersive, regardless of one's expertise; it sometimes takes an effort to get participants to break for lunch.

We also introduce soundtracks on the second day, once participants are practiced at importing media into the video editor and synchronizing new items with others. It is not a difficult subject to raise, since many participants will bring it up on their own due to their lifetime media experiences.

> We are all aware of how music in a film stirs up an emotional response. . . .
> The sudden opening of the door becomes the prelude to disaster, when the
> swelling treble of orchestrated strings calls out suspect to our ears. . . . We

know upbeat music means happy endings, slow and tremulous music means sadness is forecast, fast music means action, heroic music means battles and victorious heroes are likely. We know the stereotype.[26]

What is difficult is getting music without copyright challenges. Participants will often bring or have access to music they've purchased; this requires a discussion of copyright. At some point, enough participants will hit copyright issues that we will have a short lesson about that grim subject. There are alternatives to this problem. First, some music is available without copyright restrictions, usually because the owners deliberately or accidentally failed to copyright it. Second, participants can make and use their own music, either via digital tools like Garageband or through live performance. Third, some video-editing software comes preloaded with sample music, which can be used at least for learning purposes.

The second day ends with a challenging story circle. By now, participants are keenly aware of time pressures and can resist stopping work. Some will feel overwhelmed by the amount of work they see before them. Technical challenges loom large at this point. Instructors need to listen to these concerns, address them pragmatically, and calm the class. Technical challenges should be aired openly, summarized, and worked clearly into the next morning's plans. Some project management panic should be turned to scope management, as individual creators realize, practically, that they need to scale down overambitious elements. That four-minute video, for example, now looks doable only at three.

It is likely that some participants will stay after the instructors leave, partly because of the desire to keep honing their work in software. As fellow instructor Doug Reilly observes: "The many features some of these programs . . . also slowed the process down by offering infinite artistic variation—and infinite fiddling. It was common to see workshop participants working until late in the night perfecting their films."[27] It is also likely that others will work at home on individual computers, finding more images and recording audio or video.

Day Three

The third day begins with work. Some participants will arrive early, and jokes about staying overnight are common. Many arrive with determination to pick up where they left off. Instructors should monitor the class carefully, looking for general lulls during which the last video lessons can be taught: sound effects, advanced transitions, and titles and title cards. The latter is important socially as well as technologically, since we cannot assume that the practice of writing credits is widespread. Subtitles also appear useful for adding information to scenes where the voiceover lacks it, or for emphasis.[28] We additionally like to draw out several targets for acknowledgment: media resources, the host site, and any especially helpful colleagues.

The third day is about completing the video, finishing it no matter how unfinished it seems to its creator. We therefore push to "publish" each video on either side of the lunch break. Timing depends on how far along projects are, but a publication lesson should occur during the morning. Publication can occur in one of two main venues, DVD and the Web, so instruction needs to account for both. This includes a brief discussion about the relative virtues of each, how to burn DVDs, and differences between export formats, including file types (.mov versus wmv) and sizes.

An exhausted crew then watches all of their videos. This experience is often a powerful one for all concerned, as we become more aware of each other's work with each successive movie. Pride at completion, awareness of work as yet undone, dismay at certain effects, delight at the audience's reactions—it's a heady mix, and a climax to the workshop.

We conclude with a final story circle, one looking outward, away from the workshop. This session lets participants reflect on their accomplishments and on the workshop process. Unlike previous circles, which were focused on immediate projects, this meeting examines the next steps into the short- and medium-range future. Participants will wonder about what software and hardware to purchase or try next, where to find more information and practitioners, and what to do next with their stories. As instructors, we also ask each person for permission to use their videos in subsequent workshops; we won't do so without the creator's authorization.

Software

What digital tools does this workshop require? Hardware is easily dealt with: machines powerful enough to handle digital video applications, along with one or two other programs running simultaneously. As of this writing, that usually means laptops or desktops along with a rising proportion of netbooks. Peripheral microphones are recommended for recording audio to those machines. Handheld devices, either multipurpose phones or single-purpose devices, can be used to capture images, audio, and video. It is likely that video-editing functions will migrate to handhelds at a basic level and probably grow in capabilities.

Software is, in contrast, a broad, moving target. There is a steady ferment in application development, especially as new devices and more social media services appear. Some projects may extend into other fields, based on functional affinities. Aviary, for instance, will probably expand their photo, image, and audio services to include video at some point. At this point, we can identify software categories, offering leading examples in each, with the caveat that this information is to a degree a historical resumé.

Audio Recording and Editing

Audacity is one of the leading programs.[29] An open-source, no-cost tool, Audacity lets users record and edit multiple tracks. It works on all operating systems with reliability and stability. Audacity does look unusually plain for a multimedia application, which might help explain its lack of widespread recognition.

Web 2.0 audio tools are appearing without any one leading the market. Aviary's Myna is a good example of the type. It supports basic editing functions and runs a separate application to record audio. Like many Web 2.0 applications, it echoes some key desktop application functions, but not all.[30]

Apple's Garageband is a fine audio editor.[31] It offers an additional advantage in the form of thousands of copyright-proof music tracks, which can be mixed together to create new soundtracks.

Images

Adobe Photoshop remains the industrial standard for powerful image editing. Its lower-cost version, Express, retains more than enough power for digital storytelling uses, especially for first-time users. Adobe has launched a Web version, which follows the pattern noted above of being powerful but less fully featured.

iPhoto is another fine application, for the Apple operating system only. Like Photoshop, iPhoto supports image editing with more than enough capabilities for digital storytelling. Unlike the Adobe product, iPhoto is deeply integrated into Apple's other media products: iMovie and iDVD (see later).

Web-based image editing tools have proliferated of late. Visme lets users create basic visuals, including infographics. Pixlr offers image editing tools ranging from the basic to medium levels of complexity. Google Photos uploads and hosts your images, allowing you to edit them in basic ways. Their Assistant program will, on its own, offer to edit or animate your images as well.[32]

Video Editing

Apple's iMovie may be the best digital video editor for first-time users. Accessible and nonthreatening, it nonetheless offers enough features to satisfy the midrange user. Integration with other iLife tools means easier image importing (iPhoto) and DVD burning (iDVD). Two downsides are apparent: the most recent version has received negative reviews, and the application is only available for Apple operating system computers.

The closest Windows operating system equivalent is Windows Movie Maker. Also a basic tool aimed at first-time users, Movie Maker is accessible and offers at least a basic functionality. It is available as a free download.

Photo Story offers a less powerful, less featured, and more accessible editing experience for Windows users. It assembles a filmstrip from images you provide, then allows a basic soundtrack to be added. While not really capable of supporting the full media usage of CDS-level digital storytelling, Photo Story can serve as a quick introductory tool for users new to video editing, while letting them produce some basic results.

Final Cut is a more powerful video editor for the Apple. Like Photoshop, Final Cut is industrial quality, used professionally. It is challenging for the first-time user, but teachable by gifted instructors.

Web 2.0 video tools have appeared over the past several years, but some have also disappeared, perhaps due to the lack of a clear business model. Yahoo's Jumpcut is perhaps the most famous (or notorious) case of this phenomenon. As of this writing, the standout tool here is WeVideo. This tool allows Windows Movie Maker levels of editing, cleanly situated within the browser window. Perhaps best of all is the ability to share project files among multiple users. Latency and ability to work depends on having a good broadband connection.[33]

Google's YouTube Editor is less powerful than WeVideo, offering a more basic level of clip editing. It may be very well suited for beginners or for any user who has simple needs, such as rapidly fusing several clips together.[34]

Publication

The two major destinations for video are DVDs and Web video, especially YouTube. For the former, iDVD is the leading Apple application. It will burn files onto DVDs and also add menus, animation, and navigation. There is no one such program for the Windows world, but many, such as Nero and PowerDVD.

For Web publication, any digital video editor allows exports of file types accepted by YouTube, Vimeo, Blip, and others. Web-based video editors, like Jaycut, also allow limited hosting on their sites, along with export/download functions.

Concept Mapping

Inspiration and its children-aimed sibling, Kidspiration, are stalwarts in the field. The Brain offers a very dynamic mapping experience, allowing easy linking to media files. Tufts University's Vue has developed into a very robust platform. Mindomo is a browser-based tool, allowing multiple users to share the same map.[35]

Mobile Devices

Mobile phones and other handheld devices are increasingly capable of not only capturing but editing materials as well. SonicPics (for iPhone) lets users record audio over images. It claims the slideshow model, but can easily be used for stories.[36]

Digital Storytelling on Your Own

How do you start to make a digital story if you're not in a workshop environment? What if you would like to make a story, but are not using the CDS curriculum?

Surveying the field, we can discern two opposed schools of practice, along with a third applying digital storytelling approaches to projects that don't appear to be stories. They are divided by scale and architecture. The first method begins at a very small scale, then grows by repetition. The second starts from a larger framework and proceeds by project management.

For easy digital storytelling, begin with a small media horizon, such as a single Web page, a blog, or a Flickr account. Thinking of a story idea, create a single piece of content for it in text or image. Shoot a photo, remix a story from the public domain, or write one from scratch. Don't think of that item as a presentational PowerPoint slide, but as a mystery that can't be solved right away. Brainstorm a cryptic image, a paragraph occurring *in media res,* a character sketch for someone involved in the tale.

The starting point for overcoming a creative block is to *start with a small idea.* It is a natural tendency to want to make a novel or screenplay out of a portion of our life experiences, and to think in terms of getting all the details. But it is exactly that kind of scale that disables our memory.[37]

Then post it to the Web. Release it from your editorial grasp; you can always return to the item later. It might never be seen or read, but that isn't the point of the exercise. The idea is to start a sequence because the next step is to extend the story in time. If it's an image on Flickr, write comments to carry the story further. Or create another image and make a pool of the two. Import the image into VoiceThread and then add three comments, each in different media form. If it's a wiki page, make a second one, then a third listing the first two in order. If it's a blog post, add comments and then a new post.

Many other tools are now available for small-scale digital story creation. Cowbird lets users quickly upload images, then add captions to produce short visual stories. It may be the easiest multimedia storytelling tool currently available.[38] Comic Life lets users create comic strips, quickly combining images with thought balloons, descriptions, and frame design.[39]

Exposure emphasizes images (hence the punning name), letting users combine them with text.[40] PowToons creates simple videos with effects.[41]

What Alan Levine refers to as "short-form video" can be created by a variety of tools. Vine, for example, lets users record six-second videos; we know that a short-short story can appear in that tiny space.[42] Instagram and Flickr similarly support microvideos.

Along similar lines animated GIFs have exploded in popularity. They do not necessarily relay stories, but can host micronarratives such as one unnamed but neatly compressed ghost story.[43] In that example, we have characters (two humans, one ghost), a setting (a living room), and a plot: living people rest, a figure in a sheet appears, a human rips away the sheet, nothing appears, and the humans run away in fear. Like the six-word short story, a six-second video can conceivably contain a minimal narrative. Many tools now exist for creating animated GIFs and can be a good starting point for visually inclined first-time digital storytellers.

Social media offers a wide range of other tools. Twitter has yet to be superseded by other microblogging platforms and still exists, despite investor anxiety as of this writing. For blogging, multiple services and platforms are available, from WordPress to Blogger to Tumblr. The wiki world remains robust; Google Docs is effectively a wiki platform, perhaps the most successful in history.

Mobile devices offer a galaxy of digital storytelling tools, each presenting a different set of affordances. Shorthand, for example, helps users create "Snow Fall"-style Web 1.0 multimedia stories, as does Scrollitelling.[44]

Steller supports the composition of simpler multimedia narratives, some-what close to Cowbird in appearance.[45]

There are challenges with these platforms. Media creation, editing, and publication tools tend to be single-function entities. To start using them and to work with more than one can require multiple log-ins, getting used to different interfaces, and learning interoperability strategies. The total number of tools used in even a basic project can be daunting in compari-son to the power of a single desktop program.[46] The logic of convergence suggests some consolidation will occur in this area or that single-service providers will gradually expand their offerings into suites, but that has been slow to grow beyond the catch-all studio powers of video editors.[47]

For the bigger projects, as counterintuitive as it may seem, we can bor-row a useful framework from the world of project management. If we con-sider an incipient story in terms of its life cycle, a whole structure begins to appear and many problems start being solved. We can also use the film/video production timeline, which has been relied upon for decades. The production trinity (preproduction, production itself, and postproduction) is a superb structure for combining narrative and multiple media in a prac-tical way. The Berkeley digital storytelling curriculum also offers a well-structured creation path, as we saw above and in Chapter 2. That will influence this chapter's discussion deeply.

Combining these sources yields a multistage process:

1. Deliberate brainstorming
2. Preproduction planning
3. Production and creation
4. The social life of a digital story
5. The afterlife

The brainstorming phase is a crucial one and well worth drawing out. In my experience, people often underappreciate this stage of the creative process, either because of excitement ("I want to get on with this awesome idea!") or its opposite ("This assignment should be done as quickly and painlessly as possible"). But brainstorming time is usually well spent. Con-sider, first, that the creative state is an unusual one for most people in most of our daily lives. Coming up with a story idea shifts our mental gears, allowing free association to replace linear routines, wandering instead of taking planned routes. Inhabiting that mental space takes some time and practice. It's worth remembering how many physical and social props we now have available to enter the creative state, from inspirational music to writing retreats to physical relocation (such as the reliable coffee shop). This issue is not necessarily a technological one, but a psychological one.

Brainstorming also requires reconnecting with influences. Every creator can recall a favorite movie scene, or some story's first line, or a voice actor's best performances. When germinating a story plan, summon up such fine memories. Think of what makes them work, especially for you. Risk imitation in the spirit of homage and practice. There are many ways to prompt brainstorming and to restart the stalled creative process: see the next chapter for some resources.

After brainstorming, we enter the preproduction planning phase. Here we lay out a timeline, pushing each element of storytelling into the future, building up a practical sequence. Milestones should be set up, triggered events that give creators perspective on progress: so many words written, for example, or so many YouTube hits received. Some of these milestones can be gates, decision points where creators alter the project's course. Above all, planning means building in risk management. Assuming that something *will* go wrong in the case of a story's life span, it is very sane to allocate response resources before the story begins. For example, the Riskology group recommends that project managers bet on at least a 15 percent overrun in costs and time.[48] Budgeting can proceed accordingly, laying out money, scheduling, and person-hours.

A major story's third phase is production and creation, realizing the media aspects of the plan. This phase can involve learning new tools, be they video editors or the Inform 7 interactive fiction authoring environment. It may include acquiring copyright permissions or aggregating copyright-safe content. It can include the hard work of repeated recordings or writing.

Once the story launches, we should realize that it now takes on a social life. Recall the threefold choice from Chapter 8: creators must either embrace, tolerate, or secede from social media. This is the time to put the implications of that choice into play now that media have been produced and the story timeline activated. Creators now participate in, follow, or try to avoid the social life of a story in all its distributed complexity.

As difficult as it is to consider during the early stages of story creation, at some point the story will enter a kind of afterlife. The live game is no longer played, the file format has been outmoded, the authors no longer wish to add to the wiki, and so on. It is vital to plan for this afterlife at the earliest stages so as to minimize chaos at this fifth, final phase. Creators should decide how they will archive materials: perpetual hosting by themselves, outsourcing it to someone else, or relying on one of the major digital memory projects (Internet Archive, Google caches).

Flipping the storytelling scale, how does someone go about applying storytelling elements when they do not see themselves as engaging in story creation? That is, many of us create digital content that is something other than a narrative: PowerPoint presentations, blogs, reports. We have been answering this question throughout the book, but can summarize here:

- *Audiences require characters.* Identify, present, and transform persons.
- *We respond to mystery.* Show us leading elements of your material, but not everything, in a way that makes us want to investigate further.
- *Follow serial logic.* Audiences do not necessarily follow a sequence simply by inertia. Provide a connection between parts. Cliff-hangers, pointers to the next stage, summaries of what an audience might have missed before, anticipation, and foreshadowing can pull us forward to the next bit. Recall our epigraph from a great Victorian author, Willkie Collins, who explained how he treated audiences successfully: "Make 'em cry, make 'em laugh, make 'em wait."
- *Use multiple proscenia.* Realize that audiences increasingly assume content located in different sites and prepare materials for them, taking into account local affordances. Some viewers will appreciate the availability of options.

More on Writing in the Digital World

What else do we know about how to compose words for multimedia storytelling? We know that this area of writing is not entirely new. It builds on several overlapping, intertwined traditions of writing for other venues, including movies, TV, video, and radio.

Word choice is vital. A line attributed to Mark Twain brings things home: Word choice is the difference between lightning and a lightning bug. Specific details, rather than generic categories, summon up a story world into a reader's mind. *Porsche* means more than car, as *birch* trumps tree.[49] Sensual details are powerful, especially in helping deepen the story's impression of reality. For instance, "Smells and tastes can be very powerful. Both can evoke strong emotional memories and even physiological reactions in your listeners. . . . The use of smells and tastes help draw your listeners' bodies into experiencing your story at a visceral level."[50]

Verbs are especially powerful when a medium tends to support a small amount of text (think Twitter, or video). Anchor every sentence with an impressive main verb. Active verbs subtly add energy to a narrative. Active voice ("I threw the ball to my dog") carries more energy than passive voice ("The ball was caught by my dog"): the latter slows down a narrative—which is desirable on occasion.

Metaphors can drive a story forward. As a brainstorming technique, consider several metaphors for your topic: a promotion as a voyage, immigration as an odyssey, divorce as a musical fugue. As a voiceover, metaphors can organize a viewer/reader's experience of your multiple media. And as a developmental tool, thinking through a metaphor's various applications can spur both creativity and reflection. Consider, for example, the extraordinary use of a computer game metaphor in "A Complete History of the Soviet Union, Arranged to the Melody of Tetris."[51] The Tetris metaphor manages to cover quite a sweep from Russian history: utopianism, heroic 1930s industrial production, Stalinist terror, World War II, consumer dissatisfaction, economic reorganization, individualism versus collectivism, secrecy, and science research—all before a dark coda about post-Soviet Russia. The lyrics rapidly develop these points, while a rich flow of imagery expands them further.

As any performing musician knows, audiences tend to remember most the very beginnings and endings of a concert. We should bring a similar focus to the outer edges of our stories. That first encounter—the outer layer, if you will—powerfully shapes how (and if) an audience proceeds.

It is useful to bring to mind beginnings and endings of stories that moved you. For example, consider this powerful opening:

"Suffocate her!" the midwife told my mother when I came into the world.[52]

It's a shock, a rhetorical slap in the face, one which will repel some readers but draw others rapidly onward. That violence, the sense of family tension, the possibility of deep loss: all of these will resonate throughout Le Ly Hayslip's enormously powerful memoir of growing up during the American war in Vietnam.

Compare the opening of the film *Contact* (1997), which begins without introductory material, save three bare title cards. It plunges us into space, visually into near-Earth orbit, with a darkened North America rotating slowly underneath. Simultaneously the soundtrack blares contemporary pop music. This lasts for a few seconds and is a disorienting experience, one that asks more of the viewer's trust than most films do. The point of view then withdraws slightly from the Earth, the sun rises over the planetary limb, and the soundtrack changes to older spoken words and music. That backward motion continues as the full outline of Earth becomes visible, then dwindles. The moon, then Mars enter the frame as our motion accelerates. We flash through the asteroid belt, then past a Jovian moon, then Jupiter itself. The soundtrack also moves backward in time, with advertisements, news broadcasts, and more pop music heard from the

1970s, then the 1960s.[53] We reach the Oort cloud beyond Neptune's orbit and hear Franklin Roosevelt's Pearl Harbor address, intoning the date as 1941. Our speed accelerates still further as we race toward the edge of the Milky Way galaxy. The soundtrack falls silent as we withdraw beyond the historical start of human broadcasting. We retreat still further, to our local group, then out to what seems to be the blurry edge of the universe itself, all in a cold silence.

It's a form of the "powers of ten" story, a powerful visualization of cosmic scale. Its assertion without explanation tells us that this is the canvas of the story to follow, that science will be at its heart, and human isolation . . . but then the camera shows us a single human eye, and we plunge all the way back into the awareness of a young girl, her steady gaze, and repeated calling out of a ham radio identifier. It's a wonderful *coup de theatre*, immediately summoning the vast topical set signaled by visuals (cosmos and science) into a person's life—which is appropriate, given the subsequent narrative's anchoring on that character, who grows up to be a research astronomer. The audio track's historical arc, and the awful silence it leads to, sets us up to expect much of that character's loneliness, combined with a drive for connection.[54]

Such is the power of an effective, creative opening. We might lack the budget of a large-scale Hollywood production, but we can still write for multimedia with an eye (and ear) toward this kind of impact.

The very end of a multimedia work is where we often expect credits to be given. This is true in nondigital media, from cinema to books (printing and some assistance acknowledgments). It is good practice within digital stories to generously credit sources, colleagues, assistants, and institutions.

Both the beginning and end of a word pose a different sort of question to the creator: detailed anecdote or general concept? Each addresses a distinct type of thinking: inductive or deductive. Each has advantages—the anecdote giving us something concrete to imagine; the concept, a sense of what's at stake.

All of the foregoing addresses unitary content, either single works themselves or individual pieces considered in isolation. Writing for digital media also requires thinking through the connections between content items. The connective logic varies richly, but can be seen as varying in scale. On the one hand, a series of content items appear, perhaps across multiple platforms, in a discrete and segmented order: episodes, clips, posts. On the other hand, one story item might grow by small steps: a wiki developing, comments added to a blog post. The former is serial while the latter is accretive.

Alternatively, we can consider multiple content items in a story as a spatial problem. Think of a wiki as growing by accretion, steadily and through iteration. Layers and items are added without a readily grasped sequence.[55] Content growth can be negative, too, as wiki editors cut back previous content. Comments can be subtraction. Whole blogs and other Web sites suffer deletion. Link rot, as we have mentioned, is a part of digital story life.

The tradition of hypertext, stretching back to the 1980s (see Chapter 2), offers many guidelines and examples: branching a narrative to create different outcomes for events, hiding and revealing links, presenting narrative maps, the importance of link content.

Social media afford several additional fields of multi-item storytelling. One involves serial narrative. Historical antecedents include Victorian serial novels, pulp magazine serials, episodic radio and TV, the soap opera, and multiepisode TV story arcs.

The Problem of Copyright

One of the greatest challenges to digital storytellers is the ongoing struggle over digital copyright. This problem is complex, rapidly shifting, and sometimes very deeply entwined in policy. We can clarify the situation for storytellers by offering a fairly simply checklist to follow when faced with material you'd like to use.

First, is the material in copyright? All publishable content is either in copyright or in the public domain. Public domain materials may be used with utter freedom. Generally speaking, anything published before 1923 in the United States is in the public domain. Individual creators of material since then have dedicated some of their work to that realm as well, either deliberately or by a legal error. For example, George Romero's classic zombie film, *Night of the Living Dead* (1968), is out of copyright and freely available for remixing.

If material is under copyright, you may apply to the copyright holder for permission to use it. The owner can set conditions of price, time, or amount of material.

If you cannot reach the owners, then you may attempt to claim "fair use." This notoriously thin reed is fraught with complexity, as the law itself is very ambiguous. If you use material and are sued by the owners, you can claim a fair-use defense so long as your use passes a test:

1. Was the purpose commercial or not? (Noncommercial is better.)
2. How much of the material was used? (The more, the worse.)

3.   What kind of material was used? (Original formulations are more important than quotations from other sources.)

4.   Will your use harm future sales? (The science-fiction test)

Note the lack of quantitative measurements in this test. Ultimately a court's decision is up to a judge, and this decision only occurs if an intellectual property owner decides to sue. The decision to use material in a fair-use way is a personal one, and very political.

Otherwise, we are left with creating our own content, which we automatically own without having to register it as such, as per the Berne Convention. We can also select unproblematic content, either public domain sources or materials licensed by their owners to be shared; see Chapter 14 for examples and resources.

CHAPTER FOURTEEN

Communities, Resources, and Challenges

After following the social media theme pursued throughout this book, the reader might well expect to find digital storytelling communities and resources scattered across the Internet. Readers are likely to have already explored the Web along these lines before reaching this chapter. Some have probably added discoveries to their bookmarks, RSS feeds, and blogrolls; such is the norm of life in the social media age. This chapter will conduct that combination of exploration and sharing in print, surveying the heterogeneous array of social media resources for digital storytelling in 2017.

Such a survey encounters a series of digital storytelling challenges, starting with digital content fragility. As we first noted in the Introduction, it is the nature of the Web to lose URLs and page content. This chapter is, like the rest of the book, partly a historical placeholder describing a landscape at one point in time. Please use the Internet Archive's Wayback Machine to hunt for some archived copies. Google Web search may provide cached versions of sites. Digital storytelling practitioners, activists, and scholars sometimes provide entire or excerpted copies of stories. Try to create and share your own archive, too, to the best of your abilities and comfort level.

Another challenge concerns source diversity. Digital storytelling now spans very heterogeneous domains, as the preceding chapters have tried to show: multiple nations and regions, the major gaming industry and several small-scale movements, desktops and mobile devices, and physical objects and augmented reality. Creators and creations can tend to remain focused in one channel due to the depth, demands, and power of individual platforms. Negative media coverage of various technologies also supplies reasons not to pursue stories in other domains. Resources and communities can accordingly be confined to "silos"—limited access to sources of knowledge, inspiration, and support. This book has been an attempt to cut across those domains in pursuit of storytelling, and the following chapter is a selection of what's currently available.

Toys and Exercises

Creators seeking inspiration for storytelling can easily find story examples in all kinds of media, which can be overwhelming. The sheer quantity can stall thinking, in the classic paradox-of-choice problem.[1] This is especially true when fine stories daunt the first-time creator, as a polished work appears to be too far removed from that initial conceptual moment. In these cases, storytellers can benefit from formal exercises, prompts, and games, which provide a structured way of proceeding.

For example, Matt Madden's *99 Ways to Tell a Story* can be read as nearly 100 solutions to storytelling problems.[2] It consists entirely of variations on the single one-page vignette that begins the book. In that little passage, a man walks across his apartment, has a brief conversation, and then looks in the fridge. His microstory then gets retold for the rest of the book, reconceived and remodulated by formal twist after formal twist. The man walks, talks, and snacks with or without thought balloons, seen from above, and in a reversed timeline. Madden reruns the sequence in the mode of some famous comic artists and styles (Windsor Mckay, Jack Kirby) through the formal conventions of different genres (fantasy, science fiction, horror, romance, political cartoon, autobiography, and how-to manual) and by changing up perspective, page layout, time structure, and character point of view. Characters, objects, text, and lines are added or subtracted. Colors appear, signaling historical moments.

Reading through these iterations can spark new options for storytellers, shaking loose possibilities for those who have already begun making content. *99 Ways* is inspired by Raymond Queneau's 1947 title of the same name, which creators can exploit for the same purpose, emphasizing text.

A more conceptual or brainstorming tool is Brian Eno and Peter Schmidt's *Oblique Strategies* deck (1st ed., 1975). This set of exhortations is aimed at the creative mind as randomly selected shots of inspiration and formal revision:

- "Honor thy error as a hidden intention"
- "Use an old idea"

- "Imagine the piece as a set of disconnected events"
- "Make a blank valuable by putting it in an exquisite frame"
- "Assemble some of the elements in a group and treat the group"

These are best used when you are already in the process of making or revising a story, as they tend to address the reader in midaction.[3]

Without using any such physical tools, we can still find many practices and exercises for getting storytelling flowing. One popular method is forcing oneself to write a certain amount on a regular basis. This could be a number of words per day, a page every morning, or a paragraph after an event. The idea is simply to accustom oneself to inhabiting that expressive medium through repetition.

Nothing restricts this practice to writing, as the popularity of daily photographs and regular Webcam videos attests. Remembering to do the work, disciplining oneself to run through the process of material selection and approach, taking several photos, and selecting the best ones is an excellent way to build comfort with a camera. Several online communities exist for users to upload their daily captures and to support each other in the routine.[4] Others blog their work, like Bowdoin College's Michael Kloster: "The project began on March 27, 2002, and has no scheduled end date. With few exceptions each photograph is posted on the day it is made."[5] The same is true of daily video practice. Both photography and video repetition can include the possible bonus of habituating oneself to being on camera.

One can apply this reliable practice to social media. The practitioner habituates herself or himself to creating content on the Web on a regular basis, be it a daily photo uploaded to Flickr, a certain number of words in one's blog per day, or shooting video in the morning for editing in the afternoon. The social aspect kicks in as feedback appears, either directly in the chosen venue (blog post comments) or through other means (Facebook comment about a podcast).

More specific creative prompts are also excellent storytelling tools. For example, brevity isn't something most of us attain easily. When creating a digital story, it is actually easy to aggregate too much material to us. The vast number of images we can find on the Web or can take with cameras is a good example. Some writers find they generate too much text to use with other media. In this situation, it helps to practice a very stripped-down style. Twitter is excellent for this, with its tyrannical 140-character limit. Regular tweeting can teach the importance of a very few words.

Another such brevity practice is the six-word story game where you have to construct a full story in that many words, counting articles and conjunctions. This game is based on one such microtale written by Ernest Hemingway:

For sale: baby shoes, never used.

(Nicely parodied on Twitter:

For sale. Baby shoes. Never worn. Ya my wife said its irresponsible to spend $160 on baby sized Jordans. Just to clarify my baby is not dead)

More disturbing is a riff linked to a Twitter call for four-word dystopias:

"@Dystocalypse Baby shoes. Bloodstained. Approaching."[6]

The *Six Word Stories* site has many other examples:

Optimist drowned in half full bathtub.
Cunning terrorist only uses red wires.[7]

Trying to write one of these can be frustrating, but the process helps narrow down one's textual focus. This writing practice can be easily translated to other media. Recall the "Tell a story in 5 frames" Flickr pool. Assign yourself the task of telling a story in that many images—or fewer. You can do this with print photographs from magazines or with digital images from the Web. You can also use Alan Levine's automated Five Card Flickr Web resource.[8]

In fact, playing a game can be a fine way to get storytelling going. As we've discussed, games often provide environments or grounds for a story to be told, and players often relate stories of their experiences. Some games are openly aimed at eliciting storytelling, such as the White Wolf series of tabletop role-playing and often hyphenated games—*Vampire: The Requiem* and *Werewolf: The Forsaken*.[9] A subgenre of card games is based on goading players to tell stories based on card content, the sequence of moves, interaction between cards, the game's concept, its genre, and player creativity. Examples include *Dark Cults* (1983) and *Once Upon a Time* (1993).[10]

At a different conceptual level, Charles Cameron's ingenious HipBone games require players to build connections between moves.[11] Based on Herman Hesse's 1943 novel *The Glass Bead Game* (also *Magister Ludi*), a HipBone game consists of a series of ideas "played" in turns. Each idea is named when placed on one of a variety of boards; the player must then verbally describe its links to other already-played ideas. If you have played "the discovery of benzene" and I respond with "Wagner's Ring Cycle," I would explain the connection by describing recursion and circularity in myth. Your response would be another concept, along with its links to the previous two ideas. HipBone can easily serve as a storytelling generator for either fiction or, as in Hesse's extraordinary novel, for nonfiction understanding of the world.

Also recommended is simply playing with VoiceThread, as we noted in Chapter 5. Its ease of use and the light, yet effective way it enables quick multimedia creation can help story ideas develop.

Sources for Reflection and Inspiration

Creators can draw inspiration from the world of available digital storytelling projects. There is no single source for these, as of this writing, so we must cast our nets widely to find examples.

The TV Tropes wiki has grown into one of the most formidable storytelling resources online. Initially focused on identifying story themes and details for TV programs, the site now sprawls across film, music, gaming, and print. Entries dive from broad concepts down to obsessive details, replete with examples, and generously cross-linked to allied tropes.[12]

StoryCenter (formerly the Center for Digital Storytelling) is one of the best sources. Their YouTube channel now has a rich and growing set of examples.[13] StoryCenter's blog offers more examples, along with reflections on story.[14]

StoryCorps is a well-known audio storytelling resource. It is a service that brings together two people into a recording and editing booth, helping them tell a story about something in their mutual lives. StoryCorps then edits down those conversations into a short audio file for publication via radio and podcast. StoryCorps also has a distance option, called StoryKits, which lets people rent materials for a brief time in order to make a StoryCorps-style audio tale on their own.[15]

It is possibly the most prominent example of the CDS digital storytelling curriculum, even though it differs in deep ways from that practice. StoryCorps's emphasis on personal stories, spoken by participants or close witnesses; the condensed timeline of the result; and the use of modern, light digital tools all recall CDS. Indeed, this audio service has long had many close connections with the Bay Area originals. The audio-only focus of StoryCorps is an important difference, but so is the way StoryCorps produces the resulting stories. Instead of participants learning to create stories themselves, the recording booth records voices and then its supporting staff ultimately processes the materials. That said, StoryCorps maintains a high profile, from very public work in New York City to a partnership with National Public Radio.[16]

StoryCorps's metropolitan focus represents a fairly common emphasis for some strands of digital storytelling. The CDS approach has inspired many urban activists to help locals create their own digital narratives. For example, Streetside Stories teaches San Francisco-area children digital storytelling. Streetside works with elementary and middle-school students and teachers, helping them develop assignments and support strategies.[17]

Another fertile area for digital storytelling examples is the medical world. Some hospitals have found value in helping patients tell stories about their experiences with trauma or chronic disease. In turn, staff can relate their stories of care. For instance, *Patient Voices* provides a way for patients in the British medical system to describe their experiences as well as for staff to narrate theirs.[18]

Web-based aggregations of digital stories can be evanescent, like much of the digital world. As of this writing, *Digitales* is still alive, providing a series of stories created through a variety of platforms. And the StoryCenter site usually presents a fine set of sample stories.[19]

For the fertile field of fan fiction (Chapter 8), FFN is probably the best single location. It provides a host of stories along with reviewers and guidelines.[20]

Tapping the Hive Mind

An increasing number of digital storytelling practitioners share reflections on their work through social media. As the number grows, we can cite only a selection here.

Several blogs are deeply focused on storytelling in the digital world. *Novelr* explores large-scale storytelling in social media. *A Storied Career* discusses storytelling in general, in both analog and digital forms. The Institute for the Future of the Book's group blog offers some of the finest and most advanced thinking about digital storytelling, from changes to the publication industry to the nature of digital reading and, of course, the future of the book.[21]

Interactive fiction and gaming scholar Nick Montfort writes about new games, the experience of play, and emerging and classic themes in digital storytelling. Computer scientist, teacher, and consultant Ruben Puentedura explores both practical experience and new frontiers in digital storytelling.[22]

At a meta level, we can learn about good blogs by following interblog patterns. For example, many bloggers maintain blogrolls or lists of blogs they read and approve of. Clicking through a blogroll maintained by a trusted blogger can lead to some useful discoveries. At a different meta-blog level are "story carnivals," irregular blog posts linking to some recent digital blog posting about storytelling. There have been more than 111 of these as of the first edition of this book; alas, the practice seems to have waned since.[23]

Twitter offers a different kind of resource for the digital storytelling practitioner. Beyond telling stories with it, as we discussed in Chapter 4, or using it as a writing tool (see previous discussion), Twitter users are prone to sharing their thoughts on events and issues in pithy, accessible ways. Some fine digital storytelling Tweeple include Storytellin and, once more, Ruben Puentedura.[24]

As digital storytelling often relies on the gift of voice, we should expect to find podcast resources. LibriVox is one of the great audio achievements of our time, featuring a large and growing catalog of audiobooks. Unlike commercial audiobook enterprises such as Audible, LibriVox is run entirely by volunteers. Readers from around the world select public domain texts, read them aloud, and then podcast the results. All of the texts are out of copyright, and digital versions of them are often linked from each podcast, along with social media supplemental information. Fiction and non-fiction, from poems to multibook novels, the range of LibriVox titles is impressive. As Yochai Benkler and others have observed, it is a fine example of peer production, outflanking copyright problems, collaboratively producing items of value. LibriVox's discussion board offers an ongoing, unedited record of this kind of distributed storytelling.[25]

Discovering fine podcasts requires a combination of personal exploration and social curation, much as blogs require. When podcasts use blogs as publication platforms, they may include preferred podcasts in their blogrolls. Podcasts are also fond of reviewing and recommending other podcasts. "Social curation" means that we can check trusted sources in the social Web for pointers to audio content. In turn, we can assist others engaged on the same quest for today's theater of the mind by sharing our reflections via comments, posts, or updates.

A quieter, more streamlined venue for digital storytelling resources is social bookmarking. Social bookmarking Web sites are services where users upload links to Web content, along with small amounts of notes and selected tags. The first such service, Delicious, has been succeeded by others, such as Diigo and Pinboard ("social bookmarking for introverts").[26] We can search these sites for such tags as "digitalstorytelling," "podcasting," or "storytelling." Again, readers are invited to share their own bookmarks, contributing to the broader world of digital storytelling resources.

Several Web pages offer guides to digital storytelling and have been cited in previous chapters. The richest of all of these is Alan Levine's *50 Ways to Tell a Story*. Conceived as a way to aggregate social media storytelling tools for an academic audience, Levine's page has grown into an extraordinary, widely used, well-maintained resource.[27]

Finding Digital Materials

To some degree, all digital storytelling involves remixing. To build a story about our childhood library, for example, we would probably use someone else's media: the library's official photographs of itself, a Google Earth satellite image, one librarian's self-portrait, and an apposite musical track. These enter our story's mix alongside our own content (in this example: the creator's voiceover).

Finding and using materials is, paradoxically, both increasingly easy and difficult at the same time. On the one hand, the amount of digital content keeps growing as humans create or capture material and then publish it to the Internet. Digitization projects continue, driven by governments, individuals, corporations, and nonprofits. Tools and expressions that use potentially copyrighted content continue to proliferate. On the other hand, copyright laws are under revision, largely to tighten protection. J. D. Lasica points out that the combination of these two forces means an increasing number of people are copyright violators susceptible to takedown notices and lawsuits.[28]

One way around this tension between using and owning copyrighted content is to focus on content beyond protected intellectual property status. A growing number of people and projects use alternatives to copyright, which has resulted in a large and rich body of work the digital storyteller may exploit. The Creative Commons (CC) project supports a group of licenses, some of which are aimed at offering content for use by other creators. For example, the "Attribution" license ("by") lets any user do what they like with your work: "This license lets others distribute, remix, tweak, and build upon your work, even commercially, as long as they credit you for the original creation." The "Attribution Non-Commercial" license ("cc by-nc") narrows this down with an economic qualification: "This license lets others remix, tweak, and build upon your work non-commercially, and although their new works must also acknowledge you and be noncommercial, they don't have to license their derivative works on the same terms." Creators can make their work available to others through these licenses. Digital storytellers can take advantage of others doing precisely this and search for materials with one of the CC licenses.[29]

As of this writing, it is not as simple to search exclusively for CC-licensed content as it is to Google the broader world of content, copyrighted and otherwise. Instead, one must search from a series of domains where CC licenses are easily discovered by local search engines. The social photosharing site, Flickr, for example, aggregates CC-licensed images in a single spot, letting users easily search for usable images.[30] The Freesound audio archive hosts sound files licensed for "Sampling Plus." Barcelona's Universitat Pompeu Fabra supports this extraordinary service, which presents mp3 files in full Web 2.0 fashion: with tags, comments, previews, and downloads. More than 300,000 audio clips are available at Freesound, as of this writing.[31] The Ourmedia site has been growing a large database of tagged, alternatively licensed content for several years. It also presents helpful information on media practice.[32]

Several other sources make content available for storytelling use. The Internet Archive, whose Wayback Machine has been mentioned earlier in this book, also republishes public domain text, audio, and video clips. At last check, the Internet Archive provides copies of 369,346 movies, 1,520,413 audio recordings, and 666,912 texts, along with 2,431,321 items from public libraries, as of January 4, 2017.[33]

Gaming and Storytelling

As we noted earlier, the contemporary gaming world is enormous, which makes keeping up with it a challenging task. Pulling on the "gaming and storytelling" thread narrows down the field somewhat. Readers are advised to explore and curate resources that speak to their own interests, but a selection of leading sites can be presented here.

Game studies continues to grow, and many scholars maintain social media presences alongside their more traditional research output. They include those of Swarthmore College professor Tim Burke; leading interactive fiction scholar Nick Montfort; designer and theoretician Raph Koster; and coach/philosopher Bernie Dekoven.[34] Game designer, scholar, and activist Ian Bogost, for example, blogs and writes for *The Atlantic*.[35] Many blogs follow gaming in general, including *Kotaku* and *Joystiq*.[36] The Gamasutra news site is especially comprehensive.[37]

Some resources are focused on subsets of the gaming universe. One of the best ways to keep up with casual games is to read *Jay Is Games,* which constantly reviews new casual games while hosting copies of many and holding game design competitions.[38] Scholar Jesper Juul, from whom this book has benefited much, maintains the *Ludologist* blog.[39] For virtual worlds, the aforementioned *Terra Nova* offers continuous and thoughtful commentary. *New World Notes* is perhaps the leading blog about the *Second Life* virtual world, while the Linden Labs official blog site is the closest thing to a public record.[40] Alternate reality games have a grand central station of discussion in the Unfiction forums. The ARGNet site offers one of the leading alternate reality game blogs.[41] Andrea Phillips and Christy Dena write superbly from positions combining design practice with reflection.[42] For interactive fiction, Montfort remains the authority, blogging under the title *Grand Text Auto*. Other resources include the Interactive Fiction Archive and the annual interactive fiction contest.[43]

Workhorses

The number of story-authoring tools continues to grow as the new media expand. We covered some of those tools in Chapter 12: audio, image, and video software. What other creative implements are ready for the storyteller's hand?

In the world of gaming, the larger games are built by big teams using a variety of rich media tools, from 3-D modeling tools to rendering farms. For casual games, Adobe Flash remains the leading creative application, despite the decline in Flash player use after Apple's epochal break with them. More than a decade of professional authoring has yielded a large developers community along with substantial resources in print and online.[44] Flash had received a great deal of criticism from Apple in 2010, notably being excluded from Apple's iOS system and not being widely ported to mobile devices.[45] However, no major and widely used successor authoring tool has yet appeared, as of this writing. HTML5 is a fine standard for playing multimedia, but creating games for it requires significant back-end coding. When an HTML5 authoring tool appears, game design energies may start flowing to it.[46]

Numerous other casual game-building tools exist. To pick one example, the Massachusetts Institute of Technology's Scratch programming suite is designed to help basic users—children—start creating interactive multimedia. Having been used for several years, Scratch has a loyal and supportive online community, and one can find many examples of Scratch-built projects.[47] Another example is Venatio Creo, created by two Ursinus College students. A free download, Venatio lets users build platform adventure games.[48] For creating interactive fiction, Inform, version 7, is a superb program. It is robust and visually appealing and is connected to an energetic online support community. Inform 7 was designed to use as much natural language as possible, making it more accessible to first-time authors.[49]

For producing 3-D content, especially for machinima, the *Second Life* virtual world is a fine resource. The authoring engine is easier than many 3-D tools, such as Maya or Blender. The virtual world service explicitly assigns copyright to the individual creator, admirably. Additionally, the *Second Life* community is enormously supportive, from helping new creators build to assisting with machinima. Two-dimensional images can be exported out of the *Second Life* application, while 3-D ones need another program to record them.[50]

CHAPTER FIFTEEN

Digital Storytelling in Education

Lee is wrestling with Byzantine history. The subject is very strange to him—a bewildering mix of religion, strange place-names, complicated politics, and occasional bouts of disturbing violence. He wonders, not for the first time, why he decided to take this class as an elective. Lee is mentally very far from his intellectual home of microbiology.

Lee's instructor allowed him to create a digital story in place of a midterm paper. As with an essay, he would have to assemble materials into a coherent argument, organized into a thesis. Lee chose this option for its creative sound, but is now struggling with how to make it actually happen. The academic content is difficult, and he cannot see his way through to a final product suitable for turning in to that instructor (who seems more terrifying with every passing day).

Seeing his way through, Lee is suddenly seized by an insight. He's been thinking of the 10th- and 11th-century rulers in terms of their culture—that unusual mix of Greek, Roman, and Middle Eastern influences. But now Lee realizes that their policy debates were not about culture, but strategy. Each emperor had his own version of strategy for protecting the realm, and maybe there were really only two schools of thought, the expansionist and the defensive ones. Each had champions, like the strange and terrible Basil II, the "Bulgar killer." Those advocates struggled to shape the way Byzantium interacted with the world.

Now Lee can see characters lined up on either side of this debate: emperors and courtiers, generals both treacherous and loyal. He can track who was winning the debate at which time. Quickly he reaches for digital tools: SIMILE, to organize a timeline; his instructor's class Web page, for links; the campus library page, to look for articles; Google Images, for pictures; Word, to start getting down his ideas into words. Soon he will record his voice and assign images to support each point.

How can digital storytelling be used for teaching and learning? In a sense, this question has an obvious answer. Naturally, storytelling has been part of teaching since we started thinking about the subject, as far back as Aristotle tutoring a young soon-to-be world conqueror. Obviously, teaching has been making increasing use of digital materials, dating back to the 1960s and the first educational uses of the PLATO system.[1] Combining technology with storytelling makes deep, intuitive sense.

Stories of Learning

Multiple reasons have been advanced for integrating digital storytelling into education in the years since the CDS first began working with students. These reasons are amplified in combination with other technologies and practices.

To begin with, creating and consuming digital stories is seen as appealing to digitally immersed students. It is easy to find anecdotes about children and teenagers demonstrating greater cybercultural ease than their elders. Many institutions have shared their sense of a new generational divide. For example, Apple's education Web site refers to a "disconnect as the result of poor communication between 'digital natives,' today's students and 'digital immigrants,' many adults." Further: "These parents and educators, the digital immigrants, speak DSL, digital as a second language."[2]

It is also easy to overstate the technological fluency and range of millennial students, as many have pointed out. The "net.gen" model can quickly stretch beyond reality.[3] Yet, it is important to recognize the generational milieu represented by coming of age in the midst of social media. As the Pew Internet and American Life project has established since 2002, the majority of American teenagers are accustomed to publishing content online. For example, in 2007:

> 64% of online teens ages 12–17 . . . or 59% of all teens . . . have participated in one or more among a wide range of content-creating activities on the internet, up from 57% of online teens in a similar survey at the end of 2004.[4]

If we assume that these teens consume more than they produce, then "immersion" is a legitimate word to describe their experience. In 2005, one well-known study noted:

> Virtually all Net Gen students were using computers by the time they were 16 to 18 years of age. . . . Among children ages 8 to 18, 96 percent have gone online. Seventy-four percent have access at home, and 61 percent use the Internet on a typical day.[5]

This statistic has profound and subtle implications for teaching and learning. Connecting with students via storytelling is surely a tactic worth pursuing.

One aspect of that generational immersion is familiar to members of any demographic: information overload. The ease with which we produce and share digital content has exceeded many people's ability to process it. An industry of coping mechanisms and strategies has appeared, ranging from prayer to time management to the "Getting Things Done" lifestyle approach. Given this context, the ability to practically sift the information torrent is valuable. Learning how to sift is a skill all cybercultural denizens develop over time.[6]

Digital storytelling can be seen as one overload-coping mechanism. As we've seen in the course of this book, stories are tools for generating meaning and context. They involve a careful selection and arrangement of materials. "When facts become so widely available and instantly accessible, each one becomes less valuable. What begins to matter more is the ability to place these acts in *context* and to deliver them with *emotional impact*."[7] If this is correct, then schools have a responsibility to teach story literacy to students. As Joe Lambert and the CDS team observe, "Only people who develop effective filtering, indexing, and repackaging tools in their minds can manage to successfully and consistently articulate meaning that reconstructs a coherent story."

This is not the exclusive domain of artists, Lambert and colleagues continue:

> We think of the skilled professionals in any given field as having developed this process for their specialty. They can tell appropriate stories—the memory of cases for a trial lawyer, for example—based on having systematized a portion of their memories. But most skilled professionals have difficulty using examples outside of their respective fields, from their personal life or non-professional experience, but those who do are often described as story-tellers.[8]

On the one hand, teachers can introduce students to the creative work of making digital stories; on the other, we can all learn how to understand digital stories as they appear in our modern information ecosystems.

That sense of storytelling as a tool for presenting information points us to a related meaning: storytelling as a tool for understanding complex subjects. The process of creating a digital story can help us make sense of a cognitive domain. We must grapple with content in order to reshape it into a narrative. The Cynevin framework sees storytelling as functioning in a very specific level of human life, the world of complex networks. To go through the story creation process requires competent pattern recognition within the story's world.[9]

More than competence is suggested by the experience of teaching a digital storytelling workshop. Every time I help lead one, I witness a moment where the climate of the classroom suddenly changes. A phase change occurs, when participants switch from talking out loud (asking questions, chatting with each other) to quiet immersion in their work. This transformation from apprehension to absorption is powerful and points to the deep engagement the process elicits from students and practitioners. As one recently published guidebook observes, "The process of constructing digital stories inspires students to dig deeper into their subject, to think more complexly about it, and to communicate what they have learned in a more creative way."[10]

Because digital storytelling requires a significant amount of time, from preproduction through publication, it does not lend itself well to snap assignments. It does, however, suit project-based learning. The full timeline of work constitutes a class project, with all of the pedagogical benefits that entails. "Students who work together on long-term projects are less likely to be absent. They also develop cooperation and communication skills, practice problem-solving and critical-thinking skills, and improve their test scores."[11]

Digital storytelling serves teaching purposes other than those based on testing and skills. Empowering students is often cited as a product of the storytelling process, especially developing students' voices. Angela Thomas sees a major teaching opportunity in blog-based digital storytelling:

> For me as an English educator, it is particularly exciting to consider the opportunities for fictional blogs such as character diaries to give emergent writers the temporal space to develop their own narrative voice, the interactive space to give and receive feedback, and the identity space to explore their emerging lives as young people.[12]

Digital storytelling lets students own their creative work, taking the narrative process to themselves.

A mirror image of students practicing their own voice comes from game playing. As James Paul Gee has argued, games offer learners the opportunity to experience a world through several forms of fictional identity. Players adopt a mixture of virtual and real-world identities, which can allow a mixture of personal investment and role playing. A projective identity adds a third level of self, an aspirational one, based on a goal to attain or a tendency to cultivate.[13] If we see students as playing games that have storytelling features, then this tripartite identity play lets them ultimately explore the boundaries of their selves. If we see students as creating games or game content [virtual world items; user-created modified versions of game content or entire games (game mods)], then they enact our previous model of self achieved through creation—but also one that must engage audiences in terms of *their* identify exploration. Depending on the type of digital story, individual learners explore voice and self.

That process is sometimes team based, and therefore digital storytelling can help students practice collaborative learning. "When students write scripts together, for example, they have to decide how to blend different languages, voices, and ideas, and they have to agree on what tone and angle to use."[14] In the context of an academic culture driven by argumentative writing, storytelling offers a different approach: "Narrative by contrast comes at us collaboratively . . . inviting us gently to follow the story arm-in-arm with the listener. It is more like a dance than a battle."[15] At times, individual students assign themselves specific technical or creative functions, requiring careful project management across those differences.

Beyond individual projects, these skills and practices can then impact teaching practice in general. Collaboration, project-based learning, student voice development, immersion in content, and coping with information overload are all traits teachers and schools sometimes encourage and support. Digital storytelling practice can build on these.

Practical Pedagogies

The many pedagogies of teaching digital storytelling practice are now manifold, after years of experiment and practice. There is a wide range of diversity in implementation, given the huge variety education allows. We can summarize major approaches here, while adding specific examples from classes and teachers.

To begin with, the digital storytelling idea usually needs explication. Storytelling is part of students' lives, of course, but the paradigm can be brought into class through examples and discussion of stories. This introduction can be amplified by readings or can lead directly into digital storytelling work through reverse engineering. Peter Kittle describes his practice in terms of backward storyboarding, whereby "students in small groups . . . look through different sections of 'Daddy Duty' [a sample digital story], and identify the functions of the audio and visual attributes." Note that the small groups can then return as production teams. Moreover, this reverse storyboard changes student perceptions of the creative process: "The effect of our discussions on the structural functions of the multimodal document was that students began to read multimodal texts from the perspective of a composer, not simply a consumer."[16]

When students begin making digital stories, the overall pedagogical mode can be seen as either assessment based or constructivist. Constructivist learning appears most clearly during the process of making a story, which is, on several levels, the process of making meaningful learning. Further, a constructivist style then embeds that work in a metacognition framework, helping students make connections between their creation and their sense of learning:

> building a portfolio of learning stories through digital storytelling, of how students approached problems individually or in collaboration, detailing the steps and actions their approaches inspired, and reflecting on the insights that their eventual success, or possibly failure, reveal; [this style] provides a vivid and enjoyable mechanism for charting the development of their learning skills.[17]

An assessment pedagogy, on the other hand, focuses on digital storytelling for content mastery. The story creation process is a test of how students internalize material. In this mode, teachers distinguish deeply between form and content. Form (media craft) is very attractive in digital stories and can engage media-saturated students. It therefore needs carefully outlined assessment criteria so that students do not focus on it to the exclusion of story content. Digital stories demonstrate content mastery through the display of research. This mastery can appear in many media forms (voiceover with images, subtitled credits, etc.), and also as linked in supplemental material (sources, extra documentation).

Additionally, a digital story can be assessed for how well it carries out an argument. A story can contain a thesis (its theme or problem), supporting evidence, and a clear organization. Group projects require group-level additional assessment about individual roles and overall effectiveness of collaboration. Instructors and students both benefit from having access to assessment rubrics from the project's start, as Gail Matthews-DeNatale and others have argued. One rubric can build in peer assessment as well as instructor review. Two rubrics would be used, one for content and the other for digital form.[18] An example of this offers different ratings for purpose, audience, dramatic question, script, audio, point of view, emotion, images, economy, and credit.[19]

The direct work of creating a digital story does not have to be a single, unitary experience. Some teachers have had successes in assigning complementary assignments. Barbara Ganley, for example, taught her Middlebury College students not only to create videos but also to blog about the experience over time. We can also borrow from the portfolio approach to student composition and assume that digital stories include multiple assignment steps along with meta-level self-reflections along the way.[20] Another approach is to construct small digital storytelling assignments distributed in time, growing in complexity, and scaffolding upon each other.[21]

Many specific curricular situations call forth tailored uses of digital storytelling. For example, Doug Reilly has pioneered a study-abroad approach, which addresses the classic problem of students grappling with a rich experience once they return home; he refers to it as "predeparture and reentry programming." Reilly works with students to make short videos, using the storytelling process to organize diverse events and reflections. The growing prominence of mobile devices will probably speed this practice, Reilly notes: "I can imagine a student or group of students spending a morning scripting and shooting raw material for a digital story onsite, spending the afternoon in a cafe putting the digital story together on an iPad, and showing it in the evening at a group session."[22]

The obverse of study abroad storytelling is migrant students creating digital narratives. Story composition helps these learners reflect on their passage through nations, addressing challenges to their identity, and questioning cultural integration. Darvin and Norton urge a digital storytelling pedagogy for this population that takes into account:

1. the modes and degrees of affiliation of migrant language learners with their country of origin
2. the material conditions of these learners in their country of settlement, and
3. the extent to which the interplay of these two shape their ways of thinking and learning, their degrees of assimilation, and their investment in learning.

Clearly this is a complex practice, one that goes beyond technology alone and possibly requiring faculty to become involved with student life and other campus services.[23]

All of the preceding is based on students creating digital stories. Now we turn to faculty making their own digital stories, which can take one of several forms.

First, teachers can create digital stories about the content they teach. A decade ago, this practice would have been considered producing learning objects; in 2010, these are simply content items, learning materials. If they are made available to the open Web for use and reuse, then they are open educational resources (OER). Whatever the descriptive language, each digital story explicates one part of a subject area. Some instructors choose to create a story that dives deeply into one aspect of an issue, while others use the story medium to introduce a larger topic. In one of my workshops, a political scientist created a story introducing the concept of his specialty, African politics. In another, a French teacher composed a short story about one Francophonic nation, carefully using locally suited vocabulary to anchor the tale in this *pays*. Over time, multiple stories can be combined, of course, into a larger approach to a specialty.

Second, teachers can use stories to introduce students to themselves. For example, Williams College professor Enrique Peacock Lopez used the CDS method to explain his passion for chemistry, taking the audience through his education as a conversation with his children.[24] Naturally, these two approaches can be combined, as a teacher's storytelling voice can communicate his or her love for a subject while teaching it.

Faculty and students can work together to produce a digital story. Professor Mike Wesch and 10 of his students combined video and gaming technology to create "Falling Up," a biographical study of a retired couple's memories of their life together. The collaborative "used real field audio and video which is then embedded in a 3D environment," yielding an emotionally powerful and media-rich experience.[25]

Fitting digital storytelling practice into an academic unit requires acknowledging the demands of time. We may think of storytelling as something done quickly, perhaps through improvisation. But the full process of creation and composition requires extension in time, much as our definition of story does. The amount of time depends on what type of story is being considered. For example, the CDS curriculum can take two, but usually three entire days, as we saw in Chapter 13. This time can be distributed over a greater number of days, but the roughly 24 hours involved still need to be allocated—and connected, if separated. Less demanding technologies and platforms—writing in blogs, taking photographs, editing a wiki being relatively brief exercises—require less time. But everything else involved in story making, in establishing the story *mentality,* takes time: open discussions, brainstorming, writing, revision, hunting for media, revising again. Experiencing stories, too, soaks up time, in or outside of class. The payoffs for storytelling are impressive, but we need to be mindful of one of the costs: scheduling.

A common refrain in discussions about digital storytelling in education is the necessity of curricular integration. This requirement represents a subset of a broader conversation concerning the meaning of technology in education and the importance of making digital work evidently part of the learning mission. Storytelling cannot be seen as separate from learning, even though the mind-set may break from the ordinary classroom world of tests and standards. Story assignments, therefore, need to be interconnected with curriculum in many ways. A discipline's unique storytelling approaches can be recognized (e.g., consider the role of passive voice in science writing). Students can rummage through a subject area's media world for digital story content, which may involve teachers and librarians in helping guide learners to those online areas.

A classroom story may be distributed across a course timeline, especially if the teacher cannot afford to break out a string of days to focus on storytelling. In such cases, successive curricular steps can be linked to a sequence of storytelling work. For example, a class on the French Revolution begins with a survey of *l'ancien regime*, the prerevolutionary order. To begin work on a story about the causes of the revolution, students start to assemble media about pre-1789 France. To better do so requires learning about major aspects and issues in that field of history: class structure, the monarchy, financial problems, support for the American Revolution. This combination of academic with digital research may lead to students creating short stories such as a blog characterization, a one-minute video, or a group wiki tracing the course of financial crisis. Or the teacher may decide to refrain from that assignment and instead require students to maintain a media archive. Next, the class moves on to the events of 1789, and again the students assemble media. They may also reflect on what they've learned so far, either in narrative or nonnarrative form. As the course proceeds into the end of Louis XVI's regime, still more opportunities for stories present themselves. Students can also reflect in a metacognitive way about their learning experience so far, identifying problems and strengths and exploring their individual ways of apprehending a topic. Step by step, the course advances, with digital storytelling increments along the way.

One of the most ambitious and innovative digital storytelling pedagogical cases has been a massively open online class, or MOOC, known as DS106. The class began as a face-to-face one taught at the University of Mary Washington by Jim Groom. A devotee of the open web and inspired by the experience of early MOOCs, such as Connectivism, Groom placed all class content online for any interested party to consider. And then things took off.

A number of people started doing Groom's assignments and sharing the results. Twitter became a major communication point via the #DS106 hashtag. The popularity of the class on campus led to further iterations over the next years. Teachers started suggesting assignments, so many that the class Web site spawned a large homework prompt bank. A Twitter-organized class Web radio station appeared. Other faculty taught new sections, providing their own take on digital storytelling, sometimes by structuring their own class through a specific paradigm or according to a body of work, such as the Western, or the TV series *The Wire*. Groom and others experimented with creating new teaching personae, embodying storytelling principles while teaching them. Video content grew into a DS106 Web video channel. A handbook was collaboratively authored and shared. Wholly online versions were taught.

As of this writing, DS106 represents an astonishing amount of creativity and energy. The archives are rich and open to anyone with a Web browser. The project—or is it a movement?—should inspire any teacher interested in digital storytelling and anyone thinking about creating digital narratives.[26]

Up to this point, I have spoken only of teachers and students, but it is vital to recognize that supporting digital storytelling in schools is a more complex affair. Individual teachers may not feel comfortable supporting the full digital storytelling range of competencies, from storytelling to technology to curricular integration. Alternatively, a teacher may assert all of these, but not be able to manage them when the number of students reaches a certain level. Support strategies have appeared in several forms.

First, student peer teaching can be both useful and academically powerful. Without buying into clichés of net.gen cyberguruship, a teacher can identify several students who are especially skilled in the requisite technologies. They can then be assigned to help their classmates in whatever formal or informal manner best suits the class: in-class mentoring, titles ("Class Technologist," "Chief Edupunk"), out-of-class study groups. As students progress, they will increasingly be able to assist each other. Even without feeling or being skilled, students also make fine audiences for each other. Social learning is a hallmark of digital storytelling, and it can fit well with its classroom equivalent.

Second, other school staff can assist, depending on a campus's resources. Reference and instructional librarians can help students with finding and aggregating information and media, for instance. Media services (formerly A/V) specialists are obviously expert in manipulating media. Academic or instructional technologists are often capable of assisting the entire digital storytelling process. Again, access to such staff depends on local conditions.

I conclude this chapter on a personal note. Since I first started working in digital storytelling, it has been a delight to see the steady rise of educational uses. The number of examples continues to grow, as does the population of faculty practicing digital storytelling. They reinforce each other, inspiring more exploration and projects. As a teacher, this process is enormously gratifying and exciting. The need for resources raised by digital storytelling can sometimes be used as an argument for more such staff support.

All of these resources are on site; online communities are also valuable. As we saw in Chapter 13, there currently exist many resources and networks to help practitioners with various tools and topics. Moreover, in the age of social media, every teacher blogging or otherwise sharing an experience is another solid case from which other instructors can learn.

CHAPTER SIXTEEN

Coda: Toward the Next Wave of Digital Storytelling

In Chapters 1–3, we sketched out the first generation and ancestry of digital storytelling. Chapters 4–15 explored digital storytelling in a second generation as it moved into new platforms and evolved emergent practices, opening onto a third generation. What should we expect to see next?

Quality and assessment issues are likely to persist. Some digital stories are poor in quality for most audiences, much as oral tales can be and have been throughout history. Standards have developed for certain forms, like gaming and CDS-style digital stories, and new media studies have been developing an aesthetic. Assessing works that cut across platforms is a new field. As Henry Jenkins observes, "We do not yet have very good aesthetic criteria for evaluating works that play themselves out across multiple media." It is still early in the historical process, he says: "There have been far too few fully transmedia stories for media makers to act with any certainty about what would constitute the best uses of this new mode of storytelling."[1]

The reputation of digital storytelling as a whole remains open, if not fraught with negative potential. Media coverage has a tendency to exploit cultural anxieties and to look for horrors associated with digital media. Gaming in general is frequently subjected to lurid stories about players starving to death or otherwise acting poorly. Alternate reality gaming and live-action role-playing games occasionally encounter problems in public performance, as nonplayers experience the strangeness of a game inserted into everyday life.[2] Despite the continuing adoption of gaming throughout most populations, and probably because of that reach, we can expect a backlash to continue.

Another form of storytelling backlash may well arise in response to digital storytelling's perceived success, media hype, and positive reputation. Digital storytelling could advance up one side of Gartner's famous hype cycle,[3] then suffer a crash before returning to solid productivity. For example, a satirical listicle on Medium flays podcasts mercilessly:

> Four Journalists Discuss Politics In A Friendly, Accessible Way That Tricks You Into Thinking They're Not Sociopaths
>
> Immersive, In-Depth Reporting, Which, In This Case, Means A Report That Is Longer Than 3–5 Minutes
>
> Bullshit Science With High Production Values . . .
>
> Real Humans' Devastating Tragedy Is Turned Into A Serialized Podcast For Your Entertainment . . .
>
> Storytelling, Because Storytelling Is An Important Human Communication Form And We're All Storytellers Just Trying To Tell Our Stories To Each Other[4]

Furthermore, a too positive overly rosy impression leaves storytelling open to charges of naivete or misdirection. As David Snowden points out, stories manipulate audiences, which isn't necessarily a good or ethical thing. He goes on to recommend: "If you are going to teach storytelling . . . then honesty is the best policy. Realise that you are teaching a manipulative technique, agree [on] the grounds rules, discuss the ethics with your client."[5]

Moreover, a single story can be compelling enough to drive out other alternative stories and voices, as Chimamanda Adichie points out. As listeners, we can be powerfully shaped by stories as children, as people seeking growth and identification; successful stories can soak up those desires—which is not necessarily a good thing.[6] The way some digital storytelling platforms are acculturated as children's items, such as some games and comics, is germane here.[7]

A related problem concerns the different social understandings of digital storytelling movements. The CDS-style curriculum emphasizes building the voice and agency of creators; most game design approaches lack this kind of politics. For creators, many game production teams fold individual designers into larger teams, while the independent games movement shows few signs of CDS-style community engagement. For players, while political mobilization games exist, they are vastly outnumbered by non-activist, disengaged entertainments.[8] If these divergent trends persist, the political split in contemporary digital storytelling will deepen.

Experimental or unusual storytelling approaches may develop a different type of negative reputation, namely, of losing their power over audiences, becoming too weak to bear the burden of storytelling. Roger Caillois famously identifies a shift in how a culture's historical transformation can proceed by sapping certain games of their power:

> Each time that an advanced culture succeeds in emerging from the chaotic original, a palpable repression of the powers of vertigo and simulation [mimicry and ilinx, in Caillois's terms] is verified. They lose their traditional dominance, are pushed to the periphery of public life, reduced to roles that become more and more modern and intermittent, if not clandestine and guilty.

Their stories are thus weakened, he continues, "afford[ing] men the same eternal satisfactions, but in sublimated form, serving merely as an escape from boredom or work and entailing neither madness nor delirium."[9] That drained form of escape also entails neither meaning nor engagement. Put another way, it is the classic story of the avant-garde being domesticated in mainstreaming.

A different trend line is that of gaming's growing ubiquity. That storytelling form continues to grow, as we have discussed, and has emerged as one of the world's leading narrative platforms, penetrating into daily life. The term *gamification* describes the adoption of game practices by nongame entities, such as companies or governments using rewards programs or persuasive gaming. Moreover, the growth in persistent gameplay identity suggests that our personal histories may be increasingly bound up with the games we play.[10]

We could see game-based storytelling branching out across new technologies and multiple proscenia as games grow in popularity and technologies become gradually easier to use. *Dayz* might offer a glimpse of this, with its combination of software development, video stories, a large community, and multiplayer gaming.[11] *Minecraft* goes much further. Its "story mode" appropriately anchors players in time, thrusting them against obstacles and challenges. The low- resolution graphics have proven very attractive to legions of players. Those players have carried their creativity and stories on to epic lengths and have shared those across other media, most impressively on YouTube. The popularity of *Minecraft*'s out-of-game work, combined with the size of Twitch's streamed and recording gameplay audience, suggests game-based storytelling will expand across a variety of media.

Games may develop new social functions. *Ruby Quest* is a story that was played between a designer/game master and an audience. The former put forth a game situation and asked people for how characters should respond. That dynamic faded at certain narrative moments, then returned to the foreground for others. *Ruby* is something like a recording of a role-playing game session, but with the game mechanics made manifest and part of the plot.[12]

One trend to bear in mind is the continuing appeal of mysteries, not as a tactic but as a genre. Serial narratives might privilege mysteries, since there needs to be a hook to drive readers from piece to distributed piece. Note, for instance, the predominance of mysteries in alternate reality games and as underpinning for major console game plots.

Technological advancement offers many, many possible futures, from new platforms to additional devices. One trend we can note is that of automated storytelling. We mentioned data-driven remixes in Chapter 4 (Twist-ori, *We Feel Vine*). We can recall as well that digital video and audio editors are increasingly stocked with templates and precreated content. Google recently ramped up its autocomplete feature, for example, trying to antici-pate the searcher's quest.

Far beyond the hated "Clippy," Microsoft Word's notorious assistant ("It looks like you're writing a letter!"), are tools like OhLife.[13] This service helps a writer build an autobiographical narrative through e-mail prompts, rest-ing on a Web-based timeline. A message from OhLife to me, with the subject line "It's Thursday, Aug 5—How did your day go?" read:

> Just reply to this e-mail with your entry.
> Write about anything from today—like what you did, something you're feeling, or a conversation you had with a friend. And feel free to keep it short. A quick sentence is just fine! But if you want to write more, you can go ahead and write a longer entry too.
> After you reply to this e-mail, your entry will show up here: http://ohlife .com/today

A similar project is 750Words, which assists the writer in composition.[14] These services are nearly game-like in their careful interaction with the reader/writer, inviting us to play on.

The continuing ferment of software development produces a steady stream of new platforms, some of which do not fit into readily understand-able categories. Twitter appeared in such a fashion, and early commenta-tors struggled to assign it a recognizable pigeonhole: Microblog? Status update? One current example is Vuvox,[15] which lets users produce a hori-zontally scrolling media object, a kind of cross between timeline, collage, comic book, and side-scroller video game, although it's much simpler to make and easier to understand than that string of comparisons suggests.

Stories can unfurl through Vuvox using the techniques we've explored in this book, while its own affordances are still being explored. At a different level, the steady growth of social media means that more connections between stories are becoming visible. Influence, reception, and affiliation increasingly appear through tags, links, likes, embeds, and each new connective technology.[16]

Other tools explore the possibilities of remixing. Curated.by Storify, each tool offers ways of extracting and arranging social media content: Twitter updates, Instagram images, YouTube videos, Flickr images. The results appear along a vertical timeline.[17] Zooburst lets users build augmented reality pop-up storybooks, which can be viewed in two dimensions or three.[18]

Mobile devices are likely to continue to be fertile ground for storytelling creativity. We've discussed a variety of movements and projects in the emerging world of ubiquitous computing, from *keitai* novels to repurposed interactive fiction to multiple forms of augmented reality (Chapters 9 and 11). No single approach is likely to dominate such a broad field, but storytelling itself might well find its primary home to be on handheld mobile devices.

Storytelling consumption through mobiles is already widespread, as is media capture. But storytelling creation is shifting to mobile devices as well, as media capture, editing, and sharing tools increase in accessibility and power. Alan Levine observes that audio recording, photography, and videography are fitting this curve. At present, we assemble mobile-captured materials after an interval of time and a shift in space to laptop and desktop computer. But better production and creation tools, combined with better connectivity to both media and peers, can lead to "a miniature studio on the go." The results could include more "live" stories, stories emphasizing the present more frequently. Moreover, having such a studio in one's pocket could change the way users look at the world if parts of that world can be rapidly converted into socially shared stories.[19] We may already see the first example of this mobile digital storytelling studio with the iPhone. As Ruben Puentedura puts it, "I can do on my iPhone what [the CDS curriculum] does with desktops."[20]

Much of this mobile work is still foundational. For instance, Joseph Esposito's 2008 call for interstitial publishing remains fresh:

For "five-minute fiction" to catch on, we will need creative people who probe the nature of the interstitial medium. . . . Publishers will need to seek out writers who comprehend the new medium, who can engage a reader for five minutes, who can make the many pieces of the work congeal in the reader's mind. These writers will study readers, PDAs or smart phones in hand, standing before the spinning dryer in the laundromat, stopped at a red light, preparing to board a plane, waiting for the meeting to begin. In all of this publishers will see growth.[21]

Creating stories in a world of ubiquitous computing may no longer rely on the Romantic model of a single creator. Since so much of social media is based on different types of collaborative writing and multiple authorship, it's reasonable to expect more forms of coauthored storytelling to emerge. For example, video production is currently a single-author process; either one person assembles, edits, and publishes the content, a la Webcams or the CDS model, or a single project team produces a video as an aggregate, with each contributor working on one piece (actor, writer, voiceover, etc.). Collaborative video editing, however, is difficult, largely due to the unwieldy nature of video project files that are not easy to swap between computers. It is actually easier to hand a laptop from person to person than to shuttle huge files across a network from application to application.

The late Jumpcut service offered an elegant solution to this problem. One user saved a video mix in a Web browser, then sent its URL to a collaborator. The latter then opened the file in the Jumpcut editor. Edits could be made, then saved and accessed in turn by the original creator. It looked like a preproduction video project file could be left open for the world to edit, as a kind of Web 2.0 video wiki. This possibility was closed off in 2009, unfortunately, when Yahoo closed down Jumpcut.[22] WeVideo, mentioned above, offers a better (and still working) example.

On a far smaller scale, new experiments in collaborative writing are likely to appear. For example, CREEatives is based on writers taking turns adding individual sentences, growing a short-short story by round-robin. Perhaps that microfocus owes something to the success of Twitter's microblogging and Facebook status updates or is a form of open Exquisite Corpse.[23] Alternatively, multiple authorship might express itself through multiple voices. As a team and players co-create game content, from alternate reality games to massively multiplayer online games, we could see more projects like *The Twitter of Oz* or *Such Tweet Sorrow*. That latter romance featured five characters, each with a separate author. Readers could follow the aggregate live, or in synthetic arrangement afterward, or focus on individual character microblogging.[24]

Copyright policy struggles are also likely to persist, given the intractable nature of the problem, the depth of law, and the powers of intellectual property (IP) owners. Therefore, we may expect storytelling communities to maintain policies and practices to ward off copyright challenges. Fanfiction.net, for example, carefully structured copyright terms of service.[25]

Multiple platforms, or multiple proscenia, may well become the norm for storytelling in general. The ease of creating social media content, combined with the ever-increasing amount of social media content, should draw more content creators (and IP owners) to shift or add content to such platforms in addition to their usual venues. Several such projects appeared in 2010, including *Shadow Unit* and *The Mongoliad*. They included blogs or content published blog-style, wikis, Twitter updates, e-mail, Web widgets, physical objects, and active audience participation across all of these venues. Content is beamed at laptops, desktops, and various mobile devices. The business models for these story projects are developing.[26]

As an audience—or Clay Shirky's "those formerly known as the audience"—our ability to move between platforms through hyperlinking, media embedding, browser tabs, and growing multitasking practice should render multiplatform strategies ever more acceptable. Our growing personal immersion in cyberculture, through the combination of social media with mobile platforms, seems to be making once exotic venues quotidian. Indeed, as we have come to see unplugging, taking a media fast, or going without devices to be an unusual, nearly monastic experience, so may single-item, single-platform stories become rare. They may receive a new luster as a result, too.

Divisions may become as marked as combinations and syntheses. We have already noted the silo nature of console gaming and mobile phones, which tend to be biased toward device-specific storytelling, unlike the Web's philosophy of cross-platform compatibility. If such silos persist or grow, we may see digital storytelling marked by divisions like those between poets and novelists, between classical musicians and punks, or even between spoken languages. Beyond the politics of proprietary systems, storytelling practice may drive other divides. For example, *Second Life* versus augmented reality: "Few pervasive games employ any persistent three-dimensional virtual worlds."[27]

We should also be open to even newer and perhaps stranger forms of digital storytelling. For example, "The Interface Series" consists of a series of comments posted to Reddit threads, surrealistically independent of those threads' contents. Enterprising fellow Reddit users noticed these narrative intrusions and, in fine social media style, aggregated and organized them elsewhere on Reddit. It is not easy to classify "Interface" formally, as the story pieces appear without a shape recognizable from other stories. The narrative's contents, drawing on war, conspiracy theory, substance abuse, and science fiction, also resist easy categorization.[28]

Other social media venues have been hosting other narrative experiments. An Urban Dictionary entry for "clock spider" now contains several microstories about this disturbing and perhaps mythical creature. Some of the entries conform to the Dictionary's style, complete with a definition and examples:

Clock Spider: (n) 1. A large spider found benieth a clock in a home. 2. Big ass spider living in Cambodia 3. Future ruler of the earth and all life forms living upon it

1.   *Oh God, put the clock down! There's a Clock Spider living benieth it!*
2.   *The staple diet of a Cambodian hobo is the Clock Spider.*
3.   *Hail the Clock Spider for there is only one.*

Others avoid the format completely and simply tell a story:

the legendary clock spider, ninth leg is said to be what all religions worship, after it was severed from an epic battle with limecat. the clock spider and limecat then allied themselves to kill eternal ferret. May clock spider live forever
    that is the one and only clock spider

Some entries include images, while others link to other Urban Dictionary content, turning the latter into characters for Clock Spider consumption. In other words, Clock Spider tales are not just intrusions, but integrated into the Dictionary's larger world.[29] We can view these guerrilla microtales as expressions of the deep, persistent, human desire to tell stories and to use any new communication technology as a venue. Perhaps we will see these microtales increase in number and develop into another offshoot of digital storytelling.

Further, virtual and augmented reality combine in what some call "mixed reality." Virtual images and sounds appear within a user's immediate physical space. A Microsoft Hololens user, for example, can play the *Minecraft* game upon their real-world kitchen table. A Magic Leap user can see a dolphin leap from his living room wall or behold a solar system revolving upon her desk, or so they claim now, as of this writing, before any technology has actually been shipped.

Hololens projects give us a sample of using MR for storytelling. Basic games have already appeared, such as an alien invasion battle that breaks out in the space right around the player. I am more intrigued by "Fragments," a detective story staged in that personal space. The creators claim the application maps characters, objects, and even mystery clues directly onto the room around the Hololens hardware, down to installing thumbprints on furniture. This feature changes VR's powerful sense of setting by making that setting local rather than distant, letting a story unfold in a more familiar location. The feature might work better for location-independent stories than those relying on a specific setting.[30]

Each of these unfolding possibilities will probably play out at some level in education. Informal education can partake of any medium, of course. But such is the diversity and love of exploration in academia that creative forms of storytelling can always be attempted somewhere, to some degree, despite institutional inertia or economic pressures. Recall our Venn diagram from Chapter 3.

Each of those areas—storytelling, social media, and gaming—is in play in education as of this writing. Their overlaps are being engaged. Educators and those beyond schools should keep an eye out for emerging practices.

As we saw in Chapter 15, digital storytelling offers many advantages to various curricular situations and pedagogical styles. Such matches of academic matter with digital technologies can guide us to impending developments. Site-specific research, for example, from community engagement to teacher education to urban studies, could well be an area for augmented reality games and stories.[31] Digital literacy programs can use alternate reality games to develop players' skeptical skills. Building up a collaboratively authored networked book is already an established pedagogical practice;[32] adding storytelling elements could further student engagement while creating an interesting result. Alternatively, consider a mobile journal with some contents addressed to Google Earth and others tied to specific augmented reality sites. Perhaps Trip Journal organizes these materials.[33] A student builds this journal over time, connecting with peers, remixing media, and creating and sharing stories on the go. Her pathway through space, time, and media is partially visible to other netizens—anyone with a phone—through a mix of influence, comments, and tagging.[34] What kind of classwork best mobilizes her skills and abilities? How do instructors learn how to teach her?

At a meta level, we will see more stories *about* the new digital storytelling. Computer-mediated storytelling has appeared within other stories for some time. Urban legends about games date back decades,[35] such as the story of the madness-inducing arcade game *Polybius*:

> This game had a very limited release, one or two backwater arcades in a suburb of Portland. The history of this game is cloudy, there were all kinds of strange stories about how kids who played it got amnesia afterwards, couldn't remember their name or where they lived, etc.
> The bizarre rumors about this game are that it was supposedly developed by some kind of weird military tech offshoot group, used some kind

of proprietary behavior modification algorithms developed for the CIA or something, kids who played it woke up at night screaming, having horrible nightmares.

According to an operator who ran an arcade with one of these games, guys in black coats would come to collect "records" from the machines. They're not interested in quarters or anything, they just collected information about how the game was played.[36]

An early form of this practice is Alex Payne's "They Stopped Calling It Rendezvous" (2005), a story about a man falling in love through social media.[37] Blogs have also started appearing in suspense fiction and science fiction. In Ken MacLeod's techno-thriller *The Execution Channel* (2007), several espionage agencies maintain an overlapping series of blogs for purposes of disinformation and intelligence gathering. Each one must tell a convincing story, complete with authorial personae, in order to win a credulous audience: pretend dissident professors, everyday soldiers, conspiracy experts. Naturally enough, the reader may be led to wonder how many blogs in the world are actually such convincing stories.[38] How long before a murder mystery includes a podcaster, with clues in a wiki?

Platforms and Next Levels

If gaming is now a vast industry, could social media and CDS-style digital storytelling become only a minor literature, or simply statistically rare?[39] In Chapter 2, we surveyed some early forms of digital storytelling that broke new ground in their times: hypertext via the Storyspace and Hypercard platforms, virtual worlds in text-based MUDs and MOOs, interactive fiction (Adventure International, Infocom). And each was drastically supplanted by new technologies and practices: the Web becoming the world's most vast hypertext engine, games and *Second Life* the leading virtual worlds, games again over interactive fiction. Mobile apps outflanked the Web, gaming became enormous, and virtual and augmented reality started to grow. Perhaps what this book has described currently occupies that first historical moment, awaiting a supplanting, booming second stage. These practices are the avant-garde awaiting a transformation to some new, popular format set. Or perhaps we are living and storytelling through the moment before the onslaught of some vast, game-changing new narrative form. "Ah, those were the days before [X] changed it all!" we will reminisce. That will be a story, of course, told and retold through the new proscenia.

In the meantime, we are creating new digital stories in 2017. We can guess at the future for now, until it arrives to tell us its new stories.

Notes

The first epigraph is from Daniel H. Pink, *A Whole New Mind: Why Right-Brainers Will Rule the Future* (New York: Riverhead, 2005), 106.

Introduction

1. Others have had a similar experience: "I stared at it, thinking that it must be a fleeting phantom from an alternate and more awesome version of our world. But no, this book exists IN THIS UNIVERSE" (Wade Rockett, http://www.flickr.com/photos/waderockett/2229789094/). Now the book can be found through Amazon and eBay, scans accessed from Google Books, and multiple fan sites.

2. Beginner's All-Purpose Symbolic Instruction Code, 1964.

3. Howard Rheingold, *Tools for Thought: The History and Future of Mind-Expanding Technology,* 2nd ed. (Cambridge, MA: MIT Press, 2000).

4. Annette Simmons, *The Story Factor: Secrets of Influence from the Art of Storytelling,* 2nd ed. (New York: Basic Books, 2006).

5. David Edgerton, *The Shock of the Old: Technology and Global History since 1900* (New York: Oxford University Press, 2006).

6. Julian Bleeker, "Design Fiction: A Short Essay on Design, Science, Fact and Fiction," Near Future Laboratory, March 2009, http://drbfw5wfjlxon.cloudfront.net/writing/DesignFiction_WebEdition.pdf; Bruce Sterling, Visionary in Residence (New York: Thunder's Mouth Press, 2006).

7. https://bryanalexander.org/category/digitalstorytelling/; https://www.diigo.com/user/bryanalexander?query=digitalstorytelling; https://newdigitalstorytelling.net/.

Chapter 1

1. These examples were drawn from, respectively: http://www.fflickr.com/groups/visualstory/discuss/72157603786255599/; https://web-beta.archive.org/

web/20170205174108/http://www.project1968.com; http://askawizard.blogspot
.com/2008/11/war-of-worlds-20-post-mortem.html; and Jenna Wortham, "Twitterers Stage Mock Martian Invasion a la 'War of the Worlds,'" *Wired*, October 31,
2008, http://www.wired.com/underwire/2008/10/twitterers-stag/; https://www
.youtube.com/watch?v=czoSEn8YSwo; http://www.storycenter.org/stories/index
.php?cat=4; http:// www.metaurchins.org/book/home.htm; Dana Goodyear, "I
Novels: Young Women Develop a Genre for the Cellular Age," *New Yorker,* December 22, 2008, http://www. newyorker.com/magazine/2008/12/22/i-love-novels;
Linda Vierecke, "Young Holocaust Victim Has over 1,700 Friends on Facebook,"
Deutsche Welle, November 19, 2009, http://www.dw-world.de/dw/article/0,,49
08523,00.html.

2. The concept album is alive and well, as Dr. Dre is working on one: "An
instrumental album is something I've been wanting to do for a long time. I have
the ideas for it. I want to call it *The Planets*. I don't even know if I should be say-
ing this, but fuck it. [Laughs.] It's just my interpretation of what each planet
sounds like. I'm gonna go off on that. Just all instrumental. I've been studying the
planets and learning the personalities of each planet. I've been doing this for about
two years now just in my spare time so to speak. I wanna do it in surround
sound. It'll have to be in surround sound for Saturn to work" (http://www.vibe
.com/2010/08/dr-dre-talks-detox-waitunder-pressure-frustration-and-instrumental
-album/).

3. http://thecreatorsproject.vice.com/blog/inside-look-data-visualizing
-wwiis-death-toll.

4. Robert McKee, *Story* (New York: HarperCollins, 1997), 181ff.

5. In Scott McCloud, *Understanding Comics* (Northampton, MA: Kitchen
Sink Press, 1993), 5.

6. Story Kitchen, "Storytelling Part 1: Change of Storytelling," July 2010,
http://vimeo.com/12999733.

7. Sheila Curran Bernard, *Documentary Storytelling for Film and Videomakers,*
2nd ed. (Burlington, VT: Focal Press, 2007), 15; emphasis in original.

8. Bernard, *Documentary Storytelling,* 19.

9. Daniel H. Pink, *A Whole New Mind: Why Right-Brainers Will Rule the
Future* (New York: Riverhead, 2005), 103.

10. "Ira Glass on Storytelling," part 1, YouTube video (5:24), from a CurrentTV
interview uploaded by user kentjl on August 13, 2006, https://vimeo.com/
22972267.

11. Cognitive Edge, "Anecdote Circles," http://cognitive-edge.com/methods/
anecdote-circles/.

12. Ibid.

13. "Ira Glass on Storytelling."

14. Bernard, *Documentary Storytelling,* 25.

15. Jason Ohler, *Digital Storytelling in the Classroom: New Media Pathways to
Literacy, Learning, and Creativity* (Thousand Oaks, CA: Corwin, 2008), 72–73.

16. James Bonnet, *Stealing Fire from the Gods: The Complete Guide to Story for Writers and Filmmakers,* 2nd ed. (Studio City, CA: M. Wiese Productions, 2006).

17. McKee, *Story,* 4. See also Paul Di Filippo's clever alternate history, "Campbell's World" (1993), where Joseph, not John W., Campbell becomes editor of *Astounding Science Fiction.*

18. Annette Simmons, *The Story Factor: Secrets of Influence from the Art of Storytelling,* 2nd ed. (New York: Basic Books, 2006), 117.

19. Asking an audience to determine the sources of these lines can be a good exercise.

20. Bernard, *Documentary Storytelling,* 18.

21. These comments are not a criticism of the PowerPoint software, one of the most influential communication tools of our time. Rather, they are a critique of style, of usage rather than what enables the use.

22. Simmons, *Story Factor,* 126.

23. Simmons, *Story Factor,* 34, emphasis added; see also 45, 94.

24. Charles Baxter, *The Art of Subtext: Beyond Plot* (Saint Paul, MN: Graywolf Press, 2007), 37.

25. Ohler, *Digital Storytelling,* 53. Note Ohler's expanded sense of character, "which can be anything from a person to a group of people to an inanimate object."

26. Bernard, *Documentary Storytelling,* 21, 317.

27. Bryan Alexander and Alan Levine, "Web 2.0 Storytelling: Emergence of a New Genre," *EDUCAUSE Review* 43, no. 6 (November/December 2008), http://er.educause.edu/articles/2008/10/web-20-storytelling-emergence-of-a-new-genre.

28. I am indebted to professor Tobin Siebers for this insight.

29. http://googleblog.blogspot.com/search/label/yourgooglestories.

30. http://storyquestproject.com/.

31. See Yochai Benkler's *The Wealth of Networks: How Social Production Transforms Markets and Freedom* (New Haven, CT: Yale University Press, 2006); Clay Shirky's *Here Comes Everybody: The Power of Organizing without Organizations* (New York: Penguin, 2008); and *Cognitive Surplus: Creativity and Generosity in a Connected Age* (New York: Penguin, 2010), 45ff.

32. Lorien C. Abroms and R. Craig Lefebvre, "Obama's Wired Campaign: Lessons for Public Health Communication," *Journal of Health Communication Newsletter* 5, no. 3 (2009), https://pdfs.semanticscholar.org/f8d2/e096f00ce81eb0a5cb764e4fecde77ab1726.pdf; David Carr, "How Obama Tapped into Social Networks' Power," *New York Times,* November 9, 2008. http://www.nytimes.com/2008/11/10/business/media/10carr.html.

Chapter 2

1. Howard Rheingold, *The Virtual Community: Homesteading on the Electronic Frontier,* 2nd ed. (Cambridge, MA: MIT Press, 2000).

2. http://www.eastgate.com.

3. Janet Murray, *Hamlet on the Holodeck: The Future of Narrative in Cyberspace* (New York: Free Press, 1997), 55.

4. Harry Brown, *Videogames and Education* (Armonk, NY: M. E. Sharpe, 2008), 26.

5. Nick Montfort, *Twisty Little Passages* (Cambridge, MA: MIT Press, 2003), 85ff, 119–68.

6. Espen J. Aarseth, *Cybertext: Perspectives on Ergodic Literature* (Baltimore: Johns Hopkins University Press, 1997).

7. Christopher Hayes, "Bailout Satire," *Nation,* September 22, 2008, https://www.thenation.com/article/bailout-satire/. All typographical errors in original, as per the Nigerian scam e-mail tradition.

8. See https://web-beta.archive.org/web/20110316231322/http://www.bbc .co.uk/tellinglives/. Berners-Lee wrote: "The WWW project merges the techniques of information retrieval and hypertext to make an easy but powerful global information system. The project started with the philosophy that much academic information should be freely available to anyone" (https://www.w3.org/People/ Berners-Lee/1991/08/art-6487.txt).

9. See http://www.angelfire.com/trek/caver/page1.html for one copy. As noted, some of this content is evanescent. Finding copies of "Ted's" sometimes requires Googling the title.

10. http://www.dreamingmethods.com.

11. http://simpleton.com; http://www.grammatron.com; http://web.archive .org/web/20000818222259/; http://collection.eliterature.org/1/works/morrissey __the_jews_daughter.html, http://collection.eliterature.org/1/works/memmott __lexia_to_perplexia.html.

12. http://www.alansondheim.org/00README1st.TXT; see http://www .alansondheim.org for one catalog.

13. http://collection.eliterature.org/1/.

14. http://www.eliterature.org; http://www.net-art.org. A decent survey of net.art can be found at http://en.wikipedia.org/wiki/Net.art. See N. Katherine Hayles's *Electronic Literature: New Horizons for the Literary* (Notre Dame, IN: University of Notre Dame Press, 2008) for a fine survey.

15. http://www.textfiles.com/history/. I am indebted to Peter Naegele for drawing my attention to this material.

16. Joe Lambert, *Digital Storytelling: Capturing Lives, Creating Community* (Berkeley, CA: Digital Diner Press, 2002), 7. See also http://presentationzen.blogs .com/presentationzen/2005/07/dana_atchley_19.html.

17. Lambert, *Digital Storytelling*, 10–11.

18. Lambert, *Digital Storytelling*, 11.

19. https://www.youtube.com/watch?v=czoSEn8YSwo.

20. "DSF History," https://web-beta.archive.org/web/20160401130623/http:// dstory.com/dsf_05/history.html.

21. http://storycenter.org; see especially https://www.storycenter.org/work shops-ds/ and https://www.storycenter.org/s/cookbook_full.pdf. Note that the

term *digital storytelling*, while widely used and understood, has never been trade-marked, nor is there an alternate licensed term, like *iStorytelling*.

22. http://www.bbc.co.uk/cumbria/tellinglives/take_part.shtml; http://www.bbc.co.uk/wales/audiovideo/sites/galleries/pages/capturewales.shtml.

23. https://web.archive.org/web/20130512022053/http://mrn.placestories.com/. Thanks to Chad Berry of Berea College for bringing MRN to my attention.

24. http://storiesforchange.net.

25. Barbara Ganley, founder and director of Digital Explorations, in discussion with the author, July–August 2010.

26. See http://www.patientvoices.org.uk for examples.

27. http://lifebio.com; http://tellourlifestories.com.

28. http://www.youtube.com/user/streetsidestoriessf.

29. University of Houston, *The Educational Uses of Digital Storytelling,* http://digitalstorytelling.coe.uh.edu/; Ohio State University, https://u.osu.edu/digitalstorytelling/; Georgetown University, *Digital Stories,*; https://pilot.cndls.georgetown.edu/digitalstories/; University of Minnesota, *The Elements of Digital Story-building,* http://www.inms.umn.edu/elements/; Hamilton College, *From Digital Storytelling to Multimodal Criticism,* http://www.hamilton.edu/academics/showcase/cpdetails.cfm?CsProjID=58; Williams College, https://web-beta.archive.org/web/20110823152410/http://oit.williams.edu/itech/digitalstorytelling; Seton Hall University, "Faculty Spotlight: Dr. Michael Taylor and Creating Reflective Digital Stories to Examine the Role of Place in Environmental Outlook," http://tltc.shu.edu/mobile/2009/05/faculty-spotlight -dr-michael-taylor.html and https://web-beta.archive.org/web/20100802011722/http://tltc.shu.edu:80/mobile/2009/05/faculty-spotlight-dr-michael -taylor.html. Hunter College, http://www.hunter. cuny.edu/socwork/nrcfcpp/pass/digital-stories/index.htm; LaGuardia Community College, http://www.laguardia.edu/ctl/Digital_Storytelling.aspx. See also Kay Tee-han, *Digital Storytelling In and Out of the Classroom* (Lulu.com, 2006).

30. Ball State, http://cms.bsu.edu/academics/collegesanddepartments/telecommunications/academicsandadmissions/programsofstudy/mastersdegree; http://catalog.dsu.edu/preview_program.php?catoid=20&poid=1465#.

31. https://web-beta.archive.org/web/20110303200023/http://www.cpe.qut.edu.au/events/DSTC009.jsp

32. Peter Kittle, "Student Engagement and Multimodality: Collaboration, Schema, Identity," in *Teaching the New Writing: Technology, Change, and Assessment in the 21st-Century Classroom,* ed. Anne Herrington, Kevin Hodgson, and Charles Moran (New York: Teachers College, 2009), 169.

33. http://nitle.org.

34. For the latter, see Mauricio Tripp, "Molecular Dynamics of Lipids and Membranes," copies cached at http://web.archive.org/web/20050317120314/chem.acad. wabash.edu/~trippm/Lipids/.

35. http://en.wikipedia.org/wiki/Digital_storytelling.

Chapter 3

1. Scott Rosenberg's history of the development of Chandler offers an especially readable survey of this period; Scott Rosenberg, *Dreaming in Code: Two Dozen Programmers, Three Years, 4,732 Bugs, and One Quest for Transcendent Software* (New York: Crown, 2007).

2. Bonnie A. Nardi and Vicki L. O'Day, *Information Ecologies: Using Technology with Heart* (Cambridge, MA: MIT Press, 1999). Many discussions predicated on ecological metaphors for informatics or cyberculture owe much to Nardi and O'Day.

3. The term was introduced by the O'Reilly Web 2.0 conference in 2004, followed by Tim O'Reilly's posting "What Is Web 2.0? Design Patterns and Business Models for the Next Generation of Software," September 2005, http://www.oreilly.com/pub/a/web2/archive/what-is-web-20.html.

4. Benn Parr, "In 2009, Social Media Overtook Web 2.0," *Mashable,* December 31, 2009. http://mashable.com/2009/12/31/social-media-web-2/.

5. Compare Clay Shirky, *Cognitive Surplus: Creativity and Generosity in a Connected Age* (New York: Penguin, 2010), for a good summary of the pro-access argument, especially "The Button Marked 'Publish,'" 45ff. For the design criticism, compare Jaron Lanier, *You Are Not a Gadget: A Manifesto* (Waterville, ME: Thorndike Press, 2010).

6. U.S. IMPACT Public Library Study, 2010, http://impact.ischool.uw.edu/us-public-library-study.html.

7. Aaron Smith, "Mobile Access 2010," Pew Internet and American Life Project report, July 7, 2010, http://www.pewinternet.org/2010/07/07/mobile-access-2010/.

8. Ton Zijlstra, "Social Software Works in Triangles," *Interdependent Thoughts,* July 5, 2006, http://www.zylstra.org/blog/archives/2006/07/social_software.html.

9. Jyri Engestrom, "Why Some Social Network Services Work and Others Don't—Or: The Case for Object-Centered Sociality," April 13, 2005, http://www.zengestrom.com/blog/2005/04/why-some-social-network-services-work-and-others-dont-or-the-case-for-object-centered-sociality.html.

10. http://www.nytimes.com/projects/2012/snow-fall/#/?part=tunnel-creek.

11. http://unfathomable.epicmagazine.com/.

12. http://pinepoint.nfb.ca/#/pinepoint.

13. This discussion owes much to the fine 2004 new media and gaming seminar led by Jason Mittell.

14. Amanda Lenhart, Joseph Kahne, Ellen Middaugh, Alexandra Macgill, Chris Evans, and Jessica Vitak, "Teens, Video Games and Civics," Pew Internet and American Life report, September 16, 2008, http://www.pewinternet.org/Reports/2008/Teens-Video-Games-and-Civics.aspx.

15. Colin Campbell, "Here's How Many People Are Playing Games in America," *Polygon,* April 14, 2015, accessed April 11, 2017, http://www.polygon.com/2015/4/14/8415611/gaming-stats-2015.

16. Entertainment Software Association. "Essential Facts about the Computer and Video Game Industry." 2016. http://essentialfacts.theesa.com/Essential -Facts-2016.pdf; Chris Morris, "Average Vidgamer Older, More Affluent," *Variety .com,* June 14, 2010, http://www.variety.com/article/VR1118020564.html.

17. Assuming the Tablet PC as the first-generation tablet, from 2001.

18. Lenhart et al., "Teens, Video Games and Civics."

19. For example, see Mark Wolf, "Genre and the Video Game," in *The Medium of the Video Game,* ed. Mark Wolf (Austin: University of Texas Press, 2001), 113ff.

20. http://seriousgames.msu.edu.

21. http://www.gamesforchange.org.

22. http://www.molleindustria.org/en/oiligarchy; http://www.persuasivega mes.com/games/game.aspx?game=jetset; http://www.shakeout.org; http://www.dime nsionu.com/math/.

23. http://secondlife.com.

24. http://www.activeworlds.com; http://www.smallworlds.com; https://en .wikipedia.org/wiki/Croquet_Project; http://opensimulator.org/wiki/Main _Page.

25. Daniel Terdiman, "Virtual Magnate Shares Secrets of Success," *Cnet News,* December 20, 2006, http://news.cnet.com/Virtual-land-magnate-shares-secrets -of-her-success/2008-1043_3-6144967.html.

26. I will occasionally use "narrative" as a substitute for "story," and sometimes "narrate" for "telling a story." Distinguishing between the two has a rich tradition, dating back to Aristotelean poetics. Some schools of thought see *narrative* as the materials from which stories draw. Others focus narration on the act of relating a story. Still others add *discourse* as a third term. For the sake of clarity, economy, and the interests of the general reader, I will focus on "story" throughout this book, occasionally using "narrative" as a synonym, and defer the deep question of narrative/story distinction for another time.

27. See Jason Mittell's *Genre and Television: From Cop Shows to Cartoons in American Culture* (New York: Routledge, 2004) for a fine exploration of shifting notions of serial TV content.

28. Scott McCloud, *Understanding Comics* (Northampton, MA: Kitchen Sink Press, 1993), 7–21.

29. McCloud, *Understanding Comics,* 67.

30. The Blubrry Network is a good example of classic radio reappearing in podcast form.

31. Janet Murray, *Hamlet on the Holodeck: The Future of Narrative in Cyberspace* (New York: Free Press, 1997), 66–67.

Chapter 4

1. http://archive.org.

2. Steve Himmer, "The Labyrinth Unbound: Weblogs as Literature," in *Into the Blogosphere: Rhetoric, Community, and Culture of Weblogs,* ed. Laura J. Gurak,

Smiljana Antonijevic, Laurie Johnson, Clancy Ratliff, and Jessica Reyman (June 2004). http://conservancy.umn.edu/handle/11299/172823

3. Himmer declares the divide between blogs as fiction and nonfiction to be "irrelevant."

4. http://shes.aflightrisk.org/. See the Internet Archive for some material. See also John H. Richardson, "The Search for Isabella V.," *Esquire* January 29, 2007, http://www.esquire.com/features/ESQ1003-OCT_ISABELLA.

5. http://belledejour-uk.blogspot.com.

6. http://thesickland.blogspot.com/.

7. Bruce Sterling, "Dispatches from the Hyperlocal Future," *Wired* 15, no. 7 (June 2007), http://www.wired.com/techbiz/it/magazine/15-07/local.

8. See Chapter 10.

9. http://www.dionaea-house.com.

10. http://www.dionaea-house.com/updates.htm and http://dionaeahouse .blogspot.com.

11. http://ohdanigirl.livejournal.com.

12. http://loreenmathers.livejournal.com.

13. http://dionaeahouse.blogspot.com/2004/10/thoughts-and-theories.html.

14. http://dionaeahouse.blogspot.com/2004/10/early-start.html.

15. http://www.dionaea-house.com/aimlog.htm.

16. http://dionaeahouse.blogspot.com/2004/10/return-of-sweatsuit-man.html# comments.

17. Compare Daring Fireball's defense of not allowing comments: "What makes DF an efficient and effective soapbox is exactly that it is *not* noisy. My goal is for not a single wasted word to appear anywhere on any page of the site" (http:// daringfireball.net/2010/06/whats_fair); emphasis in original.

18. http://www.dionaea-house.com/0915.htm.

19. Angela Thomas, "Fictional Blogs," in *Uses of Blogs*, ed. Axel Burns and Joanne Jacobs (New York: Peter Lang, 2006), 201ff; https://web-beta.archive.org/ web/20170205174108/www.project1968.com; https://web-beta.archive.org/web/*/ http://www.project1968.com/janines-journal.

20. https://web-beta.archive.org/web/20170205174108/www.project1968 .com; https://web-beta.archive.org/web/*/http://www.project1968.com/janines -journal.

21. https://web-beta.archive.org/web/*/http://www.project1968.com/visiting -for-the-first-ti.html.

22. https://web-beta.archive.org/web/*/http://www.project1968.com/cast-of -project-1968.html.

23. https://web-beta.archive.org/web/*/http://www.myspace.com/project 1968

24. http://www.project1968.com/2008/09/aftermath.html.

25. http://www.project1968.com/2008/12/unstoppable.html.

26. http://www.pepysdiary.com/archive/1666/02/10/.

27. http://wwar1.blogspot.com.

28. http://orwelldiaries.wordpress.com/about/.

29. http://ww2today.com.

30. http://newsfrom1930.blogspot.com.

31. http://newsfrom1930.blogspot.com/2010/05/friday-may-1-1931-dow-15119
-758-53.html.

32. http://newsfrom1930.blogspot.com/2009/06/why-this-blog-socratic-monol
ogue_3441.html.

33. http://infocult.typepad.com/dracula/.

34. http://infocult.typepad.com/dracula/2006/05/ebb_tide_in_app.html.

35. Thomas, "Fictional Blogs," 201.

36. http://www.pepysdiary.com/archive/1666/02/10/#c274263.

37. Thomas, "Fictional Blogs," 201.

38. Chris Anderson, *The Long Tail: Why the Future of Business Is Selling Less of
More* (New York: Hyperion, 2006), 122–23.

39. Himmer, "Labyrinth Unbound."

40. https://www.washingtonpost.com/news/volokh-conspiracy/, https://pjme
dia.com/instapundit/.

41. http://www.juancole.com.

42. http://crankyprofessor.blogspot.com/.

43. http://weblogs.swarthmore.edu/burke/.

44. http://moschus.livejournal.com/141202.html.

45. Himmer, "Labyrinth Unbound."

46. http://smalltownnoir.wordpress.com/about/.

47. http://smalltownnoir.wordpress.com/2009/07/23/martin-fobes-intox
-driver-january-8-1948/.

48. http://smalltownnoir.wordpress.com/about/.

49. http://askawizard.blogspot.com/2008/11/war-of-worlds-20-post-mor
tem.html.

50. Jenna Wortham, "Twitterers Stage Mock Martian Invasion a la 'War of the
Worlds,'" *Wired* October 31, 2008, http://www.wired.com/underwire/2008/10/
twitterers-stag/.

51. http://twitter.com/zombieattack.

52. https://twitter.com/CryForByzantium.

53. http://twitter.com/CryForByzantium.

54. https://twitter.com/jfk_1960.

55. http://twitter.com/novelsin3lines.

56. http://tweeji.com. See, for example, the Arthur Rimbaud feed: http://
tweeji.com/person/Arthur_Rimbaud/.

57. Virginia Heffernan, "Being There," *New York Times,* February 10, 2009,
http://www.nytimes.com/2009/02/15/magazine/15wwln-medium-t.html.

58. https://twitter.com/DeathMedieval.

59. https://twitter.com/witchcourt.

60. https://twitter.com/MagicRealismBot.

61. https://twitter.com/MicroSFF.

62. http://twitter.com/jennyholzer.

63. http://twitter.com/oscarwilde

64. See, for example, http://twitter.com/haikuofthedead/. Zombies, once again.

65. Davar Iran Ardalan, "Poetry from Iran, One Tweet at a Time," National Public Radio, June 28, 2009, http://www.npr.org/templates/story/story.php? storyId=10 5980771. See also http://twitter.com/#!/RobinsonJeffers.

66. "TwitterVision and TwittEarth: Mapping Live Tweets on a 3D Globe," Information Aesthetics blog post, May 27, 2009, accessed April 11, 2017, http:// infosthetics.com/archives/2009/05/twittervision_and_twittearth.html.

67. http://twistori.com.

68. http://www.wefeelfine.org/methodology.html.

69. http://www.voanews.com/content/cia-recounting-of-bin-laden-raid-gets -retweets/3311263.html.

70. http://www.19.bbk.ac.uk/articles/10.16995/ntn.736/. Thanks to Julie Kane for drawing my attention to this.

71. http://www.theverge.com/2016/10/31/13476346/typewriter-musem -pictures-marcin-wichary.

72. http://c2.com/cgi/wiki is the first wiki site. The name is Hawaiian for "quick," emphasizing the ease of editing.

73. https://web-beta.archive.org/web/20070901000000*/http://artlab.lfc .edu/Corpse/LFC/index.htm.

74. I am indebted to Prof. Gregory Scranton (http://gregscranton.com) for this suggestion.

75. https://web-beta.archive.org/web/20070615000000*/http://www.amil lionpenguins.com/wiki/index.php?title=Main_Page.

76. Bruce Mason and Sue Thomas, "A Million Penguins Research Report," Institute of Creative Technologies, De Montfort University, Leicester, United Kingdom, April 24, 2008, http://www.ioct.dmu.ac.uk/projects/amillionpenguin sreport.pdf.

77. Stewart Mader, *Wikipatterns* (Indianapolis: John Wiley, 2008); Bonnie A. Nardi and Vicki L. O'Day, *Information Ecologies: Using Technology with Heart* (Cambridge, MA: MIT Press, 1999).

78. Capitalizing a letter in the middle of a word turns that word into a hyperlink within some wiki platforms. This practice used to be more prevalent than it is now, with the rise of graphic user interface wikis. Wiki culture dubbed this odd capitalization scheme "CamelCase."

79. Mason and Thomas, "Million Penguins Research Report."

80. Ibid.

81. http://www.unknowntales.net.

82. http://www.scp-wiki.net/.

83. Joe Lambert, *Digital Storytelling Cookbook* (Berkeley, CA: Digital Diner Press, 2010), 27.

84. Two major Flickr competitors are Facebook and Picasa. Google's Picasa service is increasing in content and user base as Google's social media services

continue to expand. It may supersede Flickr by the time you read this. Facebook is not primarily a photo site, unlike Flickr and Picasa, although it does host a huge amount of photographic content. It, too, might end up dwarfing Flickr. That Facebook will become simply "a photo-sharing site" is a good joke, but unlikely (https://gigaom.com/2010/07/22/fred-wilson-apple-is-evil-and-facebook-is-a -photo-sharing-site/).

85. http://www.flickr.com/groups/visualstory/.

86. URLs for this Flickr group tend to show only a string of numbers rather than any suggestive words. This could well change if Flickr changes its URL protocol.

87. http://www.flickr.com/groups/visualstory/discuss/72157594311362023/.

88. http://www.flickr.com/groups/visualstory/discuss/72157611666013264/.

89. http://www.flickr.com/groups/visualstory/discuss/72157603786255599/. See also the Library of Congress Flickr stream: http://www.flickr.com/photos/ library_of_congress/.

90. http://www.flickr.com/photos/xylonets/70970967/.

91. http://www.flickr.com/groups/visualstory/discuss/72157624387179086/ #comment72157624513901650.

92. "Alone with the Sand" (moliere1331, 2005). The story has apparently been removed since it was published.

93. http://www.poynter.org/2016/how-cir-created-an-investigative-series -just-for-instagram/426821/; https://www.instagram.com/revealnews/.

94. http://www.slideshare.net/bgblogging/intothestorm; see also http://bgex periments.wordpress.com/2007/07/13/into-the-storm/.

95. Katie Roiphe, "The Language of Fakebook," *New York Times,* August 13, 2010. http://www.nytimes.com/2010/08/15/fashion/15Culture.html?ref=fashion.

96. http://newsroom.fb.com/company-info/#statistics.

97. Some observers have noted that a well-crafted About page can tell a compelling story—see, for example, http://astoriedcareer.com/nice_twist_on_the _about_us_sto.

98. http://www.facebook.com/pages/Henio-Zytomirski-Page-No-Limited -Profile/113504528659885. See also Linda Vierecke, "Young Holocaust Victim Has Over 1,700 Friends on Facebook," http://tnn.pl/pm,3386.html; http://www .dw-world.de/dw/article/0,,4908523,00.html.

99 http://www.facebook.com/9scientist. Thanks to my son, Owain, for introducing me to this digital story.

100. http://www.facebook.com/notes/9-scientist/9/153106132737.

101. http://www.facebook.com/mydarklyng. See also http://www.slate.com/ id/2255911/entry/2255912/.

102. http://www.slate.com/id/2255954/.

103. http://twitter.com/jennarlyshoppin.

104. http://twitter.com/mydarklyng; http://www.facebook.com/profile.php ?id=100001392266442.

105. https://www.youtube.com/watch?v=2znb05_S8w8&feature=youtu.be.

Chapter 5

1. Ben Hammersley, "Audible Revolution," *Guardian,* February 11, 2004, http://www.guardian.co.uk/media/2004/feb/12/broadcasting.digitalmedia. For the best explanation, see AskANinja's "What Is Podcasting?": http://askaninja.com/news/2006/03/07/special-delivery-1-what-is-podcasting.

2. Gardner Campbell, "There's Something in the Air: Podcasting in Education," *EDUCAUSE Review* 40, no. 6 (November/December 2005): 32–47, https://net.educause.edu/ir/library/pdf/erm0561.pdf.

3. Rudolf Arnheim, "In Praise of Blindness," in *Radiotext(e)*, ed. Neil Strauss (New York: Semiotext(e), 1993), 21.

4. http://12byzantinerulers.com.

5. http://normancenturies.com. Ongoing as of this writing.

6. http://www.bbc.co.uk/radio4/features/in-our-time/.

7. The *In Our Time* archive is not always available to listeners outside of the United Kingdom. The BBC has changed the way these are offered at least once.

8. James Campanella, *The Standards of Creation* (Uvula Audio, 2008), http://www.uvulaaudio.com/books.html.

9. Mur Lafferty, *Playing for Keeps* (Podiobooks, 2007–2008), http://www.podiobooks.com/title/playing-for-keeps.

10. http://murverse.com/podcasts/fpfk.

11. http://www.radioopensource.org.

12. http://www.radioopensource.org/after-the-fall-the-rise-of-911-literature/.

13. http://www.radioopensource.org/from-the-cutting-room-911-literature/; https://web-beta.archive.org/web/*/http://www.radioopensource.org/a-911-literature-follow-up/.

14. http://librivox.org/the-yellow-sheet-by-librivox-volunteers/.

15. http://thememorypalace.us.

16. http://www.radiolab.org. Radiolab's Web site pokes fun at its emotional effects with a semisatirical yet useful tagset. Individual podcasts can be tagged as "Gut-wrenching, Heart-swelling, Knee-slapping, Mind-bending."

17. https://serialpodcast.org/.

18. https://gimletmedia.com/crimetown/; http://www.theunresolvedpodcast.com/; http://www.unsolvedpodcast.com/; http://thisiscriminal.com/.

19. http://historyofenglishpodcast.com/; http://www.missedinhistory.com/podcasts; http://www.dancarlin.com/hardcore-history-series/; http://www.revolutionspodcast.com/.

20. http://risk-show.com/; http://www.storycollider.org/; http://www.rumblestripvermont.com/.

21. https://www.flashforwardpod.com/.

22. http://www.welcometonightvale.com/.

23. http://clarkesworldmagazine.com/; http://escapepod.org/; http://podcastle.org/; http://pseudopod.org/; http://www.drabblecast.org/; http://districtofwonders.com/; http://www.wolf359.fm/.

24. http://www.tanispodcast.com/; http://theblacktapespodcast.com/.

25. http://lif-e.af/ter; http://themessagepodcast.com/.

26. http://www.limetownstories.com/.

27. https://www.youtube.com/yt/press/statistics.html.

28. See the work of Kansas State University's digital ethnography working group at http://mediatedcultures.net/youtube.htm.

29. Clay Shirky, *Cognitive Surplus: Creativity and Generosity in a Connected Age* (New York: Penguin, 2010), 64ff.

30. http://www.youtube.com/user/Fewdiodotcom.

31. http://en.wikipedia.org/wiki/Lonelygirl15 has been a solid source for background information and resources.

32. http://www.vocativ.com/327378/lonelygirl15-oral-history/.

33. A partial archive is available at http://web.archive.org/web/2007101404 2824/http://connectwithi.com/episodes.htm#1.

34. "LEGAL NOTICE: The creators of iChannel reserve the right to utilize any comments and/or suggestions left on this website as creative material for future episodes."

35. http://www.youtube.com/user/MarbleHornets.

36. http://www.youtube.com/user/totheark.

37. http://twitter.com/marblehornets.

38. For example, "Cooking with to the ark," https://www.youtube.com/watch?v=6PlnjHfgEDg.

39. http://marblehornets.wikidot.com.

40. http://tvtropes.org/pmwiki/pmwiki.php/Main/MarbleHornets.

41. http://www.facebook.com/pages/Marble-Hornets/142197209491.

42. http://forums.unfiction.com/forums/index.php?f=248.

43. A movie-style poster, for example: http://dracothrope.deviantart.com/art/Marble-Hornets-Poster-155955597.

44. https://www.youtube.com/watch?v=2I7bHClKL_k.

45. http://forums.somethingawful.com/showthread.php?threadid=3150591&userid=0&perpage=40&pagenumber=4.

46. http://voicethread.com.

Chapter 6

1. David Kushner, *Masters of Doom: How Two Guys Created an Empire and Transformed Pop Culture* (New York: Random House, 2003), 120.

2. Harry Brown offers a fine survey of this debate in the first chapter of his *Videogames and Education* (Armonk, NY: M. E. Sharpe, 2008). See also Ian Bogost's excellent sketch and response in *Unit Operations: An Approach to Videogame Criticism* (Cambridge, MA: MIT Press, 2006), 66–71.

3. Amanda Lenhart, Joseph Kahne, Ellen Middaugh, Alexandra Macgill, Chris Evans, and Jessica Vitak, "Teens, Video Games and Civics," Pew Internet and American Life report, September 16, 2008, http://www.pewinternet.org/Reports/2008/Teens-Video-Games-and-Civics.aspx.

4. For an especially creative use of Tetris for storytelling, see Chapter 13.

5. Janet Murray, *Hamlet on the Holodeck: The Future of Narrative in Cyberspace* (New York: Free Press, 1997), 99–103.

6. Murray, *Hamlet on the Holodeck,* 111–12, 125.

7. Rudolf Arnheim, "In Praise of Blindness," *Radiotext(e),* ed. Neil Strauss (New York: Semiotext(e), 1993), 21.

8. Don Carson, "Environmental Storytelling: Creating Immersive 3D Worlds Using Lessons Learned from the Theme Park Industry," *Gamasutra,* March 1, 2000, http://www.gamasutra.com/view/feature/3186/environmental_story telling_.php. Compare that with the Center for Digital Storytelling's *Cookbook* observation on character consistency: "I know when character development has been rendered ineffective when I am able to say to myself, 'You know, that character would have never said those words, or behaved in that way'"; Joe Lambert, *Digital Storytelling Cookbook* (Berkeley, CA: Digital Diner Press, 2010), 29.

9. Brown, *Videogames and Education,* 14–15, 24.

10. Jesper Juul, *Half-Real: Video Games between Real Rules and Fictional Worlds* (Cambridge, MA: MIT Press, 2005), 120 and 163ff; emphasis in original.

11. Juul, *Half-Real,* 141; emphasis in original. Compare this with the narrative play dual structures described in Katie Salen and Eric Zimmerman, *Rules of Play: Game Design Fundamentals* (Cambridge, MA: MIT Press, 2004), 382–83.

12. Carson, "Environmental Storytelling."

13. Ruben R. Puentedura, founder and president of Hippasus, in discussion with the author, July 2010.

14. Juul, *Half-Real,* 135.

15. Salen and Zimmerman, *Rules of Play,* 399–401.

16. Mark Wolf, "Narrative in the Video Game," *The Medium of the Video Game,* ed. Mark Wolf (Austin: University of Texas Press, 2001), 101.

17. Jesper Juul, *A Casual Revolution: Reinventing Video Games and Their Players* (Cambridge, MA: MIT Press, 2010), 41–49.

18. Brendan Keogh, "In Defence of the Cut-scene," *Critical Damage* blog, June 2, 2010, http://critdamage.blogspot.com/2010/06/in-defence-of-cut-scene.html.

19. Salen and Zimmerman, *Rules of Play,* 382–83.

20. James Paul Gee, "Learning about Learning from a Video Game: *Rise of Nations*" n.d., http://www.academiccolab.org/resources/documents/RON-paper.rev.pdf.

21. http://chainfactor.com/index.php. See also the *Chain Factor* wiki, http://web.archive.org/web/20100629162351/http://chainfactor.despoiler.org/index.php?title=Main_Page.

22. Brown, *Videogames and Education,* 27.

23. Salen and Zimmerman, *Rules of Play,* 381; emphasis in original.

24. Charles Baxter, *The Art of Subtext: Beyond Plot* (Saint Paul, MN: Graywolf Press, 2007), 37.

25. http://www.persuasivegames.com/games/game.aspx?game=jetset.

26. Jill Walker, "Do You Think You're Part of This? Digital Texts and the Second-Person Address," *Cybertext Yearbook 2000,* ed. Markku Eskelinen and

Raine Koskimaa, Publications of the Research Centre for Contemporary Culture (Saarijarvi: University of Jyvaskyla, 2001), http://jilltxt.net/txt/do_you _think.pdf.

27. Roger Caillois, *Man, Play, and Games,* trans. Meyer Barash (Urbana: University of Illinois Press, 2001), 21–23.

28. Scott McCloud, *Understanding Comics* (Northampton, MA: Kitchen Sink Press, 1993), 29–59, 35–36.

29. Juul, *Half-Real,* 141.

30. https://web.archive.org/web/20100701000000*/http://statistics.allface book.com/applications/leaderboard/, consulted August 2010.

31. Caillois, *Man, Play, and Games,* 89.

32. http://www.ferryhalim.com/orisinal/.

33. http://www.aooa.co.uk.

34. https://web-beta.archive.org/web/*/http://lackofbanjos.com/games/small -worlds/.

35. McCloud, *Understanding Comics.*

36. The metaphor is NickMontfort's, from his *TwistyLittlePassages* (Cambridge, MA: MIT Press, 2003), 230–31. This section owes a great deal to his pathbreaking book.

37. Montfort, *TwistyLittlePassages,* 226.

38. Matthew Baldwin, "Xyzzy," *Defective Yeti,* January 2006, http://www.def ectiveyeti.com/archives/001561.html.

39. Montfort, *Twisty Little Passages,* 25–26, 32.

40. Montfort, *Twisty Little Passages,* 34.

41. http://fallenlondon.storynexus.com/.

Chapter 7

1. Quoted in Katie Salen and Eric Zimmerman, *Rules of Play: Game Design Fundamentals* (Cambridge, MA: MIT Press, 2004), 379.

2. Quoted in Thomas Bissell, *Extra Lives: Why Video Games Matter* (New York: Pantheon, 2010), 156.

3. http://www.penumbragame.com/index.php.

4. http://frictionalgames.blogspot.com/2010/03/storytelling-through-fragments-and.html.

5. *The Spoony Experiment* is a good example of the latter, http://spoonyexperi-ment.com/category/lets-play/.

6. http://bioshock.wikia.com/wiki/BioShock_Wiki.

7. http://fallout.wikia.com/wiki/Fallout_Wiki.

8. http://roosterteeth.com/show/red-vs-blue.

9. See the Straad Players for an example, http://straad.org.uk.

10. See http://www.machinima.com/ and https://en.wikipedia.org/wiki/List _of_machinima_festivals.

11. http://aliceandkev.wordpress.com/2009/06/09/alice-and-kev/.

12. http://aliceandkev.wordpress.com/download-alice-and-kev/.

13. http://aliceandkev.wordpress.com.

14. Jesse Walker, "The Laptop Theater," *Reason,* July 2, 2010, http://reason.com/archives/2010/07/02/the-laptop-theater.

Chapter 8

1. Sarah Schmelling, "Hamlet (Facebook News Feed Edition)," *McSweeneys Internet Tendency,* July 30, 2008, https://www.mcsweeneys.net/articles/hamlet-facebook-news-feed-edition.

2. Ben Vershbow, "The Networked Book," *Forbes,* December 1, 2006, http://www.forbes.com/2006/11/30/future-books-publishing-tech-media_cz_bv_books06_1201network.html.

3. Barbara Ganley, founder and director of Digital Explorations, in discussion with the author, July–August 2010.

4. Joseph J. Esposito, "The Processed Book," *First Monday* 8, no. 3 (March 2003), http://firstmonday.org/issues/issue8_3/esposito/index.html.

5. Robert Frenay, *Pulse: The Coming Age of Systems and Machines Inspired by Living Things* (New York: Farrar, Straus & Giroux, 2006). The original *Pulse* site is now held by some entirely different entity, so the Internet Archive versions are the best records: https://web-beta.archive.org/web/*/www.pulsethebook.com/.

6. https://web-beta.archive.org/web/*/http://www.googlizationofeverything.com.

7. Joanne Jacobs, "Publishing and Blogs," *Uses of Blogs*, ed. Axel Burns and Joanne Jacobs (New York: Peter Lang, 2006), 35–36. Full disclosure: I was a member of the Smartmobs blog team for several years.

8. Jacobs, "Publishing and Blogs," 38; Dan Gillmor, *We the Media: Grassroots Journalism by the People, for the People* (Sebastopol, CA: O' Reilly, 2004), http://www.oreilly.com/wethemedia/.

9. http://napoleonsegypt.blogspot.com; Juan Cole, *Napoleon's Egypt: Invading the Middle East* (New York: Palgrave Macmillan, 2007).

10. http://pynchonwiki.com.

11. http://against-the-day.pynchonwiki.com/wiki/index.php?title=ATD_119-148.

12. http://node.tumblr.com, and now http://nodemagazine.wordpress.com.

13. https://p10.secure.hostingprod.com/@spyblog.org.uk/ssl/spookcountry/2007/08/chapter-1-white-lego.html.

14. John Sutherland, "Node Idea," *Guardian,* August 31, 2007, http://www.guardian.co.uk/education/2007/aug/31/highereducation.books.

15. Steve Ranger, "Q&A: William Gibson, Science Fiction Novelist," http://www.silicon.com/technology/networks/2007/08/06/qanda-william-gibson-science-fiction-novelist-39168006/.

16. Henry Jenkins, *Convergence Culture: Where Old and New Media Collide* (New York: New York University Press, 2006), 93ff.

17. Jenkins, *Convergence Culture,* 106, 113ff.

18. J. R. R. Tolkien, "On Fairy-Stories," in *The Tolkien Reader* (New York: Ballantine Books, 1966).

19. Johan Huizinga, *Homo Ludens: A Study of the Play Element in Culture* (Boston: Beacon Books, 1955), 9.

20. Vershbow, "Networked Book."

21. Henry Jenkins, *Textual Poachers: Television Fans and Participatory Culture* (New York: Routledge, 1992).

22. Patrick Nielsen Hayden, "H. P. Lovecraft, Founding Father of SF Fandom," December 3, 2009, http://www.tor.com/blogs/2009/12/h-p-lovecraft-founding-father -of-sf-fandom.

23. http://www.fanfiction.net.

24. http://www.rigel.org.uk/blog/000279.shtml.

25. Paul Sutherland, "Doctor Who and the Star of Doom," *Skymania,* January 27, 2010. http://www.skymania.com/wp/2010/01/doctor-who-and-star-of-doom. html/766/. Originally published in *Scientific American.*

26. http://darkerprojects.com/doctor-who/dw-special-doctor-who-and-the-silver-spiral/.

27. Bryan Alexander and Alan Levine, "Web 2.0 Storytelling: Emergence of a New Genre," *EDUCAUSE Review* 43, no. 6 (November/December 2008), http://er.educause.edu/articles/2008/10/web-20-storytelling-emergence-of-a-new -genre.

28. http://www.shadowunit.org; http://mongoliad.com.

29. http://www.playingforkeepsnovel.com.

Chapter 9

1. *Measuring the Information Society Report 2016,* International Telecommunication Union, accessed April 12, 2017, https://www.itu.int/en/ITU-D/Statis tics/Documents/publications/misr2016/MISR2016-w4.pdf.

2. James E. Katz and Mark Aakhus, *Perpetual Contact: Mobile Communication, Private Talk, Public Performance* (New York: Cambridge University Press, 2002), Introduction.

3. Mizuko Ito, Daisuke Okabe, and Misa Matsuda, ed., *Personal, Portable, Pedestrian: Mobile Phones in Japanese Life* (Cambridge, MA: MIT Press, 2005). See also Howard Rheingold, *Smart Mobs* (Cambridge, MA: Perseus, 2002).

4. Barbara Ganley, founder and director of Digital Explorations, in discussion with the author, July–August 2010.

5. Mark Weiser, "The Computer for the 21st Century," *Scientific American* 265, no. 3 (September 1991): 66–75, http://www.ubiq.com/hypertext/weiser/ SciAmDraft3.html. Note how well he anticipated trends: "Flat-panel displays containing 640×480 black-and-white pixels are now common. This is the standard size for PC's and is also about right for television. As long as laptop, palmtop and notebook computers continue to grow in popularity, display prices will fall, and

resolution and quality will rise. By the end of the decade, a 1000×800-pixel high-contrast display will be a fraction of a centimeter thick and weigh perhaps 100 grams. A small battery will provide several days of continuous use."

6. Adam Greenfield, *Everyware: The Dawning Age of Ubiquitous Computing* (Berkeley, CA: New Riders, 2006).

7. "Want to Choose Your Own Adventure? There's a Books App for That," *Guardian,* August 1, 2010, http://www.guardian.co.uk/books/2010/aug/01/choose-your-own-adventure-iphone-app.

8. Dana Goodyear, "I Novels: Young Women Develop a Genre for the Cellular Age," *New Yorker,* December 22, 2008, http://www.newyorker.com/magazine/2008/12/22/i-love-novels.

9. Ibid.

10. Joseph J. Esposito, "Interstitial Publishing: A New Market from Wasted Time," *O'Reilly Radar,* December 12, 2008, http://radar.oreilly.com/2008/12/interstitial-publishing.html. Note his insistence on phones for this kind of story instead of e-readers or tablets.

11. http://www.mozilla.com/en-US/mobile/.

12. The Apple App Store commercial slogan, "There's an app for that," may become one of the most influential ads of our time, given how thoroughly the contraction "app" has entered spoken English.

13. http://www.apple.com/iphone/apps-for-iphone/; https://play.google.com; http://www.blackberry.com/appworld/.

14. http://itunes.apple.com/us/app/ruben-lullaby/id302028937?mt=8.

15. "The 'Fighting Fantasy,' 'Gamebook Adventures' and 'Sorcery!' Series—Now with Even More Installments," *Touch Arcade,* August 20, 2010, http://toucharcade.com/2010/08/20/the-fighting-fantasy-gamebook-adventures-and-sorcery-series-now-with-even-more-installments/.

16. http://hitchery.com/.

17. https://web-beta.archive.org/web/*/http://www.portablequest.com/ and https://web-beta.archive.org/web/*/http://www.kindlequest.com/ are apparently aimed at the Kindle's very basic Web browser.

18. https://storycorps.me/; http://www.sonicpics.com; Ruben R. Puentedura, founder and president of Hippasus, in discussion with the author, July 2010.

19. I Thomas Z. Freedman, "A Kindle in Every Backpack: A Proposal for eText-books in American Schools," Democratic Leadership Council white paper, July 2009, https://tfreedmanconsulting.com/wp-content/uploads/2016/05/Freedman_Kindle-1.pdf.

20. Some best-sellers on the Kindle store have a price point near or at $0.00.

21. Greg Toppo, "School Chooses Kindle; Are Libraries for the History 'Books'?" *USA Today,* October 27, 2009, http://usatoday30.usatoday.com/news/education/2009-10-26-kindle-school-library_n.htm.

22. Claire Cain Miller, "E-Books Top Hardcovers at Amazon," *New York Times,* July 19, 2010, http://www.nytimes.com/2010/07/20/technology/20kindle.html.

23. Hyung Lee, "Kindles Yet to Woo University Users," *Daily Princetonian,* September 28, 2009, http://futureofthebook.org/blog/2009/09/29/the_kindle_gets _poor_grades_at/.

24. M. Mitchell Waldrop, *The Dream Machine* (New York: Penguin, 2001), 282, 360.

25. http://www.gartner.com/it/page.jsp?id=1313513.

26. http://www.moving-tales.com.

27. Doug Reilly, of Hobart and William Smith Colleges, in discussion with the author, July–August 2010.

28. Bruce Sterling, "Dispatches from the Hyperlocal Future," *Wired* 15, no. 7 (June 2007), http://www.wired.com/techbiz/it/magazine/15-07/local.

Chapter 10

1. The design studio explains the game at http://www.42entertainment .com/work/ilovebees. The ILoveBees site is http://www.ilovebees.com.

2. https://web-beta.archive.org/web/*/http://bangaloreworldu-in.co.cloud makers.org/index.html and https://web-beta.archive.org/web/*/http://bangalore worldu-in.co.cloudmakers.org/salla/default.html.

3. http://www.unfiction.com.

4. http://www.argn.com.

5. http://www.42entertainment.com; http://www.universecreation101.com.

6. http://www.ted.com/talks/jane_mcgonigal_gaming_can_make_a_better _world.html.

7. Nick Montfort, *Twisty Little Passages* (Cambridge, MA: MIT Press, 2003), 37ff. See also Harry Brown, *Videogames and Education* (Armonk, NY: M. E. Sharpe, 2008), 5ff.

8. Bryan Alexander, "Alternate Reality Games SIG/Whitepaper/Antecedents to Alternate Reality Games," 2006, http://www.christydena.com/wp-content/ uploads/2007/11/igda-alternaterealitygames-whitepaper-2006.pdf. Much of the following discussion flows from this paper and the amendments contributed by others, which appear in its wiki form.

9. http://www.badwolf.org.uk.

10. http://www.badwolf.org.uk/disclaimer.html.

11. See, for example, Dena's including Metacortechs in this list: http://www. christydena.com/online-essays/arg-stats/.

12. http://www.metacortechs.com.

13. The firm is located in Redland, Washington, which brought Red *mond* to mind at the time. How rapidly have Microsoft jokes lost their potency!

14. Their archive is also an excellent, rich resource for understanding the game; see http://www.metaurchins.org/book/page1.htm.

15. Ibid.

16. http://www.urgentevoke.com.

17. http://www.worldwithoutoil.org.

18. "SpaceBass" [Sean Stacey], "Undefining ARG," November 10, 2006, http://www.unfiction.com/compendium/2006/11/10/undefining-arg/.

19. For a foundational discussion, see Howard Rheingold's *The Virtual Community: Homesteading on the Electronic Frontier,* 2nd ed. (Cambridge, MA: MIT Press, 2000).

20. http://www.dionaea-house.com/default.htm.

21. http://www.dionaea-house.com/0912.htm.

Chapter 11

1. L. Johnson, A. Levine, R. Smith, and S. Stone, *The 2010 Horizon Report* (Austin, Texas: New Media Consortium, 2010), https://www.nmc.org/pdf/2010-Horizon-Report.pdf.

2. http://hurricanearchive.org.

3. http://ge.ecomagination.com/smartgrid/.

4. http://www.wikitude.org.

5. Howard Rheingold, *Smart Mobs* (Cambridge, MA: Perseus, 2002), 104.

6. J. Spohrer, "Information in Places," *IBM Systems Journal* 38, no. 4 (December 1999): 602–28.

7. Rheingold, *Smart Mobs,* 92.

8. Bruce Sterling, "At the Dawn of the Augmented Reality Industry," Address, August 20, 2009, https://www.layar.com/news/blog/2009/08/20/video-bruce-sterlings-keynote-at-the-dawn-of-the-augmented-reality-industry/; "ARE 2010 Keynote by Bruce Sterling: Bake a Big Pie!", Keynote speech, Augmented Reality Event, June 6, 2010, https://www.wired.com/2013/06/augmented-reality-bruce-sterling-keynote-at-augmented-world-expo-2013/.

9. Bruce Chatwin, *The Songlines* (New York: Penguin, 1987), 13.

10. Chatwin, *Songlines,* 107.

11. Phones may be supplemented by contact lenses. See Babak A. Parviz, "Augmented Reality in a Contact Lens: A New Generation of Contact Lenses Built with Very Small Circuits and LEDs Promises Bionic Eyesight," *IEEE Spectrum,* September 1, 2009, http://spectrum.ieee.org/biomedical/bionics/augmented-reality-in-a-contact-lens/.

12. http://brightkite.com; http://loopt.com.

13. See http://www.flickr.com/groups/1049441@N25/ for examples.

14. https://web-beta.archive.org/web/*/http://www.google.com/help/maps/favoriteplaces/business/barcode.html. Now defunct.

15. Lauren Indvik, "Microsoft Tag Shuts Down as QR Codes Struggle," *Mashable,* August 19, 2013, accessed April 12, 2017, http://mashable.com/2013/08/19/microsoft-tag-shuts-down/.

16. Bruce Sterling, *Shaping Things* (Cambridge, MA: MIT Press, 2005).

17. http://talesofthings.com.

18. https://play.google.com/store/apps/details?id=com.google.android.apps.unveil&hl=en.

19. Kit Eaton, "Wimbledon Seer App Serves Augmented Reality on a Grass Court," *Fast Company,* June 22, 2009, http://www.fastcompany.com/blog/kit-eaton /technomix/augmented-reality-hits-wimbledon-tennis-championship.

20. https://www.layar.com/news/blog/2009/12/01/layar-30-launched-5-cases-to-show-the-power-of-the-platform/.

21. http://cordis.europa.eu/project/rcn/80182_en.html.

22. https://www.wikitude.com/.

23. https://www.layar.com/news/blog/2009/12/01/layar-30-launched-5-cases -to-show-the-power-of-the-platform/.

24. http://34n118w.net.

25. http://leoalmanac.org/journal/vol_14/lea_v14_n07-08/jhight.asp.

26. http://www.murmurtoronto.ca.

27. Ibid.

28. Barbara Ganley, founder and director of Digital Explorations, in discussion with the author, July–August 2010, http://www.heartofbiddeford.org.

29. https://web-beta.archive.org/web/*/http://www.twitter-360.com/.

30. https://web-beta.archive.org/web/*/http://www.tat.se/.

31. https://link.springer.com/article/10.1007/s10956-006-9037-z.

32. Jaakko Stenros and Markus Montola, "Pervasive Game Genres," *Pervasive Games: Theory and Design*, ed. Markus Montola, Jaakko Stenros, and Annika Waern (Boston: Morgan Kaufmann, 2009), 31–46.

33. Markus Montola, "Games and Pervasive Games," *Pervasive Games*, ed. Montola, Stenros, and Waern, 12.

34. http://www.wherigo.com/. I am indebted to Jason Farmer for drawing my attention to this story-game platform.

35. http://www.wherigo.com/about.aspx.

36. https://www.google.com/sky/; http://www.ted.com/talks/blaise_aguera.html.

37. Johnson *et al.*, *2010 Horizon Report,* see note 1.

38. Amanda Lenhart and Mary Madden, "Teens, Privacy and Online Social Networks," Pew Internet and American Life Project report, April 18, 2007, http:// www.pewinternet.org/Reports/2007/Teens-Privacy-and-Online-Social-Networks .aspx.

Chapter 12

1. https://story.californiasunday.com/virtual-reality-hollywood.

2. http://www.nytimes.com/marketing/nytvr/.

3. https://www.theguardian.com/world/ng-interactive/2016/apr/27/6x9-a-virtual-experience-of-solitary-confinement.

4. http://thecreatorsproject.vice.com/blog/vr-ceremony-doom-room-lets-you -die-and-be-reborn.

5. https://www.youtube.com/watch?v=vQeN_YxstTo.

6. https://medium.com/the-mission/movies-in-vr-why-theyll-never-work-and -what-will-instead-5882d7d01f36#.r0hfeki4d.

7. https://story.californiasunday.com/virtual-reality-hollywood.

8. Ibid.

9. https://medium.com/stanford-d-school/the-storyteller-s-guide-to-the-virtual-reality-audience-19e92da57497#.7l462sua1.

10. http://www.huffingtonpost.com/jesse-damiani/storytelling-in-virtual-r_b_10448832.html.

11. https://www.youtube.com/watch?v=WxtJGX6CjZY.

12. http://www.cnbc.com/2016/12/29/episodic-virtual-reality-content-could-transform-consumer-entertainment.html.

Chapter 13

1. For the course of this chapter, I will shift narrative voice to "we" rather than first person singular. This is to emphasize the collaborative nature of what I've learned in the course of teaching digital storytelling workshops. All of them have been conducted with the generous collaboration of another instructor. Those colleagues have performed enormous labors of curricular and pedagogical invention and iteration. Those fellow teachers include fellow New Yorkers Bret Olsen and Doug Reilly. The experiences and lessons learned in this chapter also draw mightily on several leading digital storytellers and collaborators, including Barbara Ganley, Ruben Puentedura, Joan Getman, and above all, Joe Lambert.

2. "Participant" is usually a better term than "student," as it reflects a stronger participatory sense. These workshops are very interactive and deeply social.

3. Joe Lambert, *Digital Storytelling Cookbook* (Berkeley, CA: Digital Diner Press, 2010), 3.

4. Sheila Curran Bernard, *Documentary Storytelling for Film and Videomakers*, 2nd ed. (Burlington, VT: Focal Press, 2007), 25.

5. Barbara Ganley, founder and director of Digital Explorations, in discussion with the author, July–August 2010.

6. I will sometimes tell classes 100 words if they are dominated by humanities scholars. It's an even deeper, more productive shock than 150.

7. Lambert, *Digital Storytelling Cookbook*, 6–8.

8. Annette Simmons, *The Story Factor: Secrets of Influence from the Art of Storytelling*, 2nd ed. (New York: Basic Books, 2006), 4–26.

9. Lambert, *Digital Storytelling Cookbook*. For an engaging example of storyboarding, see the DVD extras to *Shrek* (2001), which show two storyboard presentations for sequences that didn't end up in the final print.

10. Joe Lambert, *Digital Storytelling: Capturing Lives, Creating Community* (Berkeley, CA: Digital Diner Press, 2002), 61.

11. Jason Ohler, *Digital Storytelling in the Classroom: New Media Pathways to Literacy, Learning, and Creativity* (Thousand Oaks, CA: Corwin, 2008), 78–80.

12. Joe Lambert, founder and executive director of the Center for Digital Storytelling, in discussion with the author, August 2010.

13. Lambert, *Digital Storytelling,* 46ff. See also Lambert, *Digital Storytelling Cookbook*, 2010, https://www.storycenter.org/cookbook/.

14. She continues: "What information or material is include or excluded? What choices are made concerning style, tone, point of view, and format?" Bernard, *Documentary Storytelling,* 4.

15. Simmons, *Story Factor,* 45.

16. Lambert, *Digital Storytelling,* 50.

17. Lambert, *Digital Storytelling,* 57.

18. Simmons, *Story Factor,* 100.

19. Lambert, *Digital Storytelling,* 59.

20. Simmons, *Story Factor,* 100.

21. Brian Harnetty, "'Boy' from 'Shawnee, Ohio,'" Vimeo, accessed November 1, 2016, https://vimeo.com/187986783. Thanks to Geoff Gevalt for pointing this example out to me.

22. Bernard, *Documentary Storytelling,* 17.

23. Lambert, *Digital Storytelling Cookbook,* 18.

24. Lambert, *Digital Storytelling Cookbook,* 18.

25. Local resources: the hosting organization may make available some materials not generally available. These could include, for example, licensed content that can be used only for the duration of the workshop.

26. Lambert, *Digital Storytelling,* 55–56.

27. Doug Reilly, of Hobart and William Smith Colleges, in discussion with the author, July–August 2010.

28. Bernard, *Documentary Storytelling,* 16–17.

29. One single technical challenge is worth noting for Audacity: the export problem. The basic Audacity download lets users export content in several file formats, *but not mp3*. It lacks a small but essential file, a codec called LAME.dll. That codec is not included because of open-source code license limitations. Copies of it are easily found, downloaded, and installed. This hurdle is a very small one to overcome, but is best dealt with before a workshop begins in order to remove it as a source of stress.

30. http://aviary.com/tools/audio-editor.

31. It's a rare Apple product to lack the "i-" prefix.

32. https://www.visme.co/; https://pixlr.com/editor/; https://photos.google.com/.

33. https://www.wevideo.com/.

34. https://www.youtube.com/editor.

35. http://www.inspiration.com; http://www.thebrain.com; http://vue.tufts.edu; http://www.mindomo.com.

36. http://www.sonicpics.com.

37. Lambert, *Digital Storytelling Cookbook,* 3; emphasis added.

38. http://cowbird.com/.

39. http://plasq.com/products/comiclife/.

40. https://exposure.co/.

41. https://www.powtoon.com/.

42. https://vine.co/.

43. http://giphy.com/gifs/xT4uQmNmedl9KArzkQ.

44. https://shorthand.com/; http://benjamin.djehouti.com/scrollitelling/.

45. https://steller.co/.

46. Bryan Alexander, Gail Matthews-DeNatale, and Gerry Bayne, "ELI in Conversation: Web 2.0 and Digital Storytelling," podcast, 2008, https://web-beta .archive.org/web/*/http://connect.educause.edu/blog/gbayne/eliinconversation web20and/46133.

47. Reilly, in discussion with the author, July–August 2010.

48. http://www.systemsguild.com/riskology/.

49. Simmons, *Story Factor,* 94.

50. Ibid., 95.

51. http://www.youtube.com/watch?v=hWTFG3J1CP8; see also http:// pigwithfaceofboy.blogspot.com/2010/08/tetris-lyrics.html.

52. Le Ly Hayslip, *When Heaven and Earth Changed Places* (New York: Plume, 1989), 1.

53. This is more poetic than accurate. An electronic signal broadcast from Earth would reach Jupiter's orbit about 35 minutes later, given the distance of almost 400 million miles and the speed of light. But it is a powerful conceit, nonetheless.

54. Also appropriate is that nobody answers her over the radio; it is her father who appears, in person, in answer to her query.

55. Tracking version changes has long been an underappreciated strength of wikis.

Chapter 14

1. Barry Schwartz, *The Paradox of Choice: Why More Is Less* (New York: Ecco, 2004). See also Joe Lambert, "Overloaded Memory Bank," in *Digital Storytelling Cookbook* (Berkeley, CA: Digital Diner Press, 2010), 1–2.

2. Matt Madden, *99 Ways to Tell a Story: Exercises in Style* (New York: Chamberlain Bros., 2005); available at http://www.exercisesinstyle.com.

3. Also available as a Twitter feed, https://twitter.com/Oblique_Chirps.

4. See, for example, http://www.flickr.com/groups/project365/pool/; https:// www.flickr.com/groups/366photos/; and http://www.dailyphotomap.com.

5. http://dailypost.bowdoin.edu.

6. https://twitter.com/radvilliany/status/788062060093382656; https:// twitter.com/esaxey/status/789049610153099264.

7. http://www.sixwordstories.net is a good resource for this. Thanks to Joan Falkenberg Getman for introducing it to me.

8. http://5card.cogdogblog.com/index.php.

9. http://www.white-wolf.com/.

10. James Wallis, "Making Games That Tell Stories," *Second Person: Role-Playing and Story in Games and Playable Media*, ed. Pat Harrigan and Noah

Wardrip-Fruin (Cambridge, MA: MIT Press, 2007), 69–80. I'm fond of this description of the Baron Munchausen game's rules: "Each player tells a story while fending off interruptions from the other [players]" (76).

11. http://home.earthlink.net/~hipbone/.

12. http://tvtropes.org/.

13. https://www.youtube.com/user/CenterOfTheStory.

14. http://www.storycenter.org/storycenter-blog.

15. http://storycorps.org; https://storycorps.org/do-it-yourself-guide/.

16. http://www.npr.org/templates/story/story.php?storyId=4516989.

17. http://streetside.org/; http://www.youtube.com/user/streetsidestoriessf.

18. http://www.patientvoices.org.uk.

19. http://digitales.us; http://storycenter.org.

20. http://www.fanfiction.net.

21. http://www.novelr.com; http://astoriedcareer.com; http://futureofthebook.org/blog/.

22. https://grandtextauto.soe.ucsc.edu/; http://www.hippasus.com/rrpweblog/. Puentedura's "Introduction to Educational Gaming" (2009) is a superb resource for anyone interested in gaming or its educational uses; see http://www.hippasus.com/rrpweblog/archives/000039.html.

23. http://www.donaldscrankshaw.com/2010/08/storyblogging-carnival-cxi.html.

24. http://twitter.com/storytellin; http://twitter.com/rubenrp.

25. http://librivox.org. See also Yochai Benkler, *The Wealth of Networks: How Social Production Transforms Markets and Freedom* (New Haven, CT: Yale University Press, 2006), and Michael Erard, "The Wealth of LibriVox," *Reason,* May 2007, http://reason.com/archives/2007/04/24/the-wealth-of-librivox.

26. The name was initially a URL joke: "delicious" as del.icio.us. https://www.diigo.com; https://pinboard.in/.

27. http://50ways.wikispaces.com/.

28. J. D. Lasica, *Darknet: Hollywood's War against the Digital Generation* (Hoboken, NJ: John Wiley, 2005); see also http://www.darknet.com.

29. http://creativecommons.org/about/licenses.

30. http://www.flickr.com/creativecommons/.

31. http://blog.freesound.org/?p=634.

32. http://www.ourmedia.org.

33. http://www.archive.org.

34. http://weblogs.swarthmore.edu/burke/; http://www.bogost.com/blog/; https://grandtextauto.soe.ucsc.edu/; http://www.deepfun.com; http://www.raphkoster.com.

35. http://bogost.com/writing/.

36. http://kotaku.com; http://www.joystiq.com.

37. http://gamasutra.com.

38. http://jayisgames.com.

39. http://www.jesperjuul.net/ludologist/.

40. http://nwn.blogs.com/nwn/; http://blogs.secondlife.com.

41. http://www.argn.com.

42. http://www.deusexmachinatio.com; http://www.christydena.com.

43. http://www.ifarchive.org; http://ifdb.tads.org; http://www.ifcomp.org.

44. http://www.adobe.com/products/flash/.. An example of a tutorial for learning Flash for game design is at http://www.kongregate.com/labs.

45. Steve Jobs, "Thoughts on Flash," April 2010, http://www.apple.com/hotnews/thoughts-on-flash/.

46. http://dev.w3.org/html5/spec/Overview.html.

47. http://scratch.mit.edu.

48. http://www.venatiocreo.com.

49. http://inform7.com.

50. http://secondlife.com.

Chapter 15

1. PLATO (Programmed Logic for Automated Teaching Operations), created and maintained at the University of Illinois starting in 1960, was an important project in the early history of networked computing.

2. http://www.apple.com/au/education/digitalkids/disconnect/landscape .html (from the archived copy at http://web.archive.org/web/20080430064447/ http://www.apple.com/au/education/digitalkids/disconnect/landscape.html). Marc Prensky's 2001 discussion is the *locus classicus* for this native/immigrant model; see Marc Prensky, "Digital Natives, Digital Immigrants," http://www.mar cprensky.com/writing/Prensky%20-%20Digital%20Natives,%20Digital%20 Immigrants%20-%20Part1.pdf.

3. See Siva Vaidhyanathan, "The Problem with 'Digital Natives,' 'Digital Immigrants,' and the 'Digital Generation,' etc.," *Googlization of Everything,* December 2007, https://web-beta.archive.org/web/*/http://www.googlizationofeverything. com/2007/12/the_problem_with_digital_nativ.php.

4. Amanda Lenhart, Mary Madden, Aaron Smith, and Alexandra Macgill, "Teens and Social Media," Pew Internet and American Life Project report, December 19, 2007, http://www.pewinternet.org/Reports/2007/Teens-and-Social-Media.aspx.

5. Diana G. Oblinger and James L. Oblinger, ed., *Educating the Net Generation* (Educause, 2005), 2.2; available at https://net.educause.edu/ir/library/pdf/ pub7101.pdf.

6. Clay Shirky, "It's Not Information Overload, It's Filter Failure," presentation to Web 2.0 Expo NY, September 2008, available at https://www.youtube .com/watch?v=LabqeJEOQyI.

7. Daniel H. Pink, *A Whole New Mind: Why Right-Brainers Will Rule the Future* (New York: Riverhead, 2005), 103.

8. Joe Lambert, *Digital Storytelling Cookbook* (Berkeley, CA: Digital Diner Press, 2010), 2.

9. http://www.cognitive-edge.com.

10. Microsoft, "Tell a Story, Become a Lifelong Learner," Digital Storytelling Learning Projects (2010), http://www.learning-v.jp/dst/images/microsoft.pdf.

11. Ibid.

12. Angela Thomas, "Fictional Blogs," *Uses of Blogs*, ed. Axel Burns and Joanne Jacobs (New York: Peter Lang, 2006), 207–08.

13. Kristian D. Stewart and Eunice Ivala, "Silence, voice, and 'other languages': Digital storytelling as a site for resistance and restoration in a South African higher education classroom." *British Journal of Educational Technology* (January 26, 2017), doi:10.1111/bjet.12540

13. James Paul Gee, *What Video Games Have to Teach Us about Learning and Literacy* (New York: Palgrave Macmillan, 2003), 51ff.

14. Microsoft, "Tell a Story," 2.

15. Kay Teehan, *Digital Storytelling In and Out of the Classroom* (Lulu.com, 2006), 8.

16. Peter Kittle, "Student Engagement and Multimodality: Collaboration, Schema, Identity," *Teaching the New Writing: Technology, Change, and Assessment in the 21st-century Classroom*, ed. Anne Herrington, Kevin Hodgson, and Charles Moran (New York: Teachers College Press, 2009), 169.

17. Joe Lambert, *Digital Storytelling: Capturing Lives, Creating Community* (Berkeley, CA: Digital Diner Press, 2002), 112.

18. Bryan Alexander, Gail Matthews-DeNatale, and Gerry Bayne, "ELI in Conversation: Web 2.0 and Digital Storytelling," podcast, 2008,. https://web-beta .archive.org/web/*/http://connect.educause.edu/blog/gbayne/eliinconversation-web20and/46133. Jason Ohler offers a good example of a media assessment rubric in his *Digital Storytelling in the Classroom: New Media Pathways to Literacy, Learning, and Creativity* (Thousand Oaks, CA: Corwin, 2008), 177ff; see also 67–68.

19. Gail Matthews-DeNatale, "Digital Storytelling: Tips and Resources," Simmons College, 2008, http://net.educause.edu/ir/library/pdf/ELI08167B.pdf. Helen Barrett offers a fine series of rubrics at http://electronicportfolios.org/digis tory/ResearchDesign.pdf.

20. Helen Barrett is probably the preeminent digital portfolio authority. Her work is very valuable, especially as she also teaches digital storytelling. See http://electronicportfolios.com/.

21. An excellent example from Tom Banaszewski can be found at http://www .infotoday.com/MMSchools/jan02/banaszewski.htm.

22. Doug Reilly, of Hobart and William Smith Colleges, in discussion with the author, July–August 2010.

23. Ron Darvin and Bonny Norton, "Transnational Identity and Migrant Language Learners: The Promise of Digital Storytelling," *Education Matters* 2, no. 1 (2014): 55–67.

24. https://web-beta.archive.org/web/*/http://oit.williams.edu/itech/digitalstorytelling/.

25. https://www.youtube.com/watch?v=BFuluIy-5QY.

26. http://ds106.us/.

Chapter 16

1. Henry Jenkins, *Convergence Culture: Where Old and New Media Collide* (New York: New York University Press, 2006), 96–97.

2. See Markus Montola's note about "dark play" in his "Games and Pervasive Games," *Pervasive Games: Theory and Design*, ed. Markus Montola, Jaakko Stenros, and Annika Waern (Boston: Morgan Kaufmann, 2009), 15.

3. http://www.gartner.com/technology/research/methodologies/hype-cycle.jsp.

4. https://medium.com/@larchuk/top-10-podcasts-of-2016-907d3d8abdf7#. 3brzhhthl.

5. David Snowden, "Be Honest, Don't Deceive Yourself," *Cognitive Edge,* October 2, 2008, http://cognitive-edge.com/blog/be-honest-dont-deceive-yourself/.

6. Chimamanda Adichie, "The Danger of a Single Story," *TED Talk,* July 2009, http://www.ted.com/talks/chimamanda_adichie_the_danger_of_a _single_story.html.

7. Compare Bissell's somewhat disturbing argument that computer games "often restore an unearned, vaguely loathsome form of innocence—an innocence derived of *not knowing anything*"; Thomas Bissell, *Extra Lives: Why Video Games Matter* (New York: Pantheon, 2010), 34, emphasis in original.

8. Joe Lambert, founder and executive director of the Center for Digital Storytelling, in discussion with the author, August 2010.

9. Roger Caillois, *Man, Play, and Games,* trans. Meyer Barash (Urbana: University of Illinois Press, 2001), 97.

10. I am indebted to my colleague, Eric Jansson, for bringing this to my attention.

11. https://www.dayz.com/.

12. http://tvtropes.org/pmwiki/pmwiki.php/Roleplay/RubyQuest.

13. http://ohlife.com. Unfortunately, defunct as of 2014.

14. http://750words.com/about. Thank you to P. F. Anderson for pointing this out to me.

15. https://web.archive.org/web/20101001000000*/http://www.vuvox.com.

16. Barbara Ganley, founder and director of Digital Explorations, in discussion with the author, July–August 2010.

17. https://web.archive.org/web/20101001000000*/http://www.curated.by; http://storify.com. Thanks to Dave Lester (https://twitter.com/davelester) for bringing these two to my attention.

18. https://web-beta.archive.org/web/*/http://www.zooburst.com/.

19. Alan Levine, formerly New Media Consortium vice president, community and CTO, in discussion with the author, July–August 2010.

20. Ruben R. Puentedura, founder and president of Hippasus, in discussion with the author, July 2010.

21. Joseph J. Esposito, "Interstitial Publishing: A New Market from Wasted Time," *O'Reilly Radar,* December 2, 2008, http://radar.oreilly.com/2008/12/ interstitial-publishing.html.

22. Its closure, as part of Yahoo's strategic reorganization, was announced via email. One copy of the final announcement can be found at http://techcrunch.com/2009/04/15/yahoo-shutting-down-the-rest-of-jumpcut-in-june/.

23. http://creeatives.wordpress.com. Thanks to Jon Breitenbucher for bringing this site to my attention.

24. https://web-beta.archive.org/web/*/https://www.visualgoodness.com/twitterOz, https://en.wikipedia.org/wiki/Such_Tweet_Sorrow, and https://twitter.com/such_tweet.

25. http://www.fanfiction.net/tos/.

26. http://shadowunit.org; http://mongoliad.com has been shuttered, with information posted to http://foreworld.com/mongoliad/.

27. Montola, "Games and Pervasive Games," 14.

28. https://www.reddit.com/r/9M9H9E9/wiki/index.

29. http://www.urbandictionary.com/define.php?term=Clock+Spider.

30. https://www.microsoft.com/microsoft-hololens/en-us/apps/fragments.

31. Markus Montola, Jaakko Stenros, and Annika Waern, "Designing Spatial Expansion," *Pervasive Games,* 79.

32. For example, the *Microbe Wiki,* authored by students across three campuses: http://microbewiki.kenyon.edu/index.php/MicrobeWiki.

33. http://www.trip-journal.com.

34. Puentedura, in discussion with the author, July 2010.

35. Jesper Juul, *Half-Real: Video Games between Real Rules and Fictional Worlds* (Cambridge, MA: MIT Press, 2005), 138–39.

36. "Polybius," *Coinop.org,* created August 3, 1998; last updated May 16, 2009; http://www.coinop.org/Game/103223/Polybius.

37. https://web-beta.archive.org/web/*/http://www.al3x.net/archives/2005/02/22/they-stopped-calling-it-rendezvous/.

38. Ken MacLeod, *The Execution Channel* (New York: Tor, 2007).

39. Gilles Deleuze and Felix Guattari, *Kafka: Toward a Minor Literature,* trans. Dana Polan (Minneapolis: University of Minnesota Press, 1986).

Bibliography

Aarseth, Espen J. *Cybertext: Perspectives on Ergodic Literature.* Baltimore: Johns Hopkins University Press, 1997.

Abroms, Lorien C., and R. Craig Lefebvre. "Obama's Wired Campaign: Lessons for Public Health Communication." *Journal of Health Communication Newsletter* 5, no. 3 (2009). https://www.ncbi.nlm.nih.gov/pubmed/19657922.

Alexander, Bryan. "Alternate Reality Games SIG/Whitepaper/Antecedents to Alternate Reality Games." 2006. http://www.christydena.com/wp-content/uploads/2007/11/igda-alternaterealitygames-whitepaper-2006.pdf.

Alexander, Bryan, and Alan Levine. "Web 2.0 Storytelling: Emergence of a New Genre." *EDUCAUSE Review* 43, no. 6 (November/December 2008). http://er.educause.edu/articles/2008/10/web-20-storytelling-emergence-of-a-new-genre.

Alexander, Bryan, Gail Matthews-DeNatale, and Gerry Bayne. "ELI in Conversation: Web 2.0 and Digital Storytelling." Podcast, 2008. https://web-beta.archive.org/web/20120527170730/http://www.educause.edu/blog/gbayne/ELIInConversationWeb20andDigit/167499.

Andersen, Ingrid, and Elizabeth J. Tisdell. "Ghost and the Machine: Bringing Untold Personal Spiritual and Cultural Experiences to Life Through the Medium of Digital Storytelling," Adult Education Research Conference Proceedings, 2016. http://newprairiepress.org/aerc/2016/papers/2.

Anderson, Chris. *The Long Tail: Why the Future of Business Is Selling Less of More.* New York: Hyperion, 2006.

Ardalan, Davar Iran. "Poetry from Iran, One Tweet at a Time." *National Public Radio,* June 28, 2009. http://www.npr.org/templates/story/story.php?storyId=105980771.

Arnheim, Rudolph. "In Praise of Blindness." In *Radiotext(e),* ed. Neil Strauss, 20–25. New York: Semiotext(e), 1993.

Baxter, Charles. *The Art of Subtext: Beyond Plot.* Saint Paul, MN: Graywolf Press, 2007.

Benkler, Yochai. *The Wealth of Networks: How Social Production Transforms Markets and Freedom*. New Haven, CT: Yale University Press, 2006.

Bernard, Sheila Curran. *Documentary Storytelling for Film and Videomakers*. 2nd ed. Burlington, VT: Focal Press, 2007.

Bissell, Thomas. *Extra Lives: Why Video Games Matter*. New York: Pantheon, 2010.

Bleeker, Julian. "Design Fiction: A Short Essay on Design, Science, Fact and Fiction." Near Future Laboratory, March 2009. http://drbfw5wfjlxon.clou dfront.net/writing/DesignFiction_WebEdition.pdf.

Bogost, Ian. *Unit Operations: An Approach to Videogame Criticism*. Cambridge, MA: MIT Press, 2006.

Bonnet, James. *Stealing Fire from the Gods: The Complete Guide to Story for Writers and Filmmakers*. 2nd ed. Studio City, CA: M. Wiese Productions, 2006.

Brown, Harry. *Videogames and Education*. Armonk, NY: M. E. Sharpe, 2008.

Caillois, Roger. *Man, Play, and Games*. Translated by Meyer Barash. Urbana: University of Illinois Press, 2001.

Campbell, Gardner. "There's Something in the Air: Podcasting in Education." *EDUCAUSE Review* 40, no. 6 (November/December 2005): 32–47. https://net.educause.edu/ir/library/pdf/erm0561.pdf

Carr, David. "How Obama Tapped into Social Networks' Power." *New York Times,* November 9, 2008. http://www.nytimes.com/2008/11/10/business/media/10carr.html.

Carson, Don. "Environmental Storytelling: Creating Immersive 3D Worlds Using Lessons Learned from the Theme Park Industry." *Gamasutra,* March 1, 2000. http://www.gamasutra.com/view/feature/3186/environmental_sto rytelling_.php.

Castañeda, Martha E. "'I am proud that I did it and it's a piece of me': Digital Storytelling in the Foreign Language Classroom." *CALICO Journal* 30, no. 1 (2013): 44–62.

Chatwin, Bruce. *The Songlines*. New York: Penguin, 1987.

Darvin, Ron, and Bonny Norton. "Transnational Identity and Migrant Language Learners: The Promise of Digital Storytelling." *Education Matters* 2, no. 1 (2014): 55–67.

Deleuze, Gilles, and Felix Guattari. *Kafka: Toward a Minor Literature*. Translated by Dana Polan. Minneapolis: University of Minnesota Press, 1986.

Di Blas, N., and P. Paolini. "Beyond the School's Boundaries: PoliCultura, a Large-Scale Digital Storytelling Initiative." *Journal of Educational Technology & Society* 16, no. 1 (2013): 15–27.

Eaton, Kit. "Wimbledon Seer App Serves Augmented Reality on a Grass Court." *Fast Company,* June 22, 2009. http://www.fastcompany.com/blog/kit-eaton/technomix/augmented-reality-hits-wimbledon-tennis-championship.

Edgerton, David. *The Shock of the Old: Technology and Global History since 1900*. New York: Oxford University Press, 2006.

Entertainment Software Association. "Essential Facts about the Computer and Video Game Industry." 2016. http://essentialfacts.theesa.com/Essential -Facts-2016.pdf.

Erard, Michael. "The Wealth of LibriVox." *Reason,* May 2007. http://reason.com/
archives/2007/04/24/the-wealth-of-librivox.

Esposito, Joseph J. "Interstitial Publishing: A New Market from Wasted Time."
O'Reilly Radar, December 2, 2008. http://radar.oreilly.com/2008/12/
interstitial-publishing.html.

Esposito, Joseph J. "The Processed Book." *First Monday* 8, no. 3 (March 2003).
http://firstmonday.org/issues/issue8_3/esposito/index.html.

Freedman, Thomas Z. "A Kindle in Every Backpack: A Proposal for eTextbooks
in American Schools." Democratic Leadership Council white paper,
July 2009. https://tfreedmanconsulting.com/wp-content/uploads/2016/05/
Freedman_Kindle-1.pdf.

Gee, James Paul. "Learning about Learning from a Video Game: *Rise of Nations"*
n.d. http://www.academiccolab.org/resources/documents/RON-paper
.rev.pdf.

Gee, James Paul. *What Video Games Have to Teach Us about Learning and Literacy.*
New York: Palgrave Macmillan, 2003.

Goodyear, Dana. "I Novels: Young Women Develop a Genre for the Cellular Age."
New Yorker, December 22, 2008. http://www.newyorker.com/magazine/
2008/12/22/i-love-novels.

Gosney, John. *Beyond Reality: A Guide to Alternate Reality Gaming.* Boston: Thom-
son, 2005.

Gray, Bronwen, Alan Young, and Tania Blomfield. "Altered Lives: Assessing the
Effectiveness of Digital Storytelling as a Form of Communication Design."
Continuum 29, no.4 (2015): 635–49. doi:10.1080/10304312.2015.1025359.

Greenfield, Adam. *Everyware: The Dawning Age of Ubiquitous Computing.* Berkeley,
CA: New Riders, 2006.

Gubrium, Aline C., Amy L. Hill, and Sarah Flicker. "A Situated Practice of Ethics
for Participatory Visual and Digital Methods in Public Health Research
and Practice: A Focus on Digital Storytelling." *American Journal of Public
Health* 104, no. 9 (2014): 1606–14.

Gubrium, Aline C., Elizabeth L. Krause, and Kasey Jernigan. "Strategic Authen-
ticity and Voice: New Ways of Seeing and Being Seen as Young Mothers
Through Digital Storytelling." *Sexuality Research and Social Policy* 11 (2014):
337–47. doi:10.1007/s13178-014-0161-x. Published online: June 3, 2014.

Hammersley, Ben. "Audible Revolution." *Guardian,* February 11, 2004. https://
www.theguardian.com/media/2004/feb/12/broadcasting.digitalmedia.

Hayes, Christopher. "Bailout Satire." *Nation,* September 22, 2008. https://www
.thenation.com/article/bailout-satire/.

Hayles, N. Katherine. *Electronic Literature: New Horizons for the Literary.* Notre
Dame, IN: University of Notre Dame Press, 2008.

Hayslip, Le Ly. *When Heaven and Earth Changed Places.* New York: Plume, 1989.

Heffernan, Virginia. "Being There." *New York Times,* February 10, 2009. http://
www.nytimes.com/2009/02/15/magazine/15wwln-medium-t.html.

Himmer, Steve. "The Labyrinth Unbound: Weblogs as Literature." In *Into the Blogosphere: Rhetoric, Community, and Culture of Weblogs,* ed. Laura J. Gurak,

Smiljana Antonijevic, Laurie Johnson, Clancy Ratliff, and Jessica Reyman. June 2004. http://conservancy.umn.edu/handle/11299/172823.

Huizinga, Johan. *Homo Ludens: A Study of the Play Element in Culture.* Boston: Beacon, 1955.

Ito, Mizuko, Daisuke Okabe, and Misa Matsuda, ed. *Personal, Portable, Pedestrian: Mobile Phones in Japanese Life.* Cambridge, MA: MIT Press, 2005.

Jacobs, Joanne. "Publishing and Blogs." In *Uses of Blogs,* ed. Axel Burns and Joanne Jacobs, 33–43. New York: Peter Lang, 2006.

Jenkins, Henry. *Convergence Culture: Where Old and New Media Collide.* New York: New York University Press, 2006.

Johnson, L., A. Levine, R. Smith, and S. Stone. *The 2010 Horizon Report.* Austin, TX: New Media Consortium, 2010.

Juul, Jesper. *A Casual Revolution: Reinventing Video Games and Their Players.* Cambridge, MA: MIT Press, 2010.

Juul, Jesper. *Half-Real: Video Games between Real Rules and Fictional Worlds.* Cambridge, MA: MIT Press, 2005.

Katz, James E., and Mark Aakhus. *Perpetual Contact: Mobile Communication, Private Talk, Public Performance.* New York: Cambridge University Press, 2002.

Kim, SoHee. "Developing Autonomous Learning for Oral Proficiency Using Digital Storytelling." *Language Learning & Technology* 18, no. 2 (2014): 20–35. http://llt.msu.edu/issues/june2014/action1.pdf, accessed February 5, 2017.

Kittle, Peter. "Student Engagement and Multimodality: Collaboration, Schema, Identity." In *Teaching the New Writing: Technology, Change, and Assessment in the 21st-Century Classroom,* ed. Anne Herrington, Kevin Hodgson, and Charles Moran, 164–80. New York: Teachers College Press, 2009.

Kushner, David. *Masters of Doom: How Two Guys Created an Empire and Transformed Pop Culture.* New York: Random House, 2003.

Lambert, Joe. *Digital Storytelling: Capturing Lives, Creating Community.* 4th ed. New York: Routledge, 2012.

Lambert, Joe. *Digital Storytelling Cookbook.* Berkeley, CA: Digital Diner Press, 2010. https://www.storycenter.org/inventory/digital-storytelling-cookbook?rq =cookbook.

Lanier, Jaron. *You Are Not a Gadget: A Manifesto.* Waterville, ME: Thorndike Press, 2010.

Lasica, J. D. *Darknet: Hollywood's War against the Digital Generation.* Hoboken, NJ: John Wiley, 2005.

Lee, Hyung. "Kindles Yet to Woo University Users." *Daily Princetonian,* September 28, 2009. https://web-beta.archive.org/web/20091101195628/http://www.dailyprincetonian.com/2009/09/28/23918

Lenette, Caroline, Leonie Cox, and Mark Brough. "Digital Storytelling as a Social Work Tool: Learning from Ethnographic Research with Women from Refugee Backgrounds." *British Journal of Social Work* 45 (2015): 988–1005. doi:10.1093/bjsw/bct184.

Lenhart, Amanda, Joseph Kahne, Ellen Middaugh, Alexandra Macgill, Chris Evans, and Jessica Vitak. "Teens, Video Games and Civics." Pew Internet and American Life report, September 16, 2008. http://www.pewinternet .org/Reports/2008/Teens-Video-Games-and-Civics.aspx.

Lenhart, Amanda, and Mary Madden. "Teens, Privacy and Online Social Networks." Pew Internet and American Life Project report, April 18, 2007. http://www.pewinternet.org/Reports/2007/Teens-Privacy-and-Online-Social-Networks.aspx.

Lenhart, Amanda, Mary Madden, Aaron Smith, and Alexandra Macgill. "Teens and Social Media." Pew Internet and American Life Project report, December 19, 2007. http://www.pewinternet.org/Reports/2007/Teens-and-Social -Media.aspx.

MacLeod, Ken. *The Execution Channel*. New York: Tor, 2007.

Madden, Matt. *99 Ways to Tell a Story: Exercises in Style*. New York: Chamberlain Bros., 2005. http://www.exercisesinstyle.com.

Mader, Stewart. *Wikipatterns*. Indianapolis: John Wiley, 2008.

Mason, Bruce, and Sue Thomas. "A Million Penguins Research Report." Institute of Creative Technologies, De Montfort University, Leicester, United Kingdom, April 24, 2008. http://www.ioct.dmu.ac.uk/documents/amillionpe nguinsreport.pdf.

Matthews-DeNatale, Gail. "Digital Storytelling: Tips and Resources." Simmons College, 2008. http://net.educause.edu/ir/library/pdf/ELI08167B.pdf.

McCloud, Scott. *Understanding Comics*. Northampton, MA: Kitchen Sink Press, 1993.

McKee, Robert. *Story*. New York: HarperCollins, 1997.

Microsoft. "Tell a Story, Become a Lifelong Learner." Digital Storytelling Learning Projects, 2010. https://learningrenaissance.files.wordpress.com/2015/ 01/digitalstorytellingebook.pdf.

Miller, Claire Cain. "E-Books Top Hardcovers at Amazon." *New York Times*, July 19, 2010. http://www.nytimes.com/2010/07/20/technology/20kindle.html.

Mittell, Jason. *Genre and Television: From Cop Shows to Cartoons in American Culture*. New York: Routledge, 2004.

Montfort, Nick. *Twisty Little Passages*. Cambridge, MA: MIT Press, 2003.

Montola, Markus, Jaakko Stenros, and Annika Waern, ed. *Pervasive Games: Theory and Design*. Boston: Morgan Kaufmann, 2009.

Morris, Chris. "Average Vidgamer Older, More Affluent." Variety.com, June 14, 2010. http://www.variety.com/article/VR1118020564.html.

Murray, Janet. *Hamlet on the Holodeck: The Future of Narrative in Cyberspace*. New York: Free Press, 1997.

Nardi, Bonnie A., and Vicki L. O' Day. *Information Ecologies: Using Technology with Heart*. Cambridge, MA: MIT Press, 1999.

Niemi, Hannele, Vilhelmiina Harju, Marianna Vivitsou, Kirsi Viitanen, Jari Multisilta, and Anne Kuokkanen. "Digital Storytelling for 21st-Century Skills in Virtual Learning Environments." *Creative Education* 5 (2014): 657–71.

Published Online May 2014 in SciRes. http://www.scirp.org/journal/ce; http://dx.doi.org/10.4236/ce.2014.59078.

Njeru, Jane W., Christi A. Patten, Marcelo M. K. Hanza, Tabetha A. Brockman, et al. "Stories for Change: Development of a Diabetes Digital Storytelling Intervention for Refugees and Immigrants to Minnesota Using Qualitative Methods." *BMC Public Health* 15 (2015): 1311. doi:10.1186/s12889-015-2628-y.

Oblinger, Diana G., and James L. Oblinger, ed. *Educating the Net Generation.* Educause, 2005. https://net.educause.edu/ir/library/pdf/pub7101.pdf.

Ohler, Jason. *Digital Storytelling in the Classroom: New Media Pathways to Literacy, Learning, and Creativity.* Thousand Oaks, CA: Corwin, 2008.

O'Reilly, Tim. "What Is Web 2.0? Design Patterns and Business Models for the Next Generation of Software." September 2005. http://oreilly.com/web2/archive/what-is-web-20.html.

Parvix, Babak A. "Augmented Reality in a Contact Lens: A New Generation of Contact Lenses Built with Very Small Circuits and LEDs Promises Bionic Eyesight." *IEEE Spectrum,* September 2009. http://spectrum.ieee.org/biomedical/bionics/augmented-reality-in-a-contact-lens/.

Pink, Daniel H. *A Whole New Mind: Why Right-Brainers Will Rule the Future.* New York: Riverhead, 2005.

Rambe, Patient, and Shepherd Mlambo. "Using Digital Storytelling to Externalise Personal Knowledge of Research Processes: The Case of a Knowledge Audio Repository." *Internet and Higher Education* 22 (April 8, 2014): 11–23.

Rheingold, Howard. *Smart Mobs.* Cambridge, MA: Perseus, 2002.

Rheingold, Howard. *Tools for Thought: The History and Future of Mind-Expanding Technology.* 2nd ed. Cambridge, MA: MIT Press, 2000.

Rheingold, Howard. *The Virtual Community: Homesteading on the Electronic Frontier.* 2nd ed. Cambridge, MA: MIT Press, 2000.

Richardson, John H. "The Search for Isabella V." *Esquire,* January 29, 2007. http://www.esquire.com/news-politics/a452/esq1003-oct-isabella/.

Roiphe, Katie. "The Language of Fakebook." *New York Times,* August 13, 2010. http://www.nytimes.com/2010/08/15/fashion/15Culture.html.

Rosenberg, Scott. *Dreaming in Code: Two Dozen Programmers, Three Years, 4,732 Bugs, and One Quest for Transcendent Software.* New York: Crown, 2007.

Salen, Katie, and Eric Zimmerman. *Rules of Play: Game Design Fundamentals.* Cambridge, MA: MIT Press, 2004.

Schwartz, Barry. *The Paradox of Choice: Why More Is Less.* New York: Ecco, 2004.

Shelby-Caffey, Crystal, Edwin Úbéda, and Bethany Jenkins. *The Reading Teacher* 68, no. 3 (2014): 191–99. doi:10.1002/trtr.1273.

Shirky, Clay. *Cognitive Surplus: Creativity and Generosity in a Connected Age.* New York: Penguin, 2010.

Shirky, Clay. *Here Comes Everybody: The Power of Organizing without Organizations.* New York: Penguin, 2008.

Shirky, Clay. "It's Not Information Overload, It's Filter Failure." Presentation to Web 2.0 Expo NY, September 2008. https://www.youtube.com/watch?v =LabqeJEOQyI.

Simmons, Annette. *The Story Factor: Secrets of Influence from the Art of Storytelling.* 2nd ed. New York: Basic Books, 2006.

Smith, Aaron. "Mobile Access 2010." Pew Internet and American Life Project report, July 7, 2010. http://pewinternet.org/Reports/2010/Mobile-Access -2010.aspx.

"SpaceBass" [Sean Stacey]. "Undefining ARG." November 10, 2006. http://www .unfiction.com/compendium/2006/11/10/undefining-arg/.

Spohrer, J. "Information in Places." *IBM Systems Journal* 38, no. 4 (December 1999): 602–28.

Sterling, Bruce. "ARE 2010 Keynote by Bruce Sterling: Bake a Big Pie!" Keynote speech, Augmented Reality Event, June 6, 2010. https://web-beta.archive. org/web/20161107192902/http://augmentedrealityevent.com/2010/06/06/ are-2010-keynote-by-bruce-sterling-build-a-big-pie.

Sterling, Bruce. "At the Dawn of the Augmented Reality Industry." Address, August 20, 2009. https://vimeo.com/6189763.

Sterling, Bruce. "Dispatches from the Hyperlocal Future." *Wired* 15, no. 7 (June 2007). http://www.wired.com/techbiz/it/magazine/15-07/local.

Sterling, Bruce. *Shaping Things.* Cambridge, MA: MIT Press, 2005.

Sterling, Bruce. *Visionary in Residence.* New York: Thunder's Mouth Press, 2006.

Story Kitchen. "Storytelling, Part 1: Change of Storytelling." July 2010. https:// vimeo.com/12999733.

Sutherland, John. "Node Idea." *Guardian,* August 30, 2007. http://www.guardian .co.uk/education/2007/aug/31/highereducation.books.

Sutherland, Paul. "Doctor Who and the Star of Doom." *Skymania*, January 27, 2010. http://www.skymania.com/wp/2010/01/doctor-who-and-star-of -doom.html/766/. Originally published in *Scientific American.*

Teehan, Kay. *Digital Storytelling In and Out of the Classroom.* Lulu.com, 2006.

Terdiman, Daniel. "Virtual Magnate Shares Secrets of Success." *Cnet News,* December 20, 2006. https://www.cnet.com/news/virtual-magnate-shares-secrets-of -success/

Thomas, Angela. "Fictional Blogs." In *Uses of Blogs*, ed. Axel Burns and Joanne Jacobs, 199–209. New York: Peter Lang, 2006.

Tolkien, J. R. R. "On Fairy-Stories." In *The Tolkien Reader.* New York: Ballantine Books, 1966.

Toppo, Greg. "School Chooses Kindle; Are Libraries for the History 'Books'?" *USA Today,* October 27, 2009. http://www.usatoday.com/news/education/2009 -10-26-kindle-school-library_N.htm.

Vershbow, Ben. "The Networked Book." *Forbes,* December 1, 2006. https://www .forbes.com/2006/11/30/future-books-publishing-tech-media_cz_bv_ books06_1201network.html.

Vierecke, Linda. "Young Holocaust Victim Has over 1,700 Friends on Facebook." *Deutsche Welle,* November 19, 2009. http://www.dw-world.de/dw/article/0,,4908523,00.html.

Vivienne, Sonja, and Jean Burgess. "The Remediation of the Personal Photograph and the Politics of Self-representation in Digital Storytelling." *Journal of Material Culture* 18, no. 3 (September 2013): 279–98. doi:10.1177/1359183513492080.

Walker, Jesse. "The Laptop Theater." *Reason,* July 2, 2010. http://reason.com/archives/2010/07/02/the-laptop-theater.

Walker, Jill. "Do You Think You're Part of This? Digital Texts and the Second-Person Address." In *Cybertext Yearbook 2000.* Publications of the Research Centre for Contemporary Culture, ed. Markku Eskelinen and Raine Koskimaa. Saarijarvi: University of Jyvaskyla, 2001. http://jilltxt.net/txt/do_you_think.pdf.

Wallis, James. "Making Games That Tell Stories." In *Second Person: Role-Playing and Story in Games and Playable Media,* ed. Pat Harrigan and Noah Wardrip-Fruin, 69–80. Cambridge, MA: MIT Press, 2007.

Weiser, Mark. "The Computer for the 21st Century," *Scientific American* 265, no. 3 (September 1991): 66–75. http://www.ubiq.com/hypertext/weiser/SciAm Draft3.html.

Wexler, Lisa, Aline Gubrium, Megan Griffin, and Gloria DiFulvio. "Promoting Positive Youth Development and Highlighting Reasons for Living in Northwest Alaska Through Digital Storytelling." *Health Promotion Practice* 14, no. 4 (July 2013): 617–23. doi:10.1177/1524839912462390.

Willox, Ashlee Cunsolo, Sherilee L. Harper, Victoria L. Edge, 'My Word': Story-telling, and Digital Media Lab. "Storytelling in a Digital Age: Digital Story-telling as an Emerging Narrative Method for Preserving and Promoting Indigenous Oral Wisdom." *Qualitative Research* 13, no. 2 (2013): 127–47. doi:10.1177/1468794112446105 qrj.sagepub.com.

Wolf, Mark. "Genre and the Video Game." In *The Medium of the Video Game,* ed. Mark Wolf. Austin: University of Texas Press, 2001.

Wortham, Jenna. "Twitterers Stage Mock Martian Invasion a la 'War of the Worlds.'" *Wired,* October 31, 2008. http://www.wired.com/underwire/2008/10/twitterers-stag/.

Index

Aarseth, Espen, 10, 19
Adobe, 107, 200
Aggregation, 32, 68, 73, 94, 136, 140, 157, 168, 197, 216, 218, 219, 232, 241
A.I. (2001), 156
Alice and Kev, 127
Alternate reality games, 155–165; antecedents of, 157–159; defined, 156. *See also* Hidden story
Amateur press association, 139
Amazon, 150–151, 245 n.1
Analog storytelling, 4–5, 14–15, 216
Android operating system, 152
Anecdote, 13, 208
Animation, 21–22, 25, 33, 101, 126, 139, 159, 168, 197, 201
Aphorisms, 65–66
Apple, 152, 200, 201, 220
Apps, 14, 15, 148–149
AR. *See* Augmented Reality (AR)
Architectural visualization, 173
Archival blogging, 56–59
Archival material, 76, 190
Arnheim, Rudolph, 82
Assassin, 175
Assassin's Creed, 123
Atchley, Dana, 23
Audacity (software), 200

Audience, 4, 6, 8, 9–13, 19, 27, 34, 39, 42, 43, 49, 58, 69–70, 73, 81–82, 87, 88, 90, 91, 92, 94, 103, 104, 106, 107, 116, 125, 132, 133, 137, 138, 140, 141, 142, 148, 152, 153, 158, 163–165, 173, 175, 179, 181–183, 187, 189, 190, 193, 194, 199, 206, 207, 227, 228, 230, 232, 235, 236, 241, 244, 247; feedback, 36, 59, 74, 75, 92, 99, 101, 135, 138, 189, 213, 226; immersion of in story, 98–103, 122–123, 181–182, 226
Audio, 21, 33, 56, 57, 81–95, 188–119, 124–125, 137, 141, 160, 163, 174, 182, 188, 190–202, 208, 215, 217; soundtrack, 91, 108, 192, 193, 197, 200, 201, 207, 208
Augmented Reality (AR), 168, 211, 239, 241–243; storytelling potential of, 167–177. *See also* Superimposed visualization
Authorship, 49, 163, 240. *See also* Wiki technology and wikis, storytelling and
Avatars, 22, 36, 39, 79; gaming and, 108–110

BBC, 84, 159, 180, 256 n.6
The Beast, 156–157

Bernard, Sheila, 6, 8, 11
Berners-Lee, Tim, 20, 248 n.8
BioShock, 38, 116, 117–127, 183
Blackwood, Algernon, 14, 93
Blair Witch Project, 158
Blog fiction, 53
Blogs and blogging, 3, 12, 14, 15,
    30, 40–62, 75, 76, 81, 85, 91, 107,
    121, 134, 135, 138, 142, 151, 153,
    161–165, 203, 209, 226, 229, 230,
    233, 244; character blogging,
    59–62; and storytelling, 48–62
Book blogging, 134–135
Borges, Jorge Luis, 158
Boundary determination, 132, 163
Brainstorming, 165, 189, 194
Brama Grodzka Cultural Center, 76
Brownworth, Lars, 82–83
Bush, Vannevar, 18

Cameron, Charles, 214–215
Campanella, James, 84
Campbell, Gardner, 82
Campbell, Joseph, 8–9
Carson, Don, 99–100
Casual games. *See* Games and gaming
Cell phone. *See* Mobile phones
Center for Digital Storytelling, 9,
    24–25, 40, 73, 85, 88, 98, 132,
    147, 174, 188, 215; Seven
    Principles, 192–193. *See also*
    StoryCenter
Chain Factor, 103
Chaotic fiction, 163–164
Characters, 5, 8, 11–12, 19, 22, 42,
    53, 55, 70, 77; in alternate reality
    games, 161–162, 164; character
    blogging, 59–62; in games, 98,
    100–106, 108, 118–124; in
    podcasting, 86–89
Chesterton, G. K., 158
Chondry, Mark, 51, 164
Choose Your Own Adventure books,
    18, 70, 118, 146, 149, 163

Chronological sequence. *See* Linear
    sequence
Cinematics. *See* Cut scenes
Codex Seraphinianus, 157–158
Cognitive Edge, 7
Coherence, 163
Collaboration, 164
Collaborative gaming. *See* Alternative
    reality games
Collaborative writing, 32, 68, 240
Collective detective stories, 156
Comic Life, 203
Commercial framework, 141
Community norms, 164
Computer games. *See* Games and
    gaming
Computer-generated imagery (CGI),
    15
Concept mapping, 143, 192, 202
Connect with I, 92–93
Console games. *See* Games and
    gaming
Constructivist learning, 228
Contact, 207–208
Content mastery, 228
Context, 26, 56, 76, 83, 105, 121, 141,
    162, 173, 190, 196, 225
Controller vibration, 36, 98, 121
Conversations, 31–32, 194, 215
Copyright, 83, 131, 196, 200,
    217–219, 221, 240; challenges, 177,
    198, 205, 209–210
Cortazar, Julio, 18
Course timeline, 231–232
Creative Commons, 131, 196, 218
Creative invisibility, 165
Credits, 198–199, 208, 228
CREEatives, 240
Curriculum, 11, 23–27, 40, 73, 174,
    192–193
Cut scenes, 101–103, 109, 118, 123,
    124
Cybercultural ease, 224
Cyberculture Ludens, 34

Data, 4, 172, 175; tags, 173
Deren, Maya, 18
Design freedom, 30
Diaries, 48–49, 56, 121, 226
Digitales, 216
Digital memoirs, 22
Digital preservation, 29
Digital storytelling: augmented reality
  and, 167–177; Center for Digital
  Storytelling model, 24–27; defined,
  3; education and, 223–233; gaming
  and, 97–126, 155–166; mobile
  devices and, 143–153; new wave,
  88; Obama administration and,
  14; possible futures of, 235–244;
  practical advice for, 187–210;
  social media and, 47–95; virtual
  reality and, 179–184
Dionaea House, 51–53, 78, 164
Discussion, 59, 68–69, 72, 78,
  83–86, 94, 97–98, 122, 134, 138,
  148, 188, 189, 217. *See also* Story
  circle; Twitter
"Dispatches from the Hyperlocal
  Future," 50–51
Distributed editing, 134–135
Doctor Who, 140, 159
Document hosting, 68
Dracula blog, 56–59
Dramatic question, 193, 228
Dreaming Methods, 21–22
Dual narrative, 106
Dual-track model, 102
du Maurier, Daphne, 9

E-books, 15, 85, 132, 141–142, 148,
  151, 163
Echo Bazaar, 112–113
Economy in storytelling, 193, 228
Editing, 31, 43, 49, 134, 146, 202,
  204, 213, 230, 239; audio, 200;
  images, 126, 196, 200; video, 188,
  194, 196–199, 201; wikis, 68–70,
  107. *See also* Distributed editing

Educational gaming, 39
Education and digital storytelling,
  26–28, 223–233
Eisner, Will, 6
Elections and storytelling, 14
Electronic Literature Organization,
  22
Elements, in games. *See* Story and
  storytelling
Emotional content, 7–8, 11–13, 23–25,
  72, 74, 75–76, 86–87, 92, 102, 103,
  116–117, 120, 127, 158, 162, 188,
  193, 197, 225, 230, 256 n.16
Empowerment, 226
Engagement, 6, 9, 11–13, 77, 91,
  99–100, 104, 125, 162, 181, 193,
  236, 237, 243
Eno, Brian, 212–213
Ergodic literature, 19–21
Esposito, Joseph, 133, 147–148, 239
Exploration, 21, 27, 38, 51, 68, 118,
  122–126
Exquisite Corpse, 69, 240
External links, 133

Facebook, 3, 31, 32, 64, 78, 94, 107,
  131, 137, 146, 213, 240. *See also*
  Single-character Facebook project
Faces of Death, 158
Fallout 3, 116–119, 121–125
Fanfiction.net, 140, 240
"Farm to Food," 76
Farmville, 107, 112
Fiction, 158. *See also* Fanfiction.net;
  Interactive fiction
Fiction/nonfiction boundary, 156,
  157
Final Cut, 201
Fincher, David, 158
Flash, 21, 78, 88, 107–108, 159, 220
Flickr, 31, 32, 44, 60, 73–76, 95,
  101, 109, 138, 147, 168, 189, 196,
  202–203, 213–214, 219, 239, 254,
  255

Forking, 70–71, 181
Fowles, John, 158
Fragmented storytelling, 118–119
Framework of discovery, 141
Frenay, Robert, 134
Freytag, Gustav, 6
Freytag triangle, 6, 117
Friction, 13, 106, 189
FTP, 30

The Game, 158, 159
Games and gaming, 34–40; casual
    games, 37, 98, 101–117, 219, 220;
    console games, 98, 100, 116,
    119, 121–122, 143; game wikis,
    120–121; resources, 219–220;
    storytelling and, 97–127. *See also*
    Serious games
Ganley, Barbara, 75, 132, 190, 229,
    249, 260, 261, 265, 266, 272
Garden model, 70–71
Gee, James Paul, 102–103, 226–227
Genre, 5, 21–22, 38–40, 88, 108, 120,
    140, 147, 163, 176, 212, 238
Gibson, William, 9–10, 18, 135
Gift of voice, 24, 85, 92, 124, 174, 193
Gillmor, Dan, 134–135
Glass, Ira, 7
Google, 12, 33, 43, 48, 83, 93, 120,
    136, 141, 145, 148, 171, 172, 176,
    201, 205, 211, 219, 238; Cardboard,
    179; Docs, 68, 203; Earth, 218,
    243; Goggles, 169; Images, 13,
    223; Maps, 58, 168; Photos, 200;
    Spreadsheets, 32; Wave, 32. *See also*
    Android operating system; Picasa;
    YouTube
GPS, 135, 145, 149, 170–171, 173
GRAMMATRON, 22
Group projects, 228–229
Guitar Hero, 107

Halo 107, 109, 119, 120, 126, 155
Halo ODST, 118–119

Hidden story, 159–163. *See also* Hoax
    and hoaxes
High Capacity Color Barcode,
    171–172
Hipbone games, 214–215
History, 56–57, 119–120
Hive mind, 216–218
Hoax and hoaxes, 3, 91, 157–158
Holeton, Richard, 18
HTML, 21, 30, 33, 51, 53, 68, 142,
    159–160
HTML5, 107, 220
Hypermedia, 18, 21, 28
Hypertext, 18–22, 133, 209; fiction
    and, 18–19; storytelling and, 21–23

Images, 25, 27, 30–35, 60, 72, 78,
    79, 95, 127, 138, 162, 167, 189,
    191–192; in augmented reality, 168,
    172, 173. *See also* Social images
Immersion, 98–102, 122–123,
    181–182, 193, 226
iMovie, 200, 201
Individual web pages, 21
Information overload, 225, 227
In Our Time, 83–85, 256 n.7
Inspiration, 14, 20, 116, 183, 204,
    212, 215–216
Instagram, 75, 203, 239
Intellectual property (IP), 93, 131,
    177, 210, 218, 240. *See also*
    Copyright
Interactive fiction, 19, 20, 44, 98,
    110–111, 117, 149, 150, 176, 205,
    220
Interactive story. *See* Interactive fiction
Internet Archive, 42, 47, 196, 205,
    211, 219
Interview, 36, 68, 83–85, 134,
    190–191
Intrigue, 85, 110, 160. *See also*
    Mystery
iOS, 142, 152, 220
iPad, 15, 37, 138, 152, 229

iPhone, 37, 146, 150, 152, 167–168, 202, 239

"Iraqi Invasion: A Text Misadventure," 110–111

ITacitus, 173

iTunes, 32, 132, 138, 141, 193

Jackson, Shelley, 18

Jenkins, Henry, 43, 136, 139, 235

Journalists, 12, 66, 67, 236

Joyce, Michael, 18

JumpCut, 32, 201, 240

Kafka, Franz, 9–10

Keitai, 144, 146–147, 239. *See also* Mobile phones

Kindle e-reader, 83, 85, 138, 142, 150–152, 262 n.17

L'Abbé, Heston, 180

Lack of control, 165

Lambert, Joe, 23–24, 27, 225, 248, 254, 258, 266, 267, 268, 270, 271, 272, 278

Landow, George, 18

Large-scale games, 98, 101, 116–127

Levine, Alan, 12, 141, 203, 214, 218, 239, 247, 272, 275

Lexia, 18–19, 21–22, 133

"Lexia to Perplexia," 22

LibriVox, 85–86, 217

Liminal states, 98–99

Linear sequence, 73–74, 117

Link rot, 29, 47, 209

Literary criticism, 131

Live stories, 239

Lonelygirl15, 90–95

Lovecraft, H. P., 158, 261 n.22

Machinarium, 109–110

Machinima, 126–127, 221

Mad City Mystery, 175

Mafia Wars, 112

Marble Hornets, 93–95

Marketing, 12, 41, 77, 78, 156, 160, 163, 176, 182

Mass Effect, 40, 116, 183

Massively multiplayer online games, 36, 240

McCloud, Scott, 42, 106, 246

McGonigal, Jane, 157

McKee, Robert, 6, 8

Meaning, 4, 6–7, 10, 13–14, 25, 26, 47, 62, 65, 73, 103, 105, 116–117, 138, 174, 192, 196, 225, 228, 230, 237

Media coverage, 212, 235

MediaWiki, 69

Memory Palace, 86

Metacortechs, 160

Metaphor, 35, 48–49, 70–71, 100–101, 117, 195, 207, 250 n.2

Microcontent, 7, 29–30, 74, 77, 134

Micronarrative, 63, 203

Microsoft, 142, 152, 238, 242, 263 n.13; Xbox, 36. *See also* High Capacity Color Barcode

Million Penguins, 70–71

Mimesis, 10–11

Mirror's Edge, 123

Mobile, definition, 133

Mobile phones, 143–153; and apps, 148–150; future of, 239–240; and storytelling, 145–153. *See also* Augmented Reality (AR); *specific devices*

Mobile Web sites, 150

"Momnotmom," 24–25

Monomyth, 8

Montfort, Nick, 6, 157

Moulthrop, Stuart, 18

Multiple proscenia, 43, 83, 88, 121, 137, 141, 182–183, 206, 237, 241

Multiple readable chunks. *See* Lexia

Multi-User Dimensions (MUDs), 17, 19, 22, 244

Murray, Janet, 44

Murray, Margaret Alice, 158

Music, 4, 5, 13, 15, 27, 34, 78, 79,
    82–84, 86, 89, 90, 100–101, 108,
    109, 115, 126, 140, 146, 148, 155,
    159, 170–171, 182, 192–195,
    197–198, 200, 204–205, 207, 215,
    218, 241
My Darklyng, 78
Myna, 200
Mystery, 8–10, 12, 54, 61, 78, 87–89,
    104–105, 110, 125–126, 158, 165,
    170, 202, 206, 242, 244
Myth, 8–9, 12, 14, 89, 169, 215, 241
Mythopoeic story, 8, 14

Narration, 25, 26, 62, 92, 192, 196;
    as alternative to story, 251 n.26.
    See also Digital storytelling; Story
    and storytelling
Narrative archaeologies, 176
Narrative impulse, 5
National Institute for Technology in
    Liberal Education (NITLE), 27
Networked book, 131–142
Neuro-linguistic programming,
    159–160
News from 1930, 56–57
Newton, Katy, 181
Nielson, Jakob, 18
99 Ways to Tell a Story, 212
Nodes, 141–142
Nonfiction, 4, 10, 12, 21–23, 48–49,
    58, 74, 76, 83, 85–88, 134,
    156–157, 173, 179, 215, 217,
    252 n.3
Novel, 3, 5, 18, 35, 48, 56–58, 63,
    70–71, 76, 78, 84, 86, 88, 105, 117,
    120, 134–135, 143, 146–147, 159,
    163, 165, 181, 202, 209, 214–217,
    239, 241, 246
Novels in Three Lines, 63–64

Obama, Barack, 14
Oblique Strategies, 212–213
Ohler, Jason, 8, 11

OhLife, 238, 272 n.13
Online communities, 213, 233
Open education resources (OER),
    229–230
Oral storytelling, 5, 34, 235. *See also*
    Podcasts and podcasting
O'Reilly, Tim, 29
Orwell, George, 9–10
Outbound links, 133
Outmoded, 47, 205

Pacing, 193–194
Paik, Nam June, 5
Patient Voices, 216
Pavic, Milorad, 18
PC gaming, 35, 37, 116
Pepys Diary, 56–59, 135, 163
Personal content, 11, 23, 119
Personal presence, 42
Phone. *See* Mobile phones
Picasa, 32, 254 n.84
Pink Floyd, 5
Plants vs Zombies, 100–104
Platforms, 99, 108–110, 113, 116,
    121, 126, 203, 208, 212, 216, 230;
    augmented reality as, 145, 167–177;
    e-readers as, 150–152; future, 238,
    241, 244; games as, 149, 220;
    mobile phone as, 143–146, 149;
    networked book as, 133, 137;
    tablets as, 152–153; virtual reality,
    179, 182
Playing for Keeps, 87
Podcasts and podcasting, 32, 42, 43,
    81–89, 138, 141, 142, 143, 163,
    183, 217
Poe, Edgar Allan, 157
Point of view, 44, 100, 105, 192, 207,
    212, 228
Pollard, Sam, 11
Pollock, Natalie, 78–79
Polybius, 243–244
Posthuman storytelling, 67
Powers of ten story, 208

Project Gutenberg, 142
Project management, 163, 165, 198, 202, 204, 227
Project MU, 160–163
Publication, 48, 57–59, 66, 90, 131, 134, 138, 148, 199, 201–202, 204, 215–217, 226
Public relations, 12
Puentedura, Ruben, 217, 239, 258 n.13
Pulse, 134
Puzzle-solving, 20, 109

QR codes, 171
Quiet Place, 51

Rabbit hole, 155, 160, 164, 165
Radio Frequency Identifier (RFID), 171–172
Radiolab, 86–87
Radio Open Source, 85
Remixing, 30, 66–67, 74, 113, 126, 140, 177, 197, 209, 218, 239, 243
Report from Iron Mountain, 157
Representation, 10–11, 42, 48, 105, 107, 109, 125, 149, 181
Rheingold, Howard, 18, 134, 169
Richardson, John, 49
Rise of Nations, 102–103
Rome: Total War, 36, 40, 116–127
Rotterdam Market Hall AR Layer, 173
Round robin story, 69, 85–86, 240
RSS, 32, 81–83, 141, 211
Ruleset, 163–164

Salen, Katie, 102, 258 n.11
Science fiction, 18, 65, 88, 89, 116, 120, 139, 140, 152, 153, 156, 168, 172, 176, 210, 212, 241, 244, 247 n.17
SCP Foundation, 72
Second Life, 39–40, 108, 126, 220, 221, 241, 244

Second-person narrative, 93, 102, 105–106, 111
Segments, 42, 146, 194
Self-representation, 48
Sequence, 6, 10, 13, 21, 42, 47, 49, 55, 68, 73–76, 82, 86, 88, 93, 95, 109, 112, 116–118, 138, 140, 147, 149, 165, 170, 182, 191, 192, 203, 205–206, 209, 212, 214, 231
Serafini, Luigi, 158
Serial logic, 206
Serial podcast, 85
Serial structure, 42, 50, 51, 54, 55, 59, 68, 85, 87, 88, 90, 92, 93, 148, 162, 165, 182, 183, 206, 208, 209, 236, 238
Serious games, 39–40
Seven Principles, CDS curriculum, 192
She's A Flight Risk, 49, 59
Sheldon, Alice, 18
Shute, David, 108
Simmons, Annette, 9
Single-character Facebook project, 76
Sitcom, 93
Slideshare, 30, 32, 75
"Small" games. *See* Games and gaming, casual games
Small Town Noir, 61–62
Small Worlds, 108–109
Smart Mobs blog, 134
Smartphones. *See* Mobile phones
Smith, Sarah, 18
Snowfall paradigm, 33
Social architecture, 29
Social bookmarking, 35, 217
Social images, 73–76
Social media, 29–33, 224; and education, 233; electoral campaigns and, 14; future of, 239–241, 243, 244; and games, 35–36, 107, 112–113, 120–121, 127, 157, 162–165; and mobile, 145–146, 149; and the networked book,

Social media (*cont.*)
131–133, 136–141; storytelling and, 42–43, 47–95, 205, 209, 218–219, 244; supplants "Web 2.0," 29; transitory state of, 47–48. *See also* Blogs and blogging; Facebook; Social bookmarking; Social images; Wiki technology and wikis
Software development, 237
Sondheim, Alan, 22, 248 n.12
Songs, 5, 125, 132, 169–170
Soukup, Karin, 181
Sound. *See* Audio
Soundarajan, Thenmozhi, 25
Soundtrack. *See* Audio
Source diversity, 211–212
Stacey, Sean, 163
Standards, academic, 231; for stories, 235; technological, 41, 88, 132, 189, 194
Standards of Creation, The, 84
Sterling, Bruce, 50, 153, 169
Story and storytelling: assessment, 228–229; autobiographical, 23, 26, 42, 88, 182, 189–193, 238; backlash against, 235–237; commentary as part of, 18, 43, 51, 53, 57, 58, 68, 70, 121, 135, 137, 143, 164; defined 5–15, 131; elements in games, 98–107; mystery and, 8–12, 78, 87, 104–105, 110, 125–126, 158, 165, 175, 202, 206; resources, 211–221; second person 105; story on rails, 118; structure, 19–22, 34–35, 41–43, 55–59, 71–72, 85, 87, 109, 112, 116, 119, 125, 149, 169, 182–3, 193–195, 204, 212. *See also* Digital storytelling
Storyboarding, 191–192, 227–228, 266 n.9
StoryCenter, 85, 88, 215
Story circle, 189, 195, 197–199
StoryCorps, 150, 215–216
Story games, 19, 213–214

Story on rails, 117–118
Storyteller, 4, 5, 12, 34, 89, 92, 95, 114, 142, 164–165, 177, 182, 195, 203, 209, 212, 218, 220, 236
Streetside Stories, 26, 216
Students, 26, 48, 69, 152–153, 175, 188–189, 216, 220, 224–225, 243
Subcreation, 137
Superimposed visualization, 168

Tablet computing, 37, 143, 152–153
Tablet PC, 37, 152, 173
Tag. *See* High Capacity Color Barcode
Tale of Things, 172
Teachers, 216, 225, 227–228, 230–233
Technological environment, 29
Technological fluency, 224
Technology, 47, 50, 57, 65, 68, 88, 91, 107, 120, 127, 131–132, 139, 144–149, 153, 157, 162–163, 168, 171, 175–176, 179, 194–195, 197, 212, 224, 230; advancement of, 238–244; workshop requirements and, 188–190
"Ted's Caving Journal," 21
Television, 9, 14, 15, 44, 47, 55, 123, 143
Tell a story in 5 frames, 73–75
Templates, 30, 238
Temporally structured archival blogging, 56–59
Text-based game–stories, 110–111
34 North 118 West, 173–174
Tolkien, J.R.R., 137, 157
Transmedia storytelling, 43, 53, 136, 160, 235
Tull, Jethro, 5
12 Byzantine Rulers, 83–84
Twitter, 3, 14, 32, 60, 62–68, 77, 79–80, 102, 107, 112, 146, 174, 175, 203, 206, 217, 231; storytelling and, 62–68, 94, 150, 213, 214, 238

Ubiquitous computing, 144–145
Urban legend, 20

Vaidhyanathan, Siva, 134
Varley, John, 18
Verbs, 66, 206
Vermont, 3, 27, 88, 167–168
Vershbow, Ben, 132, 139
Video, 5, 14, 15, 18, 22–34, 65, 73,
   80, 90–98, 102, 146, 155, 168, 172,
   187–210, 213
Videogames. *See* Games and gaming
Vinge, Vernor, 18
Vinyl records, 5
Virtual worlds, 17, 18, 19, 39–40, 99,
   126, 219–221, 227, 241
Voiceover writing, 190–196, 199, 207,
   218
VoiceThread, 95, 203, 215

Walker, Jesse, 127
Walker, Jill, 105
Walpole, Horace, 157
WarGames (1983), 18

Web 2.0, 21, 28–34, 43, 47, 75, 80,
   109, 126, 134, 200–201, 219, 247;
   coined, 29. *See also* Social media
"Welcome to Pine Point," 33–34
Wiki technology and wikis, 30, 31,
   32, 35, 36, 43, 94, 107, 120, 121,
   133, 138, 160, 165, 169, 173, 182,
   191, 203, 205, 215, 231, 244, 248;
   storytelling and, 68–73, 135–136,
   163, 208–209, 230; Wikipedia, 14,
   68, 107, 133, 163, 168, 172–173
The Wire, 14, 232
Word choice, 150, 206
Wordsworth, William, 4
World without Oil, 51

Yellow Sheet, The, 85–86
Yelp, 171–173
YouTube, 14, 20, 30, 44, 75, 76, 81,
   90–95, 133, 182, 183, 193, 202, 205,
   215, 237, 239; YouTube editor, 201

Zoeye, 22
Zytomirski, Henlo, 76–77

About the Author

Bryan Alexander, PhD, is a futurist, researcher, writer, speaker, consultant, and teacher working in the field of how technology transforms education. He completed his English language and literature doctorate at the University of Michigan in 1997; taught literature, writing, multimedia, and information technology studies at Centenary College of Louisiana; and worked with the National Institute for Technology in Liberal Education. In 2013, Alexander launched a consulting business with more than 50 clients worldwide. He also speaks widely and publishes frequently. His published work includes the first edition of *The New Digital Storytelling* and *Gearing Up for Learning Beyond K–12*. Alexander has been teaching popular digital storytelling workshops since 2003.